The word "saint" conjures up an assortment of images, many stemming from childhood catechism lessons or history classes. Pictures of St. Patrick driving the snakes from Ireland, St. George slaying the dragon, and Joan of Arc leading a battle are all part of world art culture. And the beliefs that St. Jude will answer the most desperate cause, or St. Valentine will unite two lovers, or St. Nicholas will bring presents, have become mainstays in our society. But what are the truths behind these notions?

This is a compendium for believers and non-believers. Each entry relates a particular saint's significance to history, to faith, or even to legend. They are stories of courage and sacrifice, political intrigue and intellectual devotion meant to inspire and entertain. Hopefully, they will help you, the reader, see beyond the mystique.

From the Introduction

A GUIDE TO THE SAINTS

Compiled by
Kristin E. White

IVY BOOKS • NEW YORK

Ivy Books
Published by Ballantine Books
Copyright © 1991 by Random House, Inc.

Library of Congress Catalog Card Number: 91-92202

ISBN 0-8041-0880-3

Manufactured in the United States of America

First Edition: April 1992

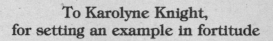

To Karolyne Knight,
for setting an example in fortitude

Introduction

The word *saint* conjures up an assortment of images, many stemming from childhood catechism lessons or history classes. Pictures of St. Patrick driving the snakes from Ireland, St. George slaying the dragon, and Joan of Arc leading a battle are all part of world art culture. And the beliefs that St. Jude will answer the most desperate cause, or St. Valentine will unite two lovers, or St. Nicholas will bring presents, have become mainstays in our society. But what are the truths behind these notions?

The phenomenon of sainthood began, of course, with the birth of Christianity. However, it wasn't until the 1600s that uniform rules for making saints were established by the papal authority. Under usual circumstances, the canonization process is long and slow. First, any Catholic can ask his local bishop to initiate canonization. If the bishop agrees, an investigation is begun into the life of the candidate; a tribunal is set up in the diocese to collect data about his or her devotion and spiritual merit. If there are witnesses, they are petitioned to testify, and any personal writings by the candidate are collected. This "proof" is then forwarded to Rome, where the congregation secretary organizes a report. The Apostolic Process—hearings where detailed testimony and data about miracles are discussed—is initiated. It is at this point that a Vatican official called the devil's advocate points out flaws, raises objections, and argues against the canonization. After the discussions are completed, a biography is drawn up and sent to the pope. Based on the number of miracles attributed to the candidate before death, he or she may be beatified. If further miracles are established, the pope may then decree final canonization and sainthood.

Sometimes a saint is dropped from the Catholic Church calendar because his or her existence cannot be proven. Therefore, in *A Guide to the Saints*, we've excluded such commonly revered saints as Barbara and Christopher, whose feast days are no longer generally celebrated.

There have also been cases of mistaken identity, or errors discovered within a saint's original *acta* (official biography). We've tried to indicate where the discrepancies occur and establish who's who in our roster of saints.

This is a compendium for believers and nonbelievers. Each entry relates a particular saint's significance to history, to faith, or even to legend. They are stories of courage and sacrifice, political intrigue and intellectual devotion, which are meant to inspire and entertain. It is hoped that they will help you, the reader, see beyond the mystique.

ADELA. Widow. c. 710–c. 734. December 24. The daughter of Dagobert II, king of the Franks, she became a nun after the death of her husband, Alberic. She was the sister of St. Irmina. She may be the widow "Adula," said to be living at Nivelles with her young son—the future father of St. Gregory of Utrecht. She founded the monastery called Pfalzel, near Trier, and became its first abbess. She was a disciple of St. Boniface.

ADELAIDE. Widow. 931–999. December 16. The daughter of Rudolph II of Upper Burgundy, she was married to Lothair at the age of sixteen, the union being part of a treaty between Rudolph and Hugh of Provence. In 950 Lothair died—he may have been poisoned—and Adelaide was imprisoned by Berengarius, her husband's successor, when she wouldn't marry his son. She was freed by Otto the Great, the German king who invaded Italy and defeated Berengarius, and married him. Otto was crowned emperor of Rome and died in 973. Their son, Otto II, succeeded. Otto's wife, Theophano, drove mother and son apart, and Adelaide was forced to leave the court. Mother and son were reconciled by St. Majolus, the abbot of Cluny. When Otto II died, he was succeeded by Otto III, with Theophano as regent. Adelaide was again driven from court, but she returned as regent when Theophano died in 991. Active in restoring monasteries, she worked to convert the Slavs. She died in a monastery she'd founded near Cologne. She is portrayed in art escaping from prison in a boat; or holding a church in her hand.

ADRIAN OF CANTERBURY. Abbot. d. 710. January 9. African by birth, he became abbot, at Nerida, near Naples. Upon the death of St. Deusdedit, the archbishop of Canterbury, Pope St. Vitalian chose Adrian to replace him because of his great learning. Adrian demurred, recommending St. Theodore instead. It was agreed he would accompany St. Theodore to England as his assistant and adviser. St. Theodore made him abbot of SS. Peter and Paul, afterward called St. Augustine's, at Canterbury, where he taught Greek and Latin. The school became famed for its teaching and was the learning place of SS. Aldhelm and Oftfor. Bede was said to have commented that some of the students spoke Latin and English equally well. St. Adrian was known for miracles that helped students in trouble with their masters, and miracles were associated with his tomb.

ADRIAN OF NICOMEDIA. Martyr. d. c. 304. September 8. A soldier in the service of the emperor at Nicomedia, he married a Christian, Natalia. Put in charge of a group of Christian prisoners, he was so moved by their courage and fortitude under torture that he proclaimed himself a Christian. He, too, was thrown into prison, into which his wife bribed her way in order to care for him and his original charges. They were condemned to death by burning, but a violent storm is said to have put out the flames. His wife was present at his death, when his body was pulled apart over an anvil. She is said to have recovered one of his severed hands and kept it until she died. When his body was taken to Argyropolis, near Constantinople, she followed, trying to evade a suitor. She lived close by and, when she died, was buried with him. He is the patron saint of arms dealers (who use anvils in their work), prison guards, and butchers, and is invoked against plagues. In art he is depicted most often with an anvil, though sometimes with a sword, lion, or hammer; he may be portrayed being thrown off a cliff into the sea, or being brought to land by dolphins.

AGATHA. Martyr, virgin. Dates uncertain. February 5. Born in Palermo or Catania, Sicily, she was a well-born girl who vowed her virginity to God. The Consul Quintian, who desired her, invoked laws against Christianity in an effort to seduce her. She was sent to a house of prostitution and there suffered mistreatment. Unswayed, she was tortured by rods, steel hooks in her sides, the rack, and fire. Lastly, her breasts were cut off, but she was miraculously healed when St. Peter appeared to her in a vision. She was finally killed when she was rolled over coals mixed with broken potsherds. Invoked against fire and the eruption of Mt. Etna (it is said that at an eruption of Mt. Etna, the people took her veil and went forth to meet the lava, which ceased to flow at their approach), she is the patron saint of nurses, wet nurses, firefighters and bell founders (possibly because bells are used to warn of fire). She is depicted in art holding a dish containing breasts, and with a knife or shears, and she may wear a long veil. In the Middle Ages, the artistic representation of breasts contained in the dish was mistaken for loaves of bread, thus originating a rite of blessing bread on her feast day.

AGNES. Martyr, virgin. d. c. 304. January 21. A wealthy and beautiful young girl, she had many suitors but denied them, having consecrated herself to God. The suitors reported her to the governor, believing that threats of torment would frighten her and convince her to recant. Racks, hooks, and fires were displayed before her, but she remained adamant. According to legend she was sent to a brothel, where it was hoped that by losing what she prized so highly, she would change her mind. When she was stripped naked, it is said that her hair spontaneously grew long to cover her. She declared that God would not allow her body to be profaned, and the men were afraid to touch her. One man who was rude to her was suddenly blinded, but she restored his sight by prayer. Her chief accuser, whom frustration had driven to become vindictive, incited the judge against her. She was killed at the age of thirteen, either by being beheaded or stabbed in the throat, and was buried by the Via Nomentana. She is the patron saint of virginal innocence. She is depicted in art with a lamb (*agnus*), a palm, or a dove with a ring in its beak.

AIDAN, AEDAN OF LINDISFARNE. Bishop. d. 651. August 31. Nothing is known for sure of his life before he became a monk of Iona. A native of Ireland, he may have studied under St. Senan before becoming a monk. Bede is virtually the only source for Aidan's biography, and he wrote particularly warmly of him. King St. Oswald, who had become a Christian during his exile at Iona, sought help from this monastery to evangelize Northumbria. The first monk sent by Iona was too severe and claimed that the Saxons were uncivilized. This monk was replaced by Aidan. Oswald gave him the isle of Lindisfarne, now called the Holy Isle, off the coast of Northumberland, to act as bishop there. St. Oswald acted as Aidan's interpreter early on. Aidan was indifferent to the gifts that were given to him by the king. At Lindisfarne he established a monastery under the rule of St. Columba, and it became known as the "English Iona." It became a center of learning and missionary activity for all of northern England, and Aidan's apostolate, furthered by miracles, was far-reaching. Aidan took twelve English boys to be reared there and trained as religious leaders; St. Chad was among them. He had great concern for children and slaves; he bought freedom for many slave boys, using alms, and educated them for the church. Aidan encouraged monastic practices such as fasting and meditation among the laity. He was known for his gentleness and asceticism, and his kindness to the poor. Both St. Oswald and his successor Oswin did everything they could to support him. Oswin and he became close friends, and Oswin once gave Aidan a horse, but Aidan gave the animal to a poor man. One story has it that during Lent, Aidan would go to the Inner Farne Island to pray and perform penance. From there, in 651, he saw Bamburgh being burned. He prayed, successfully, for the wind to change and lessen the impact of the fire. Eleven days after his friend Oswin was murdered at Gilling, Aidan himself perished. He died at the castle of Bamburgh. He was first buried in the cemetery of Lindisfarne but was later moved into the sanctuary of the church of St. Peter built on the site. In art he is portrayed giving his horse to a beggar; or calming a storm and extinguishing a fire with prayer; or with a stag at his feet (explained by a legend that by praying he rendered a deer pursued by huntsmen invisible); or as a bishop holding a crosier, with his right hand either upheld in benediction or holding a torch.

ALBERT THE GREAT. Bishop, doctor of the Church. c. 1206–1280. November 15. Born in a castle at Lauingen, Swabia, Germany, he was one of the great intellects of the medieval church. He is ranked beside Roger Bacon as one of the first and greatest natural scientists. His knowledge of physiology, chemistry, geography, astronomy, geology (one of his treatises proved the earth to be spherical), and other subjects was so broad that he was thought by some to be a magician and was called the "Universal Doctor" and

5

"the Great" in his lifetime. One of the first to recognize and cultivate the brilliance of his good friend and student St. Thomas Aquinas, he helped adapt the Scholastic method, which applied Aristotelian methods to revealed doctrine, an approach that was further developed by St. Thomas Aquinas. The son of the count of Bollstädt, he studied at the University of Padua; against family wishes he became a Dominican. He taught in Hildesheim, Freiburg-im-Breisgau, Regensburg, and Strasbourg, and then he went to Paris, where he earned a doctorate. He was made regent of the new *studia generalia* in Cologne in 1248. He was named provincial of the order in 1254 and in 1256 went to Rome, where he defended the mendicant orders against William of St. Armour and served as personal theologian to the pope. In 1257, he devoted himself solely to study, and in 1259, together with St. Thomas Aquinas and Peter of Tarentasia, drew up a new curriculum of study for the Dominicans. Against his wishes he was appointed the bishop of Regensburg in 1260. He resigned two years later and resumed teaching in Cologne. In 1277, he defended St. Thomas Aquinas, who had died in 1274, and his position against Bishop Stephen Tempier and a group of theologians at the University of Paris. Soon after he entered a period of years characterized by memory lapses and ill health. Among his works are *Summa theologie, De unitate intellectus contra Averrem, De vegetabilibus,* and *Summa de creaturis*. He is the patron saint of scientists. He is represented in art in the Dominican habit, often with St. Thomas Aquinas.

ALOYSIUS GONZAGA. 1568–1591. June 21. Born in Lombardy, he was the son of Marquis Ferrante of Castiglione, who served Philip II of Spain. He was expected to enter military service, but at the age of seven he decided to pursue a religious life. He was educated in Florence and then joined the court of the duke of Mantua, where he suffered from kidney disease that was to trouble him for the rest of his life. He began to practice severe austerities—fasting, scourging himself with a dog whip, and allowing no fires to be built while he prayed—and taught catechism to the poor of Castiglione. At the court of Don Diego, prince of the Asturias in Spain, he requested to join the Jesuits, but his angry father refused permission. In an effort to distract his son, the marquis sent him to visit the rulers of Northern Italy. Unchanged by his travels, Aloysius renewed his plea, and his father was finally persuaded and allowed him to join the Jesuits in 1585. Aware of his delicate health, the Jesuits requested that he curb his austerity measures and sent him to Milan to study. His poor health forced a return to Rome. In 1587 plague struck, and he administered to the sick in a hospital run by the Jesuits. He eventually caught the plague from patients but surprisingly recovered. He later fell into a low-grade fever, which, after he received last rites from his confessor St. Robert Bellarmine, killed him at the age of twenty-three. He is buried in the Lancellotti Chapel at the Church of St. Ignatius in Rome. He is the patron saint of Catholic youth and the protector of young students in Jesuit colleges. In art he is shown in a black habit, with a crucifix, a lily, and a disciple.

ALPHONSUS MARY LIGUORI. Blessed, Bishop, doctor of the Church. 1696–1787. August 1. Born in Marianelli, near Naples, he received a doctorate in canon and civil law at the age of sixteen from the University of Naples. He felt a vocation for the priesthood but decided to await a sign. He considered the sign to have come when, after supposedly never having lost a case in eight years of practice, he lost a case through an oversight. He became a priest and joined the Oratorians. After working as a missionary and teacher, he went to Castellamare. While leading a retreat, he met Sister Mary Celeste and became convinced that her vision of a new religious order was genuine. He reorganized her convent and founded the Redemptorines, an enclosed, penitential order. Internal rivalries caused all but one lay brother to break away from the congregation. Alphonsus founded a new congregation in Villa degli Schiavi, which drew new recruits and survived even after the church was closed as a result of persecution by the anticlerical Marquis Bernard Tanucci. The congregation grew, and Alphonsus was elected superior in 1743. He preached at missions in rural areas. He was famed for his simplicity in the pulpit and his generosity of spirit. He is said never to have refused absolution to a penitent, believing that penitents should be treated as souls to be saved rather than as malefactors. As bishop of Sant' Agatha dei Goti, he initiated programs designed to reform the clergy, monasteries, and the diocese. He worked to help the poor, and during the plague he went into debt to help the needy, even selling his father's ring. His rheumatism grew worse—portraits show him with his neck bent toward his chest—and he resigned the see in 1775. In 1780, Alphonsus submitted for royal approval a rule for the Redemptorists. The new governor, unbeknown to Alphonsus, had rewritten the rule, completely altering Alphonsus's own, which had been approved by the pope in 1750. Committing another terrible oversight similar to the one he had executed as a lawyer years before, Alphonsus did not read past the first few lines before he signed it. The rule was approved by the king of Naples. Pope Pius VI refused to admit it and declared that only the Redemptorists in the papal states were true Redemptorists. His followers were angered and disillusioned with him, and Alphonsus was replaced as superior. Disconsolate, Alphonsus experienced a period of deep depression, but he eventually reached peace, during which he is said to have made prophecies and performed miracles. He wrote *Moral Theology*, which posited a reasonable middle ground between rigorism and laxity. His devotional writings, especially *Glories of Mary*, which defended the worthwhileness of devotion to Mary, were very successful. He is the patron saint of confessors and moral theologians. He is depicted in art with rays shining upon his face from an image of the Virgin Mary; or reciting the rosary.

AMBROSE. Bishop, doctor of the Church. c. 340–397. December 7. He was largely responsible for the rise of Christianity in the West as the Roman Empire declined, and he was a courageous and untiring defender of the independence of church from state. Born in Trier, he became a lawyer in Rome, famed for his eloquence. He was appointed governor of Liguria and Aemilia c. 370. In 374, the Arian bishop of Milan died, and the Arians and Catholics fought over the vacant position. Ambrose, who was a Catholic in name, went to the cathedral to try to calm the rival parties. During a speech, a child is said to have cried, "Ambrose for bishop!" and he was unanimously elected bishop by all parties. He protested, saying he was not even baptized, but the emperor confirmed the nomination. He capitulated. He was baptized, and dedicated himself to an austere life and a study of theology. He was an admired preacher and became an articulate opponent of Arianism. He wrote extensively on the Bible, theology, and asceticism, and he wrote numerous homilies and psalms. He taught his followers to sing his hymns. Among his best-known works are *De officiis ministrorum*, a treatise on Christian ethics, *De virginibus*, written for his sister, St. Marcellina, and *De fide*. Ambrose came to be known as the "Hammer of Arianism." He was thought of with great affection by those who came into contact with him, and it was he who brought St. Augustine back to his faith and baptized him in 387. He is the patron saint of the French Army Commissariat (who are responsible for administration and procurement), beekeepers, and bishops. In art he is portrayed with a scourge, often knotted with three thongs to symbolize the Trinitarian doctrines; or with a beehive and bees, traceable to a story from his childhood when bees settled upon his face without harming him, a presage of his future eloquence.

ANASTASIA. Martyr. d. 304. December 25. She died in Dalmatia, Yugoslavia, despite her later *acta*, which made her a Roman. She was probably martyred under Diocletian, and her relics were transported to Constantinople. Much of what is known of her is unsubstantiated. She is thought to have ministered to persecuted Christians, been arrested herself, and been burned to death while staked to the ground, arms and legs outstretched. According to one legend, her death occurred on the island of Palmaria, after a ship holding her and pagan prisoners was miraculously rescued by a vision of St. Theodota. Her popularity is largely due to the fact that her memory became associated with the second mass of Christmas, and that a basilica in the Forum, *titulus Anastasiae*, was dedicated to her honor. She is the patron saint of weavers. In art she is shown burning at a stake; or on a funeral pyre.

ANDREW. Apostle, martyr. d. c. 60. November 30. Born in Bethsaida, Galilee, he was the brother of Simon Peter. He was a fisherman and an apostle of John the Baptist. He met Jesus when Jesus was baptized by John the Baptist, and then brought Peter to Jesus. He is said to have taken part in the feeding of the 5,000. The two brothers followed Jesus for a time, but when Jesus returned from Galilee, he requested that they become fishers of men. After the death of Jesus, Andrew traveled and preached, and is said to have ventured to Greece, and as far as Byzantium. Legend has it that he was crucified at Patras, Acaia, on an X-shaped saltire cross. His bones may have been taken to Scotland during invasions, which is how he became the patron saint of Scotland. According to legend, St. Regulus, who guarded his relics, was told by an angel to take them to a place indicated. He traveled in a northwesterly direction ''toward the ends of the earth'' until he was stopped by the angel at St. Andrews, where he built a church to shelter the relics, became its first bishop, and evangelized Scotland. The church became a center of pilgrimage. Crusaders took Andrew's body to Amalfi in the thirteenth century. The head was given to the pope in 1461. Considered one of the treasures of St. Peter's, the head was returned to Constantinople by Pope Paul VI. St. Andrew is the patron saint of fishermen, Russia—although he never traveled there, Greece, and Scotland. He is represented in art by the saltire cross (commonly called St. Andrew's Cross); the Latin cross; and a fishing net.

ANDREW HUBERT FOURNET. Confessor. 1752–1834. May 13. Born in Maillé, near Paris, he lived his early life frivolously, failing at several jobs. He was sent to live with an uncle who was a priest in a very poor parish. Inspired by his uncle's work, he became a protector of the poor, returned to his native town, and became a priest. During the revolution he refused to take the oath outlawing the clergy and was asked by his bishop to go to Spain for his safety. He lived there five years but returned to his flock and remained at the risk of his life. On one occasion he was forced to evade the bailiffs by impersonating a corpse, surrounded by mourning women and candles; he once was saved by a canny woman, who, when bailiffs came into the room, boxed him on the ears, chided him for not rising at their entrance, and angrily sent him out the back door. He commented later that she hit him so hard that he saw stars. After the revolution he labored as a missionary, preacher, and confessor, and with St. Elizabeth Bichier founded the congregation of the Daughters of the Cross, dedicated to nursing and teaching. Prayers to St. Andrew were said to have miraculously increased food supplies for the nuns and their charges when they were in need.

ANDREW KIM TAEGON. Blessed, martyr. d. 1846. September 21. From one of the noblest families in Korea, he was the first Korean martyred priest. He was ordained at Macao, in southern China, and returned to Korea as the first native priest. He was arrested almost immediately and was put to death.

ANGELA MERICI. Virgin. c. 1470–1540. May 31. Her first vision was said to have set her mind at rest as to the salvation of her sister, who had died without receiving the sacraments. She became a Franciscan tertiary at thirteen and lived austerely. She began teaching the poor in her native town of Desenzano, Lombardy, and her success at this led to the invitation from a wealthy couple, whom she had once helped, to begin a school in Brescia. On a trip to the Holy Land, she suddenly lost her sight. She continued her trip with devotion, and on the return trip, regained her sight at the very spot where she'd lost it. During a visit to Rome, Pope Clement VII asked her to lead a group of nursing sisters, but she declined. Assisting at mass one day, she fell into ecstasy and was said to have levitated. A vision she had experienced years before of maidens ascending to heaven on a ladder of light led her to gather young women into an informal novitiate. She placed these twenty-eight novices under the protection of St. Ursula, the patroness of medieval universities and venerated as a leader of women, on November 25, 1535. The order had no habit (members usually wore a simple black dress), took no vows, and pursued neither an enclosed nor communal life; they worked to oversee the religious education of girls, especially among the poorer classes, and to care for the sick. This first establishment of a teaching order of women in the Church was a novel idea and needed time for acceptance. The Ursulines were formally recognized by Pope Paul III four years after Angela's death. In art she is represented by the image of virgins ascending a ladder; or with St. Ursula and companions appearing to her.

ANNE. Mother of Our Lady. July 26. Nothing is known for sure about her, and the Gospels do not mention her name. Tradition has it that her childlessness was made an issue of public reproach, leading her husband, Joachim, to fast and pray for forty days. As Anne (or Hannah, meaning "grace") sat under a laurel bush, an angel came to her and told her she would bear a child. Anne responded that the child would minister to God all its life. Her child was Mary, who became the mother of Jesus. A church was erected in Anne's honor at Constantinople by Justinian I. The cult of Anne became an object of special attack by Martin Luther and the Reformers. She is the patron saint of Brittany, childless women, housewives, cabinetmakers, and miners (a result of a comparison between Mary and Christ and precious metals). In art she is represented as teaching her little daughter to read the Bible; or greeting St. Joachim at the Golden Gate.

ANSELM. Bishop, doctor of the Church. c. 1033–1109. April 21. Born in Aosta, Italy, he wished to enter a monastery at fifteen, but his father disapproved and prevented it. He lived a worldly life for a period, but while studying in Burgundy he became a disciple of Abbot Lanfranc at Bec in Normandy. He became a monk at Bec and, despite his youth, succeeded Lanfranc as prior only three years later. He became known for his patience and gentleness. He eventually became abbot and traveled to England. The English clergy nominated him to succeed Lanfranc in the see of Canterbury in 1092. He consistently resisted King William II's encroachments on ecclesiastical rights, and the king refused to approve the nomination. Anselm was not to leave Bec until 1093, and upon his arrival the king demanded an exorbitant payment in exchange for his approval of the nomination. Anselm refused to pay, and while some bishops supported the king, barons rallied to Anselm's cause.

Anselm traveled to Rome, where Pope Urban I upheld Anselm's nomination, refused Anselm's offer to resign, and ordered King William II to permit Anselm's return and to return confiscated church property. At the pope's request, Anselm was present at the Council of Bari in 1098 and defended the *Filioque,* the controversial doctrine on the procession of the Holy Spirit. Anselm returned to Canterbury at the request of King Henry II, successor to King William II, but almost immediately tangled with King Henry's wish for lay investiture. Anselm returned to Rome in 1103, where he confronted the pope on this issue. Pope Paschal II supported Anselm's refusal of the lay investiture of bishops to King Henry. King Henry threatened to exile Anselm, but a compromise was struck when Henry renounced his right to the investiture of bishops and abbots and Anselm agreed to pay homage to the king for temporal possessions. The king grew to trust Anselm so much that he made him regent while he was away in Normandy in 1108. In 1102, at a national council in Westminster, he spoke out against slavery. Anselm stands out as a link between St. Augustine of Hippo and St. Thomas Aquinas and is called the "Father of Scholasticism." He preferred to defend the faith by intellectual reason rather than scriptural arguments. The first to succcessfully incorporate the rationalism of Aristotelian dialectics into theology, he wrote on the existence of God in *Monologium* and *Proslogium.* His *Cur Deus homo?* was the most prominent treatise of the Incarnation ever written. Other writings include *De fide Trinitatis, De conceptu de virginali, Liber apologeticus pro insipiente,* letters, prayers, and meditations. He died in Canterbury in 1109. In art he is depicted as an archbishop or a Benedictine monk, admonishing an evildoer; or with Our Lady appearing to him; or with a ship; or exorcising a monk.

ANSGAR, ANSKAR, ANSCHAR, SCHARIES. Bishop. 801–865. February 3. Born near Amiens, he became a monk at Corbie monastery in Picardy, and later at

Westphalia. When the exiled King Harold returned to Denmark, he accompanied him. His success in missionary work there led King Björn of Sweden to invite him to Sweden, where he built the first Christian church in that country. He became the first archbishop of Hamburg c. 831. The pope appointed him legate to the Scandinavian countries. He labored at missionary work for the next fourteen years, building churches in Norway, Denmark, and North Germany. He saw his accomplishments obliterated when pagan Northmen invaded in 845, overran Scandinavia, and destroyed Hamburg. He was appointed the first archbishop of Bremen c. 848, and Pope Nicholas I united the see with Hamburg. Ansgar returned to Denmark and Sweden in 854 to resume missionary work. King Olaf had cast a die to decide whether to allow the entrance of Christians, an action that Ansgar mourned as callous and unbefitting. He converted King Erik of the Jutland and was called the "Apostle of the North." He was renowned for his preaching, austerity, devotion, and charity to the poor. Miracles were said to have been worked by him. The area reverted to paganism after his death. He is the patron saint of Denmark, Germany, and Iceland. He is depicted in art with converted Danes near him.

ANTHELM, ANTHELMUS. Bishop. 1107–1178. June 26. He was born in the castle of Chignin, near Chambéry. He became a priest, but after visiting the tranquil Carthusian monastery of Portes, decided to become a monk. He eventually became the abbot of Grande Chartreuse. He was responsible for guiding the Carthusians to evolve into a religious order separate from the Benedictines. Charter houses had previously been separate and independent, subject only to local bishops. He summoned the first general chapter, and Grande Chartreuse became the motherhouse. He commissioned Bl. John the Spaniard to draw up a constitution for a community of women who wished to live under Carthusian rule. After he was made prior of Portes, he ordered the bounty that had accumulated as a result of the monastery's prosperity to be distributed to those in need. He returned to Grande Chartreuse, wishing to live a solitary life, but then he actively entered the conflict over the nomination of Pope Alexander III, whom he supported, against the nomination of Emperor Frederick Barbarossa's choice, Victor IV. With the Cistercian abbot Geoffrey, Anthelm galvanized support for Pope Alexander III, who then nominated him to the see of Belley in 1163. There he set out to reform the clergy, a particular concern being that of celibacy, because some priests practiced while being openly married. When Count Humbert III violated the Church's jurisdiction over the clergy by imprisoning a priest, Anthelm sent a clergyman to handle the matter. After the priest was killed in a scuffle to rearrest him, Anthelm excommunicated the count. The pope invalidated the ban, but Anthelm would not relent and returned to Portes. Relations between the pope and Anthelm remained open, however. He established a community for women solitaries. He cared for lepers and was distributing food in a famine when he was felled by fever. Miracles were said to have occurred at his tomb, one being that, as he was lowered into the tomb, a lamp lit only for great festivals kindled spontaneously. He is represented in art in a Carthusian habit, with a miter at his feet, and above his head a lamp with the Divine Hand pointing to or kindling the flame.

ANTHONY OF PADUA. Doctor of the Church. 1195–1231. June 13. He was born Ferdinand de Bulhoes, in Lisbon, Portugal, the son of a knight serving King Alfonso II. He joined the Canons Regular of St. Augustine but asked to be transferred to the priory at Coîmbra because he found the visits of friends too distracting. He became a Franciscan in 1221 and took the name Anthony. He went to Morocco as a missionary but was forced to return because of ill health. A storm forced his ship to land in Sicily, where he attended the general chapter of 1221, at which St. Francis was present. During the chapter, he was assigned to the rural hospice of San Paolo, a choice made because its small demands were thought to be in keeping with his poor health. At an ordination to which visiting Dominicans had arrived unprepared to speak, Anthony was asked to improvise a speech because he was better educated than his fellow Franciscans. He was encouraged to speak freely. This sermon launched him as an orator. He was assigned to preach throughout Italy and was enormously successful, attracting huge crowds with his zeal and eloquence. He was appointed lector in theology for the Franciscans, became minister provincial of Emilia or Romagna, and acted as envoy from the general chapter of 1226 to Pope Gregory IX. He secured from the pope a release from his duties of office so that he could preach exclusively. He was amazingly successful as a convert maker and confessor. He was said to radiate holiness. His speeches drew such crowds that he often preached outside small churches. He settled in Padua and reformed the city, working to abolish debtors' prisons, help the poor, and convert heretics. After the death of St. Francis, he and Adam, an English friar, held out against the relaxation of Franciscan austerities. He became ill with dropsy and in 1231 went to Camposanpiero for a respite. He died in a Poor Clare convent on the way back to Padua at the age of thirty-six. He was considered one of the greatest preachers of all time, and the pope called him the "Living Ark of the Covenant" because of his marvelous memory of scripture. He is the patron saint of the poor and oppressed (alms given for his intercession are called "St. Antony's Bread"), barren women, harvests, Padua, and Flemish men. He is invoked for the retrieval of lost articles, a habit that was likely spawned by a story that a novice ran away with a psalter Anthony had been using and was forced by an apparition to return it. He is sometimes depicted in art carrying the Infant Jesus on his arm, a representation originating from an episode in which his host was said to have spied on him and seen him holding and talking to the Infant Jesus. He is also depicted holding a lily, a symbol for his knowledge of scripture, with a flame of fire in his hand or at his breast; or holding corn, in recognition of miracles he is reputed to have performed—once having preserved a field of grain from foraging birds, and on another occasion enabling a field, trampled by people who had come to listen to his sermon, to produce an abundant harvest.

ANTONY THE ABBOT. 251–356. January 17. He was born to a Christian family in Koman, south of Memphis in Upper Egypt; his parents died when he was eighteen, leaving him to care for a younger sister. He sold off his more valuable properties and gave the money to the poor, holding back enough to support himself and his sister. When later he heard read in church, "Be not solicitous for tomorrow," he distributed the rest of his property and put his sister in a convent (commonly thought to be the first mention of a nunnery). He began the life of a hermit, living in a tomb, praying, doing penance, and adhering to strict austerities. During this period, Satan is said to have repeatedly tested and tempted him, and once even to have beaten him terribly. In 285, he moved to a mountaintop and occupied a ruined fort for almost twenty years, living upon bread. When he was fifty-four, at the request of others, he came down from the mountaintop and gathered hermits who had become followers into a loose community at Fayum, thus establishing his first Christian monastery. During the persecution under Maximinus, he went to Alexandria to bolster the courage of the persecuted, wearing a white tunic so that he would be recognizable to them. When the persecution tapered off, he returned to the monastery, opened another at Pispir, and then again shut himself off, on another mountain. There he cultivated a garden and made mats and baskets. In 355, he returned to Alexandria to refute Arianism, saying that God the Son is not a creature, and that the Arians who claimed he was were heathen. There he met and became friends with St. Athanasius, who was to become his biographer. St. Jerome relates that Antony met Didymus, the blind head of a catechetical school. In St. Jerome's account of Paul, he describes Paul's meeting with Antony in the desert, during which a raven dropped a loaf of bread. He preached that the knowledge of oneself is the necessary and only step by which one can ascend to knowledge and love of God. He retired to a cave on Mt. Kolzim, and his advice was sought by people from all walks of life, including the Emperor Constantine. He asked to be secretly buried on Mt. Kolzim. The patriarch of monks, he is the patron saint of those with skin diseases, particularly St. Antony's Fire, a circumstance that probably originated from his reputation as a healer. He is also the patron saint of domestic animals and pets, and basket makers. He is depicted in art as an old man with long white hair, scantily clad, with a T-shaped Egyptian cross; or a raven; or a torch to symbolize St. Antony's Fire; or a pig. The association with the pig may have stemmed from the fact that pigs were kept by the Order of Hospitallers that grew around the Church of St. Antony at La Motte, where relics of St. Antony were kept. The Hospitallers cared for the pilgrims who came to be healed of St. Antony's Fire. Their pigs were identified by bells around their necks and were allowed to roam free. The Hospitallers sometimes gave the bells to people as a sort of lucky charm for their own beasts. The word *tantony*, which refers to the smallest of a litter of pigs or the smallest of a peal of bells is a corruption of ''St. Antony.''

ANTONY MARY CLARET. Bishop. 1807–1870. October 24. Born in Sallent, in the north of Spain, he was a weaver who entered the seminary at Vichy and was ordained in 1835. He became a Jesuit novitiate in Rome, with hopes of becoming a missionary. When his health broke down he was told to return home and preach to his countrymen. He gave retreats and missions through Catalonia for ten years and helped to establish the Carmelites of Charity. His zeal encouraged other priests, and he founded the Missionary Sons of the Immaculate Heart of Mary, known as the Claretians. He was appointed the archbishop of Santiago de Cuba, and his attempts to bring about much-needed reforms led to threats upon his life. He was wounded by an assassin who had been angered when his mistress was won back to an honest life. He returned to Spain in 1857 and became confessor to Queen Isabella II. He resigned the see and sought to avoid living at court any more than was necessary, preferring to devote himself to missionary work, preaching, and writing. He is said to have preached 10,000 sermons and written 200 books or pamphlets in his lifetime. While the rector of the Escorial, he established a science laboratory, a museum of natural history, and schools of music and language. He was reputed to have performed miraculous cures and to have had gifts of prophecy. Exiled with the queen in the revolution of 1868, he went to Rome and there he influenced the definition of papal infallibility during Vatican Council I. An attempt was made by the Spanish ambassador to bring him back to Spain but was unsuccessful. He died in the Cistercian monastery of Fontfroide. He is the patron saint of weavers; and of savings and savings banks, a result of his opening savings banks in Santiago in an effort to help the poor.

ANTONY MARY ZACCARIA. 1502–1539. July 5. Born in Cremona, he studied medicine and became a secular priest who pursued a spiritual and corporeal ministry. He worked arduously, modeling himself on St. Paul. In 1530 he founded the congregation of Clerks Regular of St. Paul, the members of which were neither monks nor friars but lived under a rule whose object was to revive spirituality and the love of divine worship. They worked among the plague-stricken Milanese, in the midst of wars, and during Luther's reforms. The group so invigorated the city's spiritual life that it was approved by Pope Clement VI in 1533. The order became known as the Barnabites when, in the last year of Antony's life, the church of St. Barnabas became the order's headquarters. Under his direction, Louisa Torelli founded the congregation of women called Angelicals, who protected and rescued girls who had fallen into disreputable lives. He died at the age of thirty-seven in Cremona.

APOLLINARIS OF RAVENNA. Bishop, martyr. First century. July 23. The first bishop of Ravenna, Italy, he was reputed to have been tortured for the faith and to have died as a result. Nothing is known for certain of his life. He may have been a native of Antioch, who at one time survived a shipwreck in Dalmatia, was driven from his see three times, went into hiding the fourth time when Emperor Vespasian banished all Christians, and was discovered and beaten by a mob. He may be a martyr only because he suffered for Christ; he may not have died of it. His shrine is at the Benedictine Abbey of Classe. He is represented in art as a bishop, holding a sword or club, standing on hot coals; or being beaten by the devil.

APOLLONIA. Martyr. d. 249. February 7. During the persecution of Christians in Alexandria under Emperor Philip, Apollonia, an aged deaconess, was seized by the populace. The mob knocked out all her teeth and then threatened to cast her into a great fire unless she renounced her Christian beliefs. She begged them for a moment to think—stalling so that they should know that what she did was of her own volition—and then leaped into the fire. St. Augustine supposed that she acted according to a particular direction of the Holy Ghost, since otherwise it would have been unlawful under Church law to take her own life. She is the patron saint of dentists and sufferers of toothache. She is depicted in art bearing a pair of pincers that hold a tooth; with a gold tooth; or with a tooth suspended from a necklace.

APOLLONIUS. d. c. 305. March 8. He was a Christian deacon at Antinoe in the Thebaid and was said to have converted Philemon, a popular musician and entertainer. According to legend, he was arrested during the persecution of Diocletian and, fearful of torture, offered the pagan Philemon four gold pieces if he would perform the rite of eating food sacrificed to false gods in his place. Philemon agreed, dressing himself in Apollonius's clothes and his hooded cloak to hide his face. Philemon appeared before the judge, who asked him to carry out the rite. The Holy Spirit entered Philemon, and he claimed himself a Christian and refused to take part in the sacrifice. The judge Arrian argued with him, and finally thinking he was speaking to Apollonius, asked that Philemon be sent for. Being unable to find Philemon, the court officers brought Philemon's brother, Theonas. Asked where his brother was, he pointed out Philemon in Apollonius's cloak. The judge saw the situation as a joke but insisted that Philemon perform the rite. Philemon refused. Arrian responded that it was foolish of him to refuse when he was not even baptized. Philemon prayed, and a cloud miraculously appeared and rained upon him. He claimed that he was thus baptized. Arrian appealed to him, begging him to think of what a terrible loss of musical skill such resistance would mean. The musician's pipes were then said to have been destroyed by Philemon himself or to have spontaneously burst into flames. Officers arrested Apollonius, proclaimed the two men as Christians, and they were condemned to death. One legend says that before the execution, Apollonius and Philemon asked that a great pot be brought before them and a living baby be placed inside it. They then asked soldiers to shoot arrows at it, which they did, the arrows piercing the pot. The baby remained unharmed. The judge then ordered that the soldiers shoot the men with arrows, but all the arrows hung suspended in the air, except one, which blinded Arrian. Despite this and several other miracles, Apollonius was said to have been tied in a sack, thrown into the sea, and drowned. Arrian's sight was said to be restored when his eyes were applied with clay from Apollonius's tomb. This led to the conversion of Arrian and four other officials. Apollonius is depicted in art on a funeral pyre; or drowning in the sea; or being crucified.

ARSENIUS THE GREAT. c. 355–c. 450. July 19. Arsenius was a Roman deacon of senatorial rank, learned in both sacred and profane knowledge. Upon the recommendation of Pope St. Damascus, Arsenius was called to Constantinople c. 383 and appointed tutor to Emperor Theodosius's children, Arcadius and Honorius. He taught the future emperors for a decade, then left the city to live with monks at Alexandria. After the death of Theodosius, saddened and sickened by his pupils' weakness of character and quarrels—for which he felt some responsibility as their former teacher—he retired to the wilderness of Skete to live as a hermit, and there he was tutored in eremitical customs by St. John the Dwarf. Initially suspicious of his dedication, St. John tested Arsenius's humility by throwing his bread upon the floor. When Arsenius ate it, undismayed, St. John became convinced of his devotion. At some point Arsenius came into a legacy of a relative who was a senator but refused the money, preferring a solitary life rather than one of luxury. He felt a lifelong guilt for the weaknesses of Arcadius and Honorius. He was forced by barbarian raids to leave Skete in 434 and spent the next ten years on the island of Canopus near Alexandria in Memphis; then he returned to Troe, where he was to die. He became known for his sanctity, and he shunned the company of others. His disciples included Alexander, Zoilus, and Daniel. He felt learning was unimportant and could even be a hindrance in a relationship with God. To an educated Roman who expressed puzzlement at the high degree of contemplation achieved by uneducated Egyptians, he responded, "We make no progress because we dwell in that exterior learning which puffs up the mind; but these illiterate Egyptians have a true sense of their own weakness, blindness and insufficiency." He was known for his simple maxims, an example being, "I have always something to repent after talking, but have never been sorry for having been silent." He continually shed tears for his and others' shortcomings, so much so that he was said to have worn away his eyelashes. When in his last hours he cried, and his brethren asked him why, he said he was afraid. He was known as "the Great," "the Deacon," and "the Roman." He is shown in art weaving baskets of palm leaves.

ATHANASIUS. Bishop, doctor of the Church. c. 297–373. May 2. He has been named in history "the Father of Orthodoxy," "Pillar of the Church," and "Champion of Christ's divinity." Born in Alexandria, he was well educated and became a deacon and secretary to Bishop Alexander of Alexandria, and a vocal opponent of Arianism. He accompanied the bishop to the Council of Nicea; the Nicene Creed formulated there is still part of Christian belief and liturgy. Upon the death of Alexander, he was made a bishop, though he was not yet thirty. He became spiritual head of the desert hermits in Ethiopia and ruled them for forty years. Arians were well represented in the imperial court, and he was exiled from his see five times. He wrote illuminating treatises on Catholic dogma and believed asceticism and virginity to be effective ways to restore the divine image in man. He aided the ascetic movement in

Egypt and was the first to introduce knowledge of monasticism to the West. From early youth, he formed a close relationship with the hermits of the desert, which was to prove providential during his exiles. Around this time a priest named Arius began to preach that the Word of God was not eternal. Eusebius of Nicomedia, an Arian bishop, tried to force Athanasius to admit Arius to communion, even going so far as to recruit the help of Emperor Constantine, whose favorite residence was in Eusebius's diocese, to pressure him. Athanasius, a weak-looking man, held out. The Meletians tried to impeach him on trumped-up charges. He was eventually cleared by the emperor. Next he was charged with the murder of a Meletian bishop, Arsenius. Everyone knew the bishop was in hiding, and he ignored the summons. He was compelled to appear before a council summoned at Tyre. The panel was packed with enemies and Arians, who made further charges. Athanasius was credited with a keen sense of humor, which helped him in confronting his adversaries. After his accusers produced a hand that they said Athanasius had cut off the murdered Arsenius, Athanasius is said to have produced the living Arsenius in court. First pointing out his face, he then drew out from the bishop's cloak first one, and then the other hand, and said, "Let no one now ask for a third, for God has only given a man two hands." After being exiled twice, he composed most of his chief theological works, including *Apologia to Constantius*, *Defense of Flight*, *Letter to the Monks*, and *History of the Arians*. He did not write the Athanasian Creed, but it was based on his writings. Athanasius returned to his see and spent the last seven years of his life in Alexandria helping to build the Nicene party. His body was taken first to Constantinople and then to Venice. One of the greatest religious leaders, courageously defending the faith against enormous odds, he was described by Cardinal Newman as "a principal instrument after the apostles by which the sacred truths of the Church have been conveyed and secured to the world." When St. Antony died, he bequeathed "a garment and a sheep skin to the bishop Athanasius.'' He is generally represented in art in a group of the Greek fathers, distinguished by name; he is also shown in a boat on the Nile; or with heretics under his feet.

AUGUSTINE OR AUSTIN OF CANTERBURY.

Bishop. d. 607. May 27. He was a Roman, the prior of St. Andrew's monastery on the Coelian Hill in Rome. In 596, Pope St. Gregory the Great sent him with thirty to forty of his monks to evangelize the English. Frightened by stories of the brutality of the Anglo-Saxons and the dangerousness of the Channel crossing, his company wanted to turn back. Augustine sought help from the pope, who sent encouragement, and the group landed on the isle of Thanet in 597. They were welcomed by King Ethelbert of Kent, then the most sophisticated of the Anglo-Saxon kingdoms, and the king was baptized within a year of their arrival. Augustine would later help him to write the earliest Anglo-Saxon written laws to survive. Augustine went to France to be consecrated bishop of the English by St. Virgilius, metropolitan of Arles, and upon his return to England was so successful in making converts that he sent to Rome for more helpers. Among them were St. Mellitus, St. Justus, and St. Paulinus, who brought with them sacred vessels, altar cloths, and books. Augustine rebuilt a church and laid the foundation for what would become the monastery of Christ Church. On land given to him by the king, he built a Benedictine monastery at Canterbury, called SS. Peter & Paul (later called St. Augustine's). He was unable to convince the bishops in Wales and Cornwall to abandon their Celtic rites and adopt the disciplines and practices of Rome. He invited leading ecclesiastics to meet him at Wessex, known as ''Augustine's Oak.'' He urged them to follow Roman rites and to cooperate with him in the evangelism of England, but fidelity to local customs and resentment against their conquerors made them refuse. A second conference, at which

Augustine is said to have failed to rise upon the arrival of the ecclesiastics, drove them further apart. He spent the rest of his days spreading the word, and he established sees at London and Rochester. He was the first archbishop of Canterbury and was called the "Apostle of the English." He adapted a gradual course of conversion outlined for him by Pope St. Gregory. The pope asked him not to destroy pagan temples and allowed that innocent pagan rites could be incorporated into Christian feasts, operating under the belief that "He who would climb to a lofty height must go by steps, not leaps." His patience became well known, as is illustrated by an episode that occurred in Dorsetshire, when a town of seafaring people attached fishtails to the backs of the Italians' robes. He was buried in the unfinished church of the monastery that would one day bear his name. He is shown in art in the black habit of the order, with a pen or book (one of his own works); or with a bishop's miter and crosier; or baptizing Ethelbert; or obtaining by prayer a fountain for baptizing.

AUGUSTINE OF HIPPO. Bishop, doctor of the Church. 354–430. August 28. He was born in Tagaste, north Africa, the son of Patricius, a pagan official, and St. Monica. In spite of his mother's early training, he lived a worldy life for many years, enjoying the theater, racehorses, and the amphitheater; and he kept a mistress for fifteen years, by whom he had a son, Adeodatus, in 372. He went to Carthage to study rhetoric with thoughts of becoming a lawyer but gave it up to follow literary pursuits. In 373, after reading Cicero's (lost) *Hortensius*, he became interested in philosophy, abandoned Christianity, and embraced Manichaeism. He taught in Carthage and Tagaste for a decade, then went to Rome in 383 and opened a school of rhetoric. He became disillusioned with Manichaeism, as a result of his students' attitudes. He became in succession an "Academicist" and a Neoplatonist. Impressed by the sermons of St. Ambrose, who answered his objections to the Bible, he turned back to Christianity. He had difficulty giving up his worldly life but was finally baptized on Easter Eve in 387. With his mother, brother, and several others, he lived a communal life of prayer and meditation. In 387, they started back to Africa, but his mother died en route at Ostia. In 388, he founded a kind of monastery at Tagaste, where he studied and meditated. He was ordained at Hippo. He established a religious community, continued his monastic life, and began to preach very successfully. In 395 he was made coadjutor to Bishop Valerius of Hippo. Since Valerius did not speak Latin, he asked Augustine to act as his mouthpiece to the Latin-speaking community, commissioning him to speak in the cathedral. This broke a precedent that only bishops could speak in cathedrals, and the practice spread. He succeeded Valerius as bishop in 396. He became a dominant figure in African Church affairs and a fierce opponent of Manichaeism, Donatism, and Pelagianism. One reform he helped to bring about was to end a custom of the rich giving feasts for the poor. These affairs invariably resulted in great drunkenness and disorderliness; his efforts led the bishop of Carthage to abolish them. He died from a fever at Hippo. His ideas dominated and molded the thinking of the Western world. He was a prolific writer, and hundreds of his treatises, letters, and sermons are of major importance in theology and philosophy. Best known are the *Confessions*, a spiritual classic about inner conflict, *City of God*, a Christian philosophy of history, *De Trinitate*, *De doctrina christiana*, and sermons on the Gospels. His soliloquies were among the books translated into Old English by King Alfred. He is referred to as the "Doctor of Grace," and he ranks with Aquinas as one of the greatest intellects the Catholic Church has ever produced. So venerated was he that his son, by virtue of being his child, was venerated as a saint as well. He was later criticized for his teaching of Predestination, which would consign unbaptized babies and others to eternal perdition, a position against which the Protestants chafed. He established a central middle ground between Jerome and Jovinian by stressing the three-fold goodness of man against the Manichaeans: these being the family, the sacraments, and fidelity. He defended the value of companionship and intimacy, and the preamble to the marriage service in the Book of Common Prayer is based on his thought. Later Church tradition rejected his position that sexual intimacy was sinful except for the purpose of reproduction. His relics were taken to Sardinia; later, Liutprand, king of the Lombards, enshrined his body in St. Peter's at Pavia. He is usually depicted among the four Latin doctors, in episcopal vestments with a pastoral staff; and his emblem is a burning heart. Often his mother is shown with him, generally wearing a gray or white coif. He is the patron saint of theologians.

BARNABAS. Apostle, martyr. 1st century. June 11. He was born a Jew in Cyprus and named Joseph. He sold his property, gave the proceeds to the apostles, who gave him the name Barnabas (meaning "man of encouragement" or "son of consolation"), and lived with the earliest converts to Christianity in Jerusalem. He was not one of the twelve chosen by Jesus, but he was given the honorary title of apostle. He persuaded the community there to accept St. Paul, whose schoolfellow he had been and whose conversion the people were initially suspicious of, as a disciple. He was sent to Antioch, Syria, to look into the community there, and he brought Paul with him from Tarsus. With Paul, he brought Antioch's donation to Jerusalem during a famine, and then he returned to Antioch with his cousin, John Mark. The three went on the first missionary journey, traveling first to Cyprus, Perga, and then Barnabas and Paul continued on to Antioch in Pisidia, while John Mark returned to Jerusalem. In Pisidia, they were so violently opposed by the Jews that they decided to preach to the pagans. They went on to Iconium, where they were stoned, and Lystra in Lycaonia, where they were first acclaimed as gods

(Barnabas was thought to be Zeus because he was so handsome) because they cured a cripple, then were stoned out of the city when the crowd turned fickle. They returned to Antioch, Syria. A dispute arose regarding the observation of Jewish rites, and Paul and Barnabas went to Jerusalem, where a council decided that pagans did not have to be circumcised to be baptized. Upon his return to Antioch, Barnabas wanted Paul and John Mark to accompany him on travels again, but Paul was angered by John Mark's abandonment of them in Perga and parted from the cousins. Barnabas and John Mark returned to Cyprus. The rift was eventually healed. Tradition has it that Barnabas preached in Alexandria and Rome, founded the Cypriote Church, and was stoned to death at Salamis in 61. Modern scholarship now credits the apocryphal *Epistle of Barnabas*, accredited to Barnabas, to a Christian in Alexandria between 70 and 100, the *Gospel of Barnabas* to an Italian Christian who became a Mohammedan, and *Acts of Barnabas*, attributed to John Mark, as having been written in the fifth century. Barnabas is the patron of Cyprus. He is generally represented carrying the Gospel in his hand, with a pilgrim's staff, and sometimes with a stone. He may also be shown being stoned or burned to death; or in company with SS. Paul or Mark, holding Mark's Gospel in his hand.

BARTHOLOMEW. Apostle, martyr. c. 50. August 24. Probably born in Cana, Galilee, his name, a patronymic, means "son of Tolmai." Nothing for certain is known of him. Many scholars assume him to have been the same person as "Nathanael," a native of Cana in Galilee, of whom Our Lord said, "Behold! an Israelite indeed, in whom there is no guile." St. Jerome said he was the only one of the twelve of noble birth, by virtue of his possible relation to Tolmai, king of Geshur. Tradition has it that he preached the Gospel of Christ in India and then went into greater Armenia. After he had converted many people there to the faith, he was flayed alive by barbarians, suspended on a cross, and by command of King Astyages was finally beheaded. The place is said to have been Albanopolis (Derbend, on the west coast of the Caspian Sea). He is said to have preached in Mesopotamia, Persia, Egypt, and elsewhere. In the fourth century, Eusebius related that St. Pantaenus, about one hundred years earlier, while going into India, found there some who still retained the knowledge of Christ and showed him a copy of St. Matthew's Gospel in Hebrew characters, which they said Bartholomew had brought into those parts when he brought the faith. "India," however, was applied by Latin and Greek writers to Arabia, Ethiopia, Libya, Parthia, Persia, and the lands of the Medes. It is most likely that Pantaenus's "India" was Ethiopia or Arabia Felix, or both. Another eastern legend relates that he met St. Philip at Hierapolis in Phrygia and traveled into Lycaonia, where St. John Chrysostom affirms that he instructed the people in the Christian faith. It's possible that he preached and died in Armenia; later writers of the country say he did, although earlier writers say little of him. His alleged relics are venerated chiefly at Beneventum and in the Church of St. Bartholomew-on-the-Tiber at Rome. An arm taken by St. Anselm to Canterbury, or given by Cnut's wife in the eleventh century, was considered very valuable and contributed greatly to his cult in England. He is the patron saint of tanners and all who work with skins, and plasterers. In art he is often represented with a butcher's flaying knife. Sometimes he carries on his arm the skin of a man with the face attached, and frequently, the Gospel of St. Matthew. In medieval days, little knives—an allusion to his martyrdom—were given away at Croyland, which was dedicated to him.

BASIL THE GREAT. Doctor of the Church. 329–379. January 2. He was born at Caesarea, the capital of Cappadocia, Asia Minor, into a family of ten, which included St. Gregory of Nyssa, St. Macrina the Younger, and St. Peter of Sebastea. His father, St. Basil the Elder, and his mother, St. Emmelia, were wealthy and landed. His early years were spent in the home of his grandmother, St. Macrina, whose teaching was to influence him greatly. He studied at Constantinople and Athens. He associated with the more serious-minded students, and his friends included St. Gregory of Nazianzus and Julian, the future emperor and apostate. He returned to Caesarea and taught rhetoric in the city for some years, but on the threshold of a brilliant career, his sister Macrina, who had helped to educate and settle her siblings, retired with their widowed mother and other women to live a community life on one of their estates at Annesi on the River Iris. Around this time, Basil was baptized and determined to serve God in poverty. He visited the principal monasteries of Egypt, Palestine, Syria, and Mesopotamia to study religious life. Julian invited him to court, but he refused. Upon his return, he settled himself in a wild spot in Pontus, separated from Annesi by the River Iris, devoting himself to prayer and study. With disciples who gathered there, he formed the first monastery in Asia Minor. His principles and rules for living have been carried down to the present day for monks of the Eastern church. Although he lived as a monk in the strict sense of the word for only five years, his legacy was as great as that of St. Benedict in the West. In 363 he was ordained a deacon and priest at Caesarea, but Archbishop Eusebius became jealous of his influence, and he returned to Pontus. In 365, St. Gregory of Nazianzus brought him out to support the faith against Arianism, and he was reconciled with Eusebius. He operated as Eusebius's right hand, while diplomatically giving him all the credit. During a drought, he used up his maternal inheritance in helping the needy, and he opened a food kitchen for the hungry. In 370, Eusebius died, and Basil was elected to replace him, much to the chagrin of the Arian Emperor Valens. Throughout this time, Basil ministered. He introduced a custom, observed during his travels, of singing psalms in church before sunrise. The crowds who attended his eloquent speeches were so huge that he himself compared them to the sea. He founded a hospital complex, including a church and hostel, that was so large it was called the Basiliad. Despite ill health, he made frequent trips to the mountainous districts. He fought simony—the purchase and sale of spiritual things—and excommunicated those involved in the prostitution trade in Cappadocia. His archdiocese became a model of organization and discipline. On the death of St. Athanasius, he became the champion of orthodoxy in the East and strove to rally Christian support, which had been weakened by Arian tyranny and troubled by schisms and dissension. His advances were misread by some as being ambitious and heretical. Appeals made to Pope St. Damascus and the Western bishops for help met with little response, and aspersions against him were made in Rome. In 378, Valens was killed in battle and Gratian succeeded, bringing an end to the Arian ascendency. This news reached Basil on his deathbed and comforted him. Worn out by his austere life-style, hard work, and a painful disease, he died. All of Caesarea—Christian and non-Christian, rich and poor alike—mourned him. Seventy-two years after his death, the Council of Chalcedon described him as "the Great Basil, the minister of grace who has expounded the truth to the whole earth." He was responsible for the victory of Nicene orthodoxy over Arianism in the Byzantine East; the denunciation of Arianism at the Council of Constantinople in 381 to 382 was largely due to his efforts. He was an articulate and prolific writer, writing hundreds of letters; many still exist. Among his better-known treatises are *On the Holy Spirit* and *Philocalia*, a selection of passages from Origen, which he compiled with Gregory. He believed that incorporating the best of secular culture, especially philosophy, was the superior approach to theology. He placed an emphasis on the benefits of communal life rather than individual acts of asceticism. He is the patriarch of Eastern monks and the patron saint of Russia. In art he is shown with a dove on his arm or hand, giving him a pen; or with the

Church in his hand; or in company with the Greek Fathers, usually distinguished by name.

BATHILDIS. Widow. d. 680. January 30. She was born in Britain and sold as a slave to the household of the mayor of the palace under King Clovis II in France. She advanced herself by her beauty and ability, married King Clovis II in 649, and bore him three sons—Clotaire III, Childeric II, and Thierry III—all of whom became kings. Upon the death of Clovis, she became regent for her first-born son and ruled capably for eight years. With St. Eligius as her adviser, she suppressed slavery, redeeming those who had been captured; helped promote religion by seconding the zeal of St. Ouen, St. Leger, and other bishops; and endowed and founded many monasteries, including Corbie, St. Denis, and Chelles. She retired to Chelles around 665 to become a nun, and she served the other nuns with great humility. Her biography was written by a contemporary. She is represented in árt as a crowned nun; a ladder to heaven, implying the pun *échelle-Chelles*, is her emblem. She may carry a broom.

BEDE, THE VENERABLE. Doctor of the Church. 673–735. May 25. Born near SS. Peter and Paul monastery at Wearmouth-Jarrow, England, he was sent there at the age of three and educated by the Abbots Benedict Biscop and Ceolfrid. He became a monk at the monastery in 703, was ordained at the age of thirty, and with the exception of a few brief visits to places probably not even outside of Northumbria, spent his whole life there, devoting himself to the study of Scripture and to teaching and writing. He is considered one of the most learned men of his time and a major influence on English literature. His best-known work, *Historia ecclesiastica*, a history of the English church and people, completed in 731, is a primary source of English history. His writings are far-reaching and include commentaries on the Pentateuch and other books of Scripture, theological and scientific treatises, historical works, and biographies of the saints. He was called "the Venerable" in acknowledgment of his wisdom and learning, and the title was formalized at the Council of Aachen in 853. His works *De Temporibus* and *De Temporum Ratione* established the idea of dating events *anno Domini* (A.D.). He is the only English doctor of the Church. As he was dying, he was translating the Gospel of John into Old English and, according to the account of his contemporary, the monk Cuthbert, he pressed forward to finish it. Alcuin claimed his relics worked miraculous cures. Durham and York are the main centers of his cult. In art he is depicted as an old monk, with a book or pen; or with a jug; or writing at a desk; or dying amidst his community. He is the patron saint of scholars.

BENEDICT. Founder. c. 480–c. 547. July 11. What is known of him derives largely from *Dialogues*, written by St. Gregory the Great. He was of good birth, born in the town of Nurcia. His twin sister Scholastica vowed herself to God from her infancy. He went to Rome to study, accompanied by a nurse/housekeeper. At that time the Church was divided by schisms and the area by war, and the country was lapsing into barbarism. Benedict grew disgusted with the immoral behavior of the city and left Rome. He went to the village Enfide, about thirty miles from Rome. He decided that it was not isolated enough and that God was calling him to a solitary life. Alone, he climbed the hills until he reached the wild and rocky Subiaco. There he found Romanus, a monk, and told him that he wanted to be a hermit. Romanus wore a sheepskin habit and lived in a cave, now the Sacro Speco, difficult both to ascend or descend. There he spent three years, fed by Romanus who sent food up to him in a basket on a rope. The first outsider to find him was a priest. While the priest had been fixing his Easter meal, he heard a voice say, "You are fixing yourself a savoury dish whilst my servant Benedict is afflicted with hunger." The priest sought Benedict out and bade him not to fast since it was Easter, of which Benedict was unaware. Benedict was next discovered by a shepherd, who first took him to be a wild beast because of his clothes. Where he lived became known, and people visited him, bringing food and asking him for advice. At one time he became tempted by thoughts of women, but he was visited by Divine Grace and repressed the temptation by rolling naked in nettles. He was never troubled by these thoughts again. He was begged to lead the monastery at Vicovaro, but the strictness of his rules proved distasteful to the monks. The jealous monks resisted and someone is said to have poisoned his drink. But when he blessed it, as he blessed everything, the jug broke apart. He returned to Subiaco, where disciples, seculars, and solitaries gathered around him. He saw the opportunity to fulfill a dream to gather ". . . as in one fold of the Lord many and different families of holy monks, dispersed in various monasteries and regions, in order to make of them one flock after His own heart, to strengthen them more, and bind them together by fraternal bonds in one house of the Lord under one regular observance, and in the permanent worship of the name of God." He settled the men in twelve wooden monasteries of twelve monks, each with its prior. They lived under no written rule but by observing Benedict's example. His fame grew, and Romans and barbarians alike, of all ranks of life, placed themselves in his care, and parents brought their sons to him to be educated and trained for monastic life. Benedict succeeded in breaking down a deeply rooted stigma against manual labor, which was bolstered by a reputed miracle in which he recovered the head of a hedge hook that had flown off a worker's tool into a lake. He believed that work was not degrading but was dignified and conducive to holiness, and he made it compulsory for plebeians and nobles alike. He left Subiaco when a jealous priest, Florentius, tried to undermine the community by slandering him and tempting them with women. Florentius is said to have poisoned a loaf of Benedict's bread, but a raven miraculously carried it away. In c. 525 Benedict traveled to Monte Cassino, which had become marshy and malarial due to barbarian raids. He fasted for forty days, preached, and made many converts. On the site of their pagan temple, he built two chapels. Around these rose what was to become the greatest abbey in history and the center of monasticism in the West. It is probable that Benedict again spent time as a hermit, but disciples soon flocked there, too. Having learned lessons from his overseeing of the monasteries at Subiaco, this time he placed the monks in one establishment, ruled over by a prior and deans. Guest rooms were added to the house for Church visitors and laymen drawn to Benedict, who had become known for his wisdom, holiness, and miracles. It is likely that at this time he composed his rule. Though it was written for the monks at Monte Cassino, it was applicable to all monks in the West. "The Holy Rule" was characterized by a renunciation of one's own will to fight under the Lord with obedience, stability, and zeal, and it prescribed a life of prayer, study, and work, while living in a community under one common father. Benedict's vision of seeing the whole world in the light of God illustrates the inspiration of his life and rule. His rule endured because it was complete and workable. He ministered to the lay community as well, curing the sick and poor, distributing alms and food, and comforting the spiritual needy; he is said to have raised the dead. When Campania suffered from famine, he gave away all the provisions in the abbey, except five loaves. He told his fearful monks, "You have not enough today but tomorrow you will have too much." The following morning, someone left bushels of flour at the gates of the monastery. He was said to have been able to read men's thoughts. He foresaw his own death, and days beforehand, told the monks to dig his grave. As soon as this was done, he was stricken with a fever. He is said to have died while his monks helped to hold him on his feet in the chapel, his hands uplifted toward heaven. He is the patriarch of Western monks. He is the patron saint of monks, Europe, Italian knights of labor, farm workers and Italian farmers (because he restored cultivation to Monte Cassino), Italian speleologists, and engineers and architects. He is invoked against poison and dying. He is represented holding a book with a broken chalice or a sieve, and with an open copy of his own rule, open at the first word, *Asculta*. His symbol is a raven with a bun in its beak.

BENEDICT II. Pope. d. 685. May 8. Not much is known of his youth except that he was born in Rome, and became an expert in Scripture and sacred chants. Elected to succeed Pope Leo II in 683, his consecration was delayed almost a year awaiting the emperor's confirmation. During his term, he amended the confirmation process to speed approval of papal elections, thus eliminating long delays. He was greatly respected by Constantine, who sent him locks of his sons' hair, making them the pope's spiritual sons. Benedict brought back to orthodoxy Macarius, the ex-patriarch of Antioch, and restored several Roman churches. He upheld the cause of St. Wilfred of York, who sought the return of his see, from which he had been deposed by St. Theodore. He ruled only eleven months. He is the patron saint of Europe.

BENEDICT OR BENET OF BISCOP. Abbot. c. 628–c. 690. January 12. Born Biscop Baducing in Northumbria of noble parents, he became a courtier at the court of King Oswiu of Northumbria. He went on a pilgrimage to Rome in 653 and upon his return decided to devote himself to spiritual studies. On the way back from a second visit to Rome, he became a monk at Lérins in 666, taking the name Benedict, and he remained there for two years strictly observing the rule. On a third trip to Rome in 669, St. Vitalian ordered him to accompany St. Theodore, the new archbishop of Canterbury, back to England. Theodore appointed him abbot of SS. Peter and Paul monastery. Two years later, he went back to Rome. In 674, he founded a monastery at the mouth of the Wear River on seventy hides of land given to him by King Egfrith. In 682, he built a second monastery, six miles away on the Tyne River, on forty hides of land given him by King Egfrith. Dedicated to St. Paul, it was called Jarrow, and the two monasteries became looked upon almost as one. On a fifth trip to Rome, he brought back treasures and Abbot John, the archcantor of St. Peter's, to teach the monks how to sing Divine Offices and Gregorian chants, and to teach Roman liturgy and uncial script. The monasteries became the centers of learning and liturgical practices, an extensive library of books, manuscripts, and religious art, unequaled in England. He devised his rule based on the rule of Benedict and those of seventeen monasteries he'd visited. Paralyzed in his lower limbs and bedridden the last three years of his life, he asked the monks to come into his room to sing psalms and joined them when he could. His biography was written by Bede, who had been entrusted to his care at seven, and whose learning was made possible by the library Benedict had built. His last exhortations were that the monks keep the library in good repair, and elect an abbot for his manner of living and teaching rather than for his membership in a particular family. His relics are thought to be at Thorney Abbey or Glastonbury. He is patron of the English Benedictines. He is portrayed in art in episcopal vestments, holding a crosier and an open book. He may be standing by the Tyne River, with two monasteries in sight.

BENEDICT JOSEPH LABRE. Confessor. 1748–1783. April 16. He was a native of Amettes, near Boulogne-sur-Mer. He came from a family of poor shopkeepers and was the oldest of many children. He was educated by an uncle, a parish priest at Erin. His uncle died of cholera after he and Benedict had ministered to other victims in the parish. He walked sixty miles to La Trappe to become a monk but was turned away because he was too young. Longing to join one of the most austere orders he could find, he tried without success to be a Cistercian and then a Carthusian. In 1770 he set out on a pilgrimage to Rome and found his vocation as a mendicant. He traveled from shrine to shrine throughout Europe, seldom begging, but living on alms and spending long hours before the Blessed Sacrament. He visited most of the leading sanctuaries, in Italy, Switzerland, France, and Spain. If he was given money, he gave it away, and he was once beaten by a man who thought he had spurned his offer of money because he gave it away. He seldom spoke and spent whole days in prayer, becoming entirely lost to his surroundings. Once he knelt in front of a crucifix so unmoving that an artist who was painting the interior of the church painted his portrait, which preserved his likeness for following generations. He traveled with only a couple of books and rarely accepted a bed. On one occasion he is reputed to have multiplied bread for the hungry, and on another to have cured an invalid. In 1774, he settled in Rome, sleeping in the Colosseum, and praying in churches. He became known as the "Saint of the Forty Hours" because he was so often present at the *Quarant Ore*. He neglected his body and his fragile health finally forced him to seek refuge in a hospice for poor men. There he was known to give away his portion of soup. He collapsed on the steps of his favorite church, the Santa Maria dei Monti, was taken to the home of a local man, and died. He is the patron saint of tramps and the homeless. He is depicted in art as a beggar, sharing his alms with other poor.

BENJAMIN. Martyr. c. 421. March 31. The king of Persia put an end to the cruel persecution of Christians under his father Sapor II, and there followed twelve years of peace. Bishop Abdas then burned down the Pyraeum, or Temple of Fire, the chief object of worship of the Persians. The king threatened to destroy all Christian churches unless Abdas rebuilt it. The bishop refused, and the king put him to death and initiated a general persecution of Christians, which continued and intensified under his son Varanes, lasting forty years. An account of the terrible cruelties was given by a contemporary, Theodoret. Benjamin, a Persian deacon, was beaten and imprisoned for a year. An ambassador from the emperor brokered his release, with the understanding that he'd stop preaching. Benjamin declared that he would not observe it and preached at the first opportunity after his release. He was rearrested. At the trial, he asked the king what he would think of a subject who would renounce his allegiance and join in a war against him. The king ordered reeds thrust under his nails and into the tenderest parts of his body and then withdrawn. After this was repeated several times, a knotted stake was inserted into his bowels to rend and tear him. He expired in terrible agony.

BERNARD OF CLAIRVAUX. Abbot, doctor of the Church. 1090–1153. August 20. Born at the family castle of Fontaines, he was the son of a Burgundian nobleman. He was sent to Châtillon on the Seine to be educated in a college of secular canons. After the death of his mother, he decided to forsake the world and the pursuit of letters, and go to Cîteaux, established fifteen years before by SS. Robert, Alberic, and Stephen—the first monastery with a strict interpretation of the Benedictine rule. He persuaded four brothers, an uncle, and other friends—a total of thirty-one men—to join him and pursue a severe religious life. They were received by Abbot St. Stephen Harding, having helped to save the monastery from near extinction. After three years, the abbot ordered him to go with twelve monks to found a new Cistercian house in the diocese of Langres in Champagne. They settled in the Vallée d'Absinthe, built a house, and lived in great hardship for a time. The land was hard, and Bernard was strict and severe in his discipline—so much so that the monks became disheartened. Bernard recognized the harshness in himself, improved the quality of meals, and condemned himself to a long silence for his fault. Afterward, he began again to preach. His reputation for holiness and wisdom grew, and the community expanded to 130 monks. The name of the valley was changed to Clairvaux, and became the motherhouse to other Cistercian monasteries. Bernard's father and another brother joined them in 1117, and Bernard himself gave them their habits. Church and lay business frequently drew Bernard out of his preferred life of retirement; he was often asked to solve disputes, and bishops referred important decisions to him because of his wisdom. His advice was looked upon with respect even by the popes. He was to become a dominant influence in the religious and political spheres of Western Europe. After the general acknowledgment of Innocent II, due largely to Bernard's support, Bernard was present at the tenth general council in Rome, the second of the Lateran. Here he met St. Malachy of Armagh, a friendship that lasted until Malachy's death nine years later. Throughout this period, Bernard had preached to his monks, and among his speeches were the famous discourses on the Song of Songs. In 1140, he preached for the first time in public, to the students of Paris. He became known for his eloquence and wit and for miracles attributed to him, and he is considered to have been one of the most energetic preachers of his time. Bernard also helped to stop *pogroms* in the Rhineland. On Christmas Day, the Seljuk Turks captured Edessa, the center of one of the four principalities of the Latin king of Jerusalem, and appeals for help were sent to Europe. Pope Eugenius asked Bernard to preach a crusade. The crusade began at Vézelay on Palm Sunday in 1146, where Queen Eleanor and many nobles became so moved by Bernard's fervor that they were the first to take the cross. There were so many followers as a result of Bernard's words that supplies of badges ran out, and he was forced to tear strips from his habit to fashion more. After rousing France, he wrote to rulers and the people of Western and Central Europe, and then went in person to Germany. Conrad III accepted the cross from him and set out with an army in May 1147, followed by Louis VII of France. But the second crusade was a disaster. Many blamed Bernard for the failure, but he faulted the crusaders' lack of faith. Early in 1153, Bernard became severely ill. At this point, he was called on for the last time to leave Clairvaux, which now supported 700 monks. The archbishop of Trier asked Bernard to reconcile the inhabitants of Metz with the duke of Lorraine, who had attacked them. Bernard drew up the treaty himself. At the time of his death, over sixty monasteries had been founded from Clairvaux. He was universally called "Doctor Mellifluous," or the "Honeysweet Doctor." He is considered one of the founders of the Cistercian Order because he helped to make it a powerful Christian movement in the West. His writing, especially *De Diligendo Deo*, one of the outstanding medieval mystical works, shaped the mysticism of the Middle Ages. His hundreds of sermons, his treatise *De consideratione*, letters, reflections on Scripture and his deep devotion to Mary and Jesus greatly influenced Christian spiritualism. He is considered the last of the Fathers of the Church. He is patron saint of Gibraltar, although the reasons for this are unclear.

BERNARDINO REALINO. 1530–1616. July 3. Born at Carpi, near Modena, he led a lively early life, but after practicing law for some years, he entered the Society of Jesus at the age of thirty-four. He was admitted at Naples by

Father Alphonso Salmeron, one of the first companions of St. Ignatius. He worked for ten years at Naples, doing pastoral work, preaching, catechizing, and helping the poor, the sick, and inmates of prisons. His holiness and fiery speaking caused him to be recognized as a saint in his lifetime and a spontaneous *cultus* sprang up, which helped to provide evidence for some of the remarkable occurrences that were testified to under oath in the process of his beatification. He was appointed rector of the college at Lecce, where he remained for the rest of his life. Six years before his death, he fell and suffered two wounds that would not heal. During his last illness, blood from a leg wound was collected in vials on account of the great veneration in which he was held. This blood behaved in various extraordinary ways. In some vessels it retained its liquidity over a century; in others it even foamed and seemed to increase in volume; in one, an observer said it "boiled" and frothed on the anniversary of his death and when brought near a reliquary containing his tongue. In 1634, his tomb was opened by an ecclesiastical authority. A good deal of tissue was left, and it was separated from the bones and put into two glass containers, which were reburied with the skeleton in the coffin. In 1711, the contents of the coffin were examined by the bishop of Lecce, in the presence of witnesses, to verify the relics. One of the glass vessels was broken, but in the other the tissues were in an apparently unaltered state but floating in a dark red liquid. The liquid was said by doctors to be blood, and they attested that its preservation and sweet smell were miraculous. Two years later, a commission of three bishops, appointed by the Congregation of Sacred Rites to examine the blood, found it to be liquid, crimson, and foaming. Don Gaetano Solazzo, who had charge of a vial (probably the vial of 1616) in the Cathedral of Lecce in 1804 left a statement saying it was liquid and had twice foamed and bubbled. Nuns saw it do the same, and a Jesuit father stated in a sworn deposition that he'd witnessed it do the same twice in 1852. These circumstances are notable because they are such a well-authenticated example of such

44

phenomena. In 1895, a biographer could find no relic of blood still in a liquid state.

BERNARDINO OF SIENA. Confessor. 1380–1444. May 20. He was the son of the governor of Massa Marittima in Tuscany. At the age of seven, his parents died, and he was entrusted to the care of an aunt, who gave him his religious training. As a teenager, he joined a confraternity of Our Lady. When plague came to Siena in 1400, Bernardino offered to take charge of the hospital, with the help of friends who were willing to risk their lives to share this duty. He worked tirelessly for four months, and although several of his companions died, he did not contract the disease. He then cared for his bedridden aunt. After her death, he set himself to prayer and fasting to learn God's will for his future. He entered the Franciscan Order, but soon asked to be moved to Colombaio outside the city, where the rule was strictly observed. He was ordained in 1404, on the Feast of the Birth of Our Lady, which was his birthday as well. Over the next twelve years he preached only occasionally. He went to Milan in 1417 to preach, and despite being a stranger to the city, he soon attracted huge congregations. The people made him promise to return the following year before they allowed him to leave to preach in Lombardy. He covered nearly all of Italy, usually on foot, preaching for two and three hours at a time, and often giving several speeches in a day. He preached devotion to the Holy Name of Jesus, displaying "IHS" for veneration and having it painted on houses. People throughout Italy spoke of the wonderful benefits of his speaking. Some detractors, however, accused him of encouraging superstitious practices and denounced him to Pope Martin V. He was cleared of the charges after an examination of his doctrine and conduct. The pope offered him the bishopric in Siena, but he declined, as he declined the bishoprics of Ferrara and Urbino in later years. In 1430 he became the vicar general of the Friars of the Strict Observance. He reformed the rule and many convents passed easily from the Conventual to the Observant rule. The original Observants had shunned scholarship (as riches), but Bernardino insisted upon instruction in theology and canon law as part of the regular curriculum. These reforms helped increase the number of observants. In 1442, he obtained permission from the pope to resign his office, and he resumed his missionary work. His health was failing, but at Massa Marittima in 1444 he preached on fifty consecutive days. Although dying, he continued his apostolic travels, setting out for Naples and preaching as he went. He got as far as Aquila, where he died. His tomb at Aquila was said to be the site of miracles. He was the most prominent missioner of the fifteenth century, and he was canonized within six years of his death. Called "the Apostle of the Holy Name," he reinvigorated and reformed the order—increasing its numbers from about 300 to 4,000, and reinstating its strict austerities. He was called "the People's Preacher" because his sermons were filled with lively and realistic depictions of everything from a bachelor's household to women's fashions. He was made the patron saint of advertisers and advertising in 1956 by Pope Pius XII because of his ability to illuminate the Catholic faith to audiences by the use of simple language and telling symbols. He is invoked against hoarseness, which he suffered in his early days of preaching, and is believed to have been cured by a prayer to the Blessed Virgin. He is represented in art holding up a sign bearing the legend "IHS," from which rays shine forth; and as a habited friar with three miters at his feet.

BIBIANA, VIVIANA OR VIBIANA. Martyr, virgin. Fourth century. December 2. A church in the city of Rome dedicated to her honor existed in the fifth century, and is said by *Liber Pontificalis* to have been dedicated by Pope St. Simplicius and to have contained her body. Her extant *acta* is untrustworthy, however, and nothing certain of her is known. Legend has it that she suffered under Emperor Julian the Apostate. She was said to have been the daughter of the ex-prefect Flavian, who had been tortured and banished to Acquapendente during the persecution of Julian the Apostate. After her father's death, his wife Dafrosa was executed and Bibiana and her sister, Demetria, were deprived of all possessions and then arrested. Upon her arrest, Demetria mysteriously died, and Bibiana was scourged to death.

BLAISE, BLASE. Bishop, martyr. d. c. 316. February 3. The bishop of Sebastea in Armenia, he was martyred in the persecutions of Licinius and Agricolaus, of Lesser Armenia. In the *acta* of St. Eustratius, said to have perished in the reign of Diocletian, it is said that Blaise received his relics, deposited them with those of St. Orestes, and executed every article of his last will and testament. This is all that can be confirmed of Blaise with any likelihood of accuracy. According to his legendary *acta*, he was born into a rich and noble family, received a Christian education, and was consecrated a bishop while quite young. When the persecutions began, he retired to a cave in a mountain, frequented only by wild beasts, in obedience to divine instructions that he become a hermit. He healed the animals when they became sick or wounded, and they sought him out for his blessing. Hunters who had been sent to capture animals for games in the amphitheater observed him surrounded by wild beasts. They seized him and took him to Agricolaus where he was imprisoned. One story has it that on the way there, they encountered a woman whose pig had been seized by a wolf, but upon Blaise's command, the wolf returned the pig untouched. The governor ordered that he be tortured and starved, but he was brought candles and food either by the woman whose pig he had saved, or by a woman whose child he had saved by removing a fishbone lodged in the child's throat. Licinius ordered that he be tortured by tearing his flesh with iron wool combs, and then beheaded. Miracles were said to occur at his shrine. He is one of the Fourteen Holy Helpers. He is the patron of those suffering throat complaints, and of wool combers. The practice of blessing throats with candles on his feast day appears to have begun in the sixteenth century; the two candles used in the rite represent the candles brought to him during his imprisonment. He is also invoked for cure of diseased cattle, and water with his blessing was given to sick cattle. In art he is represented with wool combs; or blessing wild beasts; or extracting an impediment from a child's throat; or in a cave with wild animals.

BONAVENTURE. Bishop, doctor of the Church. 1221–1274. July 15. He was born Giovanni di Fidanza in Bagnorea, Italy. According to untrustworthy legend, he was named Bonaventure by St. Francis of Assisi. He became a Franciscan in c. 1240 and studied in Paris under the Englishman Alexander de Hales ("the Unanswerable Doctor"). He taught theology and Scripture in Paris from 1248 to 1255 as master of the Franciscan school. His teaching was curtailed due to the opposition of the secular professors, who were jealous of the new mendicants' success and were perhaps made uncomfortable by their austere lives when compared unfavorably with their own. He defended the mendicant orders against attacks led by William of Saint-Armour and his book, *The Perils of the Last Times*. In response, Bonaventure wrote *Concerning the Poverty of Christ*, a treatise on holy poverty. Pope Alexander IV denounced Saint-Armour, had his book burned, and ordered a halt to the attack on the mendicants. Thus vindicated, the mendicant orders were reestablished at Paris. Bonaventure received a doctorate in theology with St. Thomas Aquinas in 1257. That same year, he was elected minister general of the Friars Minor and worked to reconcile the order that was torn by dissident factions. The severe-interpretation Spirituals valued poverty above all else, including learning. Bonaventure pursued a relaxed policy of moderation, condemning the policies of the extremist groups. At the general chapter at Narbonne in 1260, he designed a set of constitutions on the rule, which had a lasting effect on the order, and for which he is called the second founder. He traveled to Germany, France, and England as minister-general, but he refused the archbishopric of York in 1265. In 1271, he helped secure the election of Pope Gregory X. In return he was appointed cardinal-bishop of Albano—a position he could not refuse. He is said to have asked the messengers who brought the order to him at the friary of Mugello, near Florence, to wait until he had finished his task of washing the dishes. The following year, Pope Gregory called him to draw up the agenda for the fourteenth general council at Lyons to discuss the reunion of Rome with the churches of the East. St. Thomas Aquinas died on his way to the council. Bonaventure was the leading figure in the success of the council that effected the reunion, and led his last general chapter of the order between the third and fourth sessions. He died at Lyons while the council was still in session. An outstanding philosopher and theologian, he is considered one of the great minds of medieval times. Known as "the Seraphic Doctor," he wrote many famous treatises, among them *Commentary on the Sentences of Peter Lombard*, which covers the whole field of scholastic theology, the mystical works *Breviloquium*, *Itinerarium mentis ad Deum*, and *De reductione artium ad theologium*, *Perfection of Life* (written for Bl. Isabella, St. Louis IX's sister, and her nunnery of Poor Clares), *Soliloquy* and *The Threefold Way*, biblical commentaries, sermons, and the official life of St. Francis. He strongly supported the importance of study to the order and the need for the order to provide books and buildings. He confirmed the practice of the monks teaching and studying at universities, believing that the Franciscans could better fulfill a need for preaching and spiritual guidance to make up for other poorly educated clergy. Bonaventure wrote the *Life of St. Francis*, and in 1266 a general chapter invalidated all other "legends" of the saint. Bonaventure was known for his accessibility to any and all who wished to consult him, and once explained his urgency in making himself available to a simple lay brother by saying, "I am at the same time both prelate and master, and that poor brother is both my brother and master." He is portrayed in art with a cardinal's hat and a ciborium.

BONIFACE. Bishop, martyr. 680–754. June 5. Probably born at Crediton in Devonshire, England, he was baptized Winfrid. At seven he was sent to a monastery school near Exeter and at fourteen he went to the abbey at Benedictine Nursling (Hants) in Winchester. There he studied under Winbert, became a monk, and eventually became director of the school. He wrote the first Latin grammar produced in England. He was ordained and successfully taught and preached, but he wished to become a missionary to Friesland. His first missionary trip in 716 failed due to the ascendancy of the pagans and political conditions. The monks at Nursling tried to make him stay by asking him to become abbot, but he refused, and in 718 he went to Pope Gregory II in Rome and was commissioned to preach to the pagans in Germany. He changed his name to Boniface and acted as a missionary for three years, preaching with good results in Friesland and Hesse. In 722, he was recalled to Rome and consecrated regionary bishop for Germany. He impressed the pagans at Geismar when he successfully cut down the sacred Oak of Thor, an object of pagan worship that stood on the summit of Mt. Gudenberg, without being struck down by their angry gods. He went to Thuringia, established a monastery at Ohrdruf, and asked English monks and nuns to join him as missionaries to Germany. In 731, having established several monasteries and dioceses, he was made metropolitan of Germany beyond the Rhine. He was authorized to create new sees and went to Bavaria to organize a church hierarchy and establish new sees. He became a mentor and support to the Carolingians, and he reformed the Frankish Church, which Charles Martel had plundered. When he was over seventy, Boniface resigned his see in 754, in order to spend his last years reconverting the Frieslanders who had lapsed into paganism after the death of St. Willibrord. With a small company, he successfully converted large numbers in the previously unevangelized area of northeast Friesland. He was preparing for the confirmation of some of his converts at Dokkum, in the northern Netherlands, when he and his followers were attacked by a band of pagans and killed. He would not allow his companions to defend him. His bloodstained book was exhibited for centuries as a relic. His impact on English history was enormous, extending beyond the simple conversion of people to Christianity. He helped to arrange alliances between popes and emperors, and the educational and literary influence from his monasteries was significant. His body rests at Fulda. He was called "the Apostle of Germany." His emblem is a book, pierced with a sword or ax; and he is shown felling an oak tree; or with a miter and staff.

BORIS AND GLEB, OR ROMANUS AND DAVID. Martyrs. d. 1015. July 24. They were the sons of the first Christian prince in Russia, St. Vladimir of Kiev, and Anne of Constantinople, the daughter of Emperor Basil II, the Bulgar slayer. They were baptized Romanus and David. After Vladimir's death, the kingdom was to have been divided among his sons, but their oldest half brother, Svyatopolk, wished to rule alone. Boris was forewarned of his brother's plans, but when an army gathered to defend him, he called them off, explaining that he could not raise a hand against his brother who now stood in his father's place. He waited with one attendant on the bank of the Alta. He spent the night in prayer and expressed how sad it was to leave the "marvellous light" of day and his "good and beautiful body." In the morning a gang of Svyatopolk's followers attacked him with spears; on their way to Kiev with his body, they discovered he was still alive, and completed the job with swords. Svyatopolk, under a false pretense of friendliness, invited Gleb to Kiev. On the way, Gleb's boat was boarded by armed men. He begged them to spare him, refusing to fight back. When he saw he could not alter their purpose, he resigned himself to death, saying, "I am in your hands and the hands of my brother, your prince. I am being slain; I know not what for; but thou, Lord, knowest. And I know, O my Lord, that thou didst say to thine apostles that for thy name's sake hands would be laid on them and they would be betrayed by kinsmen and friends, and that brother would bring death to brother." His final death blow was said to have been delivered by his cook, who came from behind to stab his throat "like a butcher killing sheep." In 1020, another son of Vladimir, Yaroslav, usurped Svyatopolk, who died during his escape to Poland. Yaroslav buried the bodies of Boris and Gleb in the church of St. Basil at Vyshgorod. Miracles were reported at their tomb, and it became a site of pilgrimage. Although they were not considered martyrs in the traditional sense, the Russian Church perceived them as "passion bearers"—blameless men who did not wish to die but refused to defend themselves, thus submitting to death like Christ. The Greek authorities apparently did not completely understand the theory, but the popular feeling among the Russian people was so great that they agreed to canonize the brothers. Boris is the patron saint of Moscow.

BRIDGET, BRIGID, BIRGITTA, OF SWEDEN. Foundress, widow. d. 1373. July 23. She was the daughter of Birger, the wealthy governor of Upland, the principal province of Sweden, and his second wife, Ingeborg, the daughter of the governor of East Gothland. When Bridget was twelve, her mother died, and she was brought up by an aunt at Aspenäs on Lake Sommen. At fourteen she was married to the eighteen-year-old Ulf Gudmarsson, a happy marriage that lasted for twenty-eight years, and she bore eight children, one of whom was St. Catherine of Sweden. For several years, she acted as the feudal lady on her husband's estate at Ulfasa, and, uncharacteristically for women of the age, she cultivated friendships with many learned men. In 1335, she was summoned to the court of King Magnus II of Sweden, to act as the principal lady-in-waiting to his new queen, Blanche of Namur. Magnus was weak-willed and his wife was rather frivolous. Bridget made efforts to influence the immature couple. Her personal revelations, which were to make her famous later, were already guiding her opinions on subjects as various as the necessity of washing, to the terms for peace between England and France. The court remained largely deaf to her suggestions and some whispered against her. Bridget became more preoccupied with her own family when her daughter made an unfortunate marriage and her youngest son, Gudmar, died in 1340. Bridget made a pilgrimage to the shrine of St. Olaf of Norway at Trondheim. When she returned, she renewed her efforts to guide the steps of the young royal couple. Still unsuccessful in this task, she asked for a leave of absence from court and went on a pilgrimage with her husband to St. James at Compostela. During the return trip, Ulf was taken ill at Arras, where he received the last sacraments. He was restored to health, however, as Bridget had foreseen in a vision of St. Denis, and the couple vowed to devote their lives to God in religious houses. Ulf died in 1344 at the monastery of Alvastra of the Cistercian Order, where Bridget continued to live for four years, having taken upon herself the state of a penitent. When her visions and revelations became frequent, she grew afraid, fearing that she was making it up. After experiencing the same vision three times, she submitted them to Master Matthias, canon of Linköping. He pronounced her visions to have originated from God. From that point until her death, she submitted them to Peter, the prior of Alvastra, who wrote them in Latin. A vision commanded her to go to court and warn Magnus of the judgment of God on his sins. She did so, denouncing the whole royal court in her warning. Magnus briefly changed his ways, and endowed a monastery, which Bridget, in response to a vision in 1344, planned to found at Vadstena, on Lake Vattern. The monastery provided for sixty nuns, with a separate enclosure for monks, including thirteen priests (in honor of the twelve apostles and St. Paul), four deacons (representing the four doctors of the Church), and eight choir brothers not in orders, totaling the number of the Lord's apostles and disciples—eighty-five in all. She prescribed a constitution, which was said to have been dictated to her by the Savior in a vision. The men were subject to the abbess of nuns in temporal matters, but the women were subject to the men in spiritual ones, the reason for which men were asked to join. The convents were separate, and while they occupied the same church, it was designed so that the men and women could not see one another. The community was named the Order of the Most Holy Savior, or the Bridgettines, as they came to be called. Extra income was given to the poor, and ostentatious buildings were forbidden. The religious were allowed to have as many books for study as they wished, however, and the monastery was to become the intellectual center of Sweden in the fifteenth century. In 1349, Bridget traveled to Rome with her confessor, Peter of Skeninge, and others for the 1350 jubilee and to seek approval for the order. In Rome she settled down to devote herself to the poor, reform monasteries, and to lobby for the return of the popes to the city. Two churches associated with her are the churches of St. Paul's-Outside-the-Walls and San Francesco a Ripa. In St. Paul's, a crucifix of Cavallini is said to have spoken to her. In San Francesco a Ripa, she was visited by a vision of St. Francis. She took this to be an invitation to visit Assisi, which she did. She made a tour of shrines in Italy for two years. Her prophecies and revelations made reference to the prominent religious and political events of the day, both in Rome and Sweden. She refused to support Magnus in his crusade against the pagans in Latvia and Estonia, saying it was an excuse for a marauding expedition, and she wrote to Pope Clement VI, telling him that a vision demanded that he return to Rome and that he secure peace between England and France. She prophesied that the pope and emperor would be able to meet peacefully in Rome. She was famous for her criticism, even of popes. In 1371, in response to another vision, she traveled on a pilgrimage to the Holy Land, taking with her her daughter St. Catherine, her sons Charles and Birger, Alphonsus of Vadaterra, and others. Her son Charles became involved with Queen Joanna I, who despite the fact that they were both already married, wanted to marry him. Horrified, Bridget prayed ceaselessly for a resolution. It came when Charles was felled by a fever, and he died in her arms a few weeks later. He had been one of her favorite children. After the funeral, she went to Cyprus, grieving terribly. She nearly drowned in a shipwreck off Jaffa, but her journey to Holy Places was enriched by a series of comforting visions of things that had occurred there. She returned to Rome in 1373, but ailing; she died after receiving the last sacraments from her friend, Peter of Alvastra. Her visions were written up in *Revelations*. Her body was taken to Vadstena. Today, there are only twelve Bridgettine nunneries left. She is the patron saint of Sweden. She is shown in art clothed in the habit of the order, bearing a pilgrim's staff, holding a heart marked with a cross, with the Savior near her; or holding a chain or a pilgrim's flask or wallet.

BRIGID, BRIDE. Abbess, virgin. d. c. 525. February 1. Historical facts of her life are few. She was probably born in the middle of the fifth century in eastern Ireland. Her parents were said to have been baptized by St. Patrick, with whom she was to become friends. She consecrated herself to God at a young age, but reports that she was "veiled" by St. Macaille at Croghan and consecrated by

St. Mel at Armagh are unlikely. There is little reliable information about the convent she founded at Kildare ("church of the oak"), the first convent in Ireland, and the rule that was followed there. It is generally thought to have been a double monastery, housing both men and women—a common practice in Celtic lands. It's possible that she presided over both communities. She established an art school at Kildare, and the illuminated manuscripts originating there were praised. She was called "Mary of the Gael" because of her spirit of charity, and the miracles attributed to her were usually enacted in response to a call upon her pity or sense of justice. Her prayers and miracles were said to exercise a powerful influence on the growth of the early Irish Church, and she is much beloved in Ireland to this day. She is supposedly buried at Downpatrick, with SS. Columba and Patrick. A tunic reputed to have been hers, given by Gunhilda, sister of King Harold II, survives at Bruges; a relic of her shoe, made of silver and brass set with jewels, is at the National Museum in Dublin. She is the patron saint of Ireland, poets, dairymaids, blacksmiths, and healers. She is usually represented with a cow lying at her feet, a reference to a phase in her life as a cowgirl; or holding a cross and casting out the devil.

BRUNO. Founder. c. 1032–1101. October 6. Bruno was born of the prominent Hartenfaust family at Cologne. He was educated at the cathedral school of Rheims. Ordained in Cologne, he received the canonry in the Church of St. Cunibert. He was asked to come to the school of Rheims as a professor of grammar and theology in 1056. The excellence of his students furthered his reputation far beyond Rheims. After teaching for eighteen years, he was appointed chancellor of the diocese by Manasses, a clergyman with a notorious life-style. When Manasses was summoned by the pope's legate to appear at a council, he refused and was suspended. After Bruno and others accused him at this council, Manasses ordered that their houses be broken into and plundered and that their prebends be sold. Bruno and the others fled to the castle of Ebles de Roucy and remained there until the archbishop had been restored to his see—the result of a deception practiced upon Pope St. Gregory VII—at which point Bruno went to Cologne. Bruno had long since decided to pursue a solitary life despite the fact that the Church of Rheims wished to make him archbishop. He resigned his office, gave up worldly ties, and convinced some friends to join him in a life of contemplation. The company put itself under the guidance of St. Robert, abbot of Molesmes (who was later to found Cîteaux), and lived in a hermitage at Sèche-Fontaine. Bruno and six companions eventually went to St. Hugh in Grenoble in 1084 and asked him for a place where they might live remote from the world. St. Hugh assigned them a retreat in Chartreuse, signing over to them all the rights he had in that region, and promised them his assistance. The band built an oratory and small cells. This was the origin of the Order of the Carthusians, which took its name from Chartreuse. St. Hugh enforced their solitutde by forbidding outsiders to enter their lands and anyone to fish, hunt, or drive cattle in the area. They met at church for Matins and Vespers and spent much time praying in their cells. They ate only once a day, except on festival days, and their church was bare of precious metals except for a silver chalice. They copied books to earn their living, bred cattle, and scratched some sustenance out of the few cornfields they could sustain on the poor land. Three volumes survive of a Bible written there; the rest were destroyed by an avalanche soon after completion. In addition, Bruno wrote several commentaries on the Psalms and on St. Paul's Epistles. The order would become the most austere monastic organization in the Church. They had no written rule until 1127, when Guigo, the fifth prior of the order, drew one up. St. Hugh became such an admirer of Bruno that he took him for his spiritual guide and traveled often from Grenoble to consult with him. Bruno's former student, Eudes, now Pope Urban II, heard of his holy life, and wishing his counsel, sent for him to come to Rome. Meeting this wish was a great sacrifice for Bruno, who desired solitude, but he went in 1090. The pope would not allow him to return to Chartreuse because it was too far away but permitted him to retire in some remote spot in Calabria. Count Roger, brother of Robert Guiscard, gave him the valley of La Torre, where he settled with disciples he had collected in Rome. The two Calabrian hermitages Bruno founded, St. Mary's and St. Stephen's, were more organized and developed than the order at Chartreuse. He was assisted by Count Roger, with whom he had become close friends. He became ill in 1101, and expecting his death, directed his monks to record the events of his life, which his disciples wrote down. He has never been formally canonized, as the Carthusians are averse to publicity, but in 1514 leave was obtained from Pope Leo X to celebrate his feast, and in 1674, Clement X extended it to the universal church. He is portrayed in art with a shaven head, in the loose habit of the Carthusians, distinguished by a white scapular hanging down before and behind and joined at the sides by bands. He may be seated with a miter and crosier and olive branch, and there may be a crucifix before him, or a scroll with "O bonitas" issuing from his mouth.

CAESARIUS OF ARLES. Bishop. 470–543. August 27. Of a Gallo-Roman family, he was born at Chalons-sur-Saône, Burgundy. He decided to pursue an ecclesiastical career and entered the monastery at Lérins at eighteen. He acted as cellarer, but because he was a scrupulous administrator, the monks resented him. Illness caused him to leave, and while recuperating at Arles, he was noticed by his uncle Eonus, the bishop, because of his views about the use of pagan authors for study by Christian clerics. The bishop had him transferred from Lérins to his see and ordained him. He spent three years reforming surrounding monasteries, and in 503, at the age of thirty-three, he was elected to succeed his uncle as bishop of Arles. In addition to preaching successfully, he effected several reforms, fought Arianism, and declared that the Divine Office be sung in Arles churches every day. With his sister, who became an abbess, he founded the convent at Arles named for him and wrote the rule for the nuns. The rule was considered an important predecessor of the Benedictine Rule, its two fundamental precepts being stability and a completely enclosed life. The Franks captured Arles in 536, and Caesarius remained primarily at St. John's convent. He made his will in favor of the nuns there and died. He had ruled Arles for forty years and was the most famous bishop in Gaul. He is known for his roles as teacher, church leader, and scholar. He published an adaptation of Roman law, *Brevarium Alarici*, based primarily on the Theodosian code, which became the civil code of Gaul. Known for his short, accessible homilies, several of his sermons have survived, and he was the first "popular" priest whose words have come down to us. He worked zealously to establish decorum in liturgical worship. He is portrayed in art with the image of angels, extinguishing flames in a burning city.

CAJETAN, GAETANO. Founder. 1480–1547. August 7. He was born the son of Caspar, count of Thiene, and Mary di Porto, of Vicenza, in Lombardy. When he was two, his father was killed fighting for the Venetians against King Ferdinand of Naples. He went to Padua for four years, where he distinguished himself in theology and took a doctorate degree in civil and canon law in 1504. He returned to his native town, was made a senator, and in keeping with his wish to serve God as a priest, received the tonsure. In 1506, he went to Rome. Soon after, Pope Julius II made him protonotary. After Pope Julius's death, he refused the new pope's request to continue his job. He spent several years preparing for the priesthood, was ordained in 1516, and returned to Vicenza. He had revived in Rome the Confraternity of the Divine Love—an association of devout and zealous priests. In Vicenza he joined the Oratory of St. Jerome, instituted upon the plan of the Divine Love but consisting only of men in the lowest station of life. His friends were offended by this decision, seeing it as a slight to his noble family. He persisted, nevertheless, caring for the poor and those sick with terrible diseases in the hospital of incurables, whose revenues he significantly increased. He founded a similar oratory in Verona, and in 1520 he went to Venice, where he lodged in a hospital continuing his work with the needy. He stayed there three years, introducing the importance of the Blessed Sacrament, as well as frequent communion. He was distressed and saddened by the state of the clergy at this time, and in 1523, he went to Rome to confer with friends of the Oratory of Divine Love. Deciding he must revive the spirit and dedication of the clergy, he drew up a plan to institute an order of regular clergy upon the model of the Apostles, characterized by an absolute trust in divine providence. His first associates were John Peter Caraffa, then bishop of Theate and later Pope Paul IV, Paul Consiglieri, and Boniface da Colle. They lived in the community but were bound by vows and engaged in pastoral work. The new congregation was not immediately successful, and in 1527, when it still totaled only twelve members, the army of Emperor Charles V sacked Rome. The Theatines' house was nearly destroyed, and the inmates escaped to Venice. Cajeton succeeded Caraffa as superior in 1530. After three years, Caraffa was made superior again, and Cajeton was sent to Verona, where he found the clergy and laity opposing the reforms of discipline that their bishop was trying to introduce. Shortly after, he was called to Naples to establish the Clerks Regular there. His preaching and efforts effected a general improvement. During the last years of his life, with Bl.

John Marinoni, he established pawnshops (*montes pietatis*), sanctioned some time before by the Fifth Lateran Council, to extend loans to the poor. Disheartened by the suspension of the Council of Trent, he took to his bed in the summer of 1547. He is considered to be one of the great Catholic reformers. He is depicted in art with a lily in his hand; or with the Virgin Mary placing the infant Jesus in his arms.

CALLISTUS, CALIXTUS I. Martyr, pope. d. c. 222. October 14. Most of what is known of him comes from untrustworthy sources. St. Hippolytus says that when Callistus, a young slave, was put in charge of a bank by his master, a Christian named Carpophorus, he lost the money deposited with him by other Christians. He fled from Rome but was caught at Porto, where he jumped into the sea to escape capture. He was sentenced to the dreaded punishment of the mill. He was released at the request of the creditors, who hoped he might be able to recover some of the money, but was rearrested for fighting in a synagogue when he tried to collect debts from some Jews. He was sentenced to work in the mines in Sardinia but was released with other Christians at the request of Marcia, a mistress of Emperor Commodus. He was given a pension by Pope Victor I. St. Zephyrinus made Callistus supervisor of the public Christian burial grounds on the Via Appia (which would come to be called the cemetery of San Callistus) in 199. In its papal crypt most of the bishops of Rome from Zephyrinus to Eutychian, except Cornelius and Callistus, were buried. He is said to have expanded the cemetery, bringing private portions into communal possession. He was ordained by St. Zephyrinus as deacon and became his friend and advisor. After Callistus became pope by popular election of the Roman people and clergy in 217, he was denounced by St. Hippolytus (himself a nominee for the papal seat) for his doctrinal and disciplinary positions. St. Hippolytus was especially upset by the pope's admitting to communion those who had repented for murder, adultery, and fornication. St. Hippolytus and the Rigorists called Callistus a heretic, claiming that he ruled that committing a mortal sin was not sufficient to depose a bishop, that multi-married men could be admitted to the clergy, and that marriages between free women and Christian slaves were legitimate. This last was Callistus's resolution of the problem of wealthy Christian women who were unable to find suitable Christian husbands. He saw marriages to Christian slaves as a better alternative then risking excommunication for themselves and their children by marrying pagans. He was known for his gentleness and forgiveness. Hippolytus also accused him of leniency to Monarchian heretics, despite the fact that Callistus had condemned their leader, Sabelius. It is possible that Callistus was martyred around 222, perhaps during a popular uprising, but the legend that he was thrown down a well has no authority. He was buried on the Aurelian Way. The Chapel of San Callistus in Trastevere is probably a successor to the one built by the pope on a piece of land adjudged to the Christians by Alexander Severus against some innkeepers—the emperor declared that any religious rites were better than a tavern. He is depicted in art wearing a red robe with a tiara; or being thrown into a well with a millstone around his neck; or with a millstone around his neck.

CAMILLUS DE LELLIS. Founder. 1550–1614. July 14. He was born at Bocchianico, in the Abruzzi, when his mother was nearly sixty. He grew to six feet, six inches. At seventeen, he went with his father to fight the Venetians against the Turks, but he soon contracted a painful and unattractive disease in his leg that he would suffer from for the rest of his life. In 1571 he was admitted to the San Giacomo hospital for incurables in Rome as a patient and servant. He was dismissed several months later. He returned to active service in the Turkish war. In the autumn of 1574 he gambled away everything he owned in Naples—his money, arms, and even his shirt. Chastened by his penury and remembering a vow he had once made in a fit of remorse to join the Franciscans, he contracted a job as a laborer on some Capuchin buildings in Manfredonia. On Candlemas Day, when he was twenty-five, he entered the novitiate of Capuchins but could not be professed because of his leg. He was also denied by the Franciscan Recollects. He returned to the hospital, where he devoted himself to the sick, and he was eventually appointed director. Concerned by the inadequacy of the hired servants to the sick, he organized attendants who wished to nurse out of simple charity. The success of this effort provoked jealousy. To become more helpful spiritually to the sick, he sought holy orders and was ordained by Thomas Goldwell, Bishop of St. Asaph, the exiled last bishop of the old English hierarchy. He was given an annuity by Fermo Calvi, a gentleman of Rome. He decided to leave San Giacomo, against the advice of his confessor, St. Philip Neri. With two companions, he founded a congregation, prescribing short rules that required going every day to the great hospital of the Holy Ghost to serve. In 1585, he hired a larger house, extended their activities, and ordained that members should serve persons infected with the plague, those in prisons, and those dying in private houses. In 1595 and 1601, members were sent among the troops fighting in Hungary and Croatia, making them the first recorded "military field ambulance." In 1588 he was invited to Naples, and with twelve companions, founded a new house. Galleys containing plague were forbidden to dock, and Camillus and his members, now known as the Camellians, went on board to minister to the sick. Two brethren died, becoming the first martyrs of this charity. In 1591, Pope Gregory XIV approved the congregation as a religious order with the privileges of mendicants. Camillus was now suffering, in addition to his diseased leg, from several grave and painful illnesses, but refused to be waited upon. Fifteen houses and eight hospitals were founded in his lifetime. He resigned as superior of the order in 1607. He assisted at the general chapter in 1613 and visited the houses with the new superior general. In Genoa, he became very ill, but he recovered and continued his visitation of the houses. He relapsed and received the last sacraments from Cardinal Ginnasi. He revolutionized nursing, insisting upon fresh air, suitable diets, isolation of infectious patients, and spiritual assistance to the dying, for which reason the order was also called "the Fathers of a Good Death" or "Agonizantes." He is portrayed in art ministering to the sick. He is the patron saint of nurses.

CASIMIR OF POLAND. Confessor. 1458–1484. March 4. He was born the third of the thirteen children of Casimir IV, king of Poland, and Elizabeth of Austria, the daughter of Emperor Albert II of Germany. He was tutored by John Dlugosz the historian, a canon of Cracow. All the sons were close to John Dlugosz, but Casimir gained most from his teaching. Casimir was devout from childhood and lived a life of devotion, holiness, and penance. He wore a hair shirt under plain clothes, frequently slept on the ground, and prayed and meditated much of the night. He was a serene and cheerful person, with a great devotion to the poor. He gave away all he possessed to help the needy. In honor of the Blessed Virgin Mary, Casimir frequently recited the Latin hymn "*Omni die dic Mariae*," and a copy of the hymn was buried with him. Although commonly called the Hymn of St. Casimir, it was written by Bernard of Cluny in the twelfth century. In 1471, the nobles of Hungary, dissatisfied with their king, Matthias Corvinus, pleaded with King Casimir to place Casimir on the throne. Only fourteen, he was opposed to the attack, but he obeyed his father and led an army to the frontier. Hearing that the

Hungarian king had a large army, while his own was deserting because they were not being paid, he returned home. King Casimir was angered by the failure and refused him entry to Cracow, banishing him to the castle of Dobzki. He remained there for three months. He refused to ever again take up arms against Christian countries, which he felt only facilitated the progress of the Turks into Europe. He returned to his studies and prayers but was made viceroy in Poland from 1479 to 1483, while his father was away. An attempt was made to make him marry a daughter of Emperor Frederick III, but he remained true to his vow of celibacy. His austerities complicated lung trouble, and he died of tuberculosis in Grodno at the age of twenty-six. He was buried at Vilna, and his relics are in the Church of St. Stanislaus. Miracles were reported at his tomb. He is the patron saint of Lithuania, Poland, and Russia, the young people of Lithuania, nurses and nurses' associations, and the sick. He is depicted in art crowned, holding a lily; or praying at a church door at night.

CATHERINE OF ALEXANDRIA. Martyr, virgin. d. c. 310. November 25. Nothing is known for sure about her. Her *acta*, which are considered to be worthless, say she was the daughter of a patrician family of Alexandria, and that she was devoted to study, in the course of which she learned about Christ. She was converted by a vision of Our Lady and the Holy Child. When Emperor Maxentius began his persecutions, the eighteen-year-old Catherine, who was very beautiful, went to the emperor and rebuked him for his tyranny. Unable to answer her arguments, he called in fifty philosophers to confront her. After they admitted themselves to be convinced by her arguments, the emperor sentenced them to be burned. The emperor offered to marry her, but she refused. She was beaten and then imprisoned, and the emperor departed to inspect a camp. When he returned, he found that his wife and an officer had gone to visit Catherine out of curiosity and were converted, along with soldiers of the guard. All were condemned to death. Catherine was sentenced to be killed on a spiked wheel now known as the "Catherine wheel." When she was placed upon it, her bonds were miraculously loosened, the wheel broke, and the spikes flew off, killing onlookers. She was beheaded, and from her veins flowed a white, milklike liquid. Her body was said to have been carried by angels to Mt. Sinai, where a church and monastery were built. According to Alban Butler, who quotes Archbishop Falconic of Santa Severina, monastic habits were commonly called "angelical habits" and monks, "angels." It is possible, then, that it was monks who supposedly carried her to the mountain. In 527, Emperor Justinian built a fortified monastery for the hermits of Mt. Sinai, and the body of Catherine is supposed to have been taken there in the eighth or ninth century; since then it has borne her name. She is one of the Fourteen Holy Helpers and is one of the voices heard by Joan of Arc. She is the patron saint of philosophy and philosophers, learning, students—particularly women students—Christian apologists, librarians and libraries, young women, nurses, and wheelwrights. She is the patron of nurses because when she bled, her blood was said to be milk. She is symbolized in art by a spiked wheel, which may be broken; she may be shown as a young, beautiful woman, crowned, with a palm, book, or sword in her hand; or with Christ placing a ring on her finger.

CATHERINE LABOURÉ. Virgin. 1806–1876. November 28. She was born Zoe Labouré, daughter of a yeoman farmer at Fain-les-Moutiers in the Côte d'Or. She took over the running of the household at the age of eight, after the death of her mother, and for this reason she was the only one in the family who never learned to read or write. From the age of fourteen, she felt a call to the religious life. Overcoming opposition from her father, she was finally allowed to join the Sisters of Charity of St.

Vincent de Paul at Châtillon-sur-Seine in 1830, taking the name of Catherine. After her postulancy, she went to a convent in the rue du Bac in Paris. She arrived several days before the translation of relics of St. Vincent from Notre Dame to the Lazarist Church in rue de Sevres. Almost immediately, she began experiencing the series of her famous visions. The first of three major ones took place three months later. Our Lady appeared and talked with her for hours, telling her that she would have to undertake a difficult task. On November 27, Mary appeared in the same chapel in the form of a picture, standing on a globe, with shafts of light streaming from her hands, surrounded by the words "O Mary, conceived free from sin, pray for us who turn to thee!" The picture turned around, and on the reverse side appeared a capital M with a cross above it and two hearts, one thorn-crowned and one pierced with a sword, beneath. Catherine heard a voice asking her to have a medal struck, promising that all who wore the medal would receive great graces. This or similar visions were repeated several times up to September 1831. Catherine confided in her confessor, Father Aladel, and he, after making an investigation, was given permission by the archbishop of Paris, Mgr. de Quélen, to have a medal struck. In June 1832, the first 1,500 of the millions of medals to be made—now known to Catholics as the "Miraculous Medal"—were struck. In 1836, the archbishop initiated a canonical inquiry into the alleged visions. Catherine refused to appear, wishing her identity to be kept secret. Father Aladel pleaded to be allowed to keep her name anonymous. The tribunal, basing its opinion on the stability of her confessor and Catherine's character, decided to favor the authenticity of the visions. The popularity of the medal grew, especially after the conversion of Alphonse Ratisbonne in 1842. Alphonse was a Jew who, having been persuaded to wear the medal, received a vision of Our Lady in the church of Sant' Andrea delle Frate at Rome, became a priest, and founded the religious congregation known as the Fathers and Sisters of

Zion. Catherine has been described as an unremarkable person, unexcitable, and reserved. She lived from 1831 until her death at Enghien-Reuilly acting as portress, doing menial tasks like looking after the poultry, and overseeing the aged living in a hospice. Not until a few months before her death did she speak to anyone about the visions except her confessor; she confided in her superior, Sister Dufé.

CATHERINE OF SIENA.

Doctor of the Church, virgin. 1347–1380. April 29. Born in Siena, she and a twin sister—who didn't survive—were the youngest of twenty-five children. Her father was Giacomo Benincasa, a wealthy dyer, and her mother, Lapa, the daughter of a poet. She was said to have been a very happy child, who would sometimes kneel on every step to repeat a Hail Mary. At six, she is said to have had a mystical experience that assured her vocation. At twelve, her parents urged her to pay more attention to her personal appearance; to please them, for a time she agreed to have her hair dressed and to be dressed fashionably. But she soon repented this concession. She declared that she would never marry. When her parents continued to look for a husband for her, she steadfastly refused, and cut off her hair. Angered, her family scolded her continually and made her stay in the house. Since she valued privacy highly, they arranged that she would never be left alone. She bore this treatment with such patience that her father finally realized that they could not break her this way, and she was allowed to pursue the life to which she felt a calling. At fifteen she was permitted to receive what she most desired—the habit of a Dominican tertiary. In 1366, while Siena was keeping carnival, the Savior appeared to her, accompanied by the Blessed Mother and the saints. The Son placed a ring upon her hand and espoused her to himself. The ring remained visible to Catherine, but invisible to others. Shortly afterward, it was revealed to Catherine that she must go out into the world to help her neighbors, and she began gradually to

68

mix with others. Around her formed a band of friends and disciples, her fellowship or "Caterinati." These were to include an Augustinian and an English friar, William Flete. She ministered to the ill in hospitals, particularly those with especially distressing illnesses, such as leprosy and advanced cancers. Public opinion about her came to be divided. She was summoned to Florence to appear before the chapter general of the Dominicans. Accusations against Catherine and her visions were disproved and shortly after, the new lector of Siena, Bl. Raymund of Capua, was appointed her confessor. This Dominican became her director as well as her disciple. Later he became master general of the Dominicans and wrote her biography. Her reputation for holiness and wonders began to earn her enormous respect from her fellow citizens. She was referred to as "La Beata Popolana," and people in difficulty sought her out. Three Dominicans were specially charged to hear the confessions of those persuaded by her to change their lives. She was frequently called in as an arbitrator because of her success in ending feuds. She focused her efforts to support Pope Gregory XI's appeal for a crusade to take back the Holy Sepulchre from the Turks. She often wrote supportively to the pope. In 1375, she went to Pisa, where her visit caused a religious revival. While in the Church of St. Christina, she was looking at a crucifix, meditating, when rays seemed to radiate forth, piercing her hands, feet, and heart, and causing her such pain that she fainted. The wounds remained as stigmata, which were apparent only to her while she lived but became visible to others only after her death. In Pisa, she learned that the people of Florence and Perugia had joined against the Holy See and its French legates. Bologna, Viterbo, Ancona, and other cities rallied to the insurgents. Lucca, Pisa, and Siena held back, largely due to her efforts. She visited Lucca and wrote letters to all three towns. From Avignon, after unsuccessfully appealing to Florence, Pope Gregory dispatched his legate, Cardinal Robert of Geneva, with an army, and laid Florence under an interdict. The ban soon caused such hardship that the rulers sent for Catherine to accept her offer to act as mediator to the Holy See. She arrived in Avignon on June 18, 1376, and went into conference with the pope. The Florentine ambassadors, however, disclaimed her, and the pope's peace terms were so severe that the stalemate held. The popes had been absent from Rome for seventy-four years, living in Avignon, where the curia had become almost entirely French. Christians outside France and some of the most prominent men of the age had opposed the situation in vain. Gregory XI had proposed transferring the residence to Rome, but the French cardinals had deterred him. In response to his negative position, she reminded him of a vow that he had never told to anyone. Home in Siena, she wrote repeatedly to the pope, begging him to make peace in Italy. According to his wish, she went to Florence, which was still torn by strife. She remained there for some time, despite murders and confiscations, her life in danger. She retired to Siena, where she occupied herself in dictating (she did not know how to write) a book under the inspiration of the Holy Ghost, according to Raymund of Capua, her biographer. This was the celebrated mystical work, written in four treatises, known as the *Dialogue of St. Catherine*. In 1378, Urban VI was chosen pope in Rome and a rival pope, Clement VII, was set up in Avignon by cardinals who declared that Urban's election was illegal. Working to exhaustion, Catherine labored to obtain recognition for Urban, writing letters to princes and leaders in Europe. She wrote letters of encouragement to Urban, but criticized him as well for his harshness, which worked to isolate even his supporters. He asked her to come to Rome so that she might advise him. She took up residence in Rome and continued lobbying for support of his papacy. In 1380 she had a strange seizure, when a vision of the ship of the Church seemed to crush her to the earth. She never completely recovered. She next suffered a paralytic stroke, which disabled her from the waist down, and, eight days later, at the age of thirty-three, she died in the arms of Alessia Saracini. Some 400 of her letters to people of every rank still exist. She was an influential spiritual leader of the Middle Ages. She is the patron saint of Italy and Italian nurses. She is depicted in art in a Dominican habit, holding a heart and a book, wearing a crown of thorns. Her most common emblem is a lily, and she may be accepting a marriage ring from the Infant Jesus.

CATHERINE OF SWEDEN. 1331–1381. March 24.

She was born at Ulfasa, Sweden, one of the eight children of St. Bridget and her husband, Ulf Gudmarsson. She was sent to a convent to be educated at a very young age. She wished to remain in the convent to pursue a religious life, but she was married at thirteen or fourteen to Eggard Von Kürnen. She and her husband took a vow to remain celibate. She accompanied her mother to the jubilee of 1350, and while there she learned of her husband's death, which St. Bridget had prophesied. From then on she lived the life of devotion that she desired, refusing persistent suitors. In 1372 she and her mother made a pilgrimage to the Holy Land, returning by way of Rome, where St. Bridget died. Catherine returned with her mother's body to Sweden, and there she became abbess of the convent of Vadstena, founded by her mother, and the motherhouse of the Bridgettine Order. In 1375, she returned to Rome to win papal approval for the order. She succeeded in this but failed in bringing about the canonization of her mother. She died soon after her return from Rome. Her patronage is invoked as protection against abortion, perhaps because of the chastity of her life. She is commonly depicted with a hind, which, according to legend, protected her from harm on many occasions, including attacks on her chastity.

CECILIA, CECILY. Martyr, virgin. Date unknown. November 22.

Her *acta* state that she was a patrician girl born in Rome who was brought up a Christian. She wore a coarse garment beneath her clothes of rank, fasted, and vowed herself to God. Her father married her to a young patrician, Valerian. On their marriage day, when they retired, she told Valerian, "I have an angel of God watching over me. If you touch me in the way of marriage, he will be angry and you will suffer. But if you respect my maidenhood, he will love you as he loves me." Valerian replied, "Show me this angel." She told him that if he believed in the living and one true God and was baptized, he would see the angel. Valerian was then baptized by Bishop Urban. When he returned to Cecilia, he found her standing by the side of an angel. At this point, Valerian's brother, Tiburtius, appeared. He, too, was offered salvation if he would renounce false gods. Cecilia converted him, and he was baptized. From that point on, the two young men dedicated themselves to good works. Because of their ardor in burying the bodies of martyred Christians, they were arrested. The prefect Almachius told them that if they would sacrifice to the gods, they could go free. They refused, and Valerian rejoiced when he was handed over to be scourged. The prefect wanted to give them another chance, but his assessor warned him that they would simply use the interim to give away their possessions so that they couldn't be confiscated. They were beheaded in Pagus Triopius, four miles from Rome. With them was slain an officer who had declared himself a Christian after witnessing their fortitude. Cecilia buried the three and was then herself asked to refute her faith. She converted those who were sent to convince her to sacrifice to the gods. When Pope Urban visited her at home, he baptized over 400 people. In court, Almachius debated with her for some time. She was sentenced to be suffocated to death in the bathroom of her own house. The furnace was fed seven times its normal amount of fuel, but this plan failed. A soldier was sent to behead her. He struck at her neck three times, and she was left dying on the floor. She lingered for three days, during which time Christians thronged to her side, and she formally made over her house to Urban and committed her household to his care. She was buried next to the papal crypt in the catacombs of St. Callistus. What was later called the *titulus Sanctae Caeciliae* translates as "the church founded by a lady named Cecilia." She is the patron of music and musicians. There is no obvious reason why. Until the Middle Ages, St. Gregory had fulfilled that role, but when the Roman Academy of Music was established in 1584, it was put under her protection, and this devotion to her seems to have originated from this. In her *acta* it is related that "while the organs played" she, in her heart, "sang only to God." It appears that the Latin phrase *cantantibus organis* was understood to mean that she was herself playing the organ at her own wedding. From the fourteenth or fifteenth century on, she has been represented in art as sitting at an organ. She is also depicted playing a harp; or holding a palm; or crowned with roses, with a roll of music.

CHARLEMAGNE. Blessed. 742–814. January 28. He was born the son of "Pepin the Short," king of the Franks, on Christmas Day. Popular devotion to Charlemagne took root chiefly at the time of the great quarrel among the pope, Frederick Barbarossa, and the antipope Paschal III. Charlemagne's name is a somewhat extraordinary one to find among saints. He was anointed with his father and his brother Carloman by Pope Stephen II in 754. When Pepin died in 768, Charlemagne and Carloman divided the kingdom. With the death of Carloman in 771, he became the sole ruler. For the next twenty-eight years, he expanded his empire. At the request of Hadrian I, he subdued Lombardy, forcing King Desiderius to retire to a monastery. He assumed the Lombardy crown and was rewarded by the pope with the title "*patricius.*" From 772 to 785, he campaigned against the Saxons. He conquered Bavaria, the Avar kingdom and Pannonia. At home, Charlemagne organized and reformed his government, standardizing the laws, building a stable administration, and employing *missi dominici*, itinerant royal legates. He furthered ecclesiastical reforms and became a patron of letters, which resulted in his reign being labeled "the Carolingian Renaissance." He commissioned Alcuin to write against the Adoptionist heretics led by Felix of Urgel. He spurred learning by acting as a patron to the scholars who formed the Palace School. It was primarily due to Charlemagne's efforts—not the pope's—that the hierarchy, discipline, and unity of liturgy were restored; that doctrine was defined; and that education was encouraged. It is these achievements rather than his conquests that earned him fame. The high point of his reign was his coronation as the first Holy Roman Emperor by Pope Leo III on Christmas Day in 800.

CHARLES BORROMEO. Bishop, cardinal. 1538–1584. November 4. Born in a castle of Arona on Lake Maggiore, he was born into the aristocracy, the son of Gilbert Borromeo, and Margaret, a Medici, whose younger brother became Pope Pius IV. He was devout from a young age and received the clerical tonsure at twelve. His uncle, Julius Caesar Borromeo, sent him to the rich Benedictine Abbey of SS. Gratian and Felinus, at Arona. He learned Latin at Milan and attended the university at Pavia, where he studied civil and canon law under Francis Alciati, who was later promoted to cardinal through Charles's influence. He was thought to be a less than brilliant student because of a speech impediment, but he made good progress. His father made him subsist on a limited allowance from the income of the abbey, and correspondence reveals he was continually short of money to keep up his household. After the death of both his parents, he received his doctorate at the age of twenty-two. He returned to Milan, and in 1559, his uncle, Cardinal de Medici, was made pope. In 1560, the pope made his nephew cardinal-deacon—in practice, the secretary of state—and the following year, the pope nominated him to administer the vacant see in Milan. He was kept in Rome by the pope, who gave him many duties. He was named legate of Bologna, Romagna, and the March of Ancona, and protector of Portugal, the Low Countries, the Catholic cantons of Switzerland, and the Orders of St. Francis, Carmelites, Knights of Malta, and others. He was only twenty-two and only in minor orders. Despite his responsibilities, he looked after his family, and he regularly played music and engaged in sports. A patron of learning, he promoted it among the clergy and instituted in the Vatican a literary academy of clergy and laymen, some of whose conferences and studies appear among the saint's works as *Noctes Vaticanae*. He conformed to the expectations of a renaissance papal court, keeping a large household, an abundant table, and giving entertainments. He provided for the administration of the Milanese diocese to the best of his abilities from Rome. After his election to pope, Pius IV announced his intention to reassemble the Council of Trent, which had been suspended in 1552. In 1562, the council reopened. During the two years it sat, it nearly broke up several times, but Charles's support and meticulous attention to the papal legates kept it unified. In nine sessions and numerous discussion meetings, many of the most important dogmatic and disciplinary decrees of the great reforming council—notably, the drafting of the "Catechism"—were passed. The achievements and spirit of this last meeting of the council were due more to him than to any other single influence. During its assembly, Count Frederick Borromeo died, and Charles was made head of the family. It was generally assumed that he would resign his clerical state and marry. But Charles passed the responsibility of head of the family to his uncle Julius, and he received the priesthood in 1563. He was consecrated bishop soon after. Still prevented from traveling to his diocese, he remained in Rome to supervise the drafting of the Catechism and the reform of the liturgy, books, and church music. He commissioned Palestrina's mass called "Papae Marcelli." Milan had now been without a residing bishop for eighty years. Despite the efforts of Charles and his vicar, the see was in disorder. He got permission to hold a provincial council and to visit the city. Ten suffragans attended, and the quality of its regulations for observing the decrees of the Council of Trent and many other points prompted the pope to write Charles a letter of congratulation. While discharging legatine duties in Tuscany, he was summoned to the pope's deathbed. The new pope asked him to continue his duties for a time, but he resisted, wishing to attend to his diocese. He arrived in 1566 in Milan and immediately began the efforts that would eventually not only restore the diocese, but mold it into a model see. He regulated the household and sold household treasures, giving the money to the poor. He established many monuments and so aided the English college at Douai that Cardinal Allen called him its founder. He focused upon improving the morals and behavior of clergy and laity alike. He arranged retreats for the clergy, and he himself attended two a year. The regulations he made for the reform of the clergy and people in provincial councils, diocesan synods, and pastoral instructions have been studied and modeled by pastors ever since. In the face of enormous obstacles, he sought to initiate reforms regardless of rank or privilege. He directed that children in particular be instructed in Christian doctrine in Sunday school. He established the Confraternity of Christian Doctrine. His reforms were not well received by all, and he faced some violent opposition. A religious order called Humiliati, while having only a few members, possessed many monasteries and possessions and were forced to submit to his reforms. Their acceptance was not sincere, and they tried to annul the regulations but failed. Three friars plotted to assassinate him, hiring a priest, Jerome Donati Farina, to carry it out for the price of forty gold pieces, which they raised by selling church decorations. Farina waited at the door of the chapel in the archbishop's house, while Charles and his household were at evening prayers. Right after the line "It is time therefore that I return to Him that sent me" and Charles was on his knees before the altar, Farina shot him. Farina escaped. Charles, thinking himself mortally wounded, commended himself to

God. The bullet, however, only struck his clothes in the back, bruising him. After thanksgiving, Charles retired to a Carthusian monastery for a few days to consecrate his life anew to God. He then traveled to the three valleys of the diocese in the Alps, visiting each of the Catholic cantons, and removing ignorant and unworthy clergy. He converted a number of Zwinglians and restored discipline in the monasteries. A harvest failed, and Milan fell prey to a great famine. Charles raised supplies for the poor and fed 3,000 people daily for three months. He had been ill, and he changed his life-style to regain his strength but remained weak. In 1575 he went to Rome to gain a jubilee indulgence, and the following year it was published in Milan. Huge crowds of penitents came to the city. They brought the plague with them. The governor and other officials fled the city. Charles remained to care for the stricken. He assembled the superiors of the religious communities and begged them for their help. Many religious lodged in his house. The hospital of St. Gregory was inadequate and overflowed with the sick and dead, with too few to care for them. He sent for help from priests and lay helpers in the Alpine valleys, because the Milanese clergy would not go near the sick. As the plague choked off commerce, want began. He ran up huge debts. He exhausted his resources and went into debt raising supplies. Clothes were made from the flags that had been hung from his house to the cathedral during processions. Empty houses were used, and shelters were built for the sick. Altars were set up in the streets so that the sick could attend public worship from their windows. He himself ministered to the sick, in addition to supervising care in the city. The plague lasted from 1576 to 1578. Even during this period, resentful magistrates tried to make trouble between Charles and the pope. When the plague was over, Charles wanted to establish anew his cathedral chapter on the basis of a common life, but the canons refused. This led him to originate his Oblates of St. Ambrose (now the Oblates of St. Charles). In 1580, he entertained twelve young priests going on a mission trip to

England. Two preached before him—St. Ralph Sherwin and St. Edmund Campion, English martyrs. Charles preached against witchcraft and sorcery. He traveled under much strain and without enough sleep. Pope Gregory warned him not to overdo his Lenten fasting. In 1584, his health declined. After arranging for the establishment of a convalescents' home in Milan, he went to Monte Varallo to make his annual retreat, accompanied by the Jesuit Father Adorno. He told several people that he was not long for this world, and he took ill on October 24. On October 29, he started for Milan, and he arrived on All Souls' Day. He went to bed, requested the last sacraments, received them, and died quietly at the age of forty-six. He was one of the most imposing figures of the Counter-Reformation—on a par with St. Ignatius of Loyola and St. Philip Neri—and a great patron of learning and the arts. He is buried in Milan Cathedral. A spontaneous *cultus* arose immediately. He is the patron saint of catechists and catechumens. He is depicted in art with an archbishop's crosier, generally barefoot, with a rope around his neck; or with a casket and crucifix near him; or communicating with plague patients.

CHARLES LWANGA. Blessed, martyr. d. 1886. June 3. A Catholic missionary in Uganda, who stood up against the local ruler, King Mwanga, Charles Lwanga secretly baptized four of the king's pages. One of them, St. Kizito, was a thirteen-year-old he had repeatedly rescued from the pederasty of the king. The morning after the baptisms were discovered, the pages were summoned, and the Christians were ordered to stand apart from the rest. Led by Lwanga and Kizito, fifteen young men did so. All were under the age of twenty-five. They were joined by two others who had already been arrested, and by two soldiers. Asked if they intended to remain Christians, they answered, "Till death!" The king declared, "Then put them to death." Three of the youths were killed on the way to Namugongo, the place of execution, thirty-seven miles away. The rest were imprisoned for seven days while a huge pyre was prepared. On Ascension Day, they were stripped, bound, and wrapped in mats of reed. At the last minute, one boy, St. Mbaga, was killed by a blow to the neck by the chief executioner, his father. The rest of the young men were set alight. Charles Lwanga is the patron saint of African Catholic Youth action.

CHRISTINA THE ASTONISHING. Virgin. 1150–1224. July 24. Born at Brusthem in the diocese of Liège, Belgium, she was left an orphan with two older sisters. Around the age of twenty-two, she had an epileptic fit and was thought to be dead. She was carried to church in an open coffin, where a Mass of Requiem was begun. Suddenly, Christina sat up, soared to the beams of the roof, and perched there. The congregation fled in fright. The priest persuaded Christina to come down from the beam, where she is said to have taken refuge to escape the smell of sinful human bodies. She told him she had died, gone to hell, to purgatory, and then to heaven. She said she was allowed to return to earth to pray for the suffering souls in purgatory. She fled to remote places, climbed trees and towers and rocks, and even hid in ovens to escape the smell of humans. She would handle fire freely, would jump into the river in the coldest weather, and was even said to have gotten into a mill-race and been carried under the wheel. She would pray balancing on a hurdle or curled up in a ball on the ground. She was thought to be insane by many. Once she was caught by a man who struck her so hard on the leg that it was thought to be broken. She was taken to a surgeon's home where her leg was splinted, and she was chained to a pillar for her own safety. She escaped at night. On one occasion, a priest refused her communion; she ran wildly down the street and jumped into the Meuse. She dressed in rags, lived by begging in extreme poverty. She spent the last years of her life in the convent of St. Catherine at Saint-Trond. While she lived there, she was held in great respect by Louis, the count of Looz, who treated her as a friend, accepted her criticisms, and welcomed her at his castle. Bl. Mary of Oignies respected her as well, the prioress of St. Catherine's praised her obedience, and St. Lutgardis sought her advice. Her experiences were recorded by a contemporary Dominican, Cardinal James de Vitry.

CLARE OF ASSISI. Foundress, virgin. c. 1193–1253. August 11. Her mother was Ortolana di Fiumi and her father, the nobleman Faverone Offreduccio. Of her childhood and adolescence nothing is known, although she is said to have refused to marry at twelve. When she was eighteen, St. Francis came to preach the Lenten sermons at the church of San Giorgio in Assisi. Impressed by his vision of the ideal of Christian poverty, she sought him out, and he encouraged her to devote herself to God. On Palm Sunday in 1212, Clare went to the Cathedral of Assisi for the blessing of the palms. When the others went up to the altar to receive the branch of olive, she became shy and remained in her seat. The bishop saw her and came down from the altar to give her a branch. That night, she ran away to the town of Portiuncula, a mile away, where Francis lived with his small community. He and his brethren met her at the door of the Chapel of Our Lady of the Angels with lighted candles. Before the altar, she removed her fine clothes, and St. Francis cut her hair and gave her the habit of a nun, a tunic of sackcloth bound with a cord. As there was no nunnery yet, he placed her in the Benedictine convent of St. Paul, near Bastia. Friends and relatives followed to remove her from the convent. St. Francis sent her to the nunnery of Sant' Angelo di Panzo. Her sister Agnes soon joined her. Her father sent twelve armed men to remove Agnes, but Clare's prayers rendered Agnes so heavy that the men were unable to lift her. The two women held fast, and St. Francis gave the fifteen-year-old Agnes the habit. He placed them in a poorhouse next to the Church of San Damiano on the outskirts of Assisi and, against her wishes, appointed Clare superior. She was later joined by her mother and others, including three from the wealthy family of Ubaldini in Florence. She established a very rigid rule of extreme austerities and poverty. Within a few years, monasteries of nuns were founded in several places in Italy, France, Germany, Spain, and England. Bl. Agnes, the daughter of the king of Bohemia, founded a nunnery of the order in Prague, in which she took the habit. Clare and her community wore no stockings or shoes, slept on the ground, abstained from meat, and spoke only when obliged to by necessity or charity. St. Francis desired that the order should never possess rents or other property in common, and that it subsist entirely on daily contributions. Pope Gregory IX wished to lessen the harshness of this part of the rule and offered to settle a yearly revenue on the Poor Clares of San Damiano, but Clare persuaded him against it. In 1228, Pope Gregory granted the *privilegium paupertatis*, which prevented them from being forced by anyone to accept possessions and to subsist entirely on alms. Convents of Perugia and Florence also received this sanction, but other convents accepted the original mitigation. After the death of Pope Gregory, Pope Innocent IV published another recension of the rule, which in some respects brought it closer to Franciscan than Benedictine observance, but permitted the holding of property in common. He qualified it by saying that he did not wish to force this rule on any community that was not willing to accept it. Clare was not satisfied with even this, and she set about drawing up a rule that would unequivocally provide that the sisters possess no property, either individually or in common. Clare governed as abbess for forty years. Popes, cardinals, and bishops came to consult her; sick were brought to be tended by the nuns and were sometimes cured by her intercession. Thomas of Celano, who had often heard Francis warn his brethren against any imprudent association with the Poor Clares, states that she never left the walls of San Damiano. She bore twenty-seven years of various illnesses with patience, and in 1253, began a last long-drawn-out agony. Pope Innocent visited her twice and gave her absolution. She is considered to have been as great a force as St. Francis in the rapid spread of the Franciscan movement. Forty-seven convents were founded in Spain in the thirteenth century. The Poor Clares led what was easily the most austere life of any female order. She is credited with many miracles and is reputed to have saved Assisi from the besieging soldiers of Emperor Frederick II by appearing at the walls of the convent with the Blessed Sacrament. Like St. Francis, she showed a great love for animals. She is the patron saint of embroiderers because of the embroidery she did for liturgical use during her years of illnesses. She was made patron of television by Pope Pius XII in 1958. Aware of the dangers as well as the potential of TV, he chose her because one Christmas Eve, when confined to bed, she saw the crib in the church and heard singing just as if she'd been there. She is usually depicted in art with a pyx or monstrance, and she may hold a cross or lily.

CLARE OF MONTEFALCO. Virgin. c. 1268–1308. August 17. She was born in Montefalco, in the diocese of Spoleto. She lived penitentially for fifteen years in a community of hermitages under the direction of her sister Joan, an abbess. The members were secular tertiaries of St. Francis. When they wished to adopt a conventual life, however, the bishop of Spoleto gave them the Augustinian Rule. Their convent of the Holy Cross was erected in 1290 and, against her will, as her sister lay dying, Clare was elected abbess. She was reputed to have performed miracles. She also experienced ecstasies, received other spiritual gifts, and had a great devotion to the Passion of the Lord. She once said to a sister, "If you seek the cross of Christ, take my heart, there you will find the suffering Lord." When her heart was examined after her death in 1308, an image of the cross was said to have been found imprinted upon it. She is remarkable for having been said to have been visited by three divine favors. The first was the incorruption of her remains, the second was the cross and other instruments of the Passion formed solidly within her heart, and the third was the alleged liquefaction of her blood. She was called "Clare of the Cross." She was known for the faithfulness of her observance and her austerity of penance. For a breach of silence, she once stood barefoot in the snow while she said the Lord's Prayer one hundred times.

CLEMENT I. Martyr, pope. d. c. 99. November 23. Said to have been a contemporary of SS. Peter and Paul, he was the third successor of St. Peter. Origen and others refer to him as the Clement whom Paul refers to as a fellow laborer (Phil. 4:3), but this is doubtful. Details of his life are unknown. He may have been an ex-slave to the family of T. Flavius Clemens, the cousin of Emperor Domitian, and he may have been of Jewish descent. He is said to have been baptized by St. Peter. His *acta* state that, after converting a patrician named Theodora and her husband Sisinnius and 423 others, the people raised an opposition against him. He was banished by Emperor Trajan to the Crimea where he was made to work in the quarries. The nearest drinking water was six miles away, but Clement found a nearer spring for the use of the Christian captives. He preached, and soon seventy-five churches were needed to serve the converts. He was said to have been thrown into the Black Sea with an anchor tied around his neck, and that angels came and built him a tomb beneath the waves, which once a year became visible by a miraculous ebbing of the waves. It was Clement's Epistle to the fractious Corinthians that made him so famous. "Under this Clement," says St. Irenaeus, "no small sedition took place among the brethren at Corinth, and the church of Rome sent a most sufficient letter to the

Corinthians, establishing them in peace and renewing their faith, and announcing the tradition it had recently received from the apostles.'' The letter is important not only for its eloquence, historical allusions, and its evidence of Roman prestige and authority at the end of the first century, but also as a model of the pastoral letter and a homily on Christian life. It established the instance of the bishop of Rome intervening authoritatively this early in the life of the Church as the preeminent authority in the affairs of another apostolic church to settle a dispute. It also provides evidence for the residence and martyrdom of Peter and Paul at Rome. Nothing of his martyrdom or place of death are known. His death may have occurred in exile in the Crimea, but the relics that St. Cyril brought from there to Rome, after having supposedly miraculously recovered them piece by piece, with the anchor, are unlikely to have been his. These were deposited below the altar of San Clemente on the Coelian. He is the patron saint of the Guild, Fraternity and Brotherhood of the Most Glorious and Undivided Trinity of London, i.e., "Trinity House," and is the authority responsible for lighthouses and lightships. His usual emblem in art is an anchor, and he is sometimes shown robed as a pope, with a tiara and a cross with three branches.

COLETTE. Virgin. 1381–1447. March 6. She was born at Calcye, and her father, De Boilet, was a carpenter at the Abbey of Corbie in Picardy. Her parents named her Nicolette, in honor of St. Nicholas of Myra. They died when she was seventeen, leaving her in the care of the abbot. She was said to be petite and very beautiful. She tried her religious vocation with the Beguines and Benedictines but failed. She distributed her possessions to the poor and entered the third Order of St. Francis. The abbot gave her a small hermitage beside the Church of Corbie, where she lived a life of such austerity that her fame spread and people came seeking her advice. Colette had dreams and visions in which St. Francis appeared and charged her to restore the first rule of St. Clare in its original severity. She hesitated to act upon this but was struck blind for three days and dumb for three more, which she saw as a sign. Encouraged by her director, Father Henry de Baume, she left her hermitage in 1406. After trying to explain her mission to two convents, she realized that she must have better authority to accomplish her mission. She set out for Nice, barefoot and clothed in a habit of patches, to meet with Peter de Luna, acknowledged by the French during the great schism as pope under the name Benedict XIII. He welcomed her and professed her as a Poor Clare. He was so impressed with her that he made her superioress of all the convents of Minoresses that she might reform or found and a missioner to the friars and tertiaries of St. Francis. She traveled from convent to convent through France, Savoy, and Flanders. At first she was met with rude opposition and treated as a fanatic, and even accused of sorcery. She met rebuffs and curses patiently, however, and eventually began to make inroads, especially in Savoy, where her reform gained sympathizers and recruits. This reform passed to Burgundy, France, Flanders, and Spain. The first house of Poor Clares to receive the reformed rule did so in 1410. She aided St. Vincent in the work of healing the papal schism. She founded seventeen new convents, in addition to reforming many, including several houses of Franciscan friars. Impressed by her simple goodness, many people of high rank were greatly influenced by her, including James of Bourbon and Philip the Good of Burgundy. Her most famous convent is Le Puy (Haute-Loire), which has sustained an unbroken continuity. Like St. Francis, she combined a deep devotion to Christ's Passion with an appreciation and care for animals. She fasted on Fridays from 6 A.M. to 6 P.M., meditating on the Passion. Almost always after receiving Holy Communion she would fall into an hours-long ecstasy. It is said that she met St. Joan of Arc on her way with an army to besiege La Charité-sur-Loire in 1429, but there is no evidence. In Flanders, where she'd established several houses, she was seized with a last illness. She foretold her own death, received the last sacraments, and died in her convent in Ghent at sixty-seven. Her body was removed by Poor Clares when Emperor Joseph II was suppressing religious houses in Flanders; it was taken to her convent at Poligny thirty-two miles from Besançon. A branch of Poor Clares is still known as the Colettines. She is depicted in art holding a crucifix and a hook; or with SS. Francis and Clare appearing to her.

COLUMBA, COLMCILLE. Abbot. c. 521–597. June 9. Although he is one of the most famous of Scottish saints, he was born in Ireland, at Gartan in County Donegal. His father was the great-grandson to Niall of the Nine Hostages, the overlord of Ireland, and his mother, Eithne, was related to the princes of Scottish Dalriada and was a descendent of a king of Leinster. When baptized by his foster father, the priest Cruithnechan, he received the name Colm, Colum, or Columba. In later life he was called Colmcille, a name the Venerable Bede traces to *cella et Columba*, which most likely refers to the many cells or religious foundations he established. After being removed from the care of his priest guardian at Temple Douglas, he was sent to be educated at St. Finnian's famous school at Moville. By the time he left, he was a deacon. He went on to study in Leinster under the aged bard, Master Gemman. Bards preserved the records of Irish history and literature, and Columba himself was a poet. He studied further at Clonard, the famed monastic school supervised by another Finnian, who was called the "tutor of Erin's saints." Columba became one of the distinguished band of his disciples who are considered the Twelve Apostles of Erin. It was perhaps there that he was ordained a priest, but it may have been later when he was living at Glasnevin, with SS. Comgall, Kieran, and Canice, under their former fellow student, St. Mobhi. An outbreak of plague forced Mobhi to break up the school, and Columba, then twenty-five years old and fully trained, returned to Ulster. He was a tall and athletic figure, with a voice that was said to be "so loud and melodious it could be heard a mile off." Columba spent the next fifteen years traveling through Ireland, preaching, and founding more monasteries, notably those of Derry, Durrow, and Kells. He loved books and spared no efforts to obtain them. He secretly made a copy of the first copy of St. Jerome's psalter to reach Ireland, which his former master St. Finnian had obtained in Rome. Upon discovering this, St. Finnian demanded the copy. Columba refused. The case was put before King Diarmaid, the overlord of Ireland. He judged against Columba, reasoning that "To every cow her calf, and to every book, its son-book," a judgment that Columba resented. When Curnan of Connaught, after fatally injuring an opponent in a hurling match, took refuge with Columba, he was dragged from Columba's arms and killed by Diarmaid's men—defying the laws of sanctuary. A war broke out between Columba's clan and Diarmaid's followers, and it is reported in Irish *Lives* to have been instigated by Columba. After the battle of Cuil Dremne, in which thousands were slain, Columba was accused of being morally responsible for their deaths. The synod of Telltown in Meath passed a censure upon him, and but for an intervention by St. Brendan, he would have been excommunicated. Tormented by conscience, he was advised by St. Molaise to expiate his offense by exiling himself from his own country and attempting to convert as many persons as had died in the battle. Although this is the generally accepted reason for his departure, his early biographer and St. Adamnan attribute it to zeal alone. In 563, with twelve family members, he departed in a wicker coracle covered with leather, and on the eve of Pentecost, at the age of forty-two, they landed on the island of I, or Iona (the Holy Island). There he built the monastery that would be his home for the rest of his life and would be famous in Christendom for centuries. The land was given

87

to him by a kinsman, Conall, king of Scottish Dalraida, at whose invitation he may have come to Scotland. The location was ideally placed to act as a mission to the Picts of the north and the Scots of the south. At first he devoted his missionary efforts to teaching the inadequately instructed Christians of Dalraida (mostly of Irish descent), but after two years, he began to evangelize the Scottish Picts. With St. Comgall and St. Canice, he went to the castle of King Brude at Inverness. The pagan king ordered that they not be admitted, but when Columba raised his arm, the bolts were said to have withdrawn, the gates opened, and the company entered the castle. Awed by Columba's powers, the king granted him an audience and eventually grew to respect him. As overlord, he confirmed Columba's possession of Iona. Columba is credited by some as having seeded Aberdeenshire with Christianity and having evangelized nearly all of Pictland. His headquarters at Iona was visited by persons of all ranks, drawn by his reputation for sanctity, miracles, and prophecies. He lived very austerely and pressed harsh discipline upon others. It appears that he grew kinder with age, however, and an account given by St. Adamnan depicts him as a calm old man, a lover of man and beast. "He had the face of an angel; he was of an excellent nature, polished in speech, holy in deed, great in counsel . . . loving unto all . . ." was a description that would become famous. Four years before his death he suffered an illness that threatened his life, but his survival was said to be brought about by the prayers of his community. As he grew frailer, he spent much time transcribing books. On the day before he died he was copying the Psalter and had written, "They that Love the Lord shall lack no good thing," when he paused and said, "Here I must stop; let Baithin do the rest." He had named Baithin, his cousin, to succeed him as abbot. That night, when the monks went to church for Matins, they found Columba outstretched, helpless and dying, before the altar. As he was raised by his attendant, he made an effort to bless his brethren, then died. For about a century, Celtic Christians and many monasteries in western Europe upheld the Columban tradition over Roman tradition in certain matters of order and ritual, until superseded by the less stringent rule of Benedict. Monks from Iona traveled all over Europe. Columba's last blessing of the Isle of Iona proved prophetic: "Unto this place, small and mean though it be, great homage shall yet be paid, not only by the kings and peoples of the Scots, but by the rulers of barbarous and distant nations with their peoples." In 574, Aidan, the new king of Scots of Dalraida, came to Iona to be consecrated. Columba's relics were transferred to Dunkeld in 849. His "Cathach" copy of the psalms, written in his hand, is the oldest surviving example of Irish majuscule writing. He is the patron saint of Ireland. He is portrayed in art with devils fleeing from him.

CONRAD OF PIACENZA. Confessor. 1290–1351. February 19. Conrad was born of a noble family of Piacenza and lived there with his wife. Out hunting one day, he ordered his attendants to set some brushwood on fire to flush out the game. A strong wind blew the fire out of control, and it burned cornfields and buildings in neighboring villages. Unable to halt the fire, he and his attendants returned home, saying nothing. When a poor man who was discovered picking up sticks near the fire was accused of starting it and was sentenced to death, Conrad stepped forward, exculpated him, and gave himself up. He was ordered to make compensation for the damage, which cost nearly all his possessions and his wife's dowry. He saw this circumstance as a sign from God. He and his wife agreed to give their remaining possessions to the poor, and she joined the Poor Clares. He put on poor garments and joined a community of hermits who lived under the third rule of St. Francis, to which he was admitted. His piety drew visits from former fellow citizens, and to avoid publicity, he left the neighborhood. He went to Sicily and settled in the valley of Noto, where he remained for thirty years, partly in the Hospital of St. Martin and partly in the hermitage founded by William Bocherio, another noble who had become an anchorite. Toward the end of his life, seeking more solitude, he moved to the grotto of Pizzoni, three miles from Noto. In spite of his wish to live alone, word of his sanctity spread. When a famine struck, people came to him to beg for help. Through his prayers, relief was said to come at once, and from then on, he was besieged by sufferers of all kinds. When the bishop of Syracuse visited him, it was reported that while his attendants were preparing to unpack provisions they'd brought, the bishop asked Conrad smilingly whether he had anything to offer his visitors. Conrad replied that he would go and look in his cell. He returned, carrying newly made cakes, which the bishop accepted as a miracle. Conrad returned the bishop's visit and made a general confession to him. As he arrived, he was surrounded by fluttering birds, who escorted him back to Noto. When he was dying, he lay on the ground in front of the crucifix and prayed for the benefactors and people of Noto. He was buried in the church of St. Nicholas there, and his tomb became a popular shrine where many miraculous cures were said to occur. He is invoked for ruptures on account of the large number of people who were cured of hernia by his intercession. He is shown in art with small birds fluttering about him; or with stags and animals surrounding him.

CORNELIUS. Martyr, pope. d. 253. September 16. As a result of the brutality of the Decian persecutions, the Roman see was vacant for more than a year after the martyrdom of Pope St. Fabian. In 251, Cornelius was elected pope, even though Decius ''was in his hatred of bishops, uttering unspeakable threats against them and was more concerned about a new bishop of God in Rome than about a rival prince in the empire,'' according to St. Cyprian. A few months after the election of Cornelius, Novatian, a leader among the Roman clergy, set himself up as a bishop in Rome in opposition, and he denied that the Church had any power to pardon *lapsi* (lapsed Christians), no matter how repentent they might be and whatever penance they underwent. Apostasy was ranked by him with murder, adultery, fornication, and a second marriage as "unforgivable sins." Novatian became the first formal antipope and leader of a heretical sect that persisted for a several centuries in Africa. Cornelius was pastorally forgiving and believed the Church has the power to forgive repentent apostates and should readmit them to communion after penance. He was supported by St. Cyprian and the other African bishops and most of the East. At a synod of Western bishops in Rome, the teaching of Novatian was condemned, and he and his followers excommunicated. In 253, under the persecutions of Gallus, Cornelius was banished to Centum Cellae. It is most likely that he died of hardships at Centum Cellae, but according to some accounts, he was beheaded. His body was taken to Rome and buried, not in the papal cemetery but in the nearby crypt of Lucina. St. Cyprian and Cornelius had a strong and close association. In the eighth century, Cyprian's image was painted on the wall of Cornelius's crypt. A few letters of Cornelius to Cyprian, written in colloquial Latin, survive. The two are named together in the canon of the mass. In art, Cornelius is portrayed vested as a pope, holding a cow's horn or with a cow near him.

COSMAS AND DAMIAN. Martyrs. d. c. 303. September 26. All we know of them is legend. They are the most famous of those saints known in the East as *anargyroi*—"moneyless ones"—because they practiced medicine without accepting payment from their patients. They were twin brothers, born in Arabia. They studied the sciences in Syria and became well known for their skill, always practicing without charging. They lived at Aegeae on the bay of Alexandretta in Cilicia. When the persecutions under Diocletian began, it was impossible for people of their prominence to keep a low profile. They were arrested by order of Lysias, governor of Cilicia, were tortured, and beheaded. Their bodies were carried to Syria and buried at Cyrrhus, which became the center of their *cultus*. Before being beheaded, legend has it that they defied death by water, fire, and crucifixion. While hanging on their crosses, the mob stoned them, but the stones flew back at the heads of the throwers. The same happened when archers attempted to shoot them with arrows. Miraculous cures were attributed to them after their deaths. Sometimes they appeared to the ill in their sleep and prescribed to them or cured them outright. This manner of healing was also said to be experienced by pagans in the temples of Aesculapius and Serapis. Emperor Justinian I claimed he was healed by the brothers, and, out of regard for their relics, honored the city of Cyrrhus. Two churches at Constantinople are said to have been built in their honor in the early fifth century. Their basilica at Rome was dedicated c. 530. Their *cultus* was encouraged and supported by the Medicis, a number of whom were named "Cosimo," an entertaining preference in view of the saints' distaste for financial gain. They are the patron saints of doctors, physicians, surgeons, chemists, pharmacists, barbers and hairdressers (associated with medicine in the Middle Ages), and of blind people. They are usually portrayed in art as doctors of medicine with robes and instruments contemporary with the depictions; or being martyred in various ways. In the Middle Ages, their *cultus* became very popular and many stories were attributed to them. Artists depicted whole cycles of their lives. One notable example shows the grafting of a new (white) leg onto the live body of a black man with cancer.

CUNEGUND. Empress. d. c. 1033. March 3. She was trained in religion by her parents, Siegfried of Luxembourg and Hedwig. Upon her marriage to St. Henry, duke of Bavaria, the duke gave to her as a wedding present a crucifix of Eastern workmanship that is said to have been identical to one now existing in Munich. Later writers say the couple vowed on their wedding day to remain celibate, but historians may have been prompted to believe this as a result of their childlessness. Upon the death of Otto III, Henry succeeded as king of the Romans, and was crowned by St. Willigis at Mainz. In 1013, the couple went to Rome to receive the imperial crown from Pope Benedict VIII. A legend says that early in her marriage, slander led Henry to doubt Cunegund's fidelity, but she dispelled the charges by walking on hot ploughshares without being harmed. It was under the influence of Cunegund that the emperor founded the monasteries and cathedral of Bamberg, and the pope came in person to consecrate them. Cunegund obtained such privileges for the city that, by common report, ''her silken threads were a better defense than walls.'' During a serious illness, she vowed that if she recovered, she would found a convent at Kaufungen, near Cassel, in Hesse. She carried this out, and had nearly finished building a house for nuns of the Benedictine Order when Henry died. A story is told that Cunegund had a young niece, Judith or Jutta, for whom she cared a great deal and educated. When a superior was needed for the new convent, she appointed Judith. Having gained her independence, Judith became frivolous and irresponsible; it was said she was first in the refectory and last to chapel. One Sunday she failed to appear in the procession and was found eating with some of the younger sisters. Cunegund chastised her and struck her on the cheek. The marks of her fingers were said to have remained on Judith's cheek until she died, serving to convert Judith and as a warning for the whole community. In 1024, on the first anniversary of her husband's death, Cunegund invited prelates to the dedication of her church at Kaufungen. As the Gospel was sung, she offered at the altar a piece of the true cross, and, taking off her rich robes, clothed herself in a Benedictine nun's habit and was given the veil by the bishop. From that time on, she behaved as the lowest and humblest in the house. She prayed and read, and she visited and cared for the sick. After she died, her body was taken to Bamberg and she was buried with her husband. She is the patron saint of Luxembourg and Lithuania. She is portrayed in art walking over hot ploughshares or carrying one in her hand; or holding a lily with St. Henry; or holding a model of the Church of St. Stephen.

CYPRIAN. Bishop, martyr. c. 200–258. September 16. Caecilius Cyprianus, popularly known as Thascius, was pagan—born at Carthage, according to St. Jerome. He was a public orator, a teacher of rhetoric, and an advocate in the courts; and he engaged fully in the public and social life of Carthage. In middle age, he came under the influence of an old priest, Caecilian, who grew to have such confidence in Cyprian's virtue that upon the priest's death, he left his wife and son in Cyprian's care. A complete change came over Cyprian's life as a result of this association. Before his baptism, he made a vow of chastity. He gave up all pagan literature, and he studied the Holy Scriptures and the works of their best expositors, focusing particularly on the works of his compatriot, Tertullian. He was soon ordained, and in 238, he was nominated bishop of Carthage. At first he refused but then accepted the appointment. A year later, Emperor Decius began his persecutions. Years of peace had weakened the spirit of Christians, and when the edict reached Carthage, there was a stampede to the capital to register apostasies with magistrates stating falsely that they sacrificed to idols, accompanied by cries of ''Cyprian to the lions!'' by the pagans. The bishop fled to a hiding place. This action brought criticism from Rome and Africa, but he sent letters to the clergy defending his action. During his absence, Novatus, a priest who'd opposed his election, went into open schism. Some of the *lapsi* and confessors who were disciplined under Cyprian's position supported Novatus, who received the *lapsi* back to the church without penance. Cyprian denounced Novatus, and at a council convened at Carthage after the persecutions lessened, he read a treatise on the unity of the Church, *De Unitate Catholicae Ecclesiae*, his most important and influential work. Leaders of the schismatics were excommunicated. Cyprian recognized Cornelius as the true pope and supported him in Italy and Africa during the ensuing schism. With St. Dionysius, bishop of Alexandria, he rallied the bishops of the East to Cornelius. Cyprian complains often in his writing that peace had eroded Christian watchfulness and spirit, enabling entrance to many converts lacking the faith and courage to stand the trial. Between 252 and 254, a terrible plague—for which the Christians were blamed—raged in Carthage. Cyprian organized the Christians of the city and taught them that they must offer help to enemies and persecutors as well as their own people. To bolster and comfort his flock during the plague, Cyprian wrote his treatise *De mortalitate*. Where he supported Cornelius, he opposed Pope St. Stephen I in the matter of baptism conferred by heretics and schismatics; he refused to recognize their validity. Cyprian displayed considerable intolerance during this controversy, despite his public treatise on patience, and wrote many quarrelsome letters to Stephen. St. Augustine says that he atoned for this excess by his martyrdom. In August 257, Valerian passed an edict forbidding all assemblies of Christians and requiring all bishops, priests, and deacons to take part in official worship or be exiled. On August 30, Cyprian was brought before the proconsul, Paternus, who exiled him to Curubus, fifty miles away. When Galerius replaced Paternus as proconsul, he recalled Cyprian and tried him again. Cyprian refused again to offer sacrifice to pagan gods and was sentenced to be beheaded. Cyprian was a pioneer of Latin Christian literature, and his writing is characterized by his compassion, discretion, and fervor. He is mentioned in the intercession of the Roman mass, which is notable considering his disagreement with Pope St. Stephen. He is the patron of North Africa and Algeria. In art, he is shown as a bishop, holding a palm and a sword.

CYRIL AND METHODIUS. Bishops. 826–869, 815–885. February 14. The two brothers were natives of Thessalonika. The younger brother, Cyril, was baptized Constantine and assumed the name Cyril only when he received the habit of a monk. At an early age, he was sent to Constantinople, where he studied at the imperial university under Leo the Grammarian and Photius. He was ordained a deacon and eventually succeeded to the chair of Photius, and he acted as librarian at the church of Santa Sophia, earning a reputation and the label "the Philosopher." He retired for a time to a religious house, but in 861 he was sent by Emperor Michael III on a religious/political mission to convert the Khazars between the Dnieper and Volga rivers in Russia. His older brother, Methodius, who after being governor of one of the Slavic colonies in the Opsikion province, had become a monk, accompanied him on this mission, and upon his return to Greece, was elected abbot of an important monastery. In 862, an ambassador sent by Rostislav, prince of Moravia, came to Constantinople to request missionaries to teach his people in their own language, as the Germans had been unsuccessful. Photius, now patriarch of Constantinople, chose Cyril and Methodius for this mission because they were learned and knew Slavonic. Their first task was to provide characters in which the Slavonic tongue might be written. He translated the liturgical books and some of the Scriptures into Slavonic. The characters now called "cyrillic," from which we derive the present Russian, Serbian, and Bulgarian letters, were invented from the Greek letters, perhaps by followers of Cyril. The brothers set out with assistants for the court of Rostislav in 863. They used the vernacular in their preaching, which appealed to the natives. The Germans objected to this and were suspicious of missionaries from Constantinople, where heresy was common, and their dissatisfaction was backed up when the Emperor Louis the German forced Rostislav to take an oath of fealty to him. The Byzantine missionaries made many converts but were hampered by the lack of a bishop to ordain more priests. The German bishop of Passau refused to do this, and the brothers were summoned to Rome by Pope Nicholas I. They traveled at an unfortunate time; Photius had incurred excommunication and their liturgical use of Slavonic was strongly criticized. They arrived in Rome bringing the alleged relics of Pope St. Clement, which Cyril was said to have miraculously recovered from the sea in the Crimea. Pope Nicholas had died, and they were received by Adrian II. He decided to make the brothers bishops and that their neophytes were to be ordained. While in Rome, Cyril became a monk at SS. Boniface and Alexius on the Aventine, taking the name Cyril, and then died shortly after. He was buried in the church of San Clemente on the Coelian, where the alleged relics of St. Clement have been enshrined. His brother returned to teach in Moravia and was to translate the Bible into Slavonic. It is unknown whether Cyril was consecrated before his death. The present-day liturgical language of the Russians, Serbs, Ukrainians, and Bulgars is that devised by the brothers. They are the patron saints of Yugoslavia, Czechoslovakia, and of Europe. In art, Cyril is portrayed with Bulgarian converts around him; or in a long philosopher's coat; or both brothers are shown holding a church.

CYRIL OF ALEXANDRIA. Bishop, doctor of the Church. c. 376–444. June 27. He is called the "Doctor of the Incarnation." Though he had read the profane writers, he made it a rule never to advance any doctrine that he had not learned from the ancient fathers. Although his writing revealed great precision of thought, he often said that he regretted that he did not use a clearer style and write purer Greek. A native of Alexandria, he was ordained by his uncle Theophilus. Cyril accompanied him to Constantinople in 403 and was present at the Synod of the Oak that deposed John Chrysostom, whom he himself believed to be guilty. After his uncle's death in 412, he was raised to the see of Alexandria following a riot between Cyril's supporters and those of his rival Timotheus. He immediately moved to have the churches of the Novatians closed and their sacred vessels seized. He drove out the Jews and attacked the Neoplatonists, angering the governor, Orestes, although his actions were approved by Emperor Theodosius. This disagreement had a tragic outcome. Hypatia, a pagan woman, was the most influential teacher of philosophy in Alexandria, and disciples flocked to her from everywhere. Acting upon the belief that Hypatia had turned the governor against Cyril, a mob attacked her in her chariot, dragged her into the street, and tore her body into pieces. In 428, Nestorius, a priest-monk of Antioch, was made archbishop of Constantinople. He taught the clergy that there were two distinct persons in Christ: that of God and that of man, joined only by a moral union. He also held that Mary was not the Mother of God since Christ was divine and not human, and thus should not be called *theotokos*, or God bearer. Cyril sent him a mild expostulation but was answered rudely. Both appealed to Pope St. Celestine I, who condemned the doctrine and excommunicated Nestorius unless he were to publicly retract his position within ten days of receiving the sentence. Cyril was appointed to see the sentence fulfilled, and sent Nestorius his third and last summons—twelve anathemas to be signed by him as proof of his orthodoxy. Nestorius held fast, and Cyril, who enjoyed conflict, persuaded the pope to summon the third general council. Nestorius was present in town but would not appear. His sermons were read, and condemned, and a sentence of excommunication and deposition were read. Six days later, archbishop John of Antioch arrived with forty-two bishops who had been unable to reach the meeting in time. They supported

98

Nestorius, although they did not follow his practice. Instead of meeting with the council, they met together and presumed to depose Cyril, accusing him of heresy. Both sides appealed to the emperor, and he ordered that Cyril and Nestorius be arrested. When three legates from Pope Celestine arrived, they confirmed the condemnation of Nestorius, approved Cyril's conduct, and invalidated the sentence against him. Monophysite Copts, Syrians, and Ethiopians venerate Cyril as their chief teacher because, in stressing the truth of Christ's divinity, Cyril uses a terminology that sometimes appears to favor Monophysitism. He wrote treatises that clarified doctrines of the Trinity and the Incarnation, and thus prevented Nestorianism and Pelagianism from taking root in the Christian community. He is considered the most brilliant theologian of Alexandrian tradition, although his stubborn rejection and occasional misinterpretation of his opponents' beliefs have been criticized by scholars. Among his writings are commentaries on John, Luke, and the Pentateuch, treatises on dogmatic theology, an Apologia against Julian the Apostate, and letters and sermons. He is generally represented in art with the other Greek fathers, distinguished by name; or with the Virgin Mary appearing to him.

CYRIL OF JERUSALEM. Bishop, doctor of the Church. c. 315–386. March 18. His parents were probably Christians, and he was born in Jerusalem and brought up there. He was given an excellent education and was ordained a priest by the bishop of Jerusalem, St. Maximus. The bishop respected him so much that he charged him with the duty of instructing the catechumens. Cyril lectured without a book and the nineteen catechetical discourses of his that have survived are perhaps the only ones that were ever written down. They were taught to those preparing for, or those who had just received Baptism. The first year of his episcopate was notable for strange lights that were reported to appear over the city. Soon after his consecration, a dispute arose between Cyril and Bishop Acacius over precedence and jurisdiction of sees and matters of faith. Acacius had fallen under Arian heresy. Acacius called a small council of bishops of his own party, and summoned Cyril, but Cyril refused to appear. At the council Cyril was also accused of having sold church property during famine to relieve the hungry. Cyril had done this, but so had St. Augustine and St. Ambrose, and many others, without persecution. The council, however, condemned him, and he was exiled from Jerusalem. He went to Tarsus. He remained there while he awaited the hearing of an appeal he'd made to a higher court. The appeal came before the Council of Seleucia two years later. The council was comprised of semi-Arians, Arians, and a few members of the strictly orthodox party. Cyril sat among the semi-Arians, several of whom supported him during his exile. His reputation was one of great gentleness and reasonableness. Irritated by his presence, Acacius left the meeting but later returned and played an active part in the subsequent debates. Cyril, however, was vindicated and reinstated. Acacius persuaded Emperor Constantius to summon another council. A year later, he obtained a second decree of exile against Cyril. But upon the death of Constantius, his successor Julian recalled all expelled bishops. In 367, Cyril was banished a third time, when Valens expelled all bishops recalled by Julian. Around the time of the accession of Theodosius, Cyril was reinstated and remained undisturbed in his possession of his see for the last eight years of his life. Upon his return to Jerusalem he found schisms, rampant heresy, and terrible crime. The Council of Antioch sent St. Gregory of Nyssa to investigate charges against Cyril arising from his questioning of the word *homoousios*, a basic term in the Nicene Creed. St. Gregory remained only a short time, but it was long enough to compile a richly descriptive account of the corrupt morals of the holy city. He declared at the same time, however, that Cyril and his faith were orthodox. In 381, both St. Gregory and Cyril were present at the great Council

100

of Constantinople—the second ecumenical council—and as bishop of Jerusalem, Cyril took his place as a metropolitan with the patriarchs of Alexandria and Antioch. The Nicene Creed was promulgated in its amended form at this meeting, and Cyril, who subscribed to it, accepted the term *homoousios*, which had come to be regarded as the test word of orthodoxy. He had spent sixteen of his thirty-five years of episcopate in exile. He is depicted in art with a purse in his hand.

DAMASUS I. Pope. d. 384. December 11. He appears to have been born in Rome, although he may have been of Spanish extraction. But his father was a priest in Rome. Damasus never married but became a deacon in the church of St. Laurence, where his father had served. When Pope Liberius died in 366, Damasus, then about sixty, was chosen bishop of Rome. His election was highly contested, and a minority elected an antipope, Ursinus, whom they used violence to support. A bitter battle began but the civil power maintained Damasus, and Ursinus was exiled by Emperor Valentinian. The opposition was not put down immediately, however, and as late as 378, Damasus had to clear himself of a charge of incontinence cast against him by his opponents. By far the most influential action of Damasus was his patronage of St. Jerome. He commissioned Jerome to write his biblical commentaries and to revise the Latin text of the Bible, which yielded the Vulgate version of the Bible. Damasus also devoted much effort to gathering the relics and resting places of Roman martyrs, and to the restoration of sacred catacombs, and to instructions that he drew up for their care. He had placed in the papal crypt of the cemetery of St. Callistus a general epitaph that ends: ''I, Damasus, wished to be buried here, but I feared to offend the ashes of these holy ones.'' He was buried with his mother and sister at a small church he had built on the Via Ardeatina. He increased the prestige of the Roman see and successfully opposed Arians, Macedonians, Donatists, and Apollinarians. He composed many beautiful epitaphs for the tombs of the martyrs and encouraged pilgrimages to them. He enforced Valentinian's edict of 370 forbidding gifts by widows and orphans to bishops. St. Jerome, who served as his secretary for a time, called him "an incomparable man." As a biblical scholar, Damasus published the canon of Holy Scripture, specifying the authentic books of the Bible as decreed by a council in Rome in 374. He also saw to the collection and housing of papal archives. He is the patron saint of archaeologists. In art, he may hold a ring, or a screen with "*Gloria Patri*," etc., upon it; or be shown with a church door behind him.

DENIS. Bishop, martyr, d. c. 250. October 9. Writing in the sixth century, St. Gregory of Tours tells us that Denis, or Dionysius, of Paris was born in Italy and was sent in 250 with six other missionary bishops into Gaul, where he became the first bishop in Paris and where he suffered martyrdom. The "Martyrology of Jerome" mentions St. Dionysius on October 9, together with St. Rusticus and St. Eleutherius, assumed by later writers to have been the bishop's priest and deacon. Together they penetrated to Lutetia Parisiorum and established Christianity on an island in the Seine. Denis's preaching was so effective that they were arrested and, after a long imprisonment, were beheaded by Decius. Their bodies were flung into the Seine but were recovered and given an honorable burial. A chapel was later built over their tomb, and around it was built the great Benedictine Abbey of Saint-Denis, which was to become the burial place of the kings of France. The abbey was founded by King Dagobert I (d. 638), and it is possible that a century or so later the identification of St. Dionysius with Dionysius the Areopagite began to emerge. But this was not widely accepted until the time of Hilduin, the abbot of Saint-Denis. In 827, the Emperor Michael II sent copies of writings ascribed to St. Dionysius the Areopagite (likely the work of a fifth-century ecclesiastical writer) to the emperor of the West, Louis the Pious, as a present. By coincidence, the writings arrived in Paris on the eve of the feast of the patron of the abbey and were taken to Saint-Denis. Hilduin translated them into Latin, and some years later, when Louis asked for a life of St. Dionysius of Paris, the abbot presented a work that convinced Christendom for the next 700 years that Dionysius of Paris, Dionysius of Athens, and the author of the "Dionysian" writings were one and the same person. Hilduin made use of worthless and false materials in his "Areopagitica," in such a way that his motives appear suspicious. According to this story, the Areopagite comes to Rome, where Pope St. Clement I receives him and sends him to evangelize the Parisians. After the Parisians fail to kill him by wild beasts, fire, and crucifixion, they behead him, with Rusticus and Eleutherius, on Montmartre. Then the body of St. Dionysius rises to its feet and, led by angel, walks the two miles from Montmartre to where the Abbey Church of Saint-Denis now stands, carrying his head in his hands and surrounded by singing angels, and is buried there. St. Edith of Wilton built a chapel in his honor, decorated with murals of his martyrdom. He is the patron saint of Paris and France, and he is invoked against headaches. In art he is shown as a headless bishop, carrying his own mitered head, with a palm, sword, or book. His vestments may be covered with fleur-de-lis.

DOMINIC. Founder. c. 1170–1221. August 8. He was born at Calaruega in Old Castile; his father Felix, possibly of the Guzmán family, was the warden of the town, and his mother was Bl. Joan of Aza. At fourteen, he left the care of his uncle, the archpriest of Gumiel d'Izan, and entered the school of Palencia. He was made canon of the Cathedral of Osma while still a student, and after his ordination, he took up his duties there. His chapter lived a communal life under a rule of very regular observance, prayer, and penance. In 1191, during a famine, he is said to have sold all his possessions, including books, to help the poor. He became prior around 1201 at the age of thirty-one, succeeding Diego d'Azevedo. In 1204, Alfonso IX, king of Castile, sent Diego, then the bishop of Osma, to Denmark as an ambassador to negotiate a marriage for his son. Dominic accompanied him. The two passed through Languedoc, then overrun by Albigensian heretics. The owner of the house where they lodged was one. Dominic spent the entire night discussing faith with him, and the man acknowledged his errors. It is thought that from this point, Dominic knew what work God had chosen for him. He was going to reconcile heretics to the Church. After completing their mission, the bishop and he went to Rome to ask Pope Innocent III permission to preach in Russia. The pope asked them instead to oppose the heresy threatening their church at home. On their return, they visited Cîteaux, whose monks were the officially appointed organizers and preachers against Albigensianism. At Montpellier they met the abbot of Cîteaux and two monks, Peter of Castelnau and Raoul of Fontefroide, who had been in charge of missions in Languedoc. Dominic and the bishop encouraged them to follow the example of their opponents by giving up traveling with horses and retinues and staying at the best inns with servants in attendance. After showing themselves worthy of being listened to, it was suggested that they should use persuasion and discussion rather than threats and belligerence to convince their hearers. A series of conferences were held with the heretics; Dominic influenced the main body but not their leaders. The bishop returned to Osma at this point, while Dominic remained. On the feast of St. Mary Magdalen in 1206, Dominic had a sign from Heaven. As a result, within six months he founded at Prouille a monastery to house nine nuns who had been converted from heresy. A house for preaching friars was attached to it. Thus Dominic provided a supply of preachers trained to convert, a nunnery to educate girls, and a house of prayer. Dominic spent nearly ten years preaching in Languedoc as a leader, though without canonical status, of a small company of special preachers. In 1208, the murder of the papal legate, Peter of Castelnau led to the declaration by Pope Innocent of a holy war against the Albigensians. Dominic did not take part in the seven years of violence and massacres, though he followed the army and preached to the heretics. Although he had practiced the Augustinian rule, he wished to revive an apostolic spirit in the ministers of the altar. He imagined a body of religious men who would combine contemplation and education with the practical needs of preaching and public prayer. He especially wished monasteries to act as centers of learning. In 1214, Count Simon IV of Montfort gave him a castle at Casseneuil, and Dominic founded a monastery there with six followers. Bishop Fulk of Toulouse gave him an endowment in 1214 and approved the young order in 1215. A few months later, Dominic accompanied the bishop to the Fourth Lateran Council. Pope Innocent III gave his approbation of the nunnery of Prouille. His approval was on the condition that Dominic return to his brethren and agree upon which existing rule they would follow. They met at Prouille in 1216, and after consulting with colleagues, Dominic chose the rule of St. Augustine, adding certain constitutions to assist in the daily running of the order. Pope Innocent died in 1216, and Honorius III succeeded him, which put off Dominic's second journey to Rome. He finished the first friary at Toulouse, to which the bishop gave the Church of St. Romain, and the first community of Dominicans assembled to live in common under vows. Dominic arrived in Rome in the fall of 1216, and Honorius confirmed his order and its constitutions the same year. In 1217, the Friars Preachers (or Black Friars) met under their leader at Prouille. He instructed them on methods of preaching and teaching and counseled them to pursue serious and constant study. On the feast of Assumption, unexpectedly—for heresy was again gaining ground in the area—he broke up the band, dispersing them in all directions: four were sent to Spain, seven to Paris, two to Tou-

105

louse, and two were to remain at Prouille. Dominic returned to Rome. The pope gave him the church of St. Sixtus (San Sisto Vecchio). While making a foundation there, he lectured on theology and preached in St. Peter's with such eloquence that the entire city was roused. At this time, many nuns lived in Rome outside of enclosure and almost without regularity. Some lived in small monasteries, while others lived with parents or friends. Pope Innocent III had made several attempts to assemble the nuns into one house but, with all his authority, was unable to accomplish it. Honorius charged Dominic to handle this, and he succeeded. He gathered the nuns at his monastery of St. Sixtus. He accepted for his friars the house of St. Sabing; for his nuns, the house of St. Sisto. Dominic arrived in Bologna in 1219, and it was to be his primary residence for the rest of his life. In 1220, Pope Honorius confirmed Dominic's title and office as master general, and at Pentecost, the first general chapter was held at Bologna, and the final constitutions of the order were drawn up. Under Dominic's approach, the order spread rapidly, and by the second chapter in 1221, there were sixty friaries and friars had traveled into Poland, Scandinavia, and Palestine. After this second chapter, Dominic visited Cardinal Ugolino in Venice. After preaching in Hungary, he became ill, returned to Bologna, and was taken to a country location for better air. He knew he was dying, and he spoke at length to his brethren about poverty. He asked to be returned to Bologna so that he might be buried "under the feet of his brethren." The monks gathered around him to say the prayers for the dying, and at the *Subvenite*, Dominic repeated the words and died. The Order of Preachers, with that founded by St. Francis, marks the peak of the powerful spread of Christian asceticism. Dominic's demands for poverty were less poetically severe than Francis's, although he knew and respected Francis, and his order was the first to formally abandon manual labor. In addition to being a marvelous organizer, he was a man of great personal charm, and he was held in great affection by his followers. He refused a bishopric three times. His tomb at Bologna, built thirty years later by Nicholas Pisano, was embellished by Michelangelo, among others. He is depicted in art clad in the habit of the order—a white tunic and scapular and a black cloak—holding a lily. Often a star shines above his head. With him may be a dog (an early artist's pun: *domini canis*—Dominicans), and a globe, with fire. He may carry a rosary (which he was erroneously thought to have invented) and hold a tall cross.

DOMINIC SAVIO. Confessor. 1842–1857. March 9. Born in Riva, Piedmont, he was one of ten children of a peasant blacksmith and a seamstress. He grew up with a desire to be a priest. When St. John Bosco began to train youths as clergy to help him in his work caring for neglected boys at Turin, Dominic's parish priest recommended Dominic. Bosco, who would write Dominic's biography, was impressed upon meeting him. In October of 1854, at the age of twelve, Dominic became a student at the Oratory of St. Francis de Sales in Turin. He is best known for the group he organized there, called the Company of the Immaculate Conception. In addition to its devotional measures, it handled various jobs, from sweeping the floors to taking special care of boys who were misfits. Early in his stay at the oratory, Dominic halted a fight with stones between two boys. Holding a crucifix between them he said, "Before you fight, look at this, both of you, and say 'Jesus Christ was sinless, and He died forgiving His executioners; I am going to outrage him by being deliberately revengeful.' Then you can start—and throw your first stone at me." He scrupulously followed the discipline of the house, incurring resentment from some other boys from whom he expected the same behavior. Bosco's guidance probably curbed Dominic from becoming a young fanatic. He forbade Dominic to perform bodily mortifications without his permission, believing that with ". . . heat, cold, sickness (and) the tiresome ways of other people—there is quite enough mortification for boys in school life itself." He found Dominic shivering in bed one cold night with only a thin sheet. "Don't be crazy. You'll get pneumonia," he said. "Why should I?" replied Dominic. "Our Lord didn't get pneumonia in the stable at Bethlehem." On one occasion when Dominic was missing from morning until after dinner, Bosco found him in the choir of the church, standing in a cramped position by the lectern, deep in prayer. He had been there for six hours, yet he thought that early mass was not yet over. Dominic referred to these times of intense prayer as "my distractions." Bosco reports that in one strong "distraction," Dominic saw a wide, mist-shrouded plain, with a multitude of people groping about in it. To them came a pontifically vested figure carrying a torch that lighted up the whole scene, and a voice seemed to say, "This torch is the Catholic faith which shall bring light to the English people." Bosco reported this to Pope Pius IX at Dominic's request, and the pope said that it confirmed his intention to give attention to England. Dominic became known for his cheerfulness, friendliness, careful observance, and good advice. Dominic's fragile health worsened, and in 1857, he was sent home to Mondonio for a change of air. He was diagnosed with tuberculosis, and was bled, which probably hastened his death. He received the last sacraments and asked his father to read the prayers for the dying. Toward the end, he tried to sit up. "Good-bye father," he said, "the priest told me something . . . but I can't remember what. . . ." Suddenly he smiled and exclaimed, "I am seeing the most wonderful things!" and died. He was the youngest nonmartyr to receive official canonization in the history of the Church. He is the patron saint of Pueri Cantors, choirs, choirboys, boys, and juvenile delinquents.

DUNSTAN. Bishop. 909–988. May 19. Born at Baltonsborough, he was of a noble family in connection with the ruling house. He received his early education from the Irish scholars and monks at Glastonbury. While still young, he was sent to the court of King Athelstan. He had already received the tonsure, and his uncle, St. Alphege the Bald, the bishop of Winchester, encouraged him to join the religious life. Dunstan hesitated for some time and nearly got married, but after recovering from a skin condition he believed to be leprosy, he received the habit and holy orders from his uncle the same day as St. Ethelwold. He returned to Glastonbury and is thought to have built a small cell next to the old church. He engaged in prayer, study, and manual labor, making bells and sacred vessels for the church and copying or illuminating books. He is said to have excelled as a painter, embroiderer, harpist, and metal-worker. Athelstan's successor, Edmund, called him to court to act as a royal counselor and treasurer. In 943, after Edmund narrowly escaped death while hunting, he appointed Dunstan abbot of Glastonbury, endowing the monastery generously. Dunstan restored the monastery buildings and the Church of St. Peter. By introducing monks among the clerks already in residence, he enforced regular discipline without making waves. He made the abbey into a great school of learning. He revitalized other monasteries in Glastonbury. The murder of King Edmund was followed by the accession of his brother Edred, who made Dunstan one of his top advisers. In 955, Edred died and was succeeded by his sixteen-year-old nephew Edwy. On the day of his coronation, Edwy left the royal banquet to see a girl named Elgiva and her mother. For this he was sternly rebuked by Dunstan, and the prince deeply resented the chastisement. With the support of the opposing party, Dunstan was disgraced, his property confiscated, and he was exiled. He went to Ghent in Flanders, and there he came into contact with reformed continental monasticism. This experience fueled his vision of Benedictine perfection that would inspire his work from then on. A rebellion broke out in England; the north and east deposed Edwy and put his brother Edgar on the throne. Edgar recalled Dunstan and appointed him the bishop of Worcester and later that of London. On Edwy's death in 959, the kingdom was reunited under Edgar. Dunstan was made archbishop of Canterbury, and together, the two initiated a policy of reform to solidify both the Church and the country. In 961, Dunstan went to Rome to receive the pallium and was appointed by Pope John XII a legate of the Holy See. With this authority, he set about reestablishing ecclesiastical discipline, under the protection of King Edgar and assisted by St. Ethelwold, the bishop of Winchester, and St. Oswald, the bishop of Worcester and archbishop of York. They restored most of the great monasteries that had been destroyed during the Danish incursions and founded new ones. Clergy who had been living scandalous lives or boldly disregarding canonical laws of celibacy were reformed. Recalcitrant seculars were ejected and replaced by monks. Dunstan remained firm in his moral standards, even to deferring Edgar's coronation for fourteen years—likely due to a disapproval of Edgar's scandalous behavior. He modified the coronation rite, and some of his modifications survive to this day. Through sixteen years of Edgar's reign, Dunstan acted as his chief adviser, criticizing him freely, and he continued to direct the state during the short reign of the succeeding king, Edward the Martyr, Dunstan's protégé. The death of the young king, connected with the antimonastic reaction following Edgar's death, grieved Dunstan terribly. His political career now over, he returned to Canterbury to teach at the cathedral school, where visions, prophecies, and miracles were attributed to him. He was especially devoted to the Canterbury saints, whose tombs he visited at night. On the feast of Ascension in 988 the archbishop was ill but celebrated mass and preached three times to his people, to whom he declared that he would die soon. Two days later he died peacefully in his Cathedral of Christ Church, where he is buried. He is considered the reviver of monasticism in England. It has been said that the tenth century gave shape to English history, and that Dunstan gave shape to the tenth century. He composed several hymns, notably *Kyrie Rex spendens*. He is the patron saint of armorers, goldsmiths, locksmiths, and jewelers. In art, he is shown as a bishop holding the devil with a pair of pincers, often grasping him by the nose; or with a crucifix speaking to him.

DYMPNA, DYMPHNA. Martyr, virgin. c. 650. May 15. Variations of her legend are to be found in the folklore of many European countries. She was said to have been the daughter of a pagan Irish, British, or Amorite king and a Christian princess who died when she was very young, but who had had her baptized. As she grew into a young woman, her uncanny resemblance to her dead mother aroused an incestuous passion in her father. On the advice of her confessor, St. Gerebernus, she fled from home. Accompanied by Gerebernus and attended by the court jester and his wife, she took a ship to Antwerp. She then traveled southeast, through wild forest country, until she reached a small oratory dedicated to St. Martin on the site of the present-day town of Gheel. The band settled here to live as solitaries. Dympna's father had pursued her to Antwerp, and he sent spies who found them by tracing their use of foreign coins. The king tried to persuade her to return, but when she refused, the king ordered that she and Gerebernus be killed. The king's men killed the priest and their companions but hesitated to kill Dympna. The king himself struck off her head with his sword. The bodies were left on the ground. They were buried by angelic or human hands where they had perished. Great interest in her *cultus* spread when the translation of the relics of Dympna was followed by the cures of a number of epileptics, lunatics, and persons under evil influences who visited the shrine. Ever since, she has been regarded as the patroness of the mentally ill, and the inhabitants of Gheel have been known for the care they have given to those with mental illness. At the close of the thirteenth century, an infirmary was built. Today the town

111

possesses a first-class sanatorium, and it was one of the first to initiate a program through which patients live normal and useful lives in the homes of farmers or local residents, whom they assist in their labor and whose family life they share. Dympna and Gerebernus are buried in two ancient marble sarcophagi, where they were rediscovered in the thirteenth century. The body of Dympna is preserved in a silver reliquary in the church bearing her name. Only the head of Gerebernus rests there, the remains having been removed to Sonsbeck in the diocese of Munster. She is the patron saint of mental illness (once thought to be possession by the devil), asylums for the mentally ill, nurses of the mentally ill, epilepsy, possession by the devil, and sleepwalkers (sleepwalking was looked upon in the Middle Ages as a form of possession). In art she is portrayed being beheaded by a king; or praying in a cloud surrounded by a group of lunatics bound with golden chains.

EDMUND CAMPION. Martyr. c. 1540–1581. December 1. He was born the son of Edmund Campion, Sr., a bookseller, and was educated at Christ's Hospital at the expense of the Grocers' Guild. At fifteen, he received a scholarship to St. John's College, newly founded by Sir Thomas White, at Oxford. Two years later, he was appointed a junior fellow, and he gained a reputation as a great orator. He was chosen to speak at the reburial of Lady Amy Dudley (Robsart), and at the funeral of Sir Thomas White, and he was chosen by the university to give the welcoming speech to Queen Elizabeth I when she visited Oxford in 1566. He earned the respect and patronage of the queen, her counselor Cecil, and the earl of Leicester. Edmund had taken the oath of royal supremacy and he became a deacon of the Anglican Church. This decision began to trouble him, however, as he recognized that he harbored doubts about the Church. For this reason, at the end of his term as junior proctor of the university in 1596, he went to Dublin, where he helped to found a university (later Trinity College). While there, he wrote a short history of Ireland and dedicated it to Leicester. In the wake of Pope St. Pius's campaign against Elizabeth, he fell under suspicion. He returned to England in disguise in 1571 and was present at the trial of Bl. John Storey in Westminster Hall. He departed for Douai, the English college in Flanders. He was stopped for lacking a passport, but he bribed the officials with his luggage and money. At Douai he took his B.D. and was ordained a subdeacon. In 1573, he went to Rome and was admitted to the Society of Jesus. As there was no English province at this time, he was sent to Bohemia, and after his novitiate at Brno, he went to the college of Prague to teach rhetoric and other subjects. Dr. Allen (later Cardinal) convinced Pope Gregory XIII to send Jesuits to England, and in 1579, Edmund and Father Robert Persons were chosen for this mission. He set out for Rome in 1580, visited St. Charles Borromeo at Milan, and landed at Dover disguised as a jewel merchant. The Jesuits were not well received by the Catholics, who feared they would cause trouble. In London, Edmund ministered to Catholic prisoners and wrote a challenge to the Privy Council (called *Campion's Brag*), which described his mission as one "of free cost to preach the Gospel, to minister the Sacraments, to instruct the simple, to reform sinners, to confute errors; in brief, to cry alarm spiritual against foul vice and proud ignorance, wherewith many of my dear countrymen are abused." As their arrival was known to the government, he soon had to leave London and went to Berkshire, Oxfordshire, and Northhamptonshire, where he made converts. After meeting Persons in London, where persecutions had heightened, he went to Lancashire, where he preached almost daily and very successfully, always one step ahead of spies, barely escaping capture on several occasions. During this time he wrote a Latin treatise, *Decem Rationes*, which listed ten reasons why he had challenged the most learned Protestants

113

to discuss theology with him. The treatise was secretly printed on a press at the house of Dame Cecilia Stonor in Berkshire. On "Commemoration," June 27, 1581, 400 copies of it were found distributed on the benches at St. Mary's University Church at Oxford. It raised a great sensation and attempts to capture him increased. He decided to retire to Norfolk. On the way, he stayed at the house of Mrs. Yate at Lyford, and people gathered there to hear him preach. A traitor was among them, and within twelve hours the house was searched three times—and he and two other priests were discovered hiding above a gateway. He was taken to the Tower, bound, and he was labeled "Campion, the seditious Jesuit." After he spent three days in the "little ease," the earls of Bedford and Leicester tried to bribe him into recanting, without success. Other attempts failed as well, and he was racked. While still weak from torture, he was confronted by Protestant dignitaries four times. He answered them eloquently. He was racked again, this time so painfully that when he was asked the following day how he felt, he responded, "Not ill, because not at all." On November 14, he was indicted in Westminster Hall with Ralph Sherwin, Thomas Cottam, Luke Kirby, and others, on the trumped-up charge of having plotted to raise a rebellion in England. When asked to plead the charge, he was too weak to move his arms; one of his companions kissed his hand and held it up for him. Edmund defended himself and the others brilliantly, protesting their loyalty to the queen, blasting the evidence, raising doubts about the witnesses, and establishing clearly that their only crime was their faith. Although the packed jury found them guilty, it took them an hour to come to the decision. When he was condemned, Edmund said, "In condemning us you condemn all your own ancestors, all the ancient bishops and kings, all that was once the glory of England. . . . Posterity's judgment is not liable to corruption as that of those who are now going to sentence us to death." On December 1, they were taken to Tyburn, and hanged, drawn, and quartered. Some of Edmund's blood splashed on the young Henry Walpole, who would also become a Jesuit and be canonized with Edmund as one of the Forty Martyrs of England and Wales in 1970.

ELIGIUS, ELOI. Bishop. c. 588–660. December 1. He was born at Chaptelet, near Limoges. His mother, Terriga, and his father Eucherius, an artisan, were of Roman-Gallo extraction. Recognizing his son's skill at engraving and smithing, Eucherius placed him as an apprentice with Abbo, a goldsmith who was master at Limoges. When he finished his apprenticeship, Eligius crossed the Loire into France and became known to Bobbo, treasurer to Clotaire II at Paris. The king gave Eligius an order to make him a chair of state, decorated with gold and precious stones. With the materials given to him, Eligius made two chairs. The king was impressed with his honesty and his skill. Clotaire took him into his household and made him master of the mint. He became a person of rank and wore clothes embroidered with gold and adorned with precious stones; he sometimes wore nothing but silk, which was very rare in France then. But he was not corrupted by his good fortune; he gave away large amounts of money in alms. A stranger who asked the way to his house was told, "Go to such a street, and it's where you see a crowd of poor people." Eligius put off swearing an oath of allegiance to Clotaire and his excuses angered Clotaire. Clotaire finally came to understand, however, that conscience was his motive, and he assured Eligius that this was a more secure pledge of allegiance than the vows of others. Eligius ransomed many slaves, some of whom remained in his service for the rest of his life. One of them, a Saxon named Tillo, became a saint. Clotaire's son Dagobert also valued Eligius, and appointed him chief counselor in 629. Dagobert gave Eligius the estate of Solignac in his native Limousin for the foundation of a monastery, which in 632 was filled with monks who followed a combination of the rules of St. Columba and St. Benedict. Under Eligius, the monastery became known for its good work in various arts. Dagobert gave Eligius a house at Paris, which he converted to a nunnery and placed under the supervision of St. Aurea. Eligius asked for and received an additional piece of land to complete construction; when he found he had overshot the measure of the land specified, he went to the king and asked his pardon. Dagobert, taken aback at his honesty, said, "Some of my officers do not scruple to rob me of whole estates; whereas Eligius is afraid of having one inch of ground which is not his.". Eligius went on a diplomatic mission for Dagobert to the Bretons in 636 and convinced the Breton king Judicael to accept the authority of the Frankish king. Eligius was ordained in 640 and in 641 was made bishop of Noyon and Tournai by Clovis II at the same time his friend St. Audoenus was made bishop of Rouen. He became intent upon converting infidels and evangelized a large majority of the Tournai diocese and a great part of Flanders. He preached in the areas of Antwerp, Ghent, and Courtrai. The crude inhabitants shunned him as a foreigner, but he persisted. After taking care of the sick, protecting them from oppression, and undertaking other charitable causes, he won them over, and some were converted. At Noyon, he established a nunnery and brought his protégé, St. Godeberta, from Paris to govern it. He was active in promoting the *cultus* of local saints; the reliquaries of St. Martin at Tours, St. Dionysius at Saint-Denis, St. Germanus of Paris, St. Genevieve, and others are attributed to the skill of Eligius. He took an influential part in the ecclesiastical life of his day and was a valued counselor of the queen-regent, St. Bathildis. They shared a concern for slaves (she'd been sold as a slave as a child), and during the Council of Chalon, c. 677, the sale of slaves out of the kingdom was forbidden, and it was decreed that slaves must be free to rest on Sundays and holidays. Eligius foresaw his own death and told his clergy of it. Falling ill of a fever, on the sixth day he called together his household and said good-bye. He commended them to God and died a few hours later. Hearing of his illness, St. Bathildis set out from

Paris, but she arrived the morning after his death. She prepared to carry the body to her monastery at Chelles, and others wished to take it to Paris, but the people of Noyons strongly opposed the removal, and so the body remained. It was afterward moved into the cathedral. Eligius became one of the most beloved saints during the Middle Ages. Of surviving homilies accredited to him, one is notable for his warnings against pagan superstitions such as fortune-telling, watching for omens, and keeping Thursdays holy in honor of Jupiter. He is the patron saint of goldsmiths, silversmiths, metalworkers, jewelers, and craftsmen; of coin and medal collectors; of horses and veterinarians; of blacksmiths; of garage or gas-station workers. His association with horses originates from an episode that reportedly occurred after his death. A horse Eligius had been riding was inherited by a priest, but the bishop liked the horse and took it for himself. As soon as it was in the bishop's stable, it became ill, and all attempts to cure it failed. During this time, the priest had been praying that it would be returned to him. The bishop gave back the horse, useless to him, and the animal promptly recovered, a cure that was attributed to Eligius. From that time on, he was invoked on behalf of sick horses, and in some places, horses are blessed on his feast day. Gas stations may be considered a modern version of stables. His emblems are those of a metal-working contemporary with the picture (e.g., a hammer and horseshoe, a shod horse's leg, or, in one interesting example, a horse whose leg he first removed, *then* shod, and then replaced); or he wears armor and stands on an anvil; or he is dressed as a bishop and holds one of these emblems or the finer tools of a goldsmith.

ELIZABETH AND ZACHARY. First century. November 5. Elizabeth and Zachary were parents of John the Baptist. All that we know of them is limited to what is found in the first chapter of St. Luke's gospel. Zachary was a priest of the Old Covenant and Elizabeth was of the family of Aaron. Having reached middle age without children, Zachary, while officiating in the temple, had a vision of an angel who told him that in response to their prayers they should have a son, "to whom thou shalt give the name John, who should be filled with the Holy Ghost even in his mother's womb and who should bring back many of the sons of Israel to the Lord their God." When he doubted this vision, Zachary was struck dumb, but upon the birth of John, his speech was restored. Elizabeth was visited by Mary, the Mother of God, at which time Mary spoke the hymn of praise now known as the Magnificat, although a few manuscripts of the New Testament would indicate that it was Elizabeth who spoke the hymn. Tradition has it that Zachary died a martyr, killed in the Temple "between the porch and altar" by command of Herod, because he refused to disclose the whereabouts of his son. In art, Elizabeth is shown clad as an elderly lady, holding the infant St. John the Baptist; or pregnant and greeting the Virgin Mary.

ELIZABETH OF HUNGARY (THURINGIA). Queen, tertiary. 1207–1231. November 17. In the *Life* of Elizabeth, Dietrich of Apolda relates that one evening in 1207 the minnesinger Klingsohr from Transylvania announced to the Landgrave Herman of Thuringia that that night a daughter had been born to the king of Hungary, who should be exalted in holiness and become the wife of Herman's son. Elizabeth was indeed born at that time, in Pressburg, to Andrew II of Hungary and Gertrude of Andechs-Meran, the niece of St. Hedwig. For political reasons, Elizabeth was betrothed to Herman's oldest son. At the age of four, she came to the court at the castle of the Wartburg, near Eisenach, to be reared with her future husband. In 1221, when Louis (Bl. Ludwig) was twenty-one and had become landgrave in his father's place, and Elizabeth was fourteen, they were married. They had three or four children, one of whom was Bl. Gertrude of Aldenburg. Elizabeth was generous, passionate, and attractive, but she did charitable work, lived simply, and prayed a great deal. Louis supported her in this. Wartburg was located on a steep rock, which the ill were unable to climb, so Elizabeth built a hospital at its foot and often fed and cared for the patients herself. She provided for helpless children, especially orphans, founded another hospital with twenty-eight beds, and fed hundreds of persons daily, in addition to making provisions for others throughout the kingdom. Louis embarked on a crusade, departing on St. John the Baptist's day to meet the Emperor Frederick II in Apulia. He died of the plague at Otranto three months later; the news did not reach Elizabeth until after the birth of her second daughter. She was driven almost mad with grief. She was forced to leave Wartburg that winter, under circumstances that are unclear. She may have been driven out by her brother-in-law, Henry, regent for her infant son, or she may have been dismissed because of the vast revenues she had spent on her charities. In any case, she suffered much until she was taken away from Eisenach by her aunt Matilda, abbess of Kitzingen. She next visited her uncle Eckembert, bishop of Bamberg, who put his castle of Pottenstein at her disposal. She traveled there with her son Herman and the baby, leaving her daughter Sophia with the nuns at Kitzingen. Eckembert had plans for her remarriage, but she refused to consider them. She and her husband had agreed never to remarry. Early in 1228, Louis's body was brought home and buried in the abbey church at Reinhardsbrunn, and on Good Friday, in the church of the Franciscan friars at Eisenach, she became a tertiary of the third Order of St. Francis. A great influence on her was Master Conrad of Marburg, who had become her confessor in 1225. Elizabeth had developed a love of poverty from the Friars Minor but had been unable to act upon it while she was landgravine of Thuringia. At this point, her children were provided for by relatives, and she was free

119

to live in Marburg. She lived for a time in a cottage at Wehrda. Returning to Marburg, she built a small house just outside and founded a hospice to care for the sick, aged, and poor, devoting herself entirely to this work. Although Conrad prevented her from begging from door to door, divesting herself of all her goods, giving more than a certain amount in alms, and exposing herself to diseases such as leprosy, he was a hard director. He replaced her ladies-in-waiting with companions who reported all she did to him, and he punished her for disobeying his smallest commands with slaps and by hitting her with a rod, whose marks would remain for weeks. Elizabeth was chastened but not broken by this treatment, and she compared herself to a sedge in a stream during flood time: the water bears it down flat, but when the rains have gone it springs up again, strong and unhurt. She pursued menial tasks—spinning, carding, cleaning the homes of the poor, and fishing to feed them. One day a Magyar noble arrived at Marburg, and at the hospice he found Elizabeth in her plain gray gown, sitting at her spinning wheel. He asked her to return with him to the court of Hungary and leave her life of hardships, but Elizabeth would not go. She died in Thuringia shortly after at the age of twenty-four, her life probably shortened by her austerities. Her relics were translated to the Church of St. Elizabeth of Marburg, where they remained as an object of popular pilgrimage until 1539, when the relics were removed to an unknown place by the Lutheran Philip of Hesse. Miracles were reported at her tomb. She is the patron saint of Catholic charities. In art she is shown performing an act of charity; or wearing a double crown; or wearing a crown and holding two others. Her cloak may be full of roses, and she may carry a basket of food.

ELIZABETH OF PORTUGAL. Queen, tertiary, widow. 1271–1336. July 4. Elizabeth was the daughter of

Peter III, king of Aragon. She was named for her great-aunt, St. Elizabeth of Hungary, but she is known in Portugal by the Spanish form of that name, Isabella. She was married at the age of twelve to Denis, king of Portugal. He allowed her the freedom to live a pious life without joining her in her devotion. She rose early each morning to pray, made provision for pilgrims and poor strangers, and sought out and relieved the distress of those in want. She provided dowries for girls and founded many charitable establishments, including a hospital at Coîmbra, a house for penitent women at Torres Novas, a refuge for foundlings, and shelters for wayward girls. She was a good wife to her husband, whose neglect and infidelities she endured without complaint. She had two children. Her son Alfonso, who was to succeed his father, grew up rebellious, partly in response to his father's treating his illegitimate sons favorably. Twice he sought to start wars, and in both cases his mother brought about a reconciliation between the opposing parties. She was banished from the court when slanderers told the king that she favored her son. She was a gifted arbitrator, and she cut short or prevented war between Ferdinand IV of Castile, and his cousin; and between Ferdinand and her brother, James II of Aragon. She came to be called "the Peacemaker." When her husband became ill in 1324, she faithfully cared for him, leaving his room only to go to church. During his illness, the king, who had been a capable but dissolute leader, repented. He died at Santarem in 1325. After his funeral, Elizabeth made a pilgrimage to Compostela. She wished to enter a convent of Poor Clares she had founded at Coîmbra but was persuaded against it, and instead was professed in the third Order of St. Francis. She lived very simply in a house she built near her convent. She died in 1336 at Estremoz, where she had gone on a mission of reconciliation, in spite of her age and the heat. She was buried in the church of her convent of Poor Clares at Coîmbra. Miracles were reported at her tomb. She is depicted in art carrying roses in her lap in winter; or as a nun of the third Order of St. Francis, sometimes with a beggar near her or with a rose or jug in her hand.

ELIZABETH BAYLEY SETON. Foundress, widow. 1774–1821. January 4. Elizabeth was born in New York. Her mother, Catherine Charlton, was the daughter of the Episcopalian rector of St. Andrew's Church, Staten Island, and her father, Dr. Richard Bayley, was a well-known physician and a professor of anatomy at King's College (which would become Columbia University). Elizabeth's mother died when she was three, and her father gave her an unusual but far-ranging education. Her father pioneered research in surgery, diphtheria, and yellow fever, from which he died in 1801. Elizabeth married a wealthy young merchant, William Magee Seton, in 1794, and they had two sons and three daughters. Seton lost his fortune, however, and when his health deteriorated as a result, they went to live in Italy, hoping for his recuperation. He died of tuberculosis in 1803. His twenty-eight-year-old widow remained in Italy, living with friends for a time, and during this period, she became strongly attracted to Roman Catholicism through her friendship with the brothers Antonio and Filippo Filicchi. She returned to the United States and faced great opposition from her family and friends for this conversion. She resisted them, and in 1805, she was received into the Catholic Church. Estranged from her family and in financial distress, she tried to operate a boarding school in New York in order to support her children, but her religion made her unpopular. She willingly accepted the invitation from a Sulpician priest, William Valentine Du Bourg, to establish a school for girls in Baltimore. She opened St. Joseph's School in 1808. Elizabeth was not unused to this kind of endeavor. She had been greatly involved in charity work in New York, founding the Society for the Relief of Poor Widows with Small Children, and had come to be called "the Protestant Sister of Charity." In Baltimore, she organized a group of like-minded women and established a formal congregation of nuns. In 1809, a community based on the school in Baltimore, the Sisters of St. Joseph, was established and from then on, Elizabeth, who became their superior, was known as "Mother Seton." The same year, the community moved to the town of Emmitsburg in northwest Maryland, and there the sisters took over the rule of the Daughters of Charity of St. Vincent de Paul, changing the rule somewhat. From 1812 on, the congregation was known as the Daughters of Charity of St. Joseph. The sisters were very active, establishing a free school, orphanages, and hospitals. They became most well known, however, for their work with the then growing parochial school system, which was to become a jewel in the crown of the Catholic Church in the United States. In addition to her responsibilities to the congregation, Mother Seton composed music, wrote hymns, and wrote spiritual discourses. At the time of her death in Emmitsburg, her congregation, the first to be founded in the United States, had established twenty communities across the country. She was the first native-born North American to be canonized.

ELMO, ERASMUS. Bishop, martyr. d. c. 303. June 2. Nothing of him is known for certain since his *acta* were written long after his death and were based on legends that confuse him with a Syrian bishop of Antioch. He is thought to have been a bishop of Formiae, in the Campagna, a hermit on Mt. Lebanon, and martyred under Diocletian. St. Gregory the Great recorded that his relics were preserved in the Formiae cathedral in the sixth century. When Formiae was razed by the Saracens in 842, the body of Elmo was translated to Gaeta. He is best known for having been venerated as the patron saint of sailors. This may have originated from a legendary incident in which he is said to have continued to preach even after a thunderbolt struck the ground beside him. This prompted sailors, who were in danger from sudden storms and lightning, to claim him as their patron. The electrical discharges at the mastheads of ships were read as a sign of his protection and came to be called "St. Elmo's Fire." A late legend held that Elmo was martyred by having his intestines drawn out and wound around a windlass. This may have developed from his emblem of a windlass (signifying his patronage of sailors) being confused with an instrument of torture. He is the patron saint of sailors and Gaeta, and, as a result of the form of his legendary martyrdom, is invoked against the pain of women in labor, and cramp and colic, especially in children. He is depicted in art with a large opening in his body through which his intestines have been wound, or are being wound, around a windlass; or vested as a bishop holding a winch or windlass.

ENGELBERT. Bishop, martyr. 1186–1225. November 7. Born at Berg, he was the son of the count of Berg. He was made provost of several churches, including Cologne Cathedral, while still a boy studying at the cathedral school at Cologne. He was excommunicated either for taking up arms against the Emperor Otto IV or for gaining possession uncanonically of benefices. After joining the crusade against the Albigensians, the excommunication was lifted, and he was appointed archbishop of Cologne at the age of thirty. He ruled capably and well, working to restore discipline, bringing the Franciscans and Dominicans into the diocese, holding regular synods, encouraging monastic life and learning, and being attentive to the poor. He became heavily involved in politics through his support of Emperor Frederick II. The emperor appointed him chief minister and tutor to his son, and when the emperor went to Sicily in 1220, he appointed him regent during the minority of his son Henry. Engelbert crowned the twelve-year-old Henry king of the Romans in 1222. Engelbert became involved in a disagreement with his cousin, Count Frederick of Isenberg, whom he accused of stealing the property and oppressing the vassals of nuns for whom the count was acting as administrator. Traveling with an inadequate escort, Engelbert was waylaid by Frederick, other resentful nobles, and fifty soldiers at Gevelsberg, Germany, and brutally murdered. He was stabbed forty-seven times. The young King Henry had Frederick brought to justice. Engelbert is depicted in art in archiepiscopal vestments, a crosier in one hand, and an upraised sword piercing a crescent moon in his other hand.

ETHELDREDA, AUDREY. Abbess, queen. d. 679. June 23. She was born in Exning, Suffolk, the daughter of Anna, king of East Anglia, and Bertha. She was sister to Erconwald, Ethelburga, Sexburga, and Withburga, who all became saints. She was married young to Tonbert, prince of Gryvii, but she successfully convinced him to let her keep her virginity. He died three years later. Etheldreda lived in the seclusion of the island of Ely, her dowry, for the next five years. She was then brought to marry Egfrid, the son of King Oswy of Northumbria, who was then fifteen. After twelve years of marriage, Egfrid demanded his conjugal rights, but she refused, saying that she'd consecrated herself to God. The case was referred to the bishop of Northumbria, St. Wilfred, who, despite Egfrid's bribes, ruled in her favor. With Egfrid's consent, she became a nun under her aunt, St. Abba, at Coldingham Convent. The following year, she returned to Ely, and c. 672, she built a double monastery on the site of the present cathedral in Ely. Egfrid married again, and she remained there for the rest of her life. For seven years she lived a penitential life, eating only one meal per day and wearing woolen clothes instead of the finer cloth that women of rank wore. After Matins, sung at midnight, she remained in prayer until morning. She died of a tumor on her neck (the plague), which was interpreted as divine retribution for her vanity in wearing necklaces in her youth. She foretold how she would die, and how many religious would also die of the disease, which did in fact claim other nuns in the community. She was buried in a simple wooden coffin, in accordance with her wishes. Seventeen years later, her body was found incorrupt; St. Wilfrid and her physician were among the witnesses. The tumor on her neck, which had been cut out by a doctor, was found to be healed, and the linens in which she was enshrouded were fresh. Miracles were said to have been worked by her relics and linen cloths. Her body was placed in a stone sarcophagus of Roman workmanship found at Grantchester and was translated by St. Sexburga in 695. Her shrine was much visited, and she became the most popular of Anglo-Saxon saints. A great many churches were dedicated in her honor. She was translated twice more, and then the shrine was destroyed in 1541, but some relics were claimed by St. Etheldreda's Church, Ely Place, London, and her hand, discovered in 1811 in a recusant hiding place near Arundel, is claimed by St. Etheldreda's Church at Ely. At St. Audrey's Fair, necklaces of silk and lace were sold, and they were frequently of such poor quality that the word "tawdry" (a corruption of "St. Audrey") was applied to them. She is usually represented in art as an abbess, crowned, with a pastoral staff and two does, who were said to have provided the community with milk during a famine.

EUSEBIUS OF VERCELLI. Bishop. c. 283–371. August 2. He was born on Sardinia, and his father is said to have been martyred. His widowed mother took Eusebius and his sister, both infants, to Rome, where Eusebius was reared and eventually ordained a lector. He served in Vercelli, in Piedmont, with such success that he was chosen to govern it by the clergy and the people in 340. He is the first bishop of Vercelli who is known by name. He was the first in the West who combined the monastic discipline with the clerical. He himself lived a common life with clergy in the community, an example that was followed by St. Augustine. In 345, Pope Liberius assigned Eusebius and Bishop Lucifer of Cagliari to plead with the Emperor Constantius to assemble a council to try to halt the trouble between the Catholics and Arians. They were successful, and the council met in Milan in 355. Although the Catholic prelates outnumbered the Arians, Eusebius realized that the Arians would dominate by force, and he refused to attend until he was pressed to do so by Constantius himself. When the bishops were called upon to sign a condemnation of St. Athanasius, Eusebius resisted and instead presented the Nicene Creed, of which he was an author, and insisted that it be signed by all before the case of St. Athanasius was considered. This sparked a great tumult. The emperor sent for Eusebius, St. Dionysius of Milan, and Lucifer of Cagliari, and demanded that they condemn Athanasius. They supported his innocence, saying he could not be condemned without being heard, and urged that secular force not be used to coerce ecclesiastical decisions. The emperor threatened to execute them but eventually banished them instead. Eusebius was first exiled to Scythopolis in Palestine, where he was put in the charge of the Arian bishop, Patrophilus. He stayed first with St. Joseph of Palestine, who offered the only orthodox home in the town, and was visited by St. Epiphanius and others, and given money for subsistence by deputies of his church in Vercelli. After Count Joseph died, the Arians dragged Eusebius through the streets half-clothed and locked him in a small room, where they badgered him for four days to conform. Eusebius went on a hunger strike, and after fasting for four days, the Arians returned him to his lodgings. Three weeks later he was molested again; they confiscated his possessions, drove away his attendants, and dragged him away. Later he was banished to Cappadocia, and later still into the Upper Thebaid in Egypt. Upon the death of Constantius in 361, Julian recalled the banished prelates, and Eusebius traveled to Alexandria to plan with St. Athanasius how to correct the evils of the Church. He took part in a council there, and traveled to Antioch to effect the council's wish that St. Meletius should be recognized as bishop there, and the Eustathian schism be ended. Unsuccessful, Eusebius traveled over the East and through Illyricum, bolstering the wavering faith of many and bringing others back into the fold. In Italy, St. Hilary of Poitiers and Eusebius met and worked together to oppose the Arianizing Auxentius of Milan. According to St. Jerome, Vercelli "laid aside her garments of mourning" upon his long-awaited return, but nothing is known of his remaining years. Eusebius is sometimes called a martyr, but this is attributed to his sufferings and not to a violent death. A manuscript copy of the Latin Gospels that he is reputed to have copied, the Codex Vercellensis, is the oldest such manuscript in existence.

FABIAN. Martyr, pope. d. 250. January 20. In 236 he succeeded St. Antherus as pope and was bishop of Rome for fourteen years until his martyrdom under Decius. He was a layman, who, according to Eusebius, was reportedly elected because a dove flew in through a window during the election and settled on his head. This "sign" united the votes of the clergy and people. He condemned Bishop Privatus of Lambaesa, Africa, for heresy, brought the body of St. Pontian, pope and martyr, from Sardinia, and had significant restoration work done on the catacombs. The *Liber Pontificalis* credited to him the division of Rome into seven deaconries. He was the first victim of the Decian persecutions. He is described by his contemporary, St. Cyprian, as "an incomparable man, the glory of whose death corresponded with the holiness of his life." He was buried in the catacombs of St. Callistus; later, some of his relics were taken to the Basilica of St. Sebastian. The original slab that covered his first tomb, which says clearly in Greek, "Fabian, bishop, martyr," survives. He is shown in art with a dove by his side; or a tiara and a dove; or a sword or club; or kneeling at a block.

FELICITY. Martyr. d. 203. March 7. Felicity and her husband Revocatus were slaves to a twenty-two-year-old matron of noble birth, Vivia Perpetua, in Carthage. They, their mistress, and her child, and fellow catechumens, Saturninus and Secundulus, were arrested under Emperor Severus, who had forbidden fresh conversions, and imprisoned in a private home. There they were all baptized, probably by Saturus, their instructor, who joined them of his own free will. They were later transported to prison, where the pregnant Felicity gave birth to a daughter, and Secundulus died. They were tried by Hilarion, the procurator of the province, and sentenced to death at the public games in the amphitheater by being thrown before wild beasts. Felicity and Perpetua, who refused to wear the garb consecrated to Ceres, were exposed to a mad heifer. The heifer tossed Felicity, but Perpetua raised the dazed woman to her feet. The men were exposed to leopards and bears. Saturninus was mangled but not killed by a leopard. He and the women, who had remained largely unharmed, were finally taken to a place of execution where the mob had asked to see them killed. They exchanged a final kiss of peace and were sworded to death. The description of their passion, written by Perpetua and Saturninus, and their death, written by an unknown eyewitness (possibly Tertullian), are considered among the most remarkable and poignant of such accounts; they became so popular that St. Augustine protested against their being read in African churches on the same level as Scripture. They are valuable theological and historical accounts. Their feast soon gained fame in the Christian Church and is recorded in the earliest Roman and Syriac calendars. They were buried in the Basilica Majorum in Carthage. In art, the women may be shown together, with a wild cow by their side.

FERDINAND III. King. c. 1199–1252. May 30. He was born near Salamanca, the son of Alfonso IX, king of Léon, and Berengaria, the oldest daughter of Alfonso III, king of

Castile. His mother's mother was the daughter of Henry II of England, and her sister Blanche became the mother of St. Louis of France. The death of Berengaria's brother, Henry, left her heiress to the throne of Castile, but she ceded her rights to the eighteen-year-old Ferdinand. Ferdinand was a stern ruler but forgiving of personal slights. He was an excellent administrator. The archbishop of Toledo, Rodrigo Ximenes, was chancellor of Castile and his principal adviser for many years. Upon the death of his father, in 1230, Ferdinand became king of Léon. There was opposition to this, for there were supporters of the claim of his two half sisters, but his union of the two kingdoms made a recovery from the Moors possible. He campaigned against the Moors without respite for twenty-seven years, and his success won the great devotion of his people. It was in the battle of Xeres, when only ten or twelve Spanish lives were lost, that St. James was said to have been seen leading the host on a white horse. St. James's chronicle is a principal source for Ferdinand's achievements. Ferdinand's military efforts were not so much imperialistic in motivation as driven by a wish to save Christians from the dominance of infidels. Although he was a warrior, it was said of him that "he feared the curse of one old woman more than a whole army of Moors." In thanksgiving for his victories, Ferdinand rebuilt the cathedral in Burgos and converted the great mosque of Seville into a church. He restored to the Cathedral of Santiago de Compostela the bells that had been removed by the Moors. Once the Moslems and Jews submitted, he pursued a course of tolerance, while encouraging the friars to convert them. He was the founder of the famed University of Salamanca. He is the patron saint of persons in authority (rulers, governors, magistrates, etc.)—a result of his wise appointments; the poor and prisoners (over whom such persons rule); engineers, a result of his technical military skills; and the Spanish army. His emblem in art is the greyhound. He is portrayed holding a sword or an orb; as a king with a cross on his breast; or on horseback, with a Moorish prince kneeling to him.

FIACRE. Abbot. d. c. 670. September 1. It is said Fiacre was born in Ireland, lived for a time as a hermit at Kilfiachra, and then became an "exile for Christ," sailing over to France to find solitude where he might devote himself to God. He arrived at Meaux, where St. Faro, bishop of the city, gave him a hermitage in a forest that was his own patrimony, called Breuil, in the province of Brie. A legend has it that St. Faro offered him as much land as he could turn up in a day, and that Fiacre, instead of using a plow, drove furrows with the point of his staff. He cleared the land of trees and briars, made himself a cell and garden, and built an oratory in honor of the Blessed Virgin and a hospice for travelers—which developed into the village of Saint-Fiacre in Seine-et-Marne. Many sought him out for advice, and the poor looked to him for relief. He attended all cheerfully, ministering to those in the hospice, and he was said to have performed miraculous cures. Interestingly, he never allowed any women to enter his hermitage or chapel; it is thought that he had a strong distaste for them. His fame for miracles of healing endured after his death, and his shrine was visited for centuries. Among those who attributed cures to him were Mgr. Seguier, the bishop of Meaux in 1649, and John de Chatillon, the count of Blois. Anne of Austria attributed the recovery of the dangerously ill Louis XIII to the saint's intercession; in 1641, she made a pilgrimage on foot to his shrine. She also sent a token to the shrine for having safely borne her son, Louis XIV. His relics are at Meaux and are still resorted to. He is the patron saint of gardeners and horticulturists, sufferers from venereal disease (perhaps a result of his objection to women) and hemorrhoids (a medieval development which appears to have originated from a play on the French word *fic*, for small tumor), and of cabdrivers. His patronage of cabdrivers is due to the fact that the first place to offer coaches for hire was near the Hotel Saint-Fiacre in Paris. Such vehicles became known as *fiacres*. He is often represented carrying a shovel; or digging in a garden; or with a spade and open book, sometimes with a hind at his feet.

FIDELIS OF SIGMARINGEN. Martyr. 1577–1622. April 24. He was born Mark Rey in Sigmaringen in Hohenzollern, and went to the University of Freiburg-in-Breisgau, where he taught philosophy while he studied for a law degree. In 1604, he was appointed tutor to a small party of noble Swabian men who wanted to finish their education with supplementary studies in the chief cities of western Europe. During the six-year tour, he became greatly esteemed by his companions. He set them an example of religious devotion and goodness to the poor, to whom he sometimes literally gave the clothes off his back. When he returned to Germany, he took his doctorate in law and began to practice as an advocate at Ensisheim in Upper Alsace. He gained a reputation for honesty and his refusal to use the vituperative language often used then to level an opponent. His support of the cause of the poor brought about the nickname "the Poor Man's Lawyer." Repulsed by the unscrupulous measures used by his colleagues in practicing law, he decided to enter the reformed Capuchin branch of the Franciscan Order. He donated his wealth to the poor and to needy seminarians. After receiving holy orders, he took the name Fidelis. Upon completion of his theological course, he preached and heard confessions. He was appointed superior successively at Rheinfelden, Freiburg, and Feldkirch. During this last appointment, he reformed the town and outlying districts, and converted many Protestants. His reputation grew due to his dedication to the sick, many of whom he cured during an epidemic. The bishop of Chur requested that his superiors send him, with eight other Capuchins, to preach among the Protestants in the Grisons. This was the first attempt since the Reformation to recover the area from heresy. Fidelis courageously pretended to disregard threats of violence. From the very beginning, the mission made inroads, and the newly established Congregation for the Spreading of the Faith formally appointed him leader of the Grisons enterprise. His adversaries were enraged by his successes and worked to turn the peasants against him by representing him as an agent of the Austrian agent of the Austrian emperor, and avowing to him an intention to balk their national aspirations for independence. Forewarned, Fidelis spent several nights in prayer. On April 24, 1622, he preached at Grüsch. He then traveled to Sewis, where, in the middle of a sermon, someone shot at him. The bullet missed and lodged in a wall. In the following confusion the Austrian soldiers who were in the vicinity were attacked. When a Protestant offered to harbor Fidelis, Fidelis said his life was in God's hands. He attempted to return to Grüsch but was beset by his opponents who demanded that he repudiate his faith. He refused, and as his murderers attacked him with their weapons he called out to God to forgive them. A Zwinglian minister who was present became converted. Fidelis is depicted in art with a club set with spikes or a whirlbat.

FINBAR, BAIRRE, BARRY. Bishop. d. c. 633. September 25. Finbar, founder of the city and see of Cork, was born in Connaught and is said to have been the illegitimate son of a royal lady and a master smith. He was baptized Lochan, but the monks who educated him at Kilmacahil in Kilkenny called him Fionnbharr—white head—because of his blond hair. Legend has it that he went to Rome on a pilgrimage with one of his preceptors and, on the way back, passed through Wales and visited St. David in Pembrokeshire. He had no means of getting to Ireland, so David lent him a horse for the crossing, and in the Channel he sighted and signaled St. Brendan the Navigator, voyaging eastward. He is said to have gone to Rome in company with St. David and others, and that Pope St. Gregory would have made him a bishop, but that the pope was visited by a vision that revealed that Heaven had reserved this ceremony for itself. When Finbar returned to Ireland, the Lord is said to have brought a miraculous flow of oil from the ground, caught him up to Heaven, and there consecrated him bishop, anointing him with the oil that flowed around the feet of the onlookers. After preaching in various parts of southern Ireland, and living as a hermit on a small island at Lough Eiroe, Finbar established a monastery on marshy ground on the south side of the mouth of the Lee River, the *corcagh mor* from which the city of Cork derives its name. The monastery soon attracted disciples, and its school had a great influence all over southern Ireland, so much so that it was said "To this house . . . so many came . . . that it changed a desert into a great city. . . ." Accounts of Finbar are filled with surprising incidents. One story holds that when he was visited by St. Laserian, the two sat together under a hazel bush, talking of spiritual matters. St. Laserian asked Finbar for a sign that God was present. Finbar prayed, and the spring catkins on the bush above them fell off, nuts formed, grew, and ripened; he then gathered them in handfuls and poured them into St. Laserian's lap. After Finbar's death, the sun did not set for a fortnight. It would appear that he preached in Scotland, and there was formerly considerable devotion to him; the island of Barra in the Western Isles, as well as other places, took its name from him. He is said to have died at Cloyne, and his body was taken back to his church in Cork for burial. He is the patron saint of Cork, Barra, and the Outer Hebrides.

FLORA OF BEAULIEU. Blessed, virgin. 1309–1347. October 5. Flora passed a very devout childhood and resisted all her parents' attempts to find her a husband. At fourteen, she entered the priory of Beaulieu, between Figeac and the shrine of Rocamadour, which was run by the Hospitallers, nuns of the Order of St. John of Jerusalem. After dedicating herself to God, she apparently entered a state of deep depression that influenced her behavior to a degree that the other nuns found annoying. She obtained help periodically from a visiting confessor who seemed to understand her state. She experienced many mystical experiences including visions and ecstasies. It is said that one time on the feast of All Saints, she fell into an ecstasy in which she continued without eating until St. Cecilia's day, three weeks later. A fragment of the Blessed Sacrament is said to have been brought to her by an angel from a church eight miles away. She is also said to have experienced levitation. There were many accounts of her prophetic knowledge. She died at the age of thirty-eight. Miracles are said to have been performed at her tomb.

FLORIAN. Martyr. d. 304. May 4. He was an officer in the Roman army who held a high administrative post in Noricum, now part of Austria. During the Diocletian persecution, he gave himself up at Lorsch to the soldiers of the governor. After stalwartly confessing his faith, he was scourged twice, flayed alive, and thrown into the River Enns with a stone around his neck. His body was recovered and buried by a devout woman. It was removed to the Augustinian Abbey of St. Florian, near Linz. It is held that it was later translated to Rome, and Pope Lucius III, in 1138, gave some of the saint's relics to King Casimir of Poland and to the bishop of Cracow. He is the patron saint of those in danger from water and flood, and of drowning, and of Austria and Poland. In art he is shown with a hand resting on a millstone; or with a stone around his neck and thrown into a river.

FRANCES XAVIER CABRINI. Foundress, virgin. 1850–1917. November 13. She was born the youngest of thirteen children to Augustine, a farmer, and Stella Cabrini. Frances was taught by her sister Rosa, a schoolteacher, and was influenced to become a foreign missionary. Her parents wished her to become a teacher, however, and sent her to a convent boarding school at Arluno. Her parents died in 1870, and she lived with Rosa. When she tried to join the religious congregation whose school she had attended, she was refused because her health had been weakened by smallpox in 1872. She tried another congregation and was turned down again. But the priest in whose school she was teaching, Don Serrati, invited Frances to help manage a small orphanage called the House of Providence, which was being mismanaged by an eccentric foundress, Antonia Tondini, and two other women. The bishop of Lodi and Mgr. Serrati asked Frances to try to turn the institution into a religious community. Unwillingly, she agreed. From Antonia, Frances received only trouble and abuse, but she endured. With seven recruits, she took her first vows in 1877. The bishop made her superioress. Antonia's behavior became worse—she was thought to have become unbalanced—but Frances persevered another three years. At this point, the bishop himself gave up hope and closed the institution. He counseled her to found a congregation of missionary sisters, since that was what she wanted to be and he didn't know of any such order. Frances moved to an abandoned Franciscan friary at Codogno, and she drew up a rule for the community. Its main object was to be the Christian education of girls, and it would be called the Missionary Sisters of the Sacred Heart. The same year the rule was approved, and a daughter house opened at Grumello. Another opened soon in Milan. In 1887 Frances went to Rome to gain the approbation of her congregation and permission to open a house in Rome. After an initially unsuccessful interview with the cardinal vicar—the congregation was deemed to be too young for approval—Frances won him over. She was asked to open two houses in Rome, a free school and a children's home, and the first decree of approval of the Missionary Sisters was issued. The bishop of Piacenza, Mgr. Scalabrini, who had established the Society of St. Charles to work among Italian immigrants in America, suggested that Frances travel there to help these priests. She would not consider this idea, for she wanted to go to China. The archbishop of New York sent her a formal invitation. She decided to consult with the pope. Despite a fear of water, she set off across the Atlantic, landing in 1889 in New York. Although she and six other sisters were warmly welcomed, it appeared that, due to a dispute with the benefactress, the orphanage plan she was to have managed had been abandoned, and the archbishop suggested that she return home. Frances replied that the pope had sent her here and here she must stay. Within a few weeks, she had mended the rift, found a house for the sisters, and started the orphanage. In 1889 she revisited Italy, bringing with her the first two Italo-American recruits to her congregation. Nine months later, she returned, bringing reinforcements to take over West Park, on the Hudson, from the Society of Jesus. The orphanage was transferred to this house, which became the motherhouse and novitiate of the order in the United States. Next Frances traveled to Managua, Nicaragua, where under sometimes dangerous circumstances she took over an orphanage and opened a boarding school. On her way back, she visited New Orleans, and there she made a new foundation. Frances was slow in learning English, but she had great business acumen. She was sometimes overly strict and self-righteous— rejecting illegitimate children from her fee-paying schools, for example—and she was slow to recognize that non-Catholics could truly mean well. In 1892, one of Frances's greatest undertakings, Columbus Hospital, was opened in New York. After a visit to Italy, she traveled to Costa Rica, Panama, Chile, and Brazil. In Buenos Aires she opened a high school for girls. After her next visit to Italy, she traveled to France, opening her first European houses outside of Italy. By 1907, when the order was finally approved, there were over 1,000 members in eight countries. Frances had founded more than fifty houses, and numerous free schools, high schools, hospitals, and other institutions. Her health began to fail in 1911, but it was not until 1917 that she died of malaria in the convent in Chicago. She had become an American citizen in 1909 and thus became the first U.S. citizen to be canonized. She is the patron saint of emigrants and migrants.

FRANCES OF ROME. Widow. 1384–1440. March 9. She was born in the Trastevere, Rome to Paul Busso and Jacobella dei Roffredeschi, nobility who were very devout. At eleven, Frances, mature for her years, asked to be a nun, but her parents refused, wishing to arrange a fine marriage for their pretty daughter. She was betrothed to Lorenzo Ponziano and was married soon after she turned thirteen. She found her new life difficult, although she tried very hard to be a model wife. One day, her sister-in-law Vannozza found her crying. Frances confided to her her frustrated hopes, and Vannozza revealed that she too had wanted to consecrate her life to God. The two became fast friends and decided to live a perfect life under a common rule. They dressed plainly and visited the poor of Rome, relieving their distress. Their husbands did not oppose their austerities and good works. After Frances recovered from a serious illness during which she reported a vision of St. Alexis, the women devoted themselves to the sick of Santo Spiritu Hospital in Sassia. They nursed patients there, granting special attention to those suffering from the most terrible diseases. In 1400, Frances bore a son, John Baptista. The next year, her mother-in-law died, and her father-in-law asked Frances to replace her as the head of the household. Frances pleaded that Vannozza was the most proper choice as the wife of the elder brother, but Vannozza herself insisted that Frances was more suitable, and Frances capitulated. She had two more children, Agnes and Evangelist, and cared for them herself. In 1408, the troops of Ladislaus of Naples, who supported the antipope, entered Rome, and a mercenary was made governor. Frances's family supported the legitimate pope, and in a conflict, Lorenzo was stabbed. Frances nursed him back to health. The governor decided to leave the city after wreaking vengeance on the principal papal supporters. Vannozza's husband was arrested, and the child John Baptista was demanded as a hostage. While Frances was praying in the Church of Ara Coeli, however, the boy was set free under circumstances that seemed miraculous.

In 1410, the cardinals assembled at Bologna to elect a new pope, and Ladislaus again seized Rome. Lorenzo managed to escape, but his wife and family were unable to follow him. His palace was plundered, and John Baptista was taken captive. He managed to get away and join his father later. The family's possessions were destroyed, their farms raided or burned, their flocks slaughtered, and many of their peasants were killed. Frances lived in a section of her ruined home with her two younger children and Vannozza, whose husband was still incarcerated. The two women did what they could to relieve the distress of their poorer neighbors. In a plague Evangelist died. Frances turned part of the house into a hospital and was said to work great cures. She sold her jewels to help the sufferers. A year after Evangelist's death, Frances was praying when a bright light suddenly shone in the room, and Evangelist appeared, accompanied by an archangel. Evangelist told her that he was happy in Heaven and that he had come to warn her that Agnes would die. A consolation, however, would be granted to Frances: the archangel was to be her guide for twenty-three years. He would be succeeded in the last part of her life by an angel of even higher rank. Agnes soon became ill and died at the age of sixteen. Frances experienced many visions and ecstasies and made prophecies. She is said to have foreseen the end of the great schism. In 1414, the pope summoned the Council of Constance, which was to attempt to heal the great schism, and the Ponziani were called from banishment and regained their property. Lorenzo's health was broken, however, and he lived in retirement, cared for lovingly by his wife. He wished to see his son married well, and arranged a marriage with a beautiful girl named Mobilia. Mobilia proved to be tempestuous and harbored contempt for Frances, of whom she complained to her husband and his father, whom she mocked in public. In the middle of a bitter diatribe, she was struck ill, and Frances nursed her. Mobilia was won over by Frances's kindness and from then on sought to be guided by her example. The goodness of

Frances was now well known in Rome, and people sought her out to work cures and arbitrate disputes. Lorenzo, who loved her more and more as time went on, offered to release her from the obligations of married life provided that she would live under his roof. Frances was now free to form a society of women living in the world and without a rule but who would pledge to offer themselves to God and serve the poor. The plan was approved by her confessor Dom Antonio, who obtained the affiliation of the congregation to the Benedictines of Monte Oliveto, to which he belonged. Organized as the Oblates of Mary, they were afterward called the Oblates of Tor de' Specchi, after a house they had taken for a community when the order was seven years old. Frances shared in their daily life as much as she could but never allowed them to refer to her as the foundress, insisting that all should be subject to Agnes de Lellis, who was chosen as superioress. Lorenzo died three years later, and Frances retired to Tor de' Specchi. Agnes de Lellis insisted upon resigning her office to Frances, who acquiesced to become superior. One night in 1440, although she felt ill, she tried to return to the community after visiting her son and Mobilia. Her director, Dom John Matteotti, met her on the way. Taken aback by her haggard appearance, he ordered her to return to her son's house. She lingered for a week. On the evening of March 9, her face seemed to shine with an unearthly light. Her last words were "The angel has finished his task; he beckons me to follow him." Her body was removed to Santa Maria Nuova, and was buried in the chapel of the church reserved for her oblates. Her biography was written by her confessor. Santa Maria Nuova is now known as the church of Santa Francesca Romana. She is the patron saint of widows, and of motorists, which may be attributable to the fact that for the last half of her life, she had a constant vision of her guardian angel, by whose light she was able to see at night. She is portrayed in art habited in black with a white veil, accompanied by her guardian angel, and often carries a basket of food or a book of the Office of the Virgin.

FRANCIS OF ASSISI. Founder. 1181–1226. October 4.
Francis was born at Assisi in Umbria to Peter Bernardone,
a wealthy silk merchant, and Pica. Their calling him
Francesco, which means "the Frenchman," although he
was baptized John, appears to have been either because his
mother was from Provençal, or because Peter was absent on
business in France when his son was born. The young Francis was not interested in his father's business or study, and
lived a worldly, spendthrift life. He was influenced by the
ideals of chivalry, and it was with these romantic ideals of
poverty, chastity, and obedience that he would later capture
the imagination of his time. Around the age of twenty,
Francis was taken prisoner by the Perugians, who were
fighting with Assisi. When he returned, he became seriously ill. When he recovered, he decided to join the forces
of Walter de Brienne, who was fighting in southern Italy in
1205. He bought expensive equipment and a new outfit, but
when he came across a poor man who was poorly clothed,
he gave him the clothes. At Spoleto, he fell ill again, and as
he lay in bed, saw a vision of Christ who urged him to turn
back. Francis returned home facing accusations of coward-
ice. Riding one day, he met a leper, whose repulsive sores
horrified him. He got off his horse, however, and as he gave
the man alms, he kissed him. After this experience, he
visited hospitals, serving the sick, and often gave money
and his clothes to the poor. Praying one day in the Church
of San Damiano, outside the walls of Assisi, he heard a
voice coming from the crucifix, which repeated three times,
"Francis, go and repair my house, which you see is falling
down." The church was old and in disrepair, so thinking he
was being asked to restore it, he went home, and sold some
of his father's cloth. He gave the money to the priest of San
Damiano's and asked to be allowed to stay with him. The
priest agreed, but he would not accept the money. His angry
father came looking for him, but Francis hid. After days of
praying and fasting, Francis appeared again, but his looks
were so altered that people threw things at him and called
him mad. His impatient father took him home, beat him,

and locked him, bound up, in a room. His mother released him when his father was out, and Francis returned to San Damiano's. His angry father followed him there, hit him, and dramatically disinherited him. Francis said he did not regret being disinherited but that the money from the goods now belonged to God and the poor. He was summoned before the bishop of Assisi, who instructed him to return the money and to trust in God. Francis did so, stripped on the spot and gave his clothes to his father. The bishop mustered clothes and Francis thanked the household for these first alms, and put a cross on the garment with chalk. Singing the divine praises, Francis went in search of shelter. He met a band of robbers, who asked him who he was. He answered, "I am the herald of the great King." They beat him and threw him into a ditch of snow. Undeterred by this treatment, he continued singing. At a monastery he received alms and work. In the city of Gubbio, an acquaintance took him in and gave him a shabby tunic, belt, and shoes. He wore these clothes for two years, walking with a staff. He then returned to San Damiano at Assisi. He begged alms to restore the church and was mocked by townspeople who had known him as a rich man. He helped in the work of restoring the church. After helping to restore another church in the same way, he retired to a little chapel called Portiuncula, belonging to an abbey of Benedictine monks at Monte Subasio. Located two miles from Assisi, the chapel was neglected and falling down. Francis repaired it and lived nearby. On the feast of St. Matthias in 1209, Francis saw the way of his life in the gospel of the mass, which said "Do not possess gold . . . nor two coats nor shoes nor a staff. . . ." He gave away his shoes, staff, and girdle. He was left with a poor coat, which he tied with a cord. This undyed woolen dress of the shepherds and peasants in those parts would be the dress he would give to his friars. Disciples began to seek him out because of his preaching. Among them was Bernard da Quintavalle, a rich tradesman of Assisi, who sold all his possessions and gave the money to the poor. Francis gave the habit to him and to Peter of Cattaneo,

142

a canon of the cathedral, on April 16, 1209. The third to join them was the famous Brother Giles, a simple and wise man. When he had a dozen followers, Francis drew up a short informal rule, consisting chiefly of the gospel counsels of perfection. Thus, the Franciscans were founded. He sought approval for this rule from the pope in Rome in 1210. He sent for Francis, verbally approved the rule, giving the Franciscans a general commission to preach repentance. Francis gave his order the name of Friars Minor, wishing that they should be below their fellows. Francis and his company lived together in a little cottage at Rivo Torto, outside the gates of Assisi, and they left sometimes to go into the country and preach. As a result of a dispute with a peasant who wanted the cottage to house his donkey, the abbot of Monte Subasio gave the Portiuncula Chapel to Francis in 1212, upon the condition that it should always remain the head church of his order. Poverty was the foundation of the order, and Francis would not allow any property to be vested in his order, or in any community or convent of it. In 1212, Francis decided to preach to the Mohammedans. He and a companion departed for Syria, but they were driven onto the coast of Dalmatia and shipwrecked. They traveled back to Ancona as stowaways. Francis preached a year in central Italy, during which the lord of Chiusi put at the disposal of the Franciscans as a place of retreat Mt. Alvernia in the Tuscan Apennines. Francis attempted again to reach the Moslems but fell ill. Upon recovery, he returned to Italy. Small communities of Franciscans appeared throughout Umbria, Tuscany, Lombardy, and Ancona. In 1216, Francis is reported to have received from the pope the Portiuncula indulgence, or pardon of Assisi. He was in Rome again the following year and it is probably then that he met St. Dominic. Francis wanted to preach in France, but Cardinal Ugolino advised against it, so he sent Brother Pacifico and Brother Agnello, who would later bring the Franciscans to England. Missions were sent to Spain, Germany, and Hungary. The first general chapter was held at Portiuncula at Pentecost in 1217. In 1219 the chapter of Mats was held, so-called because of the number of huts made of wattles and matting put up to shelter the 5,000 friars. Francis sent some of the brethren from this chapter to Tunis and Morocco, planning to attend to the Saracens of Egypt and Syria himself. He and twelve friars left Ancona in 1219 and came to Damietta on the Nile delta, where the Crusaders were camped. He was deeply shocked by the Crusaders' immoral life-style. Against their warnings, but with permission from the papal legate, he sought out the sultan. He was brought before Malek al-Kamil. The sultan was interested in their discussions and asked him to stay with him. A few days later, the sultan sent him back to camp, but Francis refused the rich presents offered him. Disappointed by his inability to sway either the Crusaders or the Saracens, Francis went to Akka, where he visited the Holy Places. He was called back to Italy by news of changes in the order. In his absence, his two vicars, Matthew of Narni and Gregory of Naples, had introduced innovations that rendered the Franciscans more like other orders, mitigating his rule of simplicity. Francis was dismayed to find his brethren in Bologna in a fine convent. He refused to enter it, staying with the Friars Preachers. He castigated the superior and ordered the friars to leave the convent. He went to the Holy See and obtained from Honorius III the appointment of Cardinal Ugolino as protector and adviser to the Franciscans. Ugolino believed in Francis's ideas and brought his administrative experience to its aid. Francis held a general chapter in 1221 and presented a revised rule, which clearly expressed the fundamental precepts of poverty, humbleness, and evangelical freedom. His order was different from those of other poor Italian preachers of the time due to its respect for and obedience to Church authorities and doctrinal orthodoxy. Members slept on the ground, used no tables or chairs, and had very few books. It was not until later that they became an order whose theology won attention in universities. The rule approved by Pope Honorius III in 1223 was basically the same but contained certain revisions. Somewhat earlier, Francis and Cardinal

Ugolino may have drawn up a rule for the lay people who associated themselves with the Friars Minor—the Franciscan tertiaries. At Christmas in 1223, at Grecchio in the valley of Rieti, Francis decided to make a memorial of the scene of Jesus born in Bethlehem. The setting up of a crib in the hermitage was probably not the first time the crèche idea was acted out, but it is thought that Francis made it a popular tradition. In 1224, Francis retired to Mt. Alverna, living in a small cell and forbidding visitors until the feast of St. Michael. It was here that the miracle of the *stigmata* occurred, the first certain recorded incidence of such an occurrence and the most famous example. To conceal it, Francis wore shoes and stockings and covered his hands with his habit. His health worsened, he suffered pain from the *stigmata*, and his eyes were failing; in 1225, Cardinal Ugolino and the vicar Elias begged him to see the pope's physicians at Rieti. He obeyed them, and on his way he stopped for the last time to see St. Clare at San Damiano. In terrible discomfort, he wrote the "Canticle of Brother Sun," set it to music, and taught the brethren how to sing it. He went on to Monte Rainerio to undergo primitive surgery and a painful treatment, but although he received some relief, he was dying. In Assisi, doctors told him he could not live longer than a few weeks. He asked to be taken to Portiuncula and was taken there on a stretcher. He asked that they send to Rome for Lady Giacoma di Settesoli, an old friend, and to ask her to come and bring candles and a gray gown for his burial and some favorite cakes. She arrived before the messenger started. As he wished, he died lying on the ground, covered with an old habit. He was still in deacon's orders; he had never been ordained. He had asked to be buried in the criminals' cemetery on the Colle d'Inferno, but his body was taken to the Church of St. George in Assisi. It remained there until 1230, when it was secretly removed to the basilica built by Brother Elias. His relics were rediscovered in 1818 and were reburied, first in an ornate tomb, and then in 1932, in a very simple one. He is the patron saint of

Italy, Italian merchants (due to his family's business), and of ecology and ecologists. He is depicted in art in the habit of his order, a drab gown, and usually has the *stigmata*, with a winged crucifix before him; or is preaching to the birds; or is propping up a falling church; or kneeling before a crib.

FRANCIS CARACCIOLO. Confessor, founder. 1563–1608. June 4.

He was born at Villa Santa Maria, in the Abruzzi, and was given the name Ascanio. His father was related to the Neapolitan princes of Caracciolo, and his mother was related to St. Thomas Aquinas. At twenty-two, he developed a skin disease similar to leprosy, and his case was thought to be hopeless. He vowed that if he recovered, he would devote his life to God and to serving others. His speedy recovery was thought to be miraculous. He went to Naples to study for the priesthood and, after his ordination, joined the confraternity *Bianchi della Giustizia*, devoted to the care of prisoners and who prepared them to die a holy death. In 1588, John Augustine Adorno, a Genoese, set out to found an association of priests who would combine the active and contemplative life. A letter inviting the cooperation of another Ascanio Caracciolo was mistakenly delivered to Francis. Agreeing with Adorno's vision, however, Francis wished to join him, and the two made a forty-day retreat to draw up the rules for the proposed order. When they had gathered twelve followers, they went to Rome to obtain approval from the pope. Sixtus V approved their new order, the Minor Clerks Regular. They did missionary work and cared for the sick and prisoners. The next year, Caracciolo took the name of Francis, in honor of St. Francis of Assisi. The company settled in a house in a suburb of Naples, and Francis and Adorno traveled to Spain, in keeping with the pope's wishes that they establish themselves there. The court of Madrid refused permission for the house, however, and they were forced to return. They were shipwrecked on the way back, and by the time they arrived in Naples, their foundation had flourished and was unable to contain all those who wished to join it. They were invited to take over the monastery of Santa Maria Maggiore, whose former superior had joined their order. The Minor Clerks Regular worked mostly as missioners, but some worked in hospitals and prisons. Hermitages were provided for those who wished for solitude. Francis contracted a serious illness; soon after his own recovery, Adorno died at the age of forty. Against his wishes, Francis was named superior, but he swept rooms, made beds, and washed up in the kitchen just as the others did. During his life, he refused several bishoprics. Returning to Spain in 1595 and 1598, Francis successfully founded houses in Madrid, Valladolid, and Alcalá. After seven years as superior, he obtained permission from the pope to resign and became prior of Santa Maria Maggiore and master of the novices. In 1607, he gave up his administrative duties for a time of contemplation to prepare for death. He lived in a recess beneath the staircase of a Neapolitan house. Meanwhile, St. Philip Neri offered the Minor Clerks Regular a house at Agnone in the Abruzzi, and Francis was asked to help with the new establishment. He traveled there, but he soon developed a fever, which rapidly worsened. While feverish, he dictated a letter in which he exhorted his brethren to remain faithful to the rule. He then fell into meditation. An hour before sunset, he cried out "To Heaven!" A moment later, he died. Miracles, ecstasies, and prophecies have been attributed to him.

FRANCIS DE SALES. Bishop, doctor of the Church. 1567–1622. January 24. Francis was born at the family castle, Château de Sales, in Savoy. Though a sickly child, and delicate throughout his life, he was a very active person. His mother, with the help of Abbé Déage, was responsible for his early education. At eight, Francis went to the College of Annecy, and the following year he received the tonsure, having early felt a vocation. Despite this, his father expected him to pursue a secular career. At fourteen, Francis went to the University of Paris, but instead of attending the Collège de Navarre, attended by the nobility of Savoy, he attended the Jesuit Collège de Clermont, where he felt his vocation would remain strong. He was accompanied by the Abbé Déage. He excelled in rhetoric and philosophy and pursued theology vigorously. In accordance with his father's wishes, he took riding, dancing, and fencing, but his heart was set on serious studies. At twenty-four, he received his doctorate in law at Padua and returned to his family. At this point, a confrontation with his father about his future became necessary. His cousin, Canon Louis de Sales, felt that the death of the provost of the chapter of Geneva opened a position for Francis that his father might be brought to approve. Francis assumed ecclesiastical dress the day his father consented, and six months later he was ordained. The Bishop de Granier wished to send missioners in Chablais, on the south shore of Lake Geneva. The Calvinist people there were resisting the Catholicism that was being enforced by the military. Knowing the dangers, Francis volunteered, and in 1594, set out on foot, accompanied by his cousin, Canon Louis de Sàles. His father refused to give his blessing to the endeavor. They preached daily in the area. One night Francis was attacked by wolves and escaped by spending the night in a tree. Twice he was attacked by assassins, but seemingly miraculously he escaped unharmed. Few inroads were made with the people, and Francis, trying to find new ways to reach them, took to writing leaflets. These were later to form *The Controversies*. In 1595, on his way up the mountain of Voiron to restore an oratory that had been destroyed by the Bernese, he was attacked and beaten by a hostile crowd. But his sermons began to be more popular, and conversions more numerous. After three or four years, when Bishop de Granier came to visit the mission, his accomplishments were clear and impressive. It was later said by Cardinal du Perron that he himself could confute Protestantism, but that Mgr. de Sales could convert them. The bishop administered confirmation and even presided at the Forty Hours. The bishop viewed Francis as a possible coadjutor and successor and broached it to Francis. Although initially unwilling, Francis came to see it as God's will and agreed. He fell seriously ill, however, and nearly died. When he recovered, he traveled to Rome, where he was examined by Pope Clement VIII and others. His appointment as coadjutor was confirmed. Francis succeeded to the see of Geneva upon the bishop's death in 1602 and took up residence at Annecy, with a minimal household. He organized the teaching of catechism in the diocese. Children liked him and followed him around. Though very gentle, he was always firm, and he became well known for his unselfishness, charity, and sense of justice and patience. He was called the "Gentle Christ of Geneva." One of his favorite sayings was that "more flies are attracted by a spoonful of honey than by a whole barrel of vinegar." The foundation of the Order of the Visitation in 1610 was the result of the meeting of St. Jane Frances de Chantal and Francis during his preaching of Lenten sermons at Dijon in 1604. Notes of advice and instruction to a cousin by marriage, who had placed herself under his guidance, evolved into his most famous book, *The Introduction of the Devout Life*. The book, first published in 1608, was considered a spiritual gem and was translated into other languages. In 1622, Francis accepted an invitation to meet Louis XIII and the duke of Savoy at Avignon, wishing to obtain from Louis concessions for the French part of his diocese. The winter journey would be hard on him, and he seemed to anticipate that his death was not far off, so he arranged his affairs before leaving. At Avignon, his preaching was greatly in demand, and he lived as nearly as possible his usual austere life. On his trip home, he stayed for a month at Lyons in a gardener's cottage belonging to the convent of the Visitation. Though fatigued, he continued preaching in bitterly cold weather through Advent and Christmas. On St. John's day, he suffered a paralytic seizure. He regained his speech and patiently endured the treatments to prolong his life, but these were possibly so radical that they speeded his death. He received the last sacraments, and the last word he was heard to say before dying was "Jesus." His relics were translated to Annecy in 1623 and again to a new shrine in 1912. He is the patron saint of journalists, editors, writers, and the Catholic press, a patronage which Pope Pius XI deemed appropriate because of his example in *The Controversies* of "arguing forcefully, but with moderation and charity." He is portrayed in art with a sacred heart crowned with thorns above him, or with a heart in his hand.

FRANCIS DI GIROLAMA. Confessor. 1642–1716. May 11. Born in Grottaglie, near Taranto, Francis was the oldest of eleven children. At the age of twelve, he was received into the house of some secular priests. Recognizing his intelligence, the fathers promoted him to teaching catechism, and he received the tonsure at sixteen. He went to Naples to learn canon and civil law. In 1666 he was ordained a priest under a special dispensation because he was under twenty-four. He taught in the Jesuit Collegio dei Nobili for five years. At twenty-eight, having persuaded his family to consent, he entered the Society of Jesus to become a Jesuit. After being severely tested by his superiors in his first year of novitiate, he received their complete approval and was sent to help the preacher Father Agnello Bruno in his mission work. For three years the two worked tirelessly and with great success, primarily among the peasants in the province of Otranto. Francis was then recalled to Naples, finished his theological studies, and was professed. He was appointed preacher at the church known as the Gesu Nuovo in Naples. From the start, he attracted huge crowds. He was commissioned to train other missionaries and conducted at least one hundred missions in the provinces. He visited prisons, hospitals, and galleys. He converted twenty Turkish prisoners on a Spanish galley. One of his most interesting penitents was a Frenchwoman, Mary Alvira Cassier.

She had murdered her father and served in the Spanish army, impersonating a man. Under Francis, she repented and became very devout. Although he was credited with miracles, he disclaimed that they were due to his own powers, attributing numerous cures to the intercession of St. Cyrus, for whom he had a special devotion. He died at seventy-four, after a painful illness. His remains were interred in the Jesuit Church of Naples.

FRANCIS OF PAOLA. Founder. 1416–1507. April 2. Francis was born in the small town of Paola in Calabria. His parents were of modest means and very devout. At thirteen, he entered the Franciscan friary at San Marco, where he was taught to read and learned to live austerely, which he did for the rest of his life. At fourteen, he accompanied his parents on a pilgrimage, visiting Assisi and Rome. When they returned, he retired for a time to a place about a half mile from the town, and later, at the age of fifteen, to a more solitary place by the sea, where he lived in a cave as a hermit. He was eventually joined by two other men. Neighbors built them three cells and a chapel, where they sang the divine praises and where mass was said for them by a priest from a nearby church. The foundation of his order is said to have been called the Minim Friars in 1452. About seventeen years later, a church and monastery were built for them by the people of the area who had grown to love them, under the sanction of the archbishop of Cosenza. Francis maintained a regular discipline in the community. His bed was on a plank or the ground, with a log or stone for a pillow. He did not allow himself a mat until he was quite old. Charity was the motto he espoused, and humility was the virtue that he urged his followers to seek. He asked that they observe a perpetual Lent, abstaining from meat, eggs, and dairy products. The order received the approval of the Holy See in 1474. They were then sometimes called the Hermits of St. Francis of Assisi, and they were composed of uneducated men with one priest. In 1481, the dying King Louis XI of France sent for Francis, wishing the hermit to heal him, and promising to assist his order. Francis declined the invitation, but Louis appealed to Pope Sixtus IV, who ordered Francis to go. The king sent the dauphin to escort him to Plessis-les-Tours. When Louis fell on his knees before Francis and begged him to heal him, Francis told him that the lives of kings are in the hands of God and that Louis should pray to God. They had many discussions, and although Francis was an uneducated man, Philip de Commines, who was often present, wrote that he was so wise that hearers were convinced that the Holy Spirit spoke through him. He brought about a change of heart in the king, and Louis died, comforted, in his arms. For a time he was tutor to Charles VIII, who respected Francis as his father had, and asked his advice on spiritual and state matters. Francis is credited with helping to restore peace between France and Brittany, and between France and Spain. Charles built a monastery for Francis and his followers in the park of Plessias and another at Amboise, on the spot where they had first met. In Rome, he built the monastery at Santa Trinità del Monte on the Pincian Hill, to which only French Minims were admitted. Francis was so beloved that the French kings would not allow him to leave, and thus he spent the last twenty-five years of his life in that country. He became famous for prophecies and miracles. He spent the last three months of his life in solitude in his cell, preparing himself for death. On Palm Sunday, he became ill, and on Maundy Thursday, he assembled his brethren and urged them to love God, to be charitable, and to strictly observe the duties of their rule. He received the sacraments barefoot, according to the custom of the order, and died the following day. He is the patron saint of sailors, naval officers, navigators, and all people associated with the sea. This patronage originated from an incident that was said to have occurred in 1464. Francis wished to cross the Straits of Messina to Sicily but was refused a boat. He lay his cloak on the sea, tying one end to his staff to make a sail, then sailed across with his companions. His emblem in art is the word *Caritàs* in a circle of rays, and he may be portrayed standing on his cloak in the sea.

FRANCIS XAVIER. Confessor. 1506–1552. December 3. He was born in Spanish Navarre at the family castle of Xavier near Pamplona, the youngest of a big family. His first language was Basque. At eighteen, he went to the University of Paris, entered the college of St. Barbara, and received the degree of licentiate in 1528. At school he met Ignatius Loyola, and Francis would become one of the first group of Jesuits who vowed themselves to God at Montmartre in 1534. He received the priesthood at Venice three years later, and in 1540, the year the pope formally approved the Society of Jesus, St. Ignatius appointed him to join Father Simon Rodriguez on the order's first mission, to the East Indies. He joined Father Rodriguez in Lisbon, and they lived in a hospital, caring for and instructing the sick. The two also catechized in the town, and they heard confessions on Sundays and holidays at the court of the devout John III. Rodriguez was eventually retained by John, and Francis sailed, in 1541, carrying briefs from the pope that constituted Francis apostolic nuncio in the East. During the five-month journey around the Cape of Good Hope to Mozambique, where they were to winter, Francis arbitrated disagreements and other disorders on board, and he and two other Jesuits were the sole nurses during a bout of scurvy. After a journey of thirteen months, they arrived in Goa, where Francis settled at a hospital to await more companions. He ministered to those in the hospital and in prisons and walked through the streets with a bell to call children and slaves to catechism. He said a mass to lepers every Sunday, preached in public and to the Indians, and visited private homes. To facilitate the learning of the uneducated, he fitted religious statements to popular tunes. The device was very successful; the songs were soon being sung everywhere. In particular, he preached against the practice of concubinage—common among the Westerners living in the city—and cruelty to slaves. After five months, he traveled to the Pearl Fishery coast to instruct the Parava Indians. Thousands agreed to be baptized as a means to get the protection of the Portuguese against the Arabs, but they were uninstructed, and many had had no contact with Christianity at all. Francis learned the native language and preached so successfully that administering the sacrament and baptizing the multitudes sapped him to the point where he could not lift his arms. He is said to have performed miraculous cures. He lived simply on rice and water and slept on the ground in a hut. His ministry spread, and he is said to have once held off raiders by meeting them with a crucifix in his hand. Over the next few years he traveled to Malacca, Amboina, Ternate, Gilolo, and other places. He heard about Japan from Portuguese merchants and began to prepare for a mission to Japan. In 1549, he set out, accompanied by a lay brother, and they landed at Kagoshima. He set about learning Japanese, and in twelve months made one hundred converts. After visiting the fortress of Ichiku and converting the baron's wife and her steward among others, he moved on to Hirado. Well received by the *daimyô*, the missionaries made greater strides in a month than they had in a year in Kagoshima. In Yamaguchi they were not so successful, but undismayed, Francis traveled on to Kyoto, the chief city of Japan. Civil strife and the need to pay a fee to be received by the mikado hampered him, plus the fact that pious poverty was not respected in Japan. Francis changed his approach accordingly; he dressed appropriately and appeared before the *daimyô* bearing presents (among which were a music box, a clock, and a pair of spectacles). The *daimyô* were pleased, giving him permission to teach and an empty Buddhist monastery for a residence. Francis converted many. He now hoped to extend his mission to China but was compelled to first deal with abuses and problems among the missionaries and Portuguese authorities in India. In 1552, he traveled to China, landing surreptitiously on the desolate island of Sancian (now St. John's Island) since the country was closed to foreigners. While waiting to be conveyed to Canton, Francis fell ill. Treated badly by the Portuguese who had brought him there, Francis was left on the beach in a cold wind. A friendly Portuguese merchant took him to his hut. There, after daily growing weaker, he died. His body was packed in lime in a coffin and then buried. Ten weeks or more later, the grave and coffin were opened, and his body was found to be incorrupt. It was brought to Malacca, and later to Goa, where its incorruption was verified by physicians. It remains in Goa, in the Church of the Good Jesus. His right arm was detached in 1615 and taken to the church of the Gesù in Rome. Francis is called the "Apostle of the Indies and Japan" and is considered the most prolific missionary the Church has produced since St. Paul. Forty years after his arrival in Japan, there were reckoned to be 400,000 Christians. The Jesuits have credited him with more than 700,000 conversions, all the more remarkable because he often worked through interpreters. Although he has been criticized for not attempting to understand Asian religions, he was a reasonable and kind man. Notably, he never hesitated to tell the king of Portugal that the biggest hurdle to the apostolate were the trading and political Europeans. His extensive travels are remarkable in view of his propensity to seasickness. His surviving voluminous correspondence has made a detailed study of him possible. He is the patron saint of missions, of India, Pakistan, Outer Mongolia, Spanish tourism, and pelota players of Argentina (Pope Paul VI acknowledged the value of the sport for physical and mental well-being. The game is thought to be Basque in origin, and Francis is believed to have played it.). He is portrayed in art with a pilgrim's staff and beads, sometimes holding a lily; or exclaiming, "Satis est Domine, satis est"; or dying on a mat in a shed; or with angels bearing to him a crown; or carrying an Indian on his shoulders.

FULBERT. Bishop. c. 960–1029. April 10. Fulbert was born to a poor family in Italy. He later became a student at a Benedictine abbey at Rheims. He was one of their finest students, for when the celebrated Gerbert, who taught him mathematics and philosophy, became pope, he called Fulbert to Rome. When the next pope succeeded Gerbert, Fulbert returned to France, and Bishop Odo of Chartres gave him a canonry and appointed him chancellor. The cathedral schools of Chartres were given to his management, and he made them into the greatest educational center in France, attracting students from all over Europe. Fulbert himself was a true poet and scholar, with a great range of learning, including all the sciences then taught. He was chosen to succeed Bishop Roger when he died. Fulbert's influence had now become impressive, for he acted as a counselor to the spiritual and temporal leaders of France. He became a respected statesman, and was consulted by the duke of Aquitaine and the king of France. He continued to preach regularly and saw to the instruction of the territories under his jurisdiction. He was elected bishop of Chartres, and rebuilt the cathedral there when it burned down. It was built with great magnificence. All kinds of people gave him assistance, including Canute, king of England. Having a great devotion to the Virgin Mary, in whose honor he composed several hymns, he arranged that when the new cathedral opened, the newly introduced feast of her birthday be celebrated there, and that it be observed throughout the diocese. He vigorously opposed simony and the bestowing of ecclesiastical endowments upon laymen. After ruling for twenty-two years, he died. He is the author of the hymn "Ye Choirs of New Jerusalem" and sermons, hymns, and letters; several of his treatises survive.

GABRIEL THE ARCHANGEL. September 29. It was Gabriel ("man of God") who announced to the prophet the coming of the Messiah, it was he who appeared to Zachary to make known the future birth of the Precurser, and he who was sent to Mary to announce the mystery of the Incarnation. He is one of the seven archangels who stand close to God. He is the patron saint of telecommunications, television, and radio (because he was a bearer of messages); of the signals regiments of Italy, France, and Colombia; of the diplomatic services of Spain and Argentina and Argentinian ambassadors (a result of his being "God's ambassador"); and the patron of the postal services and stamp collectors. He is usually depicted as a young archangel, vested with an alb and girdle, with a lily, kneeling and holding a scroll emblazoned with the words *Ave Maria*.

GABRIEL POSSENTI. 1838–1862. February 27. Gabriel was born the eleventh of thirteen children to a lawyer. When Gabriel's mother died in his fourth year, his father had just been appointed the registrar of Spoleto. His early years were innocently worldly, although his friends referred to him as *il damerino*—"the ladies man." Before he finished his schooling, he fell dangerously ill, and he promised that if he recovered, he would enter religion. Upon his recovery, however, he did not act upon this. A year or two later, when he fell ill again, he renewed his promise. Once again he recovered. This time he fulfilled his vow, and in 1856 became a Passionist at Morrovalle, taking the name Brother Gabriel of Our Lady of Sorrows. He led a model life, seeking perfection by denial in small things, penances, and self-effacements. He was known for his continual cheerfulness. He was ordained, but he was stricken with tuberculosis and died at Isola di Gran Sasso in the Abruzzi at the age of twenty-four. He is the patron saint of students, particularly those in colleges and seminaries (acting as a model to them), of the clergy, and of young people involved in Catholic Action in Italy.

GAUDENTIUS OF BRESCIA. Bishop. d. c. 410. October 25. He was apparently educated under St. Philastrius, bishop of Brescia, and considered him his spiritual father. He made a pilgrimage to Jerusalem, hoping to escape the attention his reputation had gained him at home, and then became a monk at Caesarea in Cappadocia. During this time, St. Philastrius died, and the clergy and people of Brescia chose Gaudentius to succeed him, overruling his objections. He was consecrated by St. Ambrose c. 387. A nobleman named Benevolus, who had been disgraced by Empress Justina because he failed to support the Arians, had retired to Brescia. Due to ill health, he was unable to attend Gaudentius's Easter sermons, and he asked Gaudentius to write them down. For this reason, ten of the saint's sermons survive. In 405, Gaudentius was commissioned by Pope St. Innocent I and Emperor Honorius to go to the East to defend the cause of St. John Chrysostom before Arcadius. Gaudentius and two other bishops were badly received there and imprisoned. After their papers were taken from them, they were offered bribes to denounce St. John. They were eventually freed and returned to Italy. Gaudentius died in Italy.

GEMMA GALGANI. Virgin. 1878–1903. April 11. She was born at Borgo Nuovo di Camigliano near Lucca. Her mother died when she was seven, and from then on her life was one of domestic trials and great physical and spiritual pain. When she was eighteen, her father died, and Gemma joined the household of Matteo Giannini at Lucca. She wished to join the Passionist congregation, of which her spiritual director was a member, but she was prevented from doing so by her physical frailties, which included a condition of the spine. Between 1899 and 1901, she was subject to various supernatural phenomena, and she suffered periodically recurring *stigmata* and marks of scourging while she prayed. She experienced visions of Christ, the Blessed Virgin, and her Guardian Angel. When she spoke in ecstasies, the sound of her voice changed, and listeners recorded her words. At other times, however, she seemed to suffer possession and performed such acts as spitting on a crucifix and breaking a rosary. Throughout her life she patiently endured her spiritual and physical sufferings—which included the scorn of unbelieving relatives and townspeople—and practiced severe austerities. Her popularity increased in 1943, when her correspondence with her director was published. She was canonized, despite much opposition, based on the phenomenal nature of her religious experiences.

GENESIUS THE COMEDIAN. Martyr. d. c. 300. August 25. The story of Genesius is the same as that told of at least three other martyrs. Legend has it that when the Emperor Diocletian came to Rome, entertainments were prepared for him. In a comedy prepared for him, Genesius, one of the actors, hit upon the idea of burlesquing the ceremony of baptism. During his performance, however, Genesius was converted to Christianity. While the other actors burlesqued the ceremony of baptism, Genesius answered their questions sincerely. After being clothed in a white garment, the players shammed carrying him off to martyrdom. At this point, Genesius stood on the stage and declared his belief in God to the emperor and the audience. The emperor was enraged and ordered that he be beaten, then put into the hands of the prefect, who should force him to sacrifice to pagan gods. Genesius was racked, torn with iron hooks, and burned with torches; but he endured it stoically, crying out, "There is no other Lord besides Him whom I have seen. . . . Bitterly do I regret that I once detested His holy name and came so late to His service." Genesius was beheaded. He is the patron saint of actors and of the theatrical profession. He is depicted in art as a player being baptized on a stage, with angels around him; or as a player holding a violin, a sword, or with a clown's cap and bells.

GENEVIEVE, GENOVEFA. Virgin. c. 422–c. 500. January 3. Genevieve was born to Severus and Gerontia at Nanterre, a small village close to Paris. When St. Germanus, the bishop of Auxerre, spent a night at Nanterre, he was struck by Genevieve, who was only seven at the time. After his sermon, he asked for her parents and foretold her future sanctity. When he asked Genevieve if she wished to be a spouse of Christ and to serve God only, she asked that he bless her and consecrate her from that moment. When she was about fifteen, her parents died, and Genevieve was presented to the bishop of Paris to receive the veil. She settled with her godmother in Paris. She frequently ate only twice a week, sparingly. She experienced visions and prophecies, which initially evoked hostility from the Parisians, but the support of St. Germanus and the accuracy of her predictions eventually changed their attitudes. The Franks invaded Gaul, and King Childeric seized Paris. During a long blockade of the city, the people suffered hunger; Genevieve led a company to procure supplies and brought back from Arcis-sur-Aube and Troyes several boats filled with corn. Although Childeric remained a pagan, he grew to respect Genevieve and under her influence spared the lives of many prisoners and acted charitably in other ways. Genevieve also initiated the interest of many people to build a church in honor of St. Denis, which was afterward rebuilt with a monastery by King Dagobert in 629. Genevieve made many pilgrimages to the shrine of St. Martin at Tours, and her reputation of sanctity is said to have been so great that it even reached St. Simeon Stylites in Syria. Genevieve was listened to with respect by King Clovis, who was converted in 496, and he freed many captive prisoners at her request. When word of the march of Attila with his Huns reached the city, the Parisians planned to abandon the city, but Genevieve encouraged them to avert the disaster by praying and fasting. The citizens passed whole days in prayer with her in the baptistery. It is from this that the devotion to Genevieve appears to have originated. She reassured the people that they had the protection of Heaven, and although she was mocked by some, she proved to be right, for Attila suddenly changed the course of his march. It was at Genevieve's suggestion that Clovis began to build the church in honor of SS. Peter and Paul, and here Genevieve was enshrined. Many miracles in favor of Paris have been attributed to her intercession. She is the patron saint of Paris, of disasters, of drought and excessive rain, of fever, and of the French security forces. Devotion to her was so great that she was invoked in myriad circumstances—her shrine was carried into the cathedral in 1129 during an outbreak of what appears to have been food poisoning. Her efforts to maintain the safety of Paris led to her being made the patron of French security forces. In art she is shown as a shepherdess, usually holding a candle, which the devil is trying to extinguish (the devil is reputed to have blown out her candle when she went to pray at night in church) while an angel guards it. She may have a coin suspended around her neck.

GEORGE THE GREAT. Martyr. c. 303. April 23. Tradition has it that George was a Christian knight, born in Cappadocia. He was riding one day in the province of Lybia and came upon a city named Sylene. Near the city was a marsh, in which lived a dragon. The people had attempted to kill it but were poisoned by the creature's fetid breath. To placate the dragon, they offered it two sheep a day, but when they began to exhaust their supply of sheep, they were forced to substitute a human each day instead, using a lottery to choose the victim. At the time of George's arrival, the lot had just fallen to the king's daughter. No one volunteered to take her place, so she was dressed in bridal finery and sent to meet the dragon. Riding upon this scene, George attacked the dragon and speared it with his lance. He then fastened the princess's girdle around its neck, and the girl led the dragon into the city. The people were frightened and started to run away, but George told them not to be afraid—that if they would believe in Jesus Christ and be baptized, he would slay the dragon. The king and people agreed. George killed the dragon, and it was carried away on four ox carts. He accepted no reward for this service, but he asked the king to build churches, honor priests, and to maintain compassion for the poor. George may have been a soldier in the imperial army. There is evidence to support that he was a real martyr who suffered at Diospolis in Palestine, before the time of Constantine. It is unclear how George came to be chosen as the patron saint of England, although it is known that his cult traveled to the British Isles long before the Norman Conquest. William of Malmesbury states that SS. George and Demetrius, "the martyr knights," were seen helping the Franks at the battle of Antioch in 1098, and it appears probable that the crusaders, in particular King Richard I, who placed himself and his soldiers under George's protection, returned from the East with a belief in the power of George's intercession. King Edward III founded the Order of the Garter c. 1347, of which George has always been the patron, and for which the chapel of St. George at Windsor was built by Edward IV and Henry VII. "St. George's arms" became the basis of the uniforms of British soldiers and sailors, and George's red cross appears in the Union Jack. He is the patron saint of England, of the Order of the Garter, of the Italian cavalry (which had retained a devotion to the holy knight), of Istanbul, Aragon, Portugal, Germany, Genoa, and Venice. In the East, he is the patron of soldiers, and also the patron of husbandmen, due to a pun on the Greek form of his name. He was invoked against the plague, leprosy, and syphilis. He is depicted in art as a youth in armor, often mounted, killing or having killed a dragon. His shield and lance pennant are a red cross on a white ground.

GERALD OF AURILLAC. Confessor. 855–909. October 13. He was of noble birth and suffered a lengthy illness in his youth. For this reason, he gave much time to meditation, study, and prayer instead of the martial pursuits that would have been expected ordinarily. When he succeeded his father as count of Aurillac, he continued his life of devotion and became noted for his piety and generosity to the poor. After a pilgrimage to Rome, he built a church, under the invocation of St. Peter, and a Benedictine abbey at Aurillac, which was to become very well known. He led a life of great goodness for someone of his rank during this rather immoral period in history. He considered becoming a monk at his monastery but was persuaded against it by Gausbert, the bishop of Cahors, who counseled that he would be more useful acting as a layman who devoted himself to his neighbors and dependents. He gave a great part of his revenue to the poor and endowed the monastery generously. He dressed modestly, ate little, rose every morning at 2:00 A.M.—even when traveling—to say the first part of the Divine Office, and then he assisted at mass. He was blind for the last seven years of his life. He died at Cezenac, Quercy, and was buried at his abbey. He is the patron saint of Upper Auvergne.

GERARD OF BROGNE. Abbot. d. 959. October 3. He was born at Staves in the county of Namur and trained for the army. As a page of the count of Namur, he was sent on a special mission to the French court in 918. He remained in France and joined the Benedictines of St. Denis. He was a monk there and eleven years later went to Belgium to found an abbey on his own estate of Brogne. As instructed by a vision of St. Peter, he brought the relics of St. Eugenius to Brogne from Saint-Denis. He was abbot at the Brogne Abbey for twenty-two years and was instrumental in introducing the rule of St. Benedict into numerous houses in Flanders, Lorraine, and Champagne. He lived for a period as a recluse in a cell built near the church because he felt that the responsibilities of the community took time away from contemplation. He became active again, however, when he was called upon by the archbishop of Cambrai to reform the abbey at Saint-Chislain near Mons, Hainaut. He was so successful at this task that Count Arnulf of Flanders appointed him to a position in charge of all the abbeys in Flanders, Lorraine, and Champagne. He would spend the next twenty years reforming them. Not all the monks at the houses he guided accepted the reforms, however, and some left these monasteries for others. Toward the end of his life, he made a general visitation of all the monasteries under his charge, and then retreated to his cell at Brogne to prepare for death. He was known especially for his sweetness of temper. Gerard is depicted in art by the image of St. Peter consecrating his church; SS. Peter or Eugenius appearing to him; or holding the Church in his hand.

GERARD MAJELLA. Confessor. 1725–1755. October 16. He was born in Muro, fifty miles south of Naples, the son of a tailor. When his father died, he was apprenticed to a tailor who treated him well, but his journeyman made his life difficult. When he had mastered the trade, at which he was very skilled, he applied to join the Capuchins but was turned down because of his youth and delicate health. He became a servant in the household of the bishop of Lacedogna, a man with a bad temper who treated Gerard harshly. Gerard served the bishop well, nevertheless, until the bishop's death in 1745, at which time Gerard returned home and set up his own tailor shop. He lived with his mother and three sisters. He gave one-third of his earnings to his mother, one-third to the poor, and one-third for masses for the souls in Purgatory. He lived austerely and prayed several hours of the night. When he was twenty-three, a mission was given in Muro by some fathers of the recently founded Congregation of the Most Holy Redeemer. He asked to be made a lay brother, and despite his appearance of fragility and the reluctance of his family to let him go, he persisted in his requests, and in 1748, Father Cafaro sent him to the house of which he was rector at Deliceto. When Father Cafaro returned to the house, however, he realized he had misjudged Gerard and admitted him to the habit. Gerard worked so hard in the garden and the sacristy and was so modest that it was said that "Either he is a fool or a great saint." St. Alphonsus Liguori, founder of the order, recognized his goodness and shortened his novitiate. He was professed in 1752 and added to the usual vows the vow to always do that which should seem the more pleasing to God. He served in the infirmary, and became known for his bizarre supernatural abilities. Gerard had a gift for reading consciences, and there are many examples of his bringing secret sinners to repentance. He is also reported to have experienced ecstatic flight (he is said to have been carried through the air half a mile), bilocation (the ability to be in two places at one time), power over inanimate objects and animals, and prophecy. While in Naples, the murder of the Archpriest of Muro fifty miles away was revealed to him at the time it happened, and on many occasions he is said to have recognized and acted upon the mental wishes of persons far away. He read the conscience of the secretary of the archbishop of Conza so clearly that the man completely changed his immoral lifestyle and reconciled with his wife. Once the rector looked for Gerard in his cell and did not see him; when he saw him later in church, he asked him where he had been. Gerard responded, "In my cell." "What do you mean? I have been in there twice to look for you," the rector said. Gerard explained that he had asked God to make him invisible so that he would not be disturbed in his retreat. "I forgive you this time," the rector said. "But don't make such prayers again." One of the most unusual results of

165

his reputation for charity, goodness, and devotion is that he was allowed to become the spiritual director of several communities of nuns, an office not usually held by lay brothers. In 1753, the nuns at Deliceto went on a pilgrimage to the shrine of St. Michael at Monte Gargano. St. Gerard accompanied them and saw them safely through the nine-day trip. But a year later he was accused of lechery by a young woman whom he had befriended, Neria Caggiano. He was sent for by St. Alphonsus at Nocera. Believing it to be in accordance with his vow to do the more perfect thing, Gerard did not deny the charge. This placed St. Alphonsus, who did not believe him to be guilty, in a difficult position. Gerard was forbidden to receive communion or to have any dealings with the outside world. For several weeks, he was under suspicion; then the young woman admitted that she had lied. Soon after, Gerard went to Naples, where his reputation and miracles caused throngs of people to visit at all hours. For this reason, after four months he was sent to the house at Caposele and made porter there, a post attractive to him because of his great concern and compassion for beggars. During a hard winter that year, hundreds of people came to the door each day and were given food, clothes, and firewood. Only Gerard knew where the supplies came from. After a trip to Naples, where several cures of healing were attributed to him, he was put in charge of the new buildings at Caposele. Once when there was no money in the house with which to pay the workmen, Gerard prayed, and an unexpected sum of money was found to pay the men. He spent the summer trying to raise funds for the buildings, but the heat was hard on him, and his consumption progressed rapidly. While in bed a week at Oliveto, he cured a lay brother who had been sent to look after him. Back at Caposele, he grew worse and died at the hour and on the day he had foretold. Interestingly, while he has been praised as the model of lay brothers in their modest, quiet lives, he has at the same time been acclaimed as "the most famous wonder-worker of the eighteenth century.'' He is the patron saint of mothers and childbirth. This may be traced to his dutiful support of his widowed mother.

GERMAINE OF PIBRAC. Virgin. 1579–1601. June 15. She was born at Pibrac, a village near Toulouse, the daughter of Laurent Cousin, a farm worker. Her mother died while she was still an infant. A sickly child, she suffered scrofula among other conditions, and her right hand was deformed. Her father and his second wife treated her badly, and the girl was kept separated from her siblings. She slept in the stable or under the stairs, was fed poorly, and was sent out as a shepherdess as soon as she was capable. Germaine was very devout, however, and refused to miss mass. If mass was held while she was minding her sheep, she set her crook and her distaff in the earth, declared her flock to be under the care of her guardian angel, and went to church. Her sheep never came to any harm during her absences. She was known for her attention to children, and she shared what little food she received with the poor. Once in the winter her stepmother accused her of stealing bread and threatened her with a stick, but when Germaine opened her apron, summer flowers tumbled out. The neighbors and her parents were awed and began to treat her as a holy person. Her parents invited her to rejoin the household, but Germaine chose to continue living as before. At twenty-two, she was found dead under the stairs. Her body was buried in the Church of Pibrac and, when accidentally exhumed in 1644, was found incorrupt. It was transferred to a leaden coffin and placed in the sacristy. Sixteen years later, her body was found to be still well preserved, and miracles were attributed to her. Her relics remain in the Pibrac Church, and an annual pilgrimage is made there. She is portrayed in art as a shepherdess, with flowers in her apron, planting her distaff to keep her sheep while she goes to mass; or with a distaff and spindle, with sheep at her side.

GERTRUDE OF HELFTA. Virgin. 1256–1302. November 16. Born at Eisleben, Germany, her parents unknown, she was placed with the Benedictine nuns at Helfta—falsely designated Cistercian nuns for political reasons—in Saxony at the age of five. She became both a pupil and friend of St. Mechtilde. She took the veil and, at the age of twenty-six, began experiencing revelations. The love of the heart of Jesus is a recurring theme in the lives of both Gertrude and St. Mechtilde. It is said that in visions Gertrude twice laid her head upon the breast of Jesus and heard his heart beating. Gertrude's revelations most often occurred during the singing of the Divine Office. St. Teresa of Avila developed a strong devotion to her. Gertrude abandoned all secular studies, concentrating on the Bible and the writings of SS. Augustine, Gregory, and Bernard, and she recorded her mystical experiences, which would later appear in her *Book of Extraordinary Grace* (*Revelation of St. Gertrude*). Only the second of the five books was actually written by her; the rest were based on her notes. She recorded St. Mechtilde's visions, as well, in *Liber Specialis Gratiae*. She wrote a series of prayers for her friend, which became very popular, and through this and her other writing, she pioneered devotion to the Sacred Heart. The last ten years of her life she suffered terribly from ill health. She is considered to be one of the most important medieval mystics. She is the patron saint of the West Indies. She is depicted in art clad as an abbess holding a flaming heart; a mouse or mice may accompany her.

GILBERT OF SEMPRINGHAM. Confessor, founder. 1083–1189. February 16. He was born at Sempringham in Lincolnshire, the son of Jocelin, a wealthy Norman knight. He had some kind of physical deformity that prevented him from pursuing the knightly life that would naturally have been expected of him. He was sent to France to study, and after his return, he became a clerk in the household of

Bishop Robert Bloet of Lincoln. He was ordained a priest by Bloet's successor, Alexander. After the parsonages of Sempringham and Terrington were given to him in 1123, he turned over their revenues to the poor, keeping back only enough for basic necessities. Alexander had offered him a rich archdeaconry, but he turned it down. He drew up a rule for seven young women who lived in strict enclosure in a house adjoining the Church of St. Andrew in Sempringham. The foundation grew, and Gilbert added lay sisters and lay brothers to work the land. He went to Cîteaux in 1147 to ask the abbot to take over the foundation, but the Cistercians refused, and Gilbert was convinced by Pope Eugenius III to manage the foundation himself. He supplemented the order with canons regular to act as chaplains to the nuns. Thus originated the Gilbertines, the only medieval religious order to be founded in England. It never spread beyond Scotland and became extinct during the Reformation when Henry VIII suppressed the monasteries. At the time, there were twenty-six monasteries, but no attempt was ever made to reestablish the order. Gilbert himself built thirteen monasteries, orphanages, and leper hospitals. He traveled frequently from house to house, and he was forever active, copying manuscripts, making furniture, and building. The nuns followed the rule of St. Benedict and the canons the rule of St. Augustine. Discipline was severe. An illustration of the enforced simplicity of life was the fact that the choir office was celebrated without fanfare. Gilbert eventually became the master general of the order but resigned the office as his sight grew worse. He ate so sparingly that it was held in general wonder that he could survive at all; he kept a dish at his table and placed in it the best of the food, which was then given to the poor. He wore a hair shirt, rested by sitting, and spent much of the night in prayer. During the exile of St. Thomas of Canterbury, he and other superiors of his order were accused of having aided him. St. Thomas had evaded king's soldiers by dressing as a Sempringham lay brother. Gilbert was imprisoned but was exonerated. Gilbert was vocal in his support of St. Thomas

Becket, and although he was summoned before Henry II, he so impressed the king that he extracted a pardon and immunity for himself and his order. At the age of ninety, he was faced with the revolt of some lay brothers who claimed that there was too much work and too little food. He was supported by Pope Alexander III, but living conditions were improved. His relics are said to have been taken by King Louis VIII to Toulouse. Their alleged remains are kept in the Church of St. Sernin.

GILDAS THE WISE. Abbot. d. c. 570. January 29. He may have been born in the lower valley of the Clyde in Scotland. He is often called "Badonicus" because he was born in the year the Britons defeated the Saxons at Bath. He may have married and been widowed, but he eventually became a monk at Llaniltud in South Wales. Well-known Irish monks, including St. Finnian, became his disciples; he visited Ireland and wrote letters to far-off monasteries. Around 540 he wrote the famous work *De excidio Britanniae* with the purpose of making known "the miseries, the errors and the ruin of Britain." The work laid bare and severely criticized the lives of Britain's rulers and clerics, blaming their moral laxity for the triumph of the Anglo-Saxon invaders. Although the harshness of its rhetoric has been criticized the scriptural scholarship that it reveals is uncontested. He is considered to be the first English historian. He lived as a hermit for some time on Flatholm Island in the Bristol Channel, where he copied a missal for St. Cadoc and may have written *De excidio*. He then moved to an island near Rhuys in Brittany, where he founded a monastery, which became the center of his cult. The *De excidio* was very influential in the early Middle Ages and serves as an example of the classical and early Christian literature that was then available in England. Gildas's writings were used by Wulfstan, archbishop of York, in the eleventh century in his *Sermon of the Wolf* to the English people during the disordered reign of Ethelred the Unready. He is portrayed in art with a bell near him.

GILES. Abbot. d. c. 710. September 1. The story of St. Giles, based on an untrustworthy biography written in the tenth century, is one of the most famous of the legends of the Middle Ages. More than 160 churches were dedicated in his honor in England alone before the Reformation. It is probably true that he was a hermit of the sixth or eighth century who founded a monastery. His shrine became a great center of pilgrimage, and his cult was spread partly through the Crusaders. Legend holds that he was born in Athens, and that while a young man, he cured a sick beggar by giving him his cloak, in a manner similar to St. Martin. Uncomfortable with the attention he received from neighbors as a result of his generosity to the poor and miracles attributed to him, he traveled West. He spent two years with St. Caesarius at Arles, and then he made a hermitage in a cave in a forest near the mouth of the Rhone. Here he is said to have lived off the milk of a hind. Pursued one day in a hunt by Flavius, king of the Goths, the creature sought safety with Giles in his cave, and the dogs gave up the chase. The scenario was repeated the next day. On the third day, the king brought a bishop with him to witness the dogs' mysterious activity. This time one of the huntsmen shot an arrow toward the mouth of the cave. When the company forced their way into the cave, they discovered Giles, who had been wounded by the arrow, sitting with the hind between his knees. Flavius and the bishop asked him to explain the situation, and after he had done so, they asked for his pardon. They wished to send for a physician, but Giles refused this and all gifts they offered him. Flavius visited Giles often, and Giles asked him to found a monastery. The king agreed but only if Giles would become its abbot. The monastery was built near the cave, and its reputation eventually traveled to Charles, the king of France. The king sent for Giles and consulted him on spiritual matters but was too ashamed to admit one particular sin. While Giles was celebrating mass one Sunday, an angel is said to have appeared and laid on the altar a scroll on which was written the sin that the king had committed, and a message saying that the king would be forgiven with Giles's intercession, provided that Charles did penance and never committed the sin again. Giles gave the scroll to the king, and the king begged him to intercede for him. Giles did so. He then returned to his monastery and later traveled to Rome to commend his monks to the Holy See. In addition to many privileges, the pope gave him two carved doors of cedarwood. To illustrate his trust in Divine Providence, Giles flung the doors into the River Tiber, and they are said to have preceded him to France without harm. He was warned of his approaching death in a dream. He is one of the Fourteen Holy Helpers. His churches were often built at road junctions, so that travelers could visit them while their horses were being shod at smithies in the vicinity. Giles is the patron saint of smithies, lepers, and sufferers of influenza. His emblem in art is a hind, and he is sometimes shown with an arrow piercing his breast or leg.

GODFREY. Bishop. c. 1066–1115. November 8. When he was five years old, Godfrey was placed with the abbot of Mont-Saint-Quentin. He became a monk and was eventually ordained a priest. He became the abbot of Nogent, in Champagne, where the brethren had dwindled to six and buildings and discipline alike were run down. Under his rule the monastery prospered, and as a result, the archbishop of Rheims asked him to take over the famous Abbey of Saint-Remi. Godfrey refused. Despite his strong feelings, he was appointed bishop of Amiens in 1104, but he insisted upon continuing to live very simply. He was a stern ruler and unrelentingly fought simony and incontinence among the clergy, for which reason his life was threatened more than once. His scrupulousness caused great resentment among the laxer clergy. He became disheartened by their behavior and wished to join the Carthusians, but his people would not allow it. On his way to visit his metropolitan, he died at Soissons, where he was buried. He is portrayed in art serving the sick and embracing a poor man.

GODRIC. Hermit. 1069–1170. May 21. He was born to a poor family in Walpole in Norfolk, and became a peddler. This work carried him throughout the country, and he was eventually drawn to life at sea, which he pursued for sixteen years. He traveled to Scotland, Flanders, and Scandinavia. Over time he purchased a half share in one merchant ship, a quarter share in another, and eventually became a captain. The life he led may have been rough and somewhat unsavory, for one historian refers to him as a pirate. In any case, on a visit to Lindisfarne, he was touched by an account of the life of St. Cuthbert, and from then on he thought of the saint with devotion. He made a pilgrimage to Jerusalem and then to Compostela. He returned to England and became a house steward to a Norfolk landowner but resigned the post because of the unfair advantage taken of poorer neighbors. He made a pilgrimage to the shrine of St. Giles in Provence and then one to Rome accompanied by his mother, who is said to have made the journey barefoot. In Cumberland he acquired a psalter, which he learned by heart and which became his most valued possession. In 1105, he sold all his goods and traveled to Wolsingham, where he joined up with an elderly hermit named Aelric, with whom he spent two years. After Aelric's death, he made another pilgrimage to Jerusalem, and lived for a time with hermits in the desert of St. John the Baptist, working in a hospital for several months. In a vision, St. Cuthbert promised him a hermitage in England. After spending time at Eskedale and Durham, where he acted as a sacristan and went to school with the choirboys at St. Mary-le-Bow, he found a perfect spot to settle in Bishop Flambard's hunting grounds on the River Wear, a short distance from Durham. He spent the next sixty years in the Finchale forest, living a very austere life and practicing severe mortifications. At first he lived on roots and berries, but later he grew vegetables and milled and baked his own barley. He wore a hair shirt and a metal breastplate. Twice he nearly died, once when he was caught in a flood, and once when Scottish soldiers beat him, assuming that he had hidden valuables. Animals were said to act as his friends, and he did not fear even wolves. In winter he would bring rabbits and field mice to his hut, warm them, then set them free. Once a stag took refuge in his hut. He lived mainly alone and in silence, but he was under the guidance of the prior of Durham, who supplied him with a priest to say mass in his chapel and would send strangers to him to ask his advice. These visitors included SS. Aelred and Robert of Newminster, and a monk named Reginald who wrote a biography of him that still survives. He built a wattle oratory and later a small stone church dedicated to St. Mary. Godric received messengers from St. Thomas of Canterbury, and Pope Alexander III wrote to him. His sister, Burchwen, lived with him as a solitary for a while, but she left to become a sister in the hospital at Durham. Godric was said to have the gift of prophecy and to have foretold the death of Bishop William of Durham, and the fate of St. Thomas Becket—whom he had never met. He often saw visions of scenes occurring far away from him and was known to halt conversations in order to pray for ships in danger of shipwreck. He suffered a long illness and was nursed by Durham monks, but he died after foretelling his own death. His biographer, Reginald, recorded four songs that Godric said had been taught to him in visions of the Blessed Virgin, his dead sister, and others. They are the oldest pieces of English verse of which the musical settings survive, and are the oldest to show the use of devices of rhyme and measure instead of alliteration. He is depicted in art dressed in white, kneeling on grass and holding a rosary, while above him the Blessed Virgin and her son appear, teaching him her song.

GOHARD. Bishop, martyr. d. 843. June 25. When Northmen raided the coasts of Anglo-Saxon England and France, they attacked religious foundations, motivated by distaste for Christianity and greed for treasure held by the foundations. Massacres of the inhabitants were common. In 843, a Norman named Lambert, who had wished for the countship of Nantes but had been driven out by the citizens, returned to Nantes on a ship. The monks of a local monastery carried their ecclesiastical treasure to the church of SS. Peter and Paul, where Bishop Gohard was celebrating a feast of St. John the Baptist. The church was filled with people who had gathered there in fear of the Normans. The Normans broke down the doors and windows and murdered Gohard and the priests and monks who were present. They burned the church, sacked the city, and kidnapped leading citizens, placing a ransom on their heads. The body of Gohard was recovered, and his relics were taken to his native town of Angers. He is portrayed in art being beheaded on an altar.

GREGORY VII, OR HILDEBRAND. Pope. c. 1021–1085. May 25. Criticized in past generations as an ambitious tyrant, even to being called "Holy Satan," Gregory is now generally recognized as having pursued an uncompromising policy that was driven by a wish for justice. He was born to poor parents in Rovaco, near Saona in Tuscany and was baptized Hildebrand. His modest beginnings made him indifferent to the materialism of most ecclesiastics of the time. He was sent at a young age to Rome, where he was placed in the care of an uncle who was the superior of the monastery of St. Mary on the Aventine. He was educated at the Lateran school, and one of his teachers, John Gratian, was so impressed with him that when he became pope as Gregory VI, he appointed Hildebrand as his secretary. After the pope's death, Hildebrand retired to a monastery, which may have been Cluny, then run by St. Odilo and St. Hugh. Hildebrand would have been content to live in a monastery for life, but he was persuaded to return to Rome with St. Bruno, who was to become Pope St. Leo IX. Hildebrand acted as *economus* to the pope, restoring financial order to the treasury, order to the city, and acting as a support to the pope's efforts at reform. He was recognized, in fact, as "the power behind the throne." After the death of Alexander II in 1073, Hildebrand, by then a cardinal and archdeacon, was made pope by an overwhelming vote, and took the name Gregory VII. He was faced with a huge and thankless task of initiating vast reforms. The rulers of both the church and state at the time would work against him. Bishoprics and abbeys were sold, simony was accepted, clerical celibacy was flamboyantly disregarded, tithes and offerings were misused and even bequeathed to the children of incontinent priests. Gregory immediately denounced priests who practiced simony or were married, a move that was received with great hostility. A council assembled in Paris claimed that the new decrees were intolerable. Gregory held fast and went further, abolishing the system of lay investiture, excommunicating anyone—even a king—who should confer an investiture in connection with an ecclesiastical office. Unable to trust his own bishops, he used legates to announce and enforce his decrees. His most cunning enemy was Henry IV of Germany, who raised the clergy of Germany and northern Italy and antipapal Roman nobles against Gregory. In the midst of celebrating Christmas midnight mass in St. Mary Major's, Gregory was kidnapped and held captive for several hours until the people rescued him. A meeting of German bishops at Worms denounced him, the Lombardy bishops refused to obey him, and Henry sent an envoy to Rome to inform the cardinals that Gregory was a usurper and would be replaced by the emperor. Gregory excommunicated Henry the following day, releasing his subjects from allegiance to him, a hallmark in the history of the papacy. German nobles who felt no loyalty to Henry seized this opportunity to decide that Henry should forfeit his crown unless he received absolution from the pope within a year and appeared before a council over which Gregory should preside at Augsburg the following February. Henry decided to appear to comply, and accompanied by his wife, baby, and one attendant, crossed the Alps in terrible weather and approached the pope at the castle of Canossa. He was refused admission and spent three days, dressed as a penitent, at the gate of the castle. While there might have been suspicion of Henry's motives, nothing could be proved, and Henry was admitted, whereupon he accused himself and was absolved. Gregory's handling of this situation greatly changed the relation between church and state. In fact, Henry was merely biding his time. Nobles elected Henry's brother-in-law, Rudolph of Swabia, in his place, despite the lifting of the excommunication. Gregory wished to remain uninvolved but with time was forced to reinstate the excommunication and support Rudolph, who was killed in battle. Henry worked for the election of Guibert, the archbishop of Ravenna, as antipope, and upon Rudolph's death, invaded Italy. He attacked Rome for two years and finally took it. Gregory sought harbor in the castle of Sant' Angelo, where he was eventually rescued by an army under Robert Guiscard, the Norman duke of Calabria. The behavior of Guiscard's followers, however, distressed the Romans, and they were angry with Gregory as well because he had summoned Norman aid. Gregory went to Monte Cassino for a time and then to Salerno, out of favor and in broken health, having been abandoned by thirteen of his cardinals. Gregory made one last appeal to the people but died the following year. He forgave his enemies as he lay dying and lifted all excommunications he had declared with the exceptions of Henry IV and Guibert. "I have loved righteousness and hated iniquity and that is why I die in exile," were among his last words. He is portrayed in art with a dove upon his shoulder.

GREGORY BARBARIGO. Blessed, bishop, cardinal. 1625–1697. June 18. He was born in Venice to an old and aristocratic family. While still in his twenties, he was appointed by the Venetian government to travel with its ambassador, Luigi Contarini, to the Congress of Münster, at which the Treaty of Westphalia was signed, bringing the Thirty Years' War to an end. In Münster Gregory met the apostolic nuncio, Fabio Chigi, and earned his high respect. After Fabio became Pope Alexander VII, he became a patron and strong supporter of Gregory. In 1657, the pope nominated Gregory to the bishopric of Bergamo. He made Gregory a cardinal in 1660, and bishop of Padua in 1664. The attention and care with which Gregory ruled led to his being called a second Charles Borromeo. He supported the poor with great generosity. While very demanding of himself, he was kind to others, treating those in trouble with great compassion. He founded a college and later a seminary, which gained a great reputation. To the seminary he gave a printing press and an excellent library well stocked with scholarly works. He worked tirelessly for a reconciliation between the churches of the East and West. He died peacefully.

GREGORY THE GREAT. Doctor of the Church, pope. c. 540–604. September 3. Gregory was born into a wealthy Roman patrician family of great piety. Gregory's father, Gordian, was a senator who owned large estates and his mother, Silvia, is named as a saint in the Roman martyrology. Gregory was well educated and entered a career as a public official. He achieved the highest civil office in Rome—prefect—at around the age of thirty. Despite his success and the fact that he was one of the richest men in the city, he decided to give up worldly things and dedicate himself to God. He made his house on the Clivus Scauri into a monastery, placed it under the patronage of St. Andrew, and made a monk, Valentius, its head. Gregory was eventually ordained seventh deacon of the Roman church and then acted as a papal ambassador to the Byzantine court. He knew no Greek, however, and he retired more and more into a monastic life with some of the monks of St. Andrew's who had joined him. Probably around 586 he was summoned back to Rome by Pope Pelagius II. Despite the fact that he was one of the seven deacons of Rome, Gregory lived in his monastery and soon became abbot. He was to suffer chronic ill health as a result of the austere life he led there. He founded six monasteries on his estates in Sicily and, as deacon, abolished clerical fees for burials and ordinations, restored discipline, and removed unfit clerics. A legend recounted by Bede holds that Gregory was walking through the Roman market one day when he saw Anglo-Saxon boys up for sale and asked their nationality. He was told "They are Angles or Angli." Gregory replied, "They are well named for they have angelic faces and it becomes such to be companions with the angels in heaven." Upon learning that they were pagans, he asked what province they were from. They replied, "Deira." Then Gregory cried, "Yes, verily they shall be saved from God's ire and called to the mercy of Christ. What is the name of the king of that country?" "Aella" was the response. "Then must Alleluia be sung in Aella's land." He was so touched by their beauty and their ignorance of Christianity that he decided to preach the gospel in Britain and actually started off with some of his monks, but the people of Rome were upset by his departure and the pope sent envoys to make them return. The pope may have recalled him because Rome suffered a severe outbreak of the plague. In 590 Pelagius died of the disease. Gregory was unanimously chosen his successor. He was the first pope who had been a monk. Gregory wrote the *Regula Pastoralis*, a book on the office of a bishop, after being chided by John, the archbishop of Ravenna, for trying to avoid office. The work was enormously successful. It was translated into Greek by Anastasius, the patriarch of Antioch. St. Augustine took it to England, and 300 years later it was translated by King Alfred. At the councils he called, Charlemagne pressed bishops to study the book and arranged that each be given a copy upon his consecration. One of Gregory's first actions as pope was to buy some English slaves and educate them for service of God. He chose a company of forty missionaries from St. Andrew's and sent them to England under the guidance of St. Augustine. By doing this he initiated the spreading of the Benedictine rule among Western Europe. Gregory's *Dialogues*—a collection of visions, prophecies, miracles, and lives of Italian saints—contains the only surviving life of St. Benedict. These works helped to make Gregory one of the most prominent writers of the Middle Ages. He greatly influenced Roman liturgy; the saying of thirty successive masses for a dead person traces back to him. Gregory used his power for justice, as is illustrated by his refusal to allow the Jews to be suppressed or deprived of their synagogues. He ransomed captives from the Lombards, applauding bishops who sold church plate to raise money for this purpose, attended to the poor on a regular basis, and sought to supply Rome's needs in difficult times. The Lombards were constantly invading Italy, and it became Gregory's responsibility to defend Rome and other cities against them. For years he tried to negotiate a peace between the Byzantine emperor and the Lombards, but eventually he chose to negotiate a special truce with Agilulf for Rome and the surrounding districts. Gregory was constantly engaged in confrontations with Constantinople, trying to halt what he felt were abuses of the Italian people. He appointed governors of Italian cities, provided them with war materials, and by assuming these responsibilities, he began the exercise of temporal power by the papacy. It was he who was mainly responsible for the restoration of Rome from the wars and earthquakes that had preceded his rule. Although he enjoyed a full sense of the dignity of his office, he titled himself "Servant of the servants of God," a title that is still used by his successors. One of his last acts was to send a cloak to a bishop who suffered from the cold. Gregory was buried in St. Peter's. He was the last of the traditional Latin doctors of the Church. He is the patron saint of music and is invoked as protection against the plague. Although "Gregorian chant" is named for Gregory, his association with Church music is uncertain. He is portrayed in art vested as a pope, carrying a double-barred cross. A dove, symbolizing the Holy Spirit, may sit on his shoulder or hover near his ear, dictating to him. He may be writing, reading, or kneeling before an altar, behind which the emblems of the Lord's passion appear.

GREGORY NAZIANZEN. Bishop, doctor of the Church. c. 329–389. January 2. He was born at Nazianzus, Cappadocia, the eldest son of St. Gregory Nazianzen the Elder, who was the bishop of Nazianzus for forty-five years. He studied at Caesarea, where he was introduced to St. Basil, and then for ten years at Athens, where fellow pupils included St. Basil and the future Emperor Julian the Apostate. Gregory returned to Nazianzus but joined St. Basil at Pontus on the Iris River to live in solitude for two years. He returned home to help his aged father to administer his see. He was ordained against his will by his father in 362, ran away to Basil for ten weeks, but returned to his new duties. He wrote an *apologia* for his action, which would become a classic on the nature and responsibilities of priests. He was named bishop of Sasima around 372. It was an unfortunate appointment, for this Arian area was divided by civil strife, and Gregory, a gentle, peace-loving, and private person, was more fitted for the life of a contemplative scholar than that of an active administrator. He never went to Sasima but continued to assist his father, and after his father's death, he continued to administer the see until a new bishop was chosen. After suffering a breakdown in 375, he lived for five years at Seleucia, Isauria. While he was ill, an effort was made to depose him, but he held fast, and in 380, the newly baptized Emperor Theodosius decreed that his subjects must be orthodox and that the Arian leaders must submit or leave. Gregory was named archbishop of Constantinople. A few months after his consecration, hostilities arose again, and his election was questioned in 381 at the Council of Constantinople. Having restored orthodoxy, he resigned his office in the hopes of restoring peace. He returned to an austere private life and died in Nazianzus. He is often called "the Theologian" or "the Divine" for the depth and eloquence of his defense of orthodoxy. Among his best-known works are his sermons on the Trinity, *Five Theological Orations*, which were delivered at the Church of Anastasia, a long poem, *De vita sua*, letters, and a selection of writings by Origen, which he compiled with St. Basil. His relics were translated first to Constantinople and later to St. Peter's in Rome. He is portrayed in art with Reading, Wisdom, and Chastity appearing before him.

GUY OR GUIDO VIGNOTELLI OF CORTONA. Blessed, tertiary. c. 1185–1245. June 16. A wealthy citizen of Cortona, Guy, after hearing a sermon by St. Francis, invited him home for a meal. At the end of the meal he asked to become a disciple. He liquidated his goods and with St. Francis distributed the money among the poor. He received the habit from St. Francis, built a cell on a bridge near Cortona, and lived there. He became well known for his holiness and for his miracles, which were said to include resuscitating a girl who had drowned and multiplying food during a famine. At the age of sixty, St. Francis appeared to him in a dream and foretold his death. Guy died at the hour foretold.

HEDWIG, JADWIGA. Widow. c. 1174–1243. October 16. She was born in Bavaria, the daughter of Berthold, count of Andechs. She was aunt to St. Elizabeth of Hungary through her sister Gertrude. As a child she was placed in the

Benedictine monastery of Kitzingen in Franconia. At the age of twelve, she was married to the eighteen-year-old Henry, duke of Silesia. They had seven children. After succeeding to his father's dukedom, and under Hedwig's influence, Henry founded the monastery of Cistercian nuns at Trebnitz, the first convent of women in Silesia. The convent was built with the labor of those convicted of crimes. It was the first of a large number of such establishments founded by the couple, including houses of Augustinian canons, Cistercian monks and Dominican and Franciscan friars, by which religion and German culture were spread over their territories. Henry also founded the Hospital of the Holy Ghost in Breslau, and Hedwig founded a hospital for female lepers. Only one of their children, Gertrude, outlived Hedwig, and she became abbess of Trebnitz. After bearing her last child in 1209, Hedwig convinced her husband to a vow of continence, and from then on the two rarely lived together. It is said that Henry never again wore gold, silver, or purple, nor did he shave his beard, for which reason he was called "Henry the Bearded." Hedwig often retreated to the convent at Trebnitz, where she lived like the nuns. She wore a hair shift, and suffered painful feet from walking to church barefoot in all weathers, although she carried her shoes under her arm to put on if she met anyone. An abbot gave her a new pair of shoes and bade her wear them. In 1227, Henry engaged in fighting Conrad of Masovia for the land of Ladislaus of Sandomir who had been killed in battle. Henry triumphed and established himself at Cracow, but he was kidnapped during mass and taken by Conrad to Plock. Hedwig followed and helped bring the two to a peaceful agreement, which included the marriage of her two granddaughters to Conrad's sons. In 1238 Duke Henry died. Hedwig did not cry, and she consoled the nuns at Trebnitz. She took the habit of the nuns but not the vows, wishing to administer her property as she wished to help the needy. Her husband was succeeded by her son Henry, who came to be called "Henry the Good," but he was killed in 1240 by Mongol Tartars. Again, Hedwig comforted the others. She was said to have performed miracles, including restoring sight to a blind nun by her blessing. She predicted her own death, insisting on being anointed before anyone else would acknowledge she was in danger. She was buried at Trebnitz. She is the patron saint of Silesia. She is depicted in art with the church and a statue of the Virgin Mary in her hands; or washing the feet of the poor; or barefoot with her shoes in her hands; or in a religious habit with the robes and crown of a princess near her.

HELENA. Empress, widow. c. 250–330. August 18. She is believed to have been born at Drepanum in Bithynia and may have been the daughter of an innkeeper. The Roman general Constantius Chlorus married her despite her humble birth, but after being made emperor, he was convinced to divorce her and marry Theodora, the stepdaughter of Emperor Maximian. Helena had borne a son, Constantine the Great, who loved his mother deeply and would change the name of her native town to Helenopolis. It appears that Helena was converted to Christianity only at the age of sixty-three, after her son was proclaimed emperor. She used the imperial treasures to help the poor, and she built many churches. In addition to her compassion for the poor, she was known for her kindness to soldiers and prisoners. After Constantine became master of the East in 324, she made a pilgrimage to Palestine to places visited by Jesus. Helena oversaw the building of a church after Golgotha and the Holy Sepulchre were uncovered beneath the terrace and temple of Venus, which Emperor Hadrian had built over them. She was also driven by a desire to find the sacred cross on which Jesus died, but it is uncertain whether she took an active part in discovering the three crosses in a rock cistern to the east of Calvary. The story of her finding the true cross was the subject of Cynewulf's most celebrated poem, the ninth-century *Elene*. She spent her last days in Palestine, and Eusebius reports that she built the Basilica on the Mount of Olives and another basilica at Bethlehem. Her body was taken to Rome. The Atlantic island of St. Helena was named for her because Spanish sailors discovered it on her feast day. She is portrayed in art dressed as an empress, holding or supporting a cross, with an open book.

HENRY THE EMPEROR. Emperor. 973–1024. July 13. Henry II was born to Henry the Quarrelsome, Duke of Bavaria, and Gisela of Burgundy. He was taught by St. Wolfgang, the bishop of Ratisbon. He succeeded his father as duke in 995, and after the death of his cousin, Otto III, was chosen emperor in 1002. He engaged in many wars in order to consolidate his empire and was known to use the Church for political ends, although he did support the Church's authority. He founded the see of Bamberg in 1006 and built an impressive cathedral as a means of strengthening German power among the Wends. Although he was opposed in this by the bishops of Würzburg and Eichstätt, whose dioceses were dismantled in the process, Benedict VIII consecrated the cathedral in 1020. He was crowned emperor by Pope Benedict VIII in 1014. He repaired and restored the sees of Hildesheim, Magdeburg, Strasburg, and Meersburg with generous endowments and gave offerings to many churches. He built and endowed a monastery at Bamberg and founded other institutions to provide for the poor. On his way back from Italy after fighting the Greeks in Apulia, he was taken ill at Monte Cassino, but he is said to have been cured by the intercession of St. Benedict. He was left lame, however. He supported his friend St. Odilo and the reforms that originated at his monastery of Cluny, even going so far as to oppose his friend and former chaplain, Aribo, whom he had made archbishop of Mainz. A story has it that at one time he wished to become a monk at Saint-Vanne at Verdun. He pledged obedience to the abbot, who then commanded him, under this obedience, to continue as emperor. His work for the Church in Eastern Europe led to an interest in monastic reform. Legend says that his childless marriage with St. Cunegund was a virgin marriage, but there is no proof of this. He is the patron saint of Finland, of the Benedictine Oblates, and of kings. He is shown in art holding a lily with St. Cunegund; or holding a globe with a dove on it; or holding a church and a palm, with devils in the air; or asleep, with St. Wolfgang appearing to him; or holding the cathedral of Bamberg and a sword.

HERBERT. Hermit. d. 687. March 20. Herbert was the disciple and good friend of St. Cuthbert and lived as a hermit on an island on Lake Derwentwater. The island was named St. Herbert's Island for him. Each year Herbert would visit St. Cuthbert at Lindisfarne. The year before St. Cuthbert died, he traveled to Carlisle, and Herbert visited him there instead. St. Cuthbert told Herbert on this visit that if he had anything to ask he must do so at this time because he foresaw that he would die and that Herbert would not see him again in this world. Herbert wept and begged him not to abandon him, but to pray that since they had served God together in this world, they be taken at the same time. St. Cuthbert prayed for a moment and then predicted that this would be so. Soon afterward Herbert fell ill and his illness lasted until March 20 of the following year, when both saints died.

HERVÉ, OR HARVEY. Abbot. d. c. 575. June 17. He is one of the most popular saints in Brittany and his name is one of the commonest names given to Breton boys. Legend has it that Hervé was a blind boy born to a British bard named Hyvarnion, and a girl named Rivanon. His mother was widowed young, and when the boy was seven she gave

186

him to the care of a holy man called Arthian. Afterward, he lived with his uncle, who had founded a small monastic school at Plouvien. He helped his uncle with his farm and the students. One day, as Hervé worked in the fields, a wolf came and killed and ate the ass that was drawing the plough. A young child who was Hervé's guide cried in fear, but Hervé prayed and the wolf passed his head into the ass's harnass and finished his work. Soon after his mother's death, Hervé's uncle gave over to him the care of the community of Plouvien. The monastery prospered, but Hervé decided to establish it in another place. Surrounded by a company of monks and students, he went to León. There the bishop would have ordained him a priest, but Hervé humbly declined. From León they went west, and beside the road to Lesneven is the fountain of St. Hervé, which he is said to have caused to flow to slake the thirst of his companions. At Lanhouarneau, Hervé founded a monastery, which earned a great reputation. He lived there for the rest of his life, traveling forth periodically to preach or to act as an exorcist. His exorcisms were responsible for some of his most impressive miracles. As his monks watched beside his deathbed, they were said to have heard the music of the heavenly choirs welcoming him to Heaven. He is portrayed in art as a blind man, with a wolf and Guiharan, his child guide; and frogs may appear near him. Breton mothers threatened mischievous children with his wolf. He is invoked for eye trouble.

HILARY OF POITIERS. Bishop, doctor of the Church. 315–c. 368. January 13. He was born at Poitiers of a noble family. He was raised a pagan, and in his own writings he describes his conversion. It involved a long process of biblical study. His friend and relative, Honoratus, invited him to the recently founded monastery at Lerins, and it was there that Hilary was baptized. He joined the community and when Honoratus became bishop of Arles, he made Hilary his secretary. Hilary had been married and had a daughter Apra, and his wife was still living when he was made bishop of Poitiers around 350. He resisted the appointment, but the people insisted. Soon after, he wrote a commentary on the Gospel of St. Matthew, which survives. In 355 the Emperor Constantius and a synod required all bishops to sign the condemnation of St. Athanasius. Those who declined were banished. In reponse, Hilary wrote his "First Book to Constantius," begging him to restore peace to the Church. He went into exile in 356 and during this time did much of his writing. His most important and celebrated work is *De Trinitate*. He was one of the most prominent and esteemed theologians of his time. Although his writing could be stern and uncompromising, he was a gentle, polite, and friendly man. He wrote commentaries on the Psalms and wrote much on the Arian controversy. His writings are also useful for their historical insight. In addition, the earliest Latin hymn writing is associated with him. After three years in Phrygia, he went to Constantinople and presented the emperor with a request, which he called his "Second Book to Constantius." In it he asked permission to have a public disputation about religion with Saturninus, the initiator of his banishment. The Arians feared the outcome of such a trial and convinced the emperor to send Hilary back to Gaul. Hilary traveled through Illyricum and Italy, strengthening the morale of weaker Christians, and was well received by the people at Poitiers. He convoked a synod in Gaul and condemned the synod of Rimini in 359. Saturninus was excommunicated and deposed. Constantius died at Poitiers in 361, and the Arian persecution ended. St. Jerome called him "a fair cedar transplanted out of this world into the Church." The spring term at the Law Courts in England and at Oxford University are named for him. He is portrayed in art holding an open book of the Gospel; or as a bishop with three books; or with a child (sometimes in a cradle at his feet, raised to life by him); or with a pen or stick.

HIPPOLYTUS. Martyr. c. 170–c. 235. August 13. According to the unreliable *acta* of St. Laurence, Hippolytus was an officer in charge of the imprisoned St. Laurence and was converted and baptized by his ward. He assisted at the burial of St. Laurence, for which he was rebuked by the emperor and ordered to be scourged. He was then said to have been sentenced to be torn apart by horses—a fate suspiciously similar to that of Hippolytus, the son of Theseus. Two wild horses were found and a rope was tied between them, to which the martyr's feet were tied. He was dragged over rough land, and the Christian followers dipped up his blood with rags and gathered the pieces of his flesh. It is more likely that Hippolytus was, in fact, a learned Roman priest who was an important theological writer and probably the most important writer of his time in Italy. His most important work was *A Refutation of All Heresies*. He may have been a follower of St. Irenaeus, and St. Jerome called him "a most holy and eloquent man." Hippolytus was a rigorist and criticized Pope St. Zephyrinus for not fighting heresy zealously enough. Upon the election to the papacy of St. Callistus, to whom he was actively hostile, he allowed himself to be set up in opposition to him. He was banished with Pope St. Pontian, whom he had also once attacked, to Sardinia during the persecution of Maximinus in 235. He died from the harshness of the climate. During his exile he apparently became reconciled with the Church, because under Pope Fabian his and Pontian's bodies were brought to Rome, and he was buried in the cemetery on the Via Tiburtina. He was rediscovered as a theologian in 1551 when an excavation uncovered a third-century statue of him seated on a chair, which displayed on its sides a list of his works and his tables for calculating Easter. He is the patron saint of horses. He is portrayed in art in armor, holding a palm; or bearing a lance; or dragged and torn by horses; or holding keys as a jailer; or burying the body of St. Laurence; or holding an instrument resembling a curry comb.

HYACINTH. Confessor. 1185–1257. August 15. He was born to a noble Polish family, in the district of Oppeln, between Breslau and Cracow. He studied at Cracow, Prague, and Bologna. On a visit to Rome with his uncle Ivo of Konski, the bishop of Cracow, he met St. Dominic. It is said that he received the habit from Dominic himself around 1217 and became superior of a small company of Dominicans the same year. The band came to Cracow and was given the Church of the Holy Trinity by the bishop. Hyacinth was at this priory in 1228, and ten years later he was preaching a crusade against the Prussians. He was an active missionary and, according to his biographers, traveled widely: northeast into Lithuania, east to Kiev, southeast to the Black Sea, south to the Danube and northwest to Scandinavia. He was said to perform miracles, but some of them are similar to those attributed to other holy persons, as can be seen by his depictions in art. After the Mongols crossed the Volga in 1238, the missions that the Friars Preachers had founded were greatly damaged, and it is probable that Hyacinth helped to restore them. He died begging his brethren to esteem poverty as men that had renounced all earthly things. He is portrayed in art sailing on the sea on his cloak; or curing the bite of a scorpion; or restoring a drowned youth to life; or with either the Virgin Mary, or she and her infant son, appearing to him.

IDA OF HERZFELD. Widow. 9th century. September 4. She was reared in Charlemagne's court. Charlemagne arranged a marriage for her to a lord named Egbert, but she was widowed quite young. In her widowed state she increased her devotions to God, engaging in self-denial and austerities, and she directed most of the revenues of her estate to the poor. She built a small chapel for herself within a church that she had founded near her house at Hofstadt in Westphalia. When her son, Warin, became a monk at Corvey, Ida moved to Herzfeld, where she founded a nunnery.

It is said that she had a stone coffin made for herself and had it filled daily with food for the poor in order to remind herself of her duty to her neighbor and her own mortality. She suffered a painful illness the last years of her life but endured it with patience. She was buried in the cemetery of the Herzfeld convent. She is shown in art filling a tomb with food for the poor; or with a dove over her head; or carrying a church.

IGNATIUS. Bishop, martyr. d. c. 107. October 17. Ignatius may have been a persecutor of Christians, who then became a convert and disciple of St. John the Evangelist. He called himself both a disciple and the ''bearer of God'' (*theophoros*), so sure was he of the presence of God in himself. He appears to have taken charge of the church at Antioch. Legend holds that he was appointed and consecrated bishop by St. Peter after Peter left the deathbed of Evodius, the previous bishop. During Trajan's persecutions, Ignatius was seized by a guard of ten soldiers, bound, and taken to Rome by them. The soldiers boarded a ship that traveled along the southern and western shores of Asia Minor instead of going straight to Italy. The many stopovers enabled Ignatius to reaffirm religious fervour in various ports along the way. One deputy, Burrhus, was so helpful to Ignatius that he asked the Ephesians to allow him to accompany him as a companion. From Smyrna, Ignatius wrote four letters: to the Ephesians, to the Churches of Magnesia and Tralles—whose bishops had come to visit him—and to the Christians in Rome. The guards were anxious to leave Smyrna in order to reach Rome before the games were over; distinguished victims drew great crowds. They sailed on to Troas, where they learned that peace had been restored to the church at Antioch. There Ignatius wrote three more letters: to the Philadelphians, to the Smyrnaeans, and to St. Polycarp. As the ship approached Rome, Christians are said to have gathered to greet Ignatius, and although they wished to work for his release, he begged them not to interfere with his martyrdom. Legend has it that he arrived in Rome on the last day of the games, was rushed to the amphitheater, and was killed by lions in the arena. As he was offered to the animals, he described himself as "wheat of Christ." His relics are kept at St. Peter's in Rome. The letters of Ignatius are among the most valuable documents of the ancient Church. He is portrayed in art regarding a crucifix, with a lion at his side; or standing between two lions; or in chains; or holding a heart with "IHS" upon it; or with a heart with the "IHS" torn out by lions.

IGNATIUS OF LOYOLA. Founder. 1491–1556. July 31. He was born in the castle of Loyola at Azpeitia, the youngest child of Don Beltran, the lord of Oñaz and Loyola, and the head of one of the oldest and noblest families of the country. He first became a page at court and then joined the army. His military career was shortened when a cannon ball broke his right shin and injured his leg. The leg was badly set and was broken again by surgeons, and he limped for the rest of his life. While recuperating, he asked for a book of knightly romances, but when one could not be found, he was given books on the life of Jesus and legends of the saints. Impressed by the books, he decided to imitate the saints, and he began to practice austerities and to weep for his sins. He made a pilgrimage to the shrine at Montserrat and resolved to lead a life of penance. For a year he lived nearby, sometimes with Dominicans, sometimes in a hospice, and retreated to a cave to pray and make penance. He began to take notes of what would become the book of his *Spiritual Exercises*. In 1523, he started off to Jerusalem, begging his way there. He planned to remain in Jerusalem, but the Franciscan guardian of the Holy Places demanded that he leave for fear that his attempts to convert Moslems would result in his being kidnapped and held for ransom. He returned to Spain, studied in Barcelona for two years, and then attended the University of Alcala. He lived at a hospice, wore a coarse habit, and lived by begging. He catechized children and led prayer meetings. He was accused to the bishop's vicar general of preaching heresy and was imprisoned for forty-two days. He was exonerated but was forbidden to wear any unique dress or to instruct in religion for three years. He traveled with three companions to Salamanca, where again he fell under suspicion, was imprisoned, and was exonerated after three weeks. In midwinter, he traveled to Spain on foot, arriving in 1528. He spent the next years studying, and in 1534, at the age of forty-three, he graduated as a master of arts. Six students in divinity joined him in his spiritual exercises. The seven made a vow to observe poverty and chastity and to preach the gospel in Palestine, or offer themselves to the pope for service in any manner he saw fit. Ignatius returned home in 1535 but refused to enter the castle of Loyola, living in the poorhouse of Azpeitia instead. In 1537, the followers met Ignatius in Venice but were unable to find a ship to Palestine. They went to Rome, and Pope Paul III granted them an indult that those of them who were not priests might be ordained by any bishop they pleased. They were ordained and retreated to a cottage near Vicenza to prepare for their duties. They resolved that the chance of going to the Holy Land was slim, so they should offer their services to the pope. Ignatius and two others departed and agreed that if any should ask their affiliation, they would respond "the Company of Jesus." On the way, in a chapel at La Storta, Ignatius reportedly saw Jesus loaded with a heavy cross and was told that all would go well in Rome. Paul III instructed one brother to teach in the Sapienza and one to explain the Holy Scriptures, and Ignatius worked using his spiritual exercises to reform the people of the city. The fact that none of them spoke Italian did not hamper their efforts. It was now proposed that they form a religious order, by adding two vows—obedience, and the willingness to go wherever the pope sent them to save souls—and to appoint a superior general, whom they must obey and who in turn was subject to the Holy See. Ignatius's training as a soldier can be detected in his emphasis upon obedience and following orders of a superior. It was agreed that the celebration of the Divine Office in choir should not be one of their duties so they would be able to do their works of charity and conversion. The cardinals initially opposed the formation of the new order but changed their opinions, and in 1540, the pope approved it, calling them the Society of Jesus (the Jesuits). Ignatius was unwillingly made the first general superior and agreed to the office only in obedience to his confessor. He lived in Rome for the rest of his life, directing the order. His goals for the order included reform through education and a more frequent use of sacraments, missionary work, and a fight against heresy. He founded several establishments in the city, including a house for converted Jews and a home for penitent troubled women. St. Francis Borgia turned over a large sum for the building of the Roman College for the Jesuits in 1550, an institution that Ignatius made a model for his other colleges, seeing to it that it had the best of teachers. He also oversaw the foundation of the German College in Rome, which was originally intended for scholars from all countries where Protestantism existed. Although other universities and places of learning were established, the educational influences for which the Jesuits were to become so well known took hold by degrees. Ignatius's approach to education was progressive but authoritarian. His book of *Spiritual Exercises* was first published in Rome, with papal approval, in 1548. During the years Ignatius directed the order, it grew from ten to one thousand members throughout nine countries and provinces of Europe, in India and in Brazil. He was always ill during his last years, so the seriousness of his final sickness was not recognized. He died suddenly, without receiving the last sacraments. He is considered to have been a fundamental figure in the Counter-Reformation. He is the patron saint of retreats and spiritual exercises, and of those troubled by scruples (a patronage stemming from the rules in the *Spiritual Exercises* providing guidance in such circumstances). He is portrayed in art with his hand on the book of his constitutions, with "IHS" above him in light; or with Christ appearing to him, bearing his cross.

IRENAEUS OF LYONS. Bishop. c. 130–200. June 28. He was a native of Asia Minor and a disciple of St. Polycarp. He was well educated and learned from men who had known the Apostles or their immediate disciples. He migrated to Lyons, which had become a chief center of European trade, in order to serve as a priest at its church under its first bishop, St. Pothinus. During a sudden persecution, which resulted in the imprisonment of many church members, the church sent Irenaeus to Rome with a letter for the pope. The letter expressed the members' concern for their fellow Christians in Asia Minor and urged leniency toward the Montanists in Phrygia, a sect for whom Irenaeus felt little sympathy. He acted, however, in the interests of peace and unity. Upon his return, he was made bishop; Pothinus had been killed in the persecution. The persecution had ended, and he ruled his see for twenty years in peace, working much to evangelize neighboring lands. The spread of Gnosticism in Gaul began to take root in his diocese, and he wrote a treatise in five books, in which he set forth the doctrines of the various sects and contrasted them with the teaching of the Apostles and the Holy Scripture. He was the first great ecclesiastical writer of the West. His writings emphasize the importance of both the Old and New Testaments, the concept of the reflection of our human nature in Christ's nature, and the unity of the Gospels. Two of his principal works are *Adversus Haereses* and *Demonstration of Apostolic Preaching*. His writings give a clear indication of the traditions of the early church. Irenaeus believed that much of the interest in Gnosticism was due to the mystery that surrounded it, and he sought to "strip the fox," in his own words, in order to conquer it. His approach succeeded, for his work was translated and widely circulated, and Gnosticism's threat to the Catholic faith was arrested. Several years after his first mission to Rome, Irenaeus again acted as a go-between for a group of Christians in Asia Minor. The Quartodecimans had refused to keep Easter in accordance with the Western methods and were threatened with excommunication by Victor III. The outcome of his arbitration was a permanent peace, and the Quartodecimans eventually chose to conform to the Roman policy. Tradition makes Irenaeus a martyr, but there is no evidence of this. He died at Lyons and was buried in the crypt of St. John (now Saint Irenée), where his shrine remained until it was destroyed by Calvinists in 1562. He is shown in art with a book or casket, with a lighted torch in his hand.

IRENE. Martyr, virgin. d. 304. April 3. In 303, Emperor Diocletian issued a decree making it an offense punishable by death to possess any portion of sacred Christian writings. Irene and her sisters, Agape and Chionia, daughters of pagan parents living in Salonika, owned several volumes of Holy Scriptures, which they hid. The volumes were discovered when the sisters were arrested on another charge and the house was searched. When requested to eat meat sacrificed to pagan gods, the sisters refused, and the governor, Dulcitius, sentenced Agape and Chionia to death by burning. Irene was sent to a soldiers' brothel, where she was stripped and chained but was miraculously protected from molestation. She died either by being forced to throw herself into flames or, more likely, by being shot in the throat with an arrow.

ISAAC THE GREAT. Bishop. c. 350–440. September 9. He was a descendent of St. Gregory the Illuminator and the son of St. Nerses I, the patriarch of Armenia. He studied at Constantinople, married, and after the death of his wife, became a monk. He was made patriarch of Armenia in 390 and fought for the metropolitan rights of the Armenian Church, ending its long dependence on the Church of Caesarea in Cappadocia. He became, in actual practice, the only ruler—ecclesiastical or civil—of the Armenians. He stopped the practice of married bishops, enforced Byzantine canon law, fought Persian paganism, built churches and schools, and encouraged the growth of monasticism. He supported St. Mesrop in creating an Armenian alphabet and with him translated a large part of the Bible. He also supported the translation of the works of the Greek and Syrian doctors into Armenian, and he initiated the founding of a national liturgy. His efforts can be said to have launched Armenian literature. The Persians invaded part of his territory and forced him to retire in 428, but he returned when he was very old to rule again from his see at Ashtishat, where he died. He is considered the founder of the Armenian Church.

ISIDORE THE FARMER. Confessor. d. 1130. May 15. He was born in Madrid to poor parents and was baptized Isidore, after the famous archbishop of Seville. He became a farm laborer on the estate of the wealthy John de Vergas, and he remained on this land for the rest of his life. He married a poor girl and had a son, but the baby died young, and the couple took a vow of continence to serve God. His life was considered to be a model of simple Christian charity and faith. He prayed while at work, and he visited churches in Madrid and the area on holidays. He shared what he had—even his meals—with the poor, often giving them the more liberal portions. Tradition has it that he had a great love of animals. It is said that on a winter day he took pity on some hungry birds and poured half of his sack of corn upon the ground for the birds, despite the mocking of witnesses. When he reached the mill, however, the bag was full, and the corn, when it was ground, produced double the expected amount of flour. His wife survived him for several years, and she, too, is honored as a saint, called Santa Maria de la Cabeza. Forty years after his death, his body was transferred to a shrine, and his cult grew as a result of miracles attributed to his intercession. He is said to have appeared in a vision to King Alphonsus of Castile in 1211, and to have shown him an unknown path, which he used to surprise and defeat the Moors. He is the patron saint of Madrid, farmers and farm laborers, and the U.S. National Catholic Rural Conference. He is portrayed in art before a cross; or with an angel and white oxen near him; or holding a hoe or rake.

ITA, YTHA, IDA, MEDA, DEIRDRE. Virgin. d. c. 570. January 15. She is the most famous woman saint in Ireland after St. Brigid. She is said to have been of royal lineage, born in one of the baronies of Decies near Drum in Waterford County, and called Deirdre. An aristocrat wished to marry her, but after praying and fasting for three days, and supposedly with divine help, she convinced her father to allow her to lead the life of a maiden. She migrated to Hy Conaill, in the western part of Limerick, and founded a nunnery. She also directed a school for boys, and it is said that Brendan, who would become the famous abbot and missionary, was taught by her for years. Brendan is supposed to have once asked her what three things God especially loved. She replied, "True faith in God with a pure heart, a simple life with a religious spirit, and openhandedness inspired by charity." An Irish lullaby for the Infant Jesus is attributed to her. Many sensational miracles are also attributed to her, including one in which she is said to have reattached the head to the body of a man who'd been beheaded, and another which claimed that she lived only on food from heaven.

IVO, YVO HÉLORY OF KERMARTIN. Confessor. 1253–1303. May 19. He was born the son of a lord in

Brittany at Kermartin. At fourteen he went to Paris for a ten-year course of studies, and he gained a great reputation for his proficiency in philosophy, theology, and canon law. He began an austere regime of life, wearing a hair shirt, sleeping for short hours on a straw mat with a book or stone as a pillow, and abstaining from meat and wine. He went on to Orléans to study civil law under the famous jurist Peter de la Chapelle. After returning to Brittany, he was made a judge of the ecclesiastical court by the archdeacon of Rennes. He also received minor orders. He dispensed justice with such care and kindness that he was esteemed even by the losing sides. In time, he became official to Alan de Bruc, the bishop of Tréguier. His free defense of the poor and elicited the nickname "Advocate of the Poor." In addition to acting as judge in his own court, he pleaded for the helpless in other courts; he frequently paid their expenses and visited them in prison. Although it was the custom of the age that lawyers accept "gifts" as a matter of course, he refused these bribes. He worked to reconcile differences out of court, in order to save the parties the cost of unnecessary litigation. He was ordained a priest and was given the living at Trédrez. Three years later he resigned his legal office to devote his time to his parishioners. He became greatly in demand as a preacher, often preaching in churches other than his own. He was frequently called upon as an arbitrator. He built a hospital, nursed the sick, and distributed his harvests or their revenues to the poor. He was known to give the clothes off his back to beggars; once he gave a beggar his bed while he slept on the doorstep. His austerities became more rigorous with time, despite his failing health. He died after preaching mass on Ascension Eve. He is the patron saint of lawyers, advocates, canon lawyers, judges, and notaries, of abandoned children and orphans, and Brittany.

JAMES THE GREATER. Apostle. d. 44. July 25. He was born in Galilee, the son of Zebedee and Salome, and the brother of St. John the Evangelist. He was called James the Greater to distinguish him from the other apostle James, who was younger than he. He worked as a fisherman with his brother and father and may have lived at Bethsaida. After calling St. Peter and St. Andrew to follow him, Jesus saw James, St. John, and Zebedee mending their nets on a ship; he called them also, and they followed him. James was present at the raising of the daughter of Jairus from the dead. Jesus called James and St. John "Boanerges"—sons of thunder—apparently a comment on their quick tempers. James and St. John were the only apostles present at the Transfiguration and the Passion. After the Ascension, nothing is known for sure of his missionary activity. According to one tradition, he preached in Spain. He was the first martyr among the apostles, dying by beheading in Jerusalem under King Herod Agrippa I. He was buried in Jerusalem, but his body was said to have been translated to El Padron in Galicia, and then to Compostela, which became the greatest pilgrimage site after Jerusalem and Rome. In the Middle Ages, he was one of the most popular Spanish saints and was frequently invoked against the Mohammedans. There are stories that he made appearances during battles against the Moors. He is the patron saint of pilgrims, Spain, and Guatemala and Nicaragua (former Spanish dominions). He is portrayed in art as an elderly, bearded man, with a hat with a scallop shell (associated with Compostela); or with a shell or shells around him; or as a pilgrim with a wallet and staff; or with or being beheaded by a sword.

JAMES THE LESS. Apostle. d. c. 62. May 3. He was the son of Alpheus and thus was a first cousin of Jesus. He is called James the Less to distinguish him from the other apostle James, who was older than he. According to St. Paul, Jesus appeared to him specially before the Ascension. James's mother may have been present as Christ died on the cross. When St. Paul went to Jerusalem three years after his conversion and was still regarded suspiciously by the apostles there, it was James and St. Peter who received him with friendliness. James became the first bishop of Jerusalem. It is possible that he was the author of the Epistle of James in the New Testament, although the author speaks of the apostles in the past tense and doesn't identify himself an apostle, and the style is more sophisticated than one would expect of someone of James's modest background. At the Council of Jerusalem it was resolved that the Gentiles who became Christians did not need to be circumcised, and James said, "it hath seemed good to the Holy Ghost and to us." He was held in great esteem and was surnamed "the Just." Eusebius contended that the catastrophes that later occurred in Jerusalem were a punishment for their treatment of one "who was the most righteous of men." One account holds that he was thrown from the top of a temple and was stoned to death, living long enough to forgive his tormentors. He is the patron saint of the dying (due to his deathbed forgiveness of his murderers). He is portrayed in art being beaten with a fuller's club (used in blacksmithing); or with the emblem of a fuller's club; or with a book.

JAMES OF THE MARCH, JAMES GANGALA. d. 1476. November 28. He was born in Montebrandone in the March of Ancona. He studied law and joined the Franciscans in 1416 He gave himself severe penances and allowed himself only three hours of sleep a night. He copied most of his books himself. He studied under St. Bernardino at Siena at Fiesole and was ordained at the age of twenty-nine. He became a zealous and well-attended preacher and is said to have brought Bl. Bernardino of Feltre into the Franciscan Order. It is said he preached every day for forty years. He worked as a missionary with St. John Capistran in Italy, and in Germany, Bohemia, Poland, and Hungary. In 1426, with St. John, he was named inquisitor against the

Fraticelli by Pope St. Martin V. Their approach was harsh—some of the Fraticelli were burned at the stake—and they destroyed thirty-six Fraticelli houses, provoking opposition. James attended the Council of Basle-Florence, helping to reconcile the Observant and Conventual Franciscans. In 1456, he went to Austria and Hungary to combat the Hussites. He was offered the bishopric of Milan but turned it down, preferring to continue preaching. In 1462, as a result of a sermon he preached at Brescia in which he gave a theological opinion, he became a subject of the local inquisition. The case was controversial and James refused to appear before the Inquisition and appealed to Rome. A silence was imposed on both the Dominican inquisitors and the Franciscans, and no decision was ever reached. He spent the last three years of his life in Naples. He was a strong supporter of the establishment of charitable pawnshops. He is depicted in art with a cup and a serpent near it.

JANE FRANCES FREMIOT DE CHANTAL. Co-foundress, widow. 1572–1641. December 12. Jane was the daughter of Benigne Frémyot, president of the parliament of Burgundy. Her father was left a widower while his children were still young, and he oversaw their religious education. Jane was confirmed Frances and was given in marriage to Christopher de Chantal, at the age of twenty. Her twenty-seven-year-old husband, an expert duelist, was an officer in the French army, and through his mother was a descendent of Bl. Humbeline. Jane ran the estate with great care, and although three children died soon after birth, a boy and three girls survived. Nine years into the marriage, Baron de Chantal was wounded in a hunting accident. He lived for nine days. Jane returned with her children to her father at Dijon and lived there for one year, and then went to Monthelon, near Autun, to live with the elderly baron de Chantal. In 1604, St. Francis de Sales preached Lenten service at Dijon and she traveled to her father's house in order to hear him. She recognized him as a man she had seen in a vision and the guide for whom she had prayed. She persuaded him, initially against his will, to become her spiritual director, and under his guidance followed a strict rule of life. She cared for children and the poor who were sick and dying. She wished to enter the Carmelites, and St. Francis revealed to her his plan of forming a new establishment—the Congregation of the Visitation of the Virgin Mary. He provided a house, called the Gallery House, on the edge of Lake Annecy, and Jane and three others took the habit. They were joined by ten more. The order was intended chiefly as one for young girls, widows, and women who could not bear the austerities of older orders. The congregation would remain unenclosed so that the sisters would be more free to attend to their neighbors. This plan was not well received, however, due to Lutheran attacks on convent laxity and its seemingly relaxed rule, and St. Francis changed the plan to make it an enclosed order, under the rule of St. Augustine, to which he made some amendments. He wrote the treatise *On the Love of God* for Jane and her community. Jane often left Annecy in order to oversee the affairs of her children and the founding of new convents. After convents had been opened at Lyons, Moulins, Grenoble, and Bourges, St. Francis sent for her from Paris to open a foundation there. This Jane accomplished in 1619, despite much opposition. She was an uncompromising, sensitive, and intense woman. She ruled the convent at Paris for three years, and St. Vincent de Paul, who called her "one of the holiest souls I have ever met," oversaw the convent at the request of St. Francis. In 1622, St. Francis died, which caused her much grief, and in 1627, her son was killed fighting against the English and the Huguenots. He left a wife and an infant daughter, who would become the famous Madame de Sévigné. In 1628, a plague came, and when it reached Annecy, Jane remained in the stricken town, rallying the local authorities to meet the needs of the people and putting the resources of her convent at their disposal. In 1632, the death of Michael Favre, the confessor of St. Francis and a good friend to the Visitandines, caused her much anguish. She entered a period of depression and spiritual desolation, which is revealed in her letters. From 1635 to 1636 Jane made a visitation of the convents, which then numbered sixty-five. In 1641 she went to France at the behest of Madame de Montmorency. She was invited to Paris by Queen Anne of Austria, and was discomfited by the impressive reception she received. On her way home she fell ill, and she died in her convent at Moulins. Her body was taken to Annecy, buried near St. Francis de Sales, and was translated to a new tomb in 1912. She is shown in art holding a heart inscribed with "IHS."

JANUARIUS. Bishop, martyr. d. 304. September 19. He was a native of Naples or Benevento, and he was bishop of Benevento when the persecution of Diocletian broke out. His *acta*, however, were written much later and are unreliable. It is said that he visited some prisoners in order to comfort them and bolster their courage, and when this was revealed to the governor, he ordered that Januarius be arrested and brought before him at Nola. The bishop was accompanied by his deacon, Festus, and a lector of his church, Disiderius. These three, loaded with irons, were made to walk before the governor's chariot to Nola. They were condemned to be torn to pieces by wild beasts. In the amphitheater, however, the beasts would not touch them. They were accused of magic and sentenced to be beheaded. The sentence was carried out near Pozzuoli and the martyrs were buried near the town. His relics were removed to the Church of San Gennaro in Naples in the fifth century. During the Norman wars, they were moved twice, but in 1497 they were brought back to Naples. The sensational fame of Januarius originates from the liquefaction of the alleged relic of his blood that is kept in the chapel of the treasury of the Cathedral of Naples. Records have been kept for four hundred years of how, three times a year in connection with his three feasts (the day of the translation of his relics, his feast day, and the anniversary of a threatened eruption of Mt. Vesuvius in 1631), this relic is brought out and held by a priest near what is thought to be the martyr's head. The dark mass is said to become liquid and reddish in color, and to sometimes froth up, increasing in volume. The blood liquefied during Cardinal Cooke's visit in 1978. The last time the miracle was said not to occur upon an expected date was when Naples elected a Communist mayor. He is the patron saint of Naples. He is shown in art wearing episcopal robes, holding a palm, with Vesuvius behind him; or being thrown into a fiery furnace, or being tied to a tree, a heated oven beside him; or with vials of his blood on the book of the Gospels; or praying in the midst of flames; or lighting a fire.

JEROME. Confessor, doctor of the Church. c. 342–420. September 30. He was born in Stridon, near Aquileia. He was instructed in religion and basic reading at home and then sent to Rome, where he was tutored by the famed pagan grammarian Donatus. He became expert at Latin and Greek rhetoric and progressed in his studies, but he lost some of the religious devotion he had been raised with. He was baptized, however, by Pope Liberius. After three years in Rome, he decided to travel with a friend, Bonosus, in order to widen his studies. He went to Trier, and there he was powerfully converted to the faith. He settled in Aquileia in 370, where the bishop, St. Valerian, had attracted a clergy that was famous in the West. Jerome became friendly with many of these men, including Rufinus. He began to cause some opposition among his fellows, however, and a conflict broke up the group. Jerome decided to go East with three friends and arrived in Antioch in 374. Two of his friends became ill and died, and Jerome himself became ill. In a letter to St. Eustochium he records that in his delirium he seemed to be standing before the judgment seat of

Christ. He was then condemned for being a Ciceronian rather than a Christian. The accusation was seemingly made because he preferred pagan literature. As a result of this and a meeting with St. Malchus, Jerome retreated into the wilderness of Chalcis, where he lived in solitude for four years. During this time he suffered from ill health and fleshly temptations, but he learned Hebrew and wrote a biography of Paul of Thebes. After leaving the desert, he was ordained by Pope Damasus. He did not wish to be ordained and consented on the condition that he not have to serve any church; he wished to be a monk or a solitary. He then traveled to Constantinople to study the Scriptures under St. Gregory Nazianzen. In 382, he went to Rome with Paulinus of Antioch and St. Epiphanius to attend a council the pope was holding about the schism at Antioch. At the conclusion of the council, the pope employed him as his secretary. Jerome would later claim that he spoke through the mouth of Damasus. Together with Damasus, he helped encourage and direct the asceticism that was becoming popular among the noblewomen of Rome. His greatest achievement, however, was his work on the Holy Scriptures, which he accomplished with the pope's support and patronage. He revised the gospels and the psalms in the Old Latin version followed by the rest of the New Testament. His new translation from the Hebrew of most of the books of the Old Testament was accomplished over years of work in Bethlehem. It was a work of scholarship unequaled in the early Church. The resulting version of the Bible, called the Vulgate, was declared the official Latin text for Catholics by the Council of Trent. Almost all English Catholic translations were made from it until the mid-twentieth century, when scholars again began to use original sources. When Damasus died, however, Jerome no longer had his protection. Although he had impressed the city with his learning and devotion, he had made enemies through his imperiousness and sarcasm. He refused to suffer the fools, and he was viewed by many as cold and superior. He referred to emenders of biblical texts, for example, as "presumptuous blockheads," and because he was so learned, he brooked no opposition. Resentful and vindictive people circulated scandalous gossip about his relations with St. Paula. He decided to return East and departed in 385. He was joined later by St. Paula, her daughter St. Eustochium, and other Roman religious women who wished to exile themselves with him. They went to Egypt to visit with the monks of Nitria and Didymus, a famous blind teacher in the school of Alexandria. Helped by St. Paula's donations, a monastery for men and buildings for three communities of women were built near the basilica of the Nativity at Bethlehem. Jerome lived in a cell carved out of rock and opened a free school and a hospice. Horrified by doctrines that were being circulated in Rome, including one that espoused that the Virgin Mary had had more children by St. Joseph after the birth of Jesus, Jerome wrote two books against Jovinian, a main offender. Once again, Jerome's uncompromising severity put off some of his readers, and his "Apology to Pammachius," sometimes called his third book against Jovinian, was not much softer in tone. A few years later he became vocal against Vigilantius, whom he called Dormantius—"Sleepy"—a priest who protested against celibacy and the veneration of relics. Jerome next became entrenched in a battle against Origenism, which had the unfortunate result of causing a break with his friend Rufinus. Jerome had held great respect for Origen's learning and his writing, much of which Rufinus had translated, but changed his mind about certain of his teachings, and joined St. Epiphanius in opposing certain points. St. Augustine, distressed by this quarrel, was later to find himself in a disagreement with Jerome arising out of the exegesis of the second chapter of St. Paul's Epistle to the Galatians. He was forced to use enormous tact and diplomacy to calm the bristling Jerome, whom he had unintentionally provoked. In 404, St. Paula died, a great grief to Jerome. Rome was plundered by Alaric a few years later. In his later years he was forced to interrupt his studies when barbarians invaded and again later when the Pelagians sent persecutors to Bethlehem to assault the monks and nuns living under his direction. Some were beaten, a deacon was killed, and the monasteries were burned. In his last days, Jerome was weakened by austerities, and his sight and voice failed. He died in Bethlehem the year after St. Eustochium. He was buried under the Church of the Nativity close to SS. Paula and Eustochium, but his body was moved and now lies somewhere in St. Mary Major's in Rome. He is the patron saint of Scripture scholars, exegetes, and librarians. In art, he is shown robed as cardinal (due to services discharged for Pope Damasus), with a lion in attendance; or stripped of robes, sometimes in a monastic cave, beating his breast (a sign of voluntary penance); or as a scholar writing; or with a pen and inkwell.

JEROME EMILIANI. Confessor, founder. 1481–1537. February 8. He was born in Venice, the son of Eleanor and Angelo Emiliani. His early life was not very religious. He served in the armies of the republic, and when the League of Cambrai was formed to fight the Venetians, he was made commander of the fortress of Castelnuovo in the mountains near Treviso. When the town fell, he was captured and imprisoned in a dungeon. He prayed and miraculously escaped. He went to a church in Treviso where he hung up his chains as offerings before the altar of the Virgin Mary, to whom he vowed himself. He was made mayor of the town. He returned to Venice, however, to oversee his nephews' education and to pursue his own religious studies. He was ordained in 1518. Plague and famine had caused much hardship in the area, and Jerome directed himself to caring for those left orphaned. He gathered them into a house, supporting them at his own expense, and instructed them in religion. He fell victim to the plague himself, but he recovered and resolved to dedicate his property and time solely to others. He founded orphanages at Brescia, Bergamo, and Como, as well as a house for repentant prostitutes—one of the first of its kind—and a hospital at Verona. Around 1532, with two other priests, Jerome established a congregation of men, and at Somascha he founded a house for those whom he received into the order. The congregation was named after the town, called the Clerks Regular of Somascha, or the Somaschi, and its chief aim was the care of orphans, although it also sought to instruct young children and clerics. Jerome is said to have been the first to teach Christian doctrine to children with a question-and-answer technique of catechism. His attentive care to the poor of Somascha led them to attribute to him the gift of healing. He tried to share their lives, even working with them in the fields while talking to them of God. He died after catching an infectious disease from the sick he nursed. He is the patron saint of orphans and abandoned children. He is portrayed in art delivering a possessed child, with a chain in his hand; or with the Virgin Mary and Child appearing to him; or in a black habit, holding a key and a shackbolt.

JOACHIM. Patriarch. First century. July 26. Joachim is the usual name given to the father of the Virgin Mary. Other names attributed to him are Heli, Cleopas, Eliacim, Jonachir, and Sadoc. Nothing of him is known for sure. According to the apocryphal Gospel of James, his and his wife Anne's childlessness was held up to public reproach. He prayed and fasted for forty days in the desert, and an angel appeared to him and promised the couple a child. He died soon after witnessing the presentation of Jesus at the Temple. He was reputedly buried in Jerusalem. In later medieval times, he was frequently the subject of religious artists. He is depicted in art meeting St. Anne at the Golden Gate of Jerusalem; or leading Mary as a child; or with an angel announcing the birth of Mary.

JOAN OF ARC. Virgin. 1412–1431. May 30. She was born Jeanne, at Domremy, a small village of Champagne.

Her father, Jacques d'Arc, was a well-respected peasant farmer. Joan never learned to read or write. She was fourteen when she experienced the first of her supernatural experiences. She heard a single voice addressing her from nearby, accompanied by a blaze of light. She typically experienced her visions while watching her father's sheep. Later visions were composed of more voices, and she was able to identify the speakers as SS. Michael, Catherine, and Margaret, among others. By 1428, their messages to her had become specific. She was to present herself to Robert Baudricourt, who commanded the king's armies in the neighboring town of Vaucouleurs. Joan convinced an uncle to take her to him, but Robert laughed at her and commented that her father ought to discipline her. But the visions continued. She secretly left home and returned to Vaucouleurs. Baudricourt's doubt of her was somewhat mollified when news reached him of a serious defeat of the French—at the Battle of Herrings outside Orléans—which Joan had predicted. He sent her to the king with an escort, and she chose to travel in men's clothes for her own protection. At Chinon, Charles disguised himself, but she identified him, and by a secret sign communicated to her by her visions, she convinced him to believe in the divine origin of her mission. She asked for a troop of soldiers that she could lead to Orléans. Her request was questioned by much of the court, and she was sent to be examined by a panel of theologians at Poitiers. After a searching three-week examination, the panel advised Charles to make use of her services. She was given a force, and a special standard was made for her bearing the words "Jesus: Maria" and depicting God, to whom two angels presented a fleur-de-lis. Joan wore white armor, and the force entered Orléans on April 29. Her presence invigorated the town, and by May 8, the English forts surrounding the town were captured. She was wounded in the breast by an arrow, which enhanced her reputation. She joined in a campaign on the Loire with the duc d'Alençon, who became a good friend. The campaign was a great success, due in part to her strengthening the morale of the

210

troops, and the British were routed at Patay. Joan now pushed for the coronation of the Dauphin. On July 17, 1429, Charles VII was finally crowned, and Joan's mission as set forth by her visions was completed. From then on, she experienced only military defeats. An attack on Paris failed, mainly due to the fact that Charles had supplied neither his support nor his presence as promised, and Joan was wounded in the thigh. During a winter of truce, Joan stayed at court, where she was still viewed with skepticism. When hostilities began again, she went to Compiègne, which was holding off the Burgundians. The drawbridge was closed too soon, and Joan and some of her troops were left outside. She was dragged from her horse and taken to the duke of Burgundy, whose prisoner she remained until late autumn. King Charles made no efforts for her release. She had foretold that she would be captured by the Burgundians and handed over to the English, and so it happened. She was sold to the English leaders. The determination of the English to get rid of her is a measure of her power over her followers. The British could not execute her for fighting them in a war, so they arranged to have her sentenced as a sorceress and heretic. On February 21, 1431, she appeared before a tribunal led by Peter Cauchon, the bishop of Beauvais, who hoped the English would help to make him the archbishop of Rouen. She was interrogated about her "voices," her faith, and her wearing of male clothing. An unfair summary of her statements was made, and her visions were held to be unholy in nature, an opinion supported by the University of Paris. The tribunal declared that if she refused to retract, she would be handed over to the secular court as a heretic. She refused to recant, even after being threatened with torture. When she was brought for formal sentencing into the cemetery of St. Ouen before a huge crowd, however, she recanted to some degree, although it is uncertain how much. She was led back to prison but unaccountably reassumed the male dress that she had agreed to give up. She regained her courage and declared that all she had said during her testimony was true and that God had truly sent her. On May 30, 1431, she was led into the marketplace of Rouen to be burned at the stake. She was not yet twenty years old. Her ashes were thrown into the Seine. Twenty-three years later, her mother and two brothers appealed for a reopening of the case, which Pope Callistus III agreed to do. The trial and its verdict were quashed. She was canonized as a holy maiden, not a martyr. She was called *La Pucelle*, "the Maid of Orléans." She is the patron saint of France and French soldiers. She is portrayed in art as a bareheaded girl in armor, with a sword, a lance, or a banner with the words "Jesus: Maria" upon it; or she may wear an envisored helmet.

JOHN THE BAPTIST. Martyr, prophet. d. c. 30. June 24. He was the son of Zachariah, a Temple priest, and Elizabeth, a cousin of the Virgin Mary. His mother was past the age of childbearing when he was born. His birth and his name were foretold to Zachariah by the angel Gabriel. Zachariah was doubtful of the angel's message and asked for a further sign. He was told that he would remain dumb until the birth. Tradition maintains that John was freed from original sin and sanctified in Elizabeth's womb at the time when the Virgin Mary visited her. John began preaching and baptizing around age twenty-seven. Jews had taken part in religious washings as legal purifications, but baptism took on a new mystical significance through John. It symbolized a cleansing from sin that enabled one to join Christ's spiritual kingdom. John was called "John the Baptist" in his own lifetime. Jesus himself asked John to baptize him, not in order to be cleansed, but rather to sanctify the waters. John lived on locusts and wild honey, and he preached much in the style of the Old Testament prophets. He denounced the incestuous union of Herod Antipas with his niece and brother's wife, Herodias, and was imprisoned. When Salome, Herodias's daughter, pleased Herod with her dancing at his birthday, he promised her she could have anything she asked of him. Encouraged by her mother, she asked for the head of John the Baptist on a dish. John was executed without any trial, and his head presented to Salome. He is believed to have been buried at Sebaste (Samaria), but the tomb was desecrated by Julian the Apostate. Although various relics of his head are claimed, it is unlikely that any are authentic. He is the patron saint of monks, because his way of life was so austere and often solitary. He is depicted in art as lean and ascetic, with a rough robe or the skin of a camel, carrying a lamb or with a lamb nearby, and a tall staff often ending in a cross. He may be shown carrying his own head; or baptizing Jesus; and often carries a book or a dish with a lamb upon it. In Greek art, he usually appears with the wings of a messenger.

JOHN OF THE CROSS. Doctor of the Church. 1542–1591. December 14. John was born in Fontiveros in Old Castile to a silk weaver, whose wife, Catherine, was left penniless with three children when he died. John attended a poor school in Medina del Campo and was apprenticed to be a weaver. He had no skill for the trade, however, and became a servant in the hospital at Medina. He worked there for seven years, engaging in bodily austerities and attending the college of the Jesuits. He joined the Carmelite friars at the age of twenty-one, taking the name of John-of-St.-Matthias. He asked to follow the original Carmelite rule, without the mitigations that had been approved. He wished to become a lay brother, but this was refused him, and he was ordained a priest in 1567. St. Teresa, who was in the process of reforming the Carmelites, admired him greatly. John had wanted to become a Carthusian, longing for the order's life of solitude and prayer, but Teresa convinced him that his vocation lay with the Carmelites. She had received permission to found two reformed houses, and after the first was founded, in Duruelo, John entered it. When he renewed his profession, he took the name John-of-the-

Cross. More houses were founded, and John was made rector of one at Alcalá, a college of the university. John entered a stage of spiritual doubt and earthly temptations. Teresa became prioress of the unreformed convent of the Incarnation at Avila and sent for John to be its spiritual director and confessor. His confessional was sought out by seculars as well, and he is said to have performed miracles. There were disagreements and bad feeling between the reformed Discalced—"barefoot"—and Mitigated Carmelites, however, and John was ordered by the provincial of Castile to return to his original friary at Medina. He refused, saying that he held his office from the papal nuncio and not the order. Armed men broke down his door and carried him off. He was taken to Toledo to remove him from the loyal people at Avila and was pressed to abandon the reform. After refusing, he was locked up in a small, dark cell. He was beaten publicly in chapter, by order of Jerome Tostado, vicar general of the Carmelites in Spain and a consultor of the Inquisition, and was scarred for life. He wrote his earliest poems about this time of suffering, including *The Spiritual Canticle*. He escaped after nine months, going first to the reformed friary of Beas de Segura, and later to the hermitage of Monte Calvario. After the Discalceds were recognized and a separate province established, he founded and became head of a Discalced college at Baeza in 1579. In 1581, he was made prior of Los Martires, near Granada. He began the writings that were to make him a doctor of the Church. After the death of St. Teresa in 1582, disagreements among the Discalceds arose. He attempted to initiate reforms in the monasteries, believing that the religious's vocation was contemplative in nature and that they should not leave the houses to preach, and opposition grew against him. He founded more friaries, and when he finished his term of office as vicar of Andalusia, he went to Granada as prior. Father Nicholas Doria received a brief from the Holy See approving a further separation of the Discalceds from the Mitigated Carmelites. Nicholas was made vicar general, and the one province was divided into six. John was made a consultor of one. John spoke in support of nuns who were upset by the changes and favored the moderate views of Father Jerome Gracián, who had been deprived of authority. Nicholas stripped John of his offices and made him a simple friar, sending him off to the remote friary of La Peñuela. He stayed there for several months in contemplation. Unfortunately, a friar whose activities he had criticized while vicar provincial still felt resentment, and traveled about the province, making inquiries about John's life and conduct. He trumped up charges against him and claimed that he could have him expelled from the order. John fell ill, and the provincial gave him a choice of going to Baeza or Ubeda. At Ubeda, the prior was another friar whom he had criticized years before; he chose this house. The journey exhausted him, and the prior treated him badly, forbidding any visitors and providing him only ordinary food, despite his weakness. The prior was reprimanded by the provincial for his behavior and eventually came to repent it. But after suffering for three months, John died. His writings were among the masterpieces of Spanish literature and Catholic mysticism, and he was one of Spain's foremost poets. He is the patron saint of mystics. He is depicted in art with a large cross on his shoulders; or as a Carmelite with a pen and manuscript, looking at a crucifix; or with Jesus appearing to him, bearing his cross.

JOHN DAMASCENE. Confessor, doctor of the Church. 676–749. December 4. John's father was the chief of the revenue department in the government of the Moslem rulers of Damascus. Christians could hold high office, although they were subject to a poll tax and other conditions. He also acted as the representative of the Christians at the court of the caliph, Abdul Malek. The surname, al-Mansur, was given to him by the Arabs and was passed on to his son. John was baptized as an infant and tutored by a Sicilian monk called Cosmas, whom the Arabs had captured, and for whom John's father paid a great price. Taught alongside John was an adopted boy also called Cosmas, who would become a poet and singer and would later accompany John to become a monk. In youth, John aspired only to the career of his father, which had become a hereditary post, and he succeeded him and filled the post for several years. He was known for his humility, among other virtues. But he eventually resigned and became a monk, with Cosmas, in the laura of St. Sabas near Jerusalem around 726. John became a leading defender of the Catholic position and aroused the anger of the Byzantine emperor, who, however, could not touch him since he was under the caliph's protection. John and Cosmas occupied their spare time writing books and hymns, but the brethren were put off by these activities, particularly the writing and singing of hymns. The patriarch of Jerusalem, John V, approved of them, however, and first made Cosmas bishop of Majuma, then ordained John and brought him to Jerusalem. John returned to the monastery soon afterward, and wrote works defending icons, which earned him the ire of Leo the Isaurian, who in 726 had issued an edict prohibiting the veneration of images. John spent his entire life under Mohammedan rule, and was safe from his detractors. He spent the remainder of his life writing theology and poetry and died an old man. The elegance of his Greek led to his being called "Chrysorrhoas"—gold pouring. His work *De Fide Orthodoxa* is one of the most prominent theological works of antiquity, and he is considered the greatest hymn writer, with the possible exception of St. Romanus, of the Eastern Church. He was the author of the first real compendium of theology, the *Fount of Wisdom*. He was the last of the Greek Fathers. He was an almost exact contemporary of Bede and was much like him in his devotion to scholarly pursuits.

JOHN BAPTIST DE ROSSI. Confessor. 1698–1764.
May 23. He was born in the village of Voltaggio in the
diocese of Genoa. When John was ten, a nobleman and his
wife who summered at Voltaggio took him back to Genoa to
be trained in their home. He stayed for three years, and
during that time he gained the good opinion of two Capuchin friars who visited his patrons. They told his uncle, the
minister provincial of the Capuchins, of the boy's potential.
The result was that his cousin Lorenzo Rossi, a canon of
Santa Maria in Cosmedin, invited him to come to Rome.
John entered the Roman College at thirteen. He completed
the classical course but began practicing severe mortifications after reading an ascetical book. Their severity, combined with a heavy course load, led to a breakdown, and he
was forced to leave the college. He recuperated and completed his training at Minerva but was never again very
strong. At twenty-three he was ordained, and he celebrated
his first mass in the Roman College. He had visited hospitals as a student, and now he focused more attention upon
them. He concentrated especially on the hospice of St.
Galla, an overnight place for paupers that had been founded
by Pope Celestine III. He divided his labors among this
place, the hospital of the Trinità dei Pellegrini, and serving
the people of the area. He instructed the cattlemen from the
country who came to the marketplace, and he sought to help
homeless women and girls who lived in the streets. He was
penniless except for paltry mass stipends, but with a local
donation and a donation from the pope, he rented a house
behind the hospice and made it a refuge, placing it under the
protection of St. Aloysius Gonzaga. In 1731, Canon Rossi
obtained the position of assistant priest at Santa Maria in
Cosmedin for John. The church had not been well attended,
but John now drew throngs of penitents to his confessional.
He was so sought after as a confessor that he was released
from his choir obligation. When Canon Rossi died in 1736,
the canonry was given to John, who used the compensation
from the office to buy the church an organ and to pay an
organist. He chose to live in an attic, giving the house that

had been his legacy from his cousin to the chapter. Pope Benedict XIV chose John to instruct prison officials and other state officials, including the public hangman. His preaching was in great demand, and he was often asked to give addresses in religious houses. His frail health compelled him in 1763 to move to the Trinità dei Pellegrini, and the same year he suffered a stroke and received the last sacraments. He recovered enough to resume celebrating mass, but in 1764, he suffered another seizure. The hospital of the Trinità undertook to pay for the poor priest's burial. His funeral was attended by 260 priests. Archbishop Lercari of Adrianople spoke at the requiem, and the papal choir sang.

JOHN EUDES. Founder. 1601–1680. August 19. He was born, seemingly the result of the prayers of his previously childless parents, in Ri in Normandy. His father was a yeoman farmer. He was baptized John and was sent to the Jesuit college at Caen when he was fourteen. John's parents expected him to marry and take on his father's estate, but John took a private vow of celibacy and in 1621 received minor orders. He returned to Caen to study theology, initially intending to enroll himself among the parochial clergy. Instead, he joined the Congregation of the Oratory of France and was accepted in 1623. He so impressed the founder, Bérulle, that he was permitted to preach while still in minor orders. After a year in Paris, John was sent to Aubervilliers to be instructed by Charles de Condren. Plague broke out in Normandy two years later, and John went to work among the sufferers for two months. He was then sent to the Oratory of Caen. Plague came to the city in 1631, and again he went out to help the victims. To avoid infecting his brethren, he lived in a large cask in the middle of a field, his food being supplied by a nearby convent. For the next ten years he was engaged primarily in giving missions. He was disturbed by the uneasy position of women and girls who left the troubled life of

218

fallen women to become penitents. He found them temporary homes, but this approach was inadequate. In 1641, a house was rented to shelter these women until they could find work, but he realized that it was necessary for the organization to be directed by a religious congregation. He offered this job to the Visitandines of Caen, and they accepted it. In 1643, he left the Oratorians, feeling that the clergy needed reform and that until seminaries were established, the Congregation of the Oratory would not fulfill its potential. Although he found support for this concept among some Oratorians, the superior general did not agree with his plan. John conceived the idea of a new congregation of secular priests who should conduct seminaries. This was founded in 1643 and called the Congregation of Jesus and Mary, or Eudists. Its rule was modeled on that of the Oratory and the secular priests were not bound by vows. Unfortunately, the congregation met some opposition, especially from the Jansenists and French Oratorians, and when John sought papal approval he did not receive it. The bishop of Courtances invited John to establish a seminary in 1650, and in 1651 he was asked to give a mission at the Church of Saint-Sulpice in Paris. While in Paris, the news came that the sisters at the refuge in Caen became a separate congregation, under the name Sisters of Our Lady of Charity of the Refuge, and from these originated the Good Shepherd Nuns, whose fourth vow—to care for fallen women—resulted in their establishing reformatories. In 1667, the Refuge sisters were recognized by the pope as an institute to work among troubled women. John founded seminaries at Evreux, Rennes, Lisieux, and Rouen. In 1670, he published the book *The Devotion to the Adorable Heart of Jesus*, which included a mass and office of the Sacred Heart of Jesus. The first feast of the Sacred Heart of Jesus was observed in the seminary chapel at Rennes. John was the originator of the liturgical cult of the Sacred Heart. In 1674, Pope Clement X issued briefs of indulgences for the confraternities of the Hearts of Jesus and Mary erected in Eudist seminaries. The last years of his life were spent working on *The Admirable Heart of the Most Holy Mother of God*, and he completed it a month before his death. Several years of frail health together with preaching in cold weather out in the open weakened John, and he died. The Eudists were almost snuffed out by the French Revolution, but they were reconstituted in 1826 and their chief objective became secondary education.

JOHN THE EVANGELIST. Apostle. d. c. 100. December 27. He was born in Galilee, the son of Zebedee, and the younger brother of St. James the Greater and was said to be the youngest of the Apostles of Christ. He was a fisherman. He witnessed special events such as the raising of Jairus's daughter, the healing of Peter's mother-in-law, the Transfiguration, and the Agony in the Garden. Jesus called St. James and John "Boanerges"—sons of thunder—as a result of their passionate natures. They wished to call down fire from Heaven on the Samaritans who rejected Christ, and they were willing to suffer as witnesses to Jesus' sufferings. As a result of their zeal, James was martyred and John was said to suffer under Domitian's persecution. John was chosen to go with Peter to prepare the Last Supper, and at that supper, was told by Jesus who would betray him. He was the only apostle who was present at the foot of the cross with Mary and the other women. After the Resurrection, John took the Virgin Mary as his adopted mother, according to Jesus' dying wish. Tradition has it that John is the author of the Fourth Gospel. As one of the prominent members of the early Church, he participated in the preaching, organization, and imprisonment of Peter, to whom he looked as a superior. He (with Peter and James) was referred to by Paul as "these leaders, these pillars" of the church in Jerusalem. Tradition has it that he was taken to Rome during the persecution of Domitian and was thrown into a cauldron of boiling oil, but he miraculously survived. He was exiled to the island of Patmos, where he experienced the revelation that he wrote down in *The Apocalypse*. He eventually settled at Ephesus and died old, the only apostle who didn't suffer martyrdom. In medieval times, his statue appeared on the rood beam in churches. He is the patron saint of protection against poison, which originates from the legend that he was offered a poisoned cup by the high priest of Diana, and he drank without incurring harm. He is also the patron saint of Asiatic Turkey. He is represented in art holding a chalice from which a snake or dragon is emerging (an allusion to the poisoned cup); or as a young man with a book; or with an eagle (representing the soaring majesty of the gospel); or in a cauldron of boiling oil.

JOHN FISHER. Bishop, cardinal, martyr. 1469–1535. June 22. He was born in Beverley, Yorkshire, the son of a textiles merchant, who died when he was still a boy. He was sent to Cambridge at the age of fourteen, where he performed with excellence. He was elected a fellow of Michaelhouse and was ordained a priest under a special dispensation at the age of twenty-two. He became doctor of divinity, master of Michaelhouse, and vice chancellor of the university. He became the chaplain of the king's mother, Lady Margaret Beaufort, in 1502. He was such an articulate preacher that he was chosen as panegyrist of King Henry VII and Lady Margaret. Under his direction, Lady Margaret founded Christ's College and St. John's College at Cambridge, and established there and at Oxford a Lady Margaret Divinity Chair. John was the first to fill the chair at Cambridge. At the time he attended Cambridge, the library had dwindled to 300 volumes, and no Greek or Hebrew was taught. Under his direction, Greek and Hebrew became part of the curriculum, scholarships were endowed, and he brought Erasmus to the university as a lecturer. He was elected chancellor in 1504 and remained so until his death. Although only thirty-five, he was nominated bishop of Rochester by King Henry VII, a position he accepted warily, as it added greatly to his responsibilities. He was a devoted and attentive bishop at a time in history when most bishops were not worthy of admiration. During this time, he continued to write books and pursue his own studies, beginning to learn Greek at the age of forty-eight, and Hebrew at fifty-one. He lived austerely, sleeping and eating little, and he kept a skull in front of him at meals to remind himself of mortality. He formed one of the most exceptional libraries in Europe with the intention of bequeathing it to the university. His learning and oratorical excellence led him to be chosen to speak against Lutheranism when it began making inroads, and his refutations of Luther's doctrines were the first to be published. He sought to reform the clergy, criticizing their laxness and the underhanded ways in which many gained their positions. He opposed King Henry VIII's attempt to nullify his marriage to Catherine, and was chosen as one of the queen's counselors in the suit. He criticized the measures against the clergy that were being forced through the Commons, and he refused to grant that Henry was head of the Church in England, but he suggested adding the words "So far as the law of Christ allows" to the corresponding oath, which smoothed the path of many who signed. Despite being imprisoned for two short periods, and being the object of poisoning and shooting attempts, he persisted in espousing his views. Thomas Cromwell unsuccessfully tried to link him with Elizabeth Barton, a nun who had trances and made personal attacks upon Henry for trying to divorce the queen. He was summoned to Lambeth, despite being ill, to sign the oath of the bill of succession. He refused, because it was in essence an oath of supremacy. He was arrested and taken to the Tower, his property was confiscated, and he was stripped of his offices. His illness made him appear twenty years older than he was. A confidential messenger from Henry asked him to declare, for the king's ear alone, his opinion on royal supremacy. His negative opinion sealed his conviction. His trial was fixed, but some of the judges cried as he was sentenced to death. A few days later, John was awakened at five in the morning and told that he was to be executed that day. He asked to rest a little longer and slept for two hours. He dressed, putting on a fur mantle, and carrying his New Testament, he walked with great difficulty, because of excessive weakness, to the execution block. After saying that he was dying for the faith and asking the people to pray that he might have courage, he was beheaded with an ax. He was buried in the churchyard of All Hallows, Barking, without rites or a shroud. His head was exhibited on London Bridge for two weeks, then was thrown into the Thames. In art he is shown robed as a cardinal, with haggard ascetic features; or with an axe or his hat at his feet.

JOHN OF GOD. Founder. 1495–1550. March 8. He was born at Montemoro Nuovo in Portugal and received a pious upbringing. He spent some time serving the bailiff of the count of Oroprusa in Castile. He enlisted in a company of soldiers mustered by the count in 1522, then served in the wars between the French and the Spaniards, and in Hungary against the Turks. After the company broke up, he worked as a shepherd near Seville. Around the age of forty he became penitent about his past life and decided to make amends by dedicating himself to God. He initially thought of going to Africa to rescue Christian slaves. In Gibraltar he decided to become a peddler of sacred pictures and books. His business prospered, and in 1538 he opened a shop in Granada. After hearing Bl. John of Avila preach on St. Sebastian's Day, he was so touched that he cried aloud and beat his breast, begging for mercy. He ran about the streets, behaving like a lunatic, and the townspeople threw sticks and stones at him. He returned to his shop, gave away his stock, and took to wandering the streets in distraction. Some people took him to Bl. John of Avila, who advised him and offered his support. John was calm for a while but fell into wild behavior again and was taken to an insane asylum, where the customary brutal treatments were applied to bring him to sanity. John of Avila heard of his fate and visited him, telling him that he had practiced his penance long enough and that he should address himself to doing something more useful for himself and his neighbor. John was calmed by this, remained at the hospital, and attended the sick until 1539. He then began selling wood to earn money to feed the poor and hired a house as a refuge for the sick poor. His success at caring for the sick impressed the city, and his dedication brought in donations for carrying on his work. Thus was begun the foundation of the Order of Brothers of St. John of God. He had not intended to ·found a religious order, and the rules were drawn up six years after his death. He fell ill from the exhaustion of working hard for ten years and from efforts to save his wood and to rescue a drowning man in a flood. He hid his illness and continued in his duties, but the news finally got out. He named Antony Martin superior over his helpers. He remained so long in front of the Blessed Sacrament that the Lady Anne Ossorio took him home with her by force. He worried that while Jesus drank gall, he, a miserable sinner, was being fed good food. The magistrates begged him to bless his fellow townsfolk, but he said that he was a sinner. The archbishop finally convinced him to confer his blessing. He died on his knees before the altar of his hospital chapel. He was buried by the archbishop. He is the patron saint of the sick, of hospitals, and of nurses, printers, and booksellers. He is depicted in art with a pomegranate with a cross at the top in his hand; or with an alms chest; or carrying sick persons; or washing Jesus's feet as a pilgrim.

JOHN GUALBERT. Abbot. c. 993–1073. July 12. He was born in Florence, the son of the nobleman Visdomini. He spent his youth· in worldly amusement and was bred to be a soldier. Hugh, his older brother, was murdered, and John felt that it was his duty to avenge him. On Good Friday he met the murderer in a narrow passage and drew his sword; the man fell upon his knees. Remembering Christ and how he prayed for his murderers while on the cross, John put away his sword and embraced the man. He went on to the monastery of San Miniato and prayed. As he did so, the crucifix is said to have bowed its head, which he took to be a sign of approval for his action. He asked to be admitted to the congregation. Despite the abbot's fears of John's father's disapproval, John cut off his hair, borrowed a habit, and began the life of a penitent. When the abbot died, John, fearing he would be chosen to succeed him, left the monastery with a companion in search of solitude. While visiting the hermitage of Camoldoli, he decided to establish his own foundation. He did so in Vallis Umbrosa, near Fiesole, building a small monastery and forming a community that followed the rule of St. Benedict. He added constitutions, including the provision for lay brothers—probably the first such incidence—and the elimination of manual labor for choir monks. He was dedicated to poverty and humility, declining even to receive minor orders, and insisted that monastery buildings be simple in architecture. He was generous to the poor and often gave away the stores of the monastery. The area in which the monastery was located was wild and barren, but the monks planted fir and pine trees and transformed it into parkland. He was known for his wisdom, miracles, and prophecies, and many came to seek his advice, including Pope St. Leo IX, who traveled specially to Passignano to talk with him. Pope Alexander II attributed the eradication of simony in his country to him. He died at Passignano at one of his foundations. He is the patron saint of foresters and park keepers. He is portrayed in art clothed as a Vallombrosan Benedictine; or with a crucifix bending toward him; or with a church and a picture of Jesus in his hand; or standing on the devil.

JOHN JOSEPH-OF-THE-CROSS. Confessor. 1654–1734. March 5. He was born on the island of Ischia to the devout Joseph Calosirto and Laura Garguilo, and was baptized Carlo Caetano. Five of their seven sons became religious. After meeting two Spanish Franciscan friars of the Alcantarine reform, Carlo went to their convent, Santa Lucia del Monte of Naples. Father Carlo-of-the-Wounds-of-Jesus put him through a difficult nine-month program of self-mortification and training, and he took the religious habit at sixteen. The impression he made upon his superiors is illustrated by the fact that when the Neapolitan Alcantarines built a monastery at Piedimonte di Alife, John was asked to start a tradition of regular observance, though he was only twenty and not yet a priest. He was ordained a priest in 1677, although he had wished to remain a deacon like St. Francis of Assisi. He was an especially sensitive and wise confessor. He arranged for the building of some hermitages apart from the monastery where the brethren could spend periods of time in greater solitude and simplicity. He was sent to the motherhouse to become the novice master. A compassionate and astute man, he was careful not to tax the novices with austerities, and he required them to have regular recreational periods. He was transferred to Piedimonte where he was made superior. He experienced a period of depression, but he was soothed by a vision of a deceased monk who assured him that he would pass safely through it. He began to be known for miracles, which included healing and providing food for the monastery. When he returned home to see his dying mother, he was received by the townspeople as a saint. He served as novice master again, then again as superior. He became seriously ill as a result of his harsh life-style but recovered. The pope had required that the higher offices in the order should always be filled by Spaniards, and the Italians looked to John Joseph for direction. Through his efforts, the Italians were finally granted permission to form themselves into a separate province. He attended to the full range of their needs, helping to provide them with the most basic necessities. In 1722, the two Neapolitan houses were returned, and John returned to Santa Lucia. He had foretold that he would die there. After he received a divine message that his death was approaching, he spoke freely of it, while continuing about his ordinary duties. He suffered a seizure, and died five days later. He was buried at Santa Lucia del Monte, and his tomb soon became a popular site of pilgrimage.

JOHN OF KANTI OR JOHN CANTIUS. Confessor.

c. 1390–1473. December 23. He was born to country people in Kanti, in Poland. He was sent to the University of Cracow, where he was ordained a priest and was appointed to a chair. He led a life so strict and austere that acquaintances warned him to be careful of his health. He shared his earnings with the poor, who often "cleared him right out." He told students to fight all false opinions but to do so in a moderate and polite way. Rivals, jealous of his reputation as a teacher and preacher, arranged to have him sent as a parish priest to Olkusz. He worked hard but was intimidated by the responsibility of caring for souls, and his parishioners were not enamored of him. By the time he was recalled to Cracow, however, their attitudes had changed. He was appointed a professor of Sacred Scripture and taught for the rest of his life. He was so respected that his doctoral gown was used for many years to vest each candidate when a degree was conferred. He was well known both to the rich and poor of Cracow. He continued his austere life-style, eating no meat, and sleeping on the floor; he carried his luggage and traveled by foot when he visited Rome. Miracles were attributed to him. As he was dying, he comforted the grieving. He died on Christmas Eve. He is the patron saint of Poland and Lithuania. He is portrayed in art giving his garments to the poor.

JOHN LEONARDI. Founder. 1550–1609. October 9.

He started his career as a pharmacist's assistant in Lucca. He became a member of a confraternity founded by Bl.

John Colombini and studied for ordination. After being ordained, he ministered a great deal in hospitals and prisons. Several laymen came to assist him, and their headquarters became the church of St. Mary della Rosa in Lucca, and their home a house nearby. In keeping with the spirit of reform of the time, John and his company decided to form a congregation of secular priests. The idea of secular priests was not well received in Lucca for political reasons, and John was henceforth exiled from the city, with the exception of visits he made there under special papal protection. In 1580 he quietly took the Church of Santa Maria Cortelandini for his congregation, which in 1583 was recognized by the bishop of Lucca, with the pope's approval, as an association of secular priests with simple vows. The order's present name—the Clerks Regular of the Mother of God—was not granted until 1621. St. Philip Neri supported John and gave to him his property at San Girolamo della Carita—and his cat. For a time the congregation of St. Joseph Calasanctius was merged with John's. The congregation accomplished so much good that it was confirmed by Clement VIII in 1595. The pope also appointed John commissary apostolic to direct the reform of the monks of Vallombrosa and Monte Vergine. John's constitution required that the order never have more than fifteen churches. John is considered to be one of the founders of the College of Propoganda Fide in Rome. Clement gave John the Church of Santa Maria in Portico. After being infected while nursing plague victims, John died.

JOHN NEPOMUCEN. Martyr. c. 1340–1393. May 16. He was born in Bohemia to a family named Wölflein or Welflin, but his name was taken from his birthplace, Nepomuk. He attended the recently founded University of Prague and then occupied various religious posts, eventually being appointed vicar general to the archbishop of Prague. The Emperor Charles IV was succeeded by his son

Wenceslas, an unpredictable, vindictive, and cruel man. Unsubstantiated tradition has it that John became confessor to the emperor's wife Sophie, whom the emperor mistakenly suspected of adultery, and who resented John because he would not reveal Sophie's confessions. In 1393, wishing to furnish one of his favorites with a bishopric, Wenceslas decided to found a new diocese at Kladrau, and to confiscate the church and revenues of the Benedictine Abbey of Kladrau after the death of its aged abbot in order to finance the new diocese. John and the archbishop strongly opposed this and arranged to swiftly elect and ratify a new superior after the abbot's passing. The king initially came to some agreement with the archbishop through envoys, but then he ordered John and other representatives to be tortured. He personally tortured John with a burning torch. He released the victims under the vow that they should not reveal what had happened. But John was already dying, and so he was gagged and his body trussed up "like a wheel," with his heels tied to his head, and thrown in the River Moldau. His body washed ashore, was recognized, and was buried in the Cathedral of St. Vitus. Mounted at the place on the bridge from which he was thrown is a metal plate with seven stars, an allusion to the legend that on the night he was murdered, seven stars hovered over the water. He is the patron saint of Czechoslovakia and Bohemia, of confessors, and of bridges, and he is invoked against slander. He is depicted in art standing on a bridge; or with a bridge and river near him; or with a padlock and a finger to his lips; or with the empress confessing to him, with stars around his head; or floating on a river under a bridge; or in prison, manacled, with angels; or in a doctor's four-horned biretta, with his finger to his lips and stars around his head.

JOHN NEPOMUCENE NEUMANN. Bishop, founder. 1811–1860. January 5. He was born in Prachitz in Bohemia, the son of a German father, Philip, and a Czech mother, Agnes. As a young boy he showed great intellect as well as a vocation for religion. He was educated in Budweis and began at the diocesan seminary in 1831. He continued studying theology at the Charles Ferdinand University in Prague. The abundance of clergy in his home diocese prevented his being ordained to minister there, so he decided to go to America as a missionary. He was ordained in New York by Bishop James Dubois, and he engaged in pastoral work in the district of Niagara for four years. He then joined the Redemptorists, and for a short while directed the American division of the order. His main activity was establishing schools. He was appointed the bishop of Philadelphia by Pope Pius IX in 1852, and he set about expanding the parochial school system. The population of his schools increased enormously after he attracted a number of teaching orders to staff them, and he built many new parishes, introduced the devotion of the Forty Hours, began work on a cathedral, and saw to the care of orphans and the needy. He founded the sisters of the Third Order of St. Francis. He wrote much during this time—including articles for newspapers—and produced two catechisms that were very popular in America in the nineteenth century. He continued to compose his most important works in German, although he was fluent in seven other languages. He died on the street in Philadelphia.

JOHN FRANCIS REGIS. 1597–1640. June 16. He was born at Fontcouverte in the diocese of Narbonne into a family of landed gentry. He attended the Jesuit college Béziers and sought admittance into the Society of Jesus in 1615. After a successful year as a novice, he went to study at Carhors and Tournon. While in Tournon, he accompanied the father who served the town of Andance on Sundays and holidays, and his catechism instruction was so effective that he inspired the parents through their children. He went to Toulouse in 1628 to begin his theology course, and he spent much of his nights in prayer. He was ordained in 1631 and was chosen to be a missionary. He worked in Languedoc, throughout the Vivarais, and ended in the Velay. He spent the summers in towns and the winters in the countryside. His approach to preaching was simple and homely, and he attracted large crowds, comprised of all ranks of people. He focused especially on the poor, however, saying, "the rich never lack confessors." There was little he would not do for the poor, and when he was warned that by doing so he appeared foolish, he responded, "So much the better." He often missed meals because he was so caught up in his work, which included visiting prisons and hospitals. In Montpellier he converted several Huguenots and many lapsed Catholics, organized women to oversee prison conditions, and brought many troubled women back to an honest life. He gained the confidence of the people by speaking to them in their own dialect. The regions of the Vivarais had experienced much civil and religious discord, and the people had become uncivilized. Churches were neglected and some parishes had not received the sacrament for twenty years. In the course of a three-year ministry launched by Bishop de la Baume and his assistants, with John traveling a day or so ahead of them, the mission returned the area to religious observance, in addition to converting a large number of Protestants. Charges made by those who resented his zeal came close to causing his recall, but the bishop recognized that the accusations were false. He organized a social service, setting up a granary for the poor and a refuge for troubled women and girls, and organized nurses and guardians of the poor, and overseers of prisons. The refuge for women and girls was endangered by the vindictive slander of the unprincipled persons who had lost the female supply they wished to exploit, and his activities were stopped for a time. At this time he became known for miracles, which are said to have included curing a blind boy and man, and multiplying the supply of corn in his granary. Although he foresaw his death, he set out in terrible weather to give a mission. He and his companion, whom he had predicted would return from the journey while he himself would not, lost their way and camped in a ruined house, where John contracted pleurisy. Ill as he was, he continued his journey the next day to La Louvesc and opened his mission. He preached many times and spent the rest of the time in penance. He fainted twice while in the confessional and was taken to the curé's house, where he died. His body is at La Louvesc, and his tomb is a site of pilgrimage. He is the patron saint of marriage (due to his work among prostitutes), of illegitimate children, and social workers, especially medical social workers.

JOHN BAPTIST VIANNEY. Confessor. 1786–1859. August 4. He was a shepherd of sheep and cattle on his father Matthew Vianney's farm. Because of the French Revolution, he made his first communion secretly at the age of thirteen; shortly after, mass was allowed to be offered again in public. At seventeen he asked to pursue his vocation as a priest, but he was not permitted to attend the presbytery school established by Abbé Balley in Ecully until he was twenty. His studies were difficult for him, especially Latin, partly due to his scanty education; and since his name was not entered on the roll of exempt students, he was drafted into the army. He was taken ill and hospitalized, and the company left without him. Barely recovered, he was drafted again. Because he went to a church to pray, he again missed the company's departure, and he set out to catch up with it. A stranger seized his knapsack while he was resting and ordered him to follow. He learned the man was a deserter and that many other deserters were hiding in the area. He reported himself to the mayor, who pointed out to him that since he was already considered a deserter, his best course was to remain in hiding, and the mayor found a place for him at his own cousin's house. For fourteen months, he hid in a stable under a hayloft, narrowly escaping detection several times, once even feeling a sword as it was plunged into the hay. In 1810, the emperor declared an amnesty for deserters. After his brother joined the army as a substitute for him, John returned home. He received the tonsure in 1811 and was sent for a year's study to a seminary in Verrières. He worked hard and was sent on to the larger seminary at Lyons. Hard work was not enough to compensate for his scholarly shortcomings here, however, and he left the seminary and was tutored by Abbé Balley at Ecully. He received minor orders and the subdiaconate in 1814, returned for more tutoring to Balley, and received the diaconate, and then the priesthood. He became a curate to the abbé. In 1817, Abbé Balley died, and John was made parish priest of Ars-en-Dombes, a small, remote parish. He visited every household, carefully composed sermons, and exhorted against blasphemy and obscenity, uttering the offensive words so that his congregation knew precisely to what he was alluding. He preached against dancing—going so far as to deny absolution to those who persisted—as well as indecent clothing, and labored to abolish working on Sunday. In 1824 he opened a free school for girls, run by two women whom he had sent to be convent trained, and an offshoot of the school was La Providence, a refuge for orphans and other destitute children. People of all ranks began to make pilgrimages to Ars to see him, and he received many long-distance requests for counseling. From 1830 to 1845, the average number of visitors in a day was over 300; a special booking office was opened in Lyons to service the visitors. He spent up to twelve hours a day in the confessional in winter and up to sixteen hours in summer. He was gifted with a penetrating knowledge of those who confessed. He was occasionally tormented by evil spirits. He dressed poorly and slept and ate little. He yearned always for a life of solitude, particularly that of a Carthusian monk, and he actually fled the village three times. Once, after he suffered a serious illness, the bishop of Belley made him an honorary canon of the chapter against his will; John sold his vestment to raise money for a charitable purpose.

He was made a knight of the Imperial Order of the Legion of Honour but refused to be invested and to wear the imperial cross. In 1853 he attempted one last time to flee from Ars, but he was prevailed upon to return after an appeal was made on behalf of people who were unable to do without him. In the twelve months before his death, thousands of pilgrims visited the seventy-three-year-old "Curé of Ars." The pressure was too taxing, and after the bishop of Belley hurriedly made his way to his bedside, he died. He is the patron saint of priests and parochial clergy.

JOSAPHAT. Bishop, martyr. c 1580–1623. November 12. He was born in Vladimir in Volhynia, the son of a burgess, and baptized John. He was educated in Vladimir and then apprenticed to a merchant of Vilna. He spent his free time learning Church Slavonic so that he could assist more ably at divine worship and recite some of the lengthy Byzantine office each day. He was encouraged by Peter Arcudius, the rector of the oriental college at Vilna, and two Jesuits. Although he was never interested in trade, his master offered him a partnership in the business and his daughter in marriage. He refused both. Deciding to become a monk, John entered the monastery of the Holy Trinity at Vilna. There was a great schism in the area at this time due to the difference in the rites of the Catholic Holy See and Byzantine Christian rites. Josaphat persuaded Joseph Benjamin Rutsky, a convert from Calvinism, to join him at the monastery. The two strategized together how to promote a union and reform Ruthenian monastic observance. John, having taken the name Josaphat, was ordained deacon and priest and soon built a reputation as a preacher, especially on the subject of reunion with Rome. He lived simply and engaged in such extreme mortifications that he was chastised by even the most austere monks. The abbot held separatist views; Josaphat's studies were cut short, and he was sent out to help in the foundation of new houses in Poland.

Rutsky became metropolitan of Kiev in 1614, and Josaphat replaced him as abbot at Vilna. Josaphat accompanied Rutsky to his new cathedral and visited the monastery of The Caves at Kiev. The monks threatened to throw Josaphat, a reformer, into the river, because they were content under their relaxed rule. He was unable to reform them, but his character generated their goodwill. In 1617, Josaphat became bishop of Vitebsk, with the right to succeed the archbishop of Polotsk, who favored the dissidents. He succeeded to a see in schism whose property and morals had been neglected. He held synods, published a catechism, set down rules for the clergy, fought the interference of laymen in ecclesiastical affairs, and preached and tended his flock as personally as he could. He had greatly restored the see by 1620. Unfortunately, a dissident hierarchy of bishops was set up side by side with the Catholic one, and Meletius Smotritsky was sent as archbishop to Polotsk. Meletius passed the word that Josaphat had "turned Latin," that his people would be forced to do the same, and that Catholicism was not the traditional Christianity of the Ruthenian people. Returning from Warsaw, Josaphat found that some of his support in the city was becoming shaky; the monk Silvester had persuaded Vitebsk, Mogilev, and Orcha to the side of Meletius. When the king of Poland proclaimed that Josaphat was the legitimate archbishop of Polotsk, there were riots, and Josaphat's life was threatened. Josaphat did not receive support from the Latin bishops of Poland because he maintained Byzantine rites and customs. Afraid of the potential for political unrest due to these disturbances, Leo Sapieha, a Catholic and the chancellor of Lithuania, believed that the unrest was Josaphat's doing, and he accused him of violence, endangering the kingdom, and closing down non-Catholic churches, among other things. Thus Josaphat faced opposition and misunderstanding both from Catholics and non-Catholics, but he stoically held firm and determined to appear in Vitebsk in person, despite the danger. He declined a military escort. Although Meletius most likely wished only to drive Josaphat from the diocese, his followers hatched a plot to assassinate him. The priest Elias agreed to go to the archbishop's home and insult the archbishop and his religion to his servants. After this occurred several times, Josaphat gave his servants permission to seize the man if he showed up. They did this, locking him in a room, and Josaphat's enemies seized upon the action as a rallying point. A mob assembled, demanding the release of Elias and that Josaphat be punished. Josaphat let Elias go with a warning, but the people broke into his home and beat his attendants. Josaphat went out to them to beg that they not harm his servants and was beaten over the head with a halberd and shot. His body was dragged and thrown into the River Dvina. He was the first Eastern saint to be formally canonized. He is shown in art with a chalice; or crown; or as a winged deacon.

JOSEPH. Patriarch. First century. March 19. He was of royal descent and was the husband of the Virgin Mary. He defended her good name and acted as foster father to Jesus. He saw to Jesus' education and taught him his trade, carpentry. The apocryphal Protevangelium of James holds that he was an old man when Jesus was born, but this appears unlikely when one considers the fact that he reared Jesus and fulfilled the family duties. 'Joseph's disappointment upon learning of Mary's pregnancy was said to be assuaged by an angelic vision, and he was the recipient of two more visions: one telling him to seek refuge in Egypt to escape Herod's persecution, and the second, to return to Palestine. He is the patron saint of the Universal Church (as head of the Holy family), fathers, of opposition to atheistic Communism (he was a worker), of workers, carpenters, doubters (he married Mary despite her pregnancy), travelers, house hunters, of a happy death (he is said to have died before Jesus and Mary), Austria, Bohemia, Canada, Mexico, Belgium, Peru, Russia, South Vietnam, and missions to the Chinese. In art, he usually appears with Mary or Jesus, and is shown as an old man carrying a lily or some instrument of carpentry.

JOSEPH OF ARIMATHEA. Confessor. First century. March 17. He was a follower of Jesus in secret because he was afraid of persecution from Jewish officials. He attended the Crucifixion, and legend has it that he caught Jesus' blood as he hung from the cross. He persuaded Pontius Pilate to let him have Jesus' body, wrapped it in linen and herbs, and laid it in a tomb carved in a rock in the side of a hill. Medieval legend has it that he accompanied Philip to Gaul to preach and was sent to England as the leader of twelve missionaries. It is said that the company, inspired by Gabriel the archangel, built a church in honor of the Virgin Mary on an island called Yniswitrin, given to them by the king of England. The church eventually evolved into Glastonbury Abbey. Miraculous cures were said to have been worked by Joseph; the Holy Thorn, which flowers at Christmas, is said to have grown from his staff. Joseph is said to have died and been buried on the island, although this is unlikely. He is reputed to have inherited the chalice used at the Last Supper; what is said to be the *Sacro Catino*—or Holy Grail—is at San Lorenzo, Genoa. He is the patron saint of undertakers. He is portrayed in art as a very old man, carrying a pot of ointment or a flowering staff or a pair of altar cruets (carrying the blood and sweat of Jesus).

JOSEPH CALASANZ OR CALASANCTIUS. Founder. 1556–1648. August 25. He was born in his father's castle near Peralta de la Sal in Aragon, the youngest of five children born to Pedro Calasanz and Maria Gaston.

He was sent to study at Estadilla, where his devotion was mocked by fellow students. His father wished him to be a soldier, but Joseph persuaded him to send him to the University of Lerida, where he took a doctorate in law. He continued his theology studies at Alcalá and was ordained a priest in 1583. He was appointed vicar general of the district of Trempe. So well did he carry out his duties that he was commissioned to deal with the Pyrenean part of the diocese. This remote area was religiously and morally lax, and he set about reforming the clergy. After achieving this, he returned to Trempe and was eventually made vicar general of the diocese. Feeling a pull to a different vocation, however, he resigned his offices, divided his property among his sisters, the poor, and endowments for charitable institutions—holding back a suitable income for himself—and, in keeping with a vision he had experienced, departed for Rome. During the plague of 1595 he competed with St. Camillus, his friend, as to who should do more for those suffering. His real interest, however, was the education of destitute children. He became a member of the Confraternity of Christian Doctrine, who taught children and adults on Sundays and holidays. He realized the inadequacy of this approach and wished to organize some kind of regular instruction. His requests of parish teachers to admit the poor to their classes without fees were turned down; the teachers demanded a rise in pay, which the Roman senate would not grant. He approached the Jesuits and Dominicans for help, but they were already greatly occupied. Joseph decided that it was God's will that he take this work upon himself. He was offered two rooms by a parish priest of Santa Dorotea, and a public free school was opened, the first of its kind in Rome. The school had a hundred pupils within a week, and more came, so he engaged paid teachers from among the clergy of the city. It was moved to a new location in 1599, and he lived at the school with the other masters, acting as superior. After the pupils increased to 700, another house was taken, adjoining the church of Sant' Andrea della Valle. He became lame after falling while hanging a bell in the courtyard. The school was endowed by Pope Clement VIII, and noblemen began to send their children as students. This caused jealousy, and parish teachers and others criticized the school, which culminated in a surprise inspection of the institution by Cardinals Antoniani and Baronius. Their report resulted in Clement's taking the school under his protection. Despite constant opposition, the institution thrived, and in 1611, a *palazzo* was bought to house the nearly 1,000 pupils near the church of San Pantaleone. Among the pupils were Jews, whom Joseph had invited to attend. Other schools were established, and in 1621, the teachers were recognized as an order, the Clerks Regular of the Religious Schools, with Joseph named superior general. Throughout this period he continued to care for the sick and needy as well. Mario Sozzi, a priest who was admitted to the order and had worked his way up, denounced Joseph to the Holy Office. Cardinal Cesarini ordered Father Mario's papers seized, and the people of the father's congregation, encouraged by Sozzi, had Joseph arrested. Cardinal Cesarini prevented his being imprisoned. Father Mario, however, was unpunished, and he continued to connive against Joseph, spreading the word that Joseph was too old to carry out his duties, and succeeding by unscrupulous means in having him suspended from the generalate. Joseph was treated in a humiliating fashion, and the order fell into disorder. In 1643, Sozzi was succeeded by Father Cherubini, who followed the same treacherous policies. Joseph endured this with patience, counseling the order to be loyal to Cherubini because he was their superior. In one instance, he actually protected Cherubini from angry younger members. The Holy See arranged for an investigation of the situation, and Joseph was reinstated as superior general. Jealous dissidents within the order, however, who had the support of a relative of the pope, persevered in their troublemaking, and in 1646, Pope Innocent X published a brief that diminished the Clerks Regular to a simple society of priests subject to their respective bishops. When informed of the turn events had taken, Joseph's comment was simply, "The Lord gave and the Lord hath taken away. Blessed be the name of the Lord." The new constitutions were drawn up by Cherubini. Soon afterward, however, Cherubini was convicted by the auditors of the Rota for improper administration of the Nazarene College. He was disgraced and left Rome, but he returned a year later, repentent, and reconciled with Joseph, who attended him at his deathbed. Joseph died a few months later and was buried in the Church of San Pantaleone at ninety-two, in the knowledge that his good work had seemingly come to nothing. The foundation, however, was restored as an order in 1669. Today it is commonly called the Piarists or Scolopi, after *Le Scuole Pie*—religious schools. Joseph was called "a second Job" by Pope Benedict. He is the patron saint of Christian schools. He is shown in art holding a lily and miter, with a cardinal's hat before him, sometimes with the Virgin Mary and Infant appearing to him.

JOSEPH COTTOLENGO. Confessor, founder. 1786–1842. April 29. He was born at Brà, near Turin. He was ordained, became canon of the church of *Corpus Domini*, and engaged in pastoral work. After the death of a poor woman due to a lack of medical facilities, he opened, with no capital, a small hospital for the poor. He organized the volunteers who staffed it into the Brothers of St. Vincent and the Daughters of St. Vincent (Vincentian Sisters). It grew, and during the cholera epidemic of 1831, it was transferred to a suburb of Valdocco and came to be called *Piccola Casa*, or the Little House of Divine Providence. It continued to expand as he added almshouses, refuges, orphanages, asylums, and workshops, until it became the size of a town. He depended entirely upon alms for its support, never kept accounts, and made no investments; he spent the money as it came in. The people to whom the institution ministered grew to include the old, the deaf, the blind, the crippled, the insane, and troubled girls. He founded the Daughters of Compassion, the Hermits of the Holy Rosary, and the Priests of the Holy Trinity. He died of typhoid at Chieri, Italy. The Cottolengo Charitable Institute has branches in several parts of the world.

JOSEPH OF CUPERTINO. Confessor. 1602–1663. September 18. He was born in Cupertino, a small village between Brindisi and Otranto. He was born in a shed because his poor father, a carpenter, had recently sold the house to meet his debts. His father died, and his mother looked upon Joseph as a burden and treated him accordingly. He became absentminded, forgetting even to eat, and earned the nickname "Bocaperta," the gaper, because he wandered in a daze about the town. Although he had a short temper, he was devoted to religious duties. He was apprenticed to a shoemaker but was not very skilled. At seventeen, he tried to gain admittance to the Conventual Franciscans and was refused. He joined the Capuchins as a lay brother, but he forgot what he was told to do, dropped plates, and let the kitchen fire go out; he was dismissed within a year. After being refused help from a wealthy uncle, he returned home. His mother got her brother, a Conventual Franciscan, to get him a job as a servant to the order at Grottella. Given a tertiary habit, he worked in the stables. A change could be seen in him, and his hard work, mortifications, and acts of penance resulted in his being admitted to the religious in 1625. He became a novice, but although his life-style impressed the brethren, he did not make easy progress in his studies. He was ordained a priest in 1628 and did not eat bread or drink wine for five years, eating herbs on Fridays that were so unpalatable that no one else could eat them. He fasted rigorously and was given manual work in keeping with his capabilities. But from the time of his ordination, he experienced ecstasies and supernatural encounters, and he

241

worked cures that have not been equaled in any other reasonably authenticated account of a saint. During his stay at Grottella, over seventy occasions of his levitation are recorded. It is said that he would fly from the church door to the altar over the heads of worshipers. The most impressive account occurred while the friars were building a calvary. The middle cross was thirty-six feet high and was so heavy that ten men couldn't lift it. Joseph is said to have "flown seventy yards from the door of the house to the cross, picked it up in his arms as if it were a straw" and put it into place. The Lutheran duke of Brunswick was converted after seeing him in ecstasies at mass. While in his trances, blows, pinpricks, and burning would not awaken him. The brethren resented the publicity, and for thirty-five years he was not permitted to celebrate mass in public, to keep choir, to eat with the brethren, or to attend public functions. His supernatural experiences disturbed many, and when he attracted crowds while passing through Bari, he was excoriated. The vicar general sent an accusation to the inquisitors of Naples. Joseph was ordered to appear before them. The inquisitors did not find any reason for censure, but they sent him to the minister general in Rome. He was initially received coldly, but the minister general was won over by his innocence and modesty and took him to see Pope Urban VIII. Joseph went into an ecstasy during the interview, and the pope declared that if Joseph died before him, he would testify to the miracle that he had witnessed. He was sent to Assisi, where again his superiors treated him as a fraud. He stayed there thirteen years, experiencing for a time a spiritual depression during which he was tortured by temptations. He became incapacitated by his condition and was called to Rome by the minister general. During the journey, he improved. The minister general kept him for three weeks and then sent him back to Assisi. For unknown reasons, the Inquisition of Perugia was instructed to send Joseph to the Capuchins in a remote monastery in the hills of Pietrarossa in 1653. The solitude there was the equivalent of being incarcerated, for he was cut off from the world and confined in many ways by the monks, who prevented him even from receiving letters. Pilgrims soon located him, however, and traveled to see "The Flying Friar." In 1655 the chapter general of the Conventual Franciscans asked that he be returned to Assisi, but Pope Alexander VII responded that one St. Francis at Assisi was enough. In 1657, however, he was permitted to move to the Conventual house at Osimo. The seclusion was strictest here, and only certain religious were allowed to visit him in his cell. He remained always simple and humble, and he was said to have both a great affinity for animals and the ability to read consciences. He experienced supernatural events until his death, despite the efforts to repress him. He is the patron saint of students and degree candidates, and of aviators and astronauts. He is portrayed in art raised above the ground before an image of the Virgin Mary.

JUDE. Apostle. First century. October 28. Jude or Judas, also called Thaddeus or Lebbeus, "the brother of James," is usually regarded as the brother of St. James the Less, and therefore was related by blood to Jesus. Nothing is known of how or when he became a disciple of Christ. After the Last Supper, when Christ promised to manifest himself to his hearers, Jude asked him why he did not manifest himself to the rest of the world. Christ answered that he and the Father would visit all who love him, and that "we will come to him, and will make our abode with him." What happened to Jude after the Ascension and the descent of the Holy Spirit is unknown. According to a Western tradition, he preached in Mesopotamia and was martyred with St. Simon in Persia. Some scholars contend that Jude the apostle and Jude the author of the *Epistle of Jude* are different people. He is the patron saint of those in desperate situations. A tenuous explanation of this is that, due to a confusion of him with Judas, the follower who betrayed Christ, Jude was not invoked unless all else failed.

JULIA BILLIART. Virgin, foundress. 1751–1816. April
8. She was born to a family of prosperous peasant farmers
who also owned a small shop at Cuvilly in Picardy. Cuvilly
was her birthplace. At fourteen, she took a vow of chastity
and dedicated herself to the service and instruction of the
poor. She was mysteriously paralyzed and became an invalid. In 1790, the curé of Cuvilly was replaced by a priest
who had taken the oath prescribed by the revolutionary
authorities, and Julia rallied the people to boycott him. She
also helped find refuges for fugitive priests, and for this
reason was taken to Compiègne, where she had to change
addresses often for her safety. A friend brought her to
Amiens to the house of Viscount Blin de Bourdon after the
Reign of Terror. She met Frances Blin de Bourdon, Vis-
countess de Gézaincourt, who became her friend and
worked with her. Heightened persecution forced Julia and
Frances to move to a house belonging to the Doria family at
Bettencourt. There she met Father Joseph Varin, who was
convinced that Julia was meant to achieve great works; and
after returning to Amiens, they laid the foundations of the
Institute of Notre Dame, whose objects were to see to the
religious instruction of poor children, the Christian education of girls of all classes, and the training of religious
teachers. The rules were somewhat innovative, requiring
the abolition of the distinction between choir and lay sisters.
At a mission held by the Fathers of the Faith of Amiens in
1804, the teaching of the women was given to the Sisters of
Notre Dame. At the end of the mission, Father Enfantin
asked Julia to join him in a novena without telling her why,
and on the feast of the Sacred Heart, he ordered her to walk.
After being an invalid for over twenty years, she got up and
realized that she was cured. Now fully functional, she
worked to extend the new foundation and to assist at missions conducted by the Fathers of the Faith in other towns.
She did this until the work was halted by the government.
The educational work continued, however, and convents
were opened at Namur, Ghent, and Tournai. Unfortunately,
Father Varin's post of confessor to the Sisters was

filled by a young priest who estranged Julia from the bishop of Amiens, and the bishop pressed for her withdrawal from his diocese. She retired to the house at Namur, joined by nearly all the sisters, where she was well received by the bishop of Namur. Soon she was vindicated and invited to return to Amiens, but since it was too difficult to restore the foundation there, Namur became the motherhouse. As of 1816, it was clear that Julia's health was failing rapidly. While repeating the *Magnificat*, she died.

JUSTIN DE JACOBIS. Blessed, bishop, confessor. 1800–1860. July 31. He was born at San Fele in Lucania and was brought up in Naples. He was known for his youthful piety and became a Vincentian. He was chosen by the Congregation de Propoganda Fide as prefect-apostolic for Ethiopia. In 1838 he departed for Africa with some companions. He adapted his life-style to that of the country, and despite persecution, imprisonment, and hardships, he worked hard and with great dedication, founding missions and creating a native clergy. His converts are numbered at 12,000, including Bl. Ghebre Michael. In 1849, he was pressed to accept the title of vicar-apostolic and episcopal ordination. He barely escaped the martyrdom that Bl. Ghebre Michael suffered. He died on the roadside near Halai. He is the true founder of the Abyssinian mission. He was a man of great tact, and Cardinal Messaia wrote of him, "God chose him to be a teacher even more by example than by words."

JUSTIN MARTYR, JUSTIN THE PHILOSOPHER. Martyr. c. 100–165. June 1. He was a layman and the first great Christian philosopher who wrote works of sizable length. His own writing gives details of his life. According to his account, he was a native of Flavia Neapolis, and his pagan parents were of Greek origin. He was given a liberal education and devoted himself particularly to rhetoric, poetry, and history. He then moved on to the study of philosophy, and he studied the system of the Stoics, then gave it up because it taught nothing of God. He applied to the school of Pythagoras but was told that a preliminary knowledge of music, geometry, and astronomy would be required. He came into contact with a respected Platonist, however, who led him to the science of God. One day, while wandering near the seashore, reflecting upon one of Plato's maxims, he saw an impressive-looking old man, whom he engaged in a discussion about the maxim. The man told him of a philosophy nobler and more fulfilling than any he had yet studied—one that had been revealed by God to the Hebrew prophets and had culminated in Jesus Christ. Justin was inspired to study the Scriptures and to learn about the Christians. He is said to have become converted by his reading and by observing the heroism of martyrs. He became a Christian around the age of thirty and was baptized perhaps at Ephesus or Alexandria, both cities that he visited. In his teaching as well as his writing, he described the faith of the Christians and what took place at their meetings, an approach that most early Christians avoided in order to protect their rites from profanation. He apparently traveled much and held disputations with pagans, heretics, and Jews. At last he came to Rome, where he opened a Christian school, with Tatian as one of his students. At some point he presented his *Apology* to the Emperor Marcus Aurelius. He argued in public with a Cynic named Crescens, whom he accused of ignorance and misrepresentation. It is believed that it was through the machinations of Crescens's followers that Justin was arrested. He was brought before Rusticus, and records of his trial still exist. He stated his beliefs openly and refused to sacrifice to the gods. He was sentenced to be scourged and beheaded. Six other Christians, including a woman, died with him. He is the patron saint of philosophers and philosophy, and apologists. He is depicted in art with an ax or a sword.

KATERI TEKÁKWITHA. Blessed, virgin. 1656–1680.
April 17. She was born in the village of Osserneon (Au-
riesville), New York, the daughter of a Christian Al-
gonquin. She was orphaned when her family died during an
epidemic of smallpox, and the disease left her with a pocked
face and impaired eyesight. She was captured by Iroquois
Indians and married to a pagan Mohawk chieftain. Converted and baptized in 1676 by Fr. Jacques de Lamberville,
a Jesuit missionary, she became afraid for her life due to the
disapproval of her relatives and the other Indians. She ran
away from the village in 1677 and traveled through 200
miles of wilderness to the Christian Indian village of Sault
Ste. Marie, near Montreal. She made her First Communion
on Christmas that year and took a vow of chastity in 1679.
She became known for her spirituality and austere life-style,
and miracles were attributed to her. She was called the
"Lily of the Mohawks." She died at Caughnawaga, Canada, and her grave became a pilgrimage site for Christian
Native Americans and French colonists. She was the first
Native American proposed for canonization.

KEVIN, COEMGEN, CAOIMHGHIN. Abbot. d. c.
618. June 3. Tradition has it that he was born at the Fort of
the White Fountain in Leinster, Ireland, and was of a noble
family that had been ousted from the kingship. He was
baptized by St. Cronan and was educated by St. Petroc of
Cornwall, who was then in Ireland. After being ordained,
he became a hermit at the Valley of the Two Lanes in
Glendalough, lived in a cave ("St. Kevin's Bed"), and
used the Teampull na Skellig (the rock church), a Bronze
Age rock tomb. He spent seven years there and then was
persuaded to give up his life of solitude. He went to Disert-
Coemgen and founded a monastery for his followers. Later,
he returned to Glendalough. He made a pilgrimage to Rome
and brought back relics for his foundation at Glendalough,
of which he was abbot. He was a friend of St. Kieran of

Clonmacnois and claimed that he visited him before his death and that the saint gave him his bell. He trained the son of King Colman of Ui Faelain. Many sensational miracles were attributed to him, including his reputedly feeding his community with salmon brought to him by an otter. He was said to have been 120 years old when he died. Glendalough became an important center of pilgrimage. He is the patron saint of Dublin. He is depicted in art with a blackbird, which is said to have laid an egg in his hand while it was outstretched in prayer, the saint remaining in this position until the egg hatched.

LAURENCE OF BRINDISI. Confessor, doctor of the Church. 1559–1619. July 21. He was born in Brindisi in the kingdom of Naples to a Venetian family. He was educated by local Conventual Franciscans and then by his uncle in the College of St. Mark in Venice. He became a Capuchin Franciscan, taking the name Laurence, at the age of sixteen. He studied at the University of Padua, where he demonstrated an incredible gift for languages, learning Greek, Hebrew, German, Bohemian, French, and Spanish, and excelled at Bible studies. He gave a Lenten course of sermons while still a deacon, and after being ordained, he preached successfully in Padua, Verona, Vicenza, and elsewhere in northern Italy. He became definitor general of the order in Rome in 1596. Pope Clement VIII commissioned him to work to convert Jews; his facility with Hebrew contributed greatly to his success at this task. He accompanied Bl. Benedict of Urbino to Germany to establish the Capuchins as a means of counteracting the spread of Lutheranism. They nursed plague victims and established monasteries at Prague, Vienna, and Gorizea. He was then elected minister general of the Capuchins. He was sent by the emperor, Rudolf II, to unite the German princes against the Turks. As a result of his efforts, an army was mustered, and he was appointed chaplain general. Before the battle of Szekes-Fehervar in 1601, the generals consulted him on strategy. He advised an attack, rallied the troops, and rode before the army with a crucifix. The victory was attributed to him. He was commissioned by the emperor to persuade Philip III of Spain to join the Catholic League, and in the course of this task, he founded a house of Capuchins in Madrid. He was then sent to Munich as nuncio of the Holy See at the court of Maximilian of Bavaria, head of the League, from which location, in addition to his other duties, he administered two provinces of his order. After acting as a diplomat in two more royal tangles, he returned to the monastery at Caserta in 1618, desiring a more solitary life. Representatives from Naples came to him, however, and asked him to intercede for them with King Philip about the Spanish viceroy, the duke of Osuna, whose dictatorial methods they feared would cause a rebellion. Although he was ill and tired and predicted that he would not return alive, he agreed. He was forced to travel to Lisbon in the heat of summer. There he convinced the king of the seriousness of the case, and the duke was recalled. After accomplishing his aim, he returned to his lodging and died on his birthday. He was buried in the cemetery of the Poor Clares at Villafranca. His written works included some controversial pieces against the Lutherans, sermons, and a commentary on Genesis.

LAURENCE OF ROME. Martyr. d. 258. August 10. All that is known for certain of Laurence, the deacon of Pope St. Sixtus II, is that he was martyred four days after the pope during the persecutions of Emperor Valerian. Accounts written long after his death and legends have provided additional details. He may have been born in Huesca, Spain. According to these accounts, as the pope was led to execution, Laurence followed him. Before the pope died, he predicted that Laurence would join him soon after. When he heard this, he sold many Church possessions, distributing the money to the poor. He then went through the city, gathering together the poor who were supported by the Church. On the third day he took them to the prefect and invited him to see the treasure of the Church. The prefect, disturbed by the motley and unhappy group he saw before him, angrily asked where the treasure was. Laurence pointed to the crowd and told him they were the Church treasures. This angered the prefect further, and he ordered a gridiron to be prepared to burn Laurence alive. Laurence was stripped and bound upon the gridiron, over a slow fire. After prolonged suffering, he is said to have commented, "Let my body be turned; one side is broiled enough." He was turned over, and later, said, "It is cooked enough. You may eat." After praying for the conversion of Rome, he died. He became one of the most venerated martyrs of the Roman Church. He was buried in the cemetery of Cyriaca *in agro Verano* on the Via Tiburtina, on the site of what is now the church of St. Laurence-outside-the-Walls. Pope Vitalian sent some of his relics to King Oswiu of Northumbria. Laurence's intercession was reputed to cause the victories of Christian armies in the battle of Lechfeld against the Magyars in 955, and at Saint-Quentin, in 1557. He is the patron saint of cooks. He is portrayed in art carrying a long cross on his shoulder and a gospel book in his hand, and his emblems are the gridiron and a money purse (symbolizing his almsgiving).

LAURENCE RUIZ. Martyr. b. c. 1600. He was born in Manila, the Philippines. He was a pious married layman, and he joined a secret Dominican mission to Japan. A storm drove the company onto the island of Okinawa. There they were tortured to death by the Japanese. Dying with him were Bl. Michael Aozaraza, Bl. Antony Gonzales, Bl. William Cowtet, Bl. Vincent Shiwozuka, and Bl. Lazarus of Kyoto.

LEO THE GREAT. Doctor of the Church, pope. d. 461. November 10. He appears to have been born in Rome, although his family was Tuscan. That he was well educated is apparent from his writing. He became a deacon under St. Celestine I and later under Sixtus III; St. Cyril wrote directly to him, and Cassian dedicated his treatise against Nestorius to him. In 440, Leo was sent to arbitrate a dispute between two imperial generals in Gaul, and he was still there when a disputation came to announce the death of Pope Sixtus III and his own succession to the papacy. He immediately set about advancing and consolidating the Roman see. The principal writings of his that survive are sermons, and they encourage various acts of Christian social charity and elaborate upon Christian doctrine. The 143 surviving letters written by him show a decisive and firm man. In 448, he received a letter from an abbot in Constantinople, Eutyches, complaining about the revival of Nestorian heresy, and later, a protest by Eutyches against the fact that St. Flavian had excommunicated him. Communication with St. Flavian revealed that Eutyches denied the two natures of Christ—making him a heretic—and a council was summoned at Ephesus by Emperor Theodosius, with the superficial intention of investigating the matter. The synod, dubbed "the Robber Synod," was packed with Eutyches's friends and acquitted him while condemning St. Flavian. Dioscorus, the patriarch of Alexandria, prevented the papal legates from reading aloud a letter Leo had sent. St. Flavian died from violence stemming from his deposition. Two years later, St. Flavian was vindicated in a general council at Chalcedon attended by 600 bishops and Leo's representatives. Dioscorus was excommunicated and deposed. The letter Leo had written to St. Flavian setting out his doctrine on the Nestorian and Eutyches issue, called "The Dogmatic Letter" or "The Tome of St. Leo," which had been repressed by Dioscorus, was proclaimed to the council. Leo's clarification of the issue of the two-fold nature of Christ would become the Church line on the subject. When Attila and his Huns, after plundering Milan and destroying Pavia, set out for Rome, Leo set out to meet them. Leo convinced Attila in an interview not to attack—to accept an annual tribute from the city instead. Three years later, the Vandal Genseric attacked and sacked the city, but Leo persuaded him against killing the inhabitants and burning the city. After the Vandals departed, Leo ministered to the people, replacing the treasures of the churches, and he sent priests with money to the captives whom the Vandals took with them. In his lifetime he gained the respect of people of all ranks, from emperors to barbarians, and his sageness and effectiveness were to influence the concept of the papacy for centuries. His relics are preserved in the Vatican Basilica. He is depicted in art with SS. Peter and Paul confronting Attila; or on horseback, with Attila and his soldiers kneeling before him; or praying at the tomb of St. Peter.

LEONARD CASONOVA OF PORT MAURICE. Confessor. 1676–1751. November 26. He was born at Porto Maurizio, Italy, and was baptized Paul Jerome. He entered the Jesuit Roman College at the age of thirteen. The uncle with whom he lived wished him to become a physician, and when Paul refused, he disowned him. He joined the Franciscans of the Strict Observance at Ponticelli in 1697 and took the name of Leonard. He studied at the Observant St. Bonaventure's in Rome and was ordained in 1703. In 1709 he went to the St. Francesco del Monte monastery in Florence, and using it as a base, preached successfully throughout Tuscany. He became guardian of San Francesco and founded a retreat for the religious at Incontro. He directed missions in the area around Rome for six years. In 1736 he became guardian at St. Bonaventure's but was permitted to resign the office in 1737 in order to continue his missions, which drew enormous crowds. He encouraged the Stations of the Cross—he was said to have set up nearly 600 stations throughout Italy—and was devoted to the Blessed Sacrament, the Sacred Heart, and Mary. He acted as spiritual director of Clementina Sobieska, the wife of King James III, claimant to the English throne. In 1744 Pope Benedict XIV sent him to Corsica to preach and restore peace, but the Corsicans remained resistant, believing him to be an instrument of the ruling Genoese. He returned to Rome in 1751 to St. Bonaventure's and, completely worn out by his labors, died. He is the patron of parish missions.

LEONARD OF NOBLAC. Abbot. d. c. 559. November 6. He was one of the most popular saints of Western Europe in the late Middle Ages, but the account of his life is unreliable because it was not written until the eleventh century. Tradition has it that he was a Frankish nobleman who was converted to the faith by St. Regimius. His godfather was King Clovis I, who offered Leonard a bishopric, which he declined. Instead he went to the monastery of Micy in Orléans and became a monk. In search of an even more solitary life, he went to a forest near Limoges, built a cell, and lived on vegetables and fruit. Clovis was hunting in the forest one day, and his queen, who had accompanied him, went into a difficult labor. Leonard prayed for her, and the child was delivered safely. To show his appreciation, the king gave him as much land as he could ride around in a night on his donkey. On this land Leonard formed a community. It thrived and became the Abbey of Noblac, which is now called the town of Saint-Léonard. He worked to convert those in the area, became known for his miracles, and died at Noblac. He is the patron saint of childbirth, prisoners (Clovis promised to free every prisoner whom Leonard could visit), prisoners of war (Bohemond, the crusader prince of Antioch, was released from a Moslem prison in 1103 and visited Noblac to make an offering in gratitude), and those in danger from brigands, robbers, and thieves (perhaps because the public was in danger from the very prisoners whom Leonard was responsible for freeing). He is shown in art vested as an abbot, holding chains, fetters or locks, while freeing prisoners.

LOUIS IX OF FRANCE. King. 1214–1270. August 25. He was born at Poissy, son to Louis VIII, and Blanche, the daughter of Alfonso of Castile and Eleanor of England. He was raised by Blanche in a religious atmosphere. His father became king when Louis was eight years old but died in 1226; Blanche was named regent for her son. Blanche was forced to deal with the ambition of barons, but she proved perservering, and Louis was compassionate to rebels. At nineteen, he married Margaret, the daughter of Raymund Berenger, count of Provence. Her sisters were married to Henry III, king of England, Richard of Cornwall, and Charles, Louis's brother. The couple had eleven children. In 1235, Louis took over the duties of king, although he still used his mother as a counselor. He was generous to the poor, forbade usury, commanded that anyone who committed blasphemy should be branded (an important Parisian was branded under this order), protected vassals against lords, and forbade feuding among the lords. He reformed the administration and built the first French navy. He was known as an impartial judge and was often sought out as an arbitrator. The Abbey of Royaumont was the first of many foundations, cathedrals, and universities that he built or helped to launch. At times Thomas Aquinas and other friars were his guests, and Robert de Sorbonne, the founder of the Sorbonne, was a good friend. Baldwin II, the Latin emperor at Constantinople, gave Louis the relic of Christ's Crown of Thorns in 1239. He razed his Chapel of St. Nicholas and built the Sainte Chapelle to harbor the relic. He brought Carthusians to Paris and gave them the palace of Vauvert and joined his mother in founding the convent of Maubuisson. Louis defeated Henry III of England at Taillebourg in 1242 and made a truce with him. Seventeen years later he made another treaty with Henry in which Henry gave up all rights to Normandy, Anjou, Maine, Touraine, and Poitou, and Louis yielded Limousin and Périgord to him. In 1244 Louis decided to go on crusade in the East. At the thirteenth general council at Lyons, benefices were taxed in order to finance this. Louis departed in 1248 and was joined by the earl of Salisbury and 200 English knights. They took Damietta, in the delta of the Nile, and Louis entered the city barefoot as an act of humility. They attacked the Saracens six months later, but due to floods and a lack of cooperation, Louis was taken prisoner and his army cut down. He endured his imprisonment patiently, reciting the Divine Office daily, and was eventually released when Mamluk emirs overthrew the sultan. He traveled to Palestine with the remnants of his army and visited many holy places. He returned to France when his mother, who had been acting as regent in his place for six years, died. In 1267 he announced another crusade. He departed in 1270, but soon after landing in Tunis, he and his son caught typhoid fever. He received the last sacraments, and as he lay dying, he urged the Greek ambassadors to reunite with the Roman Church. His bones and heart were taken back to France to the Abbey-Church of St. Denis. They were scattered during the Revolution. He is the patron saint of the French monarchy, French soldiers, button makers, Franciscan tertiaries, and stonemasons, sculptors, masons, and workers in marble (due to his ecclesiastical building). In art he is shown clad in royal robes, often decorated with fleurs-de-lis, holding a cross, crown of thorns, or other emblems of the Savior's Passion.

LOUISE DE MARILLAC. Widow, co-foundress. 1591–1660. March 15. She was born to an aristocratic country family, probably at Ferrières-en-Brie, near Meaux. Her mother died while she was young, but she was well educated by her father and the Dominican nuns of Poissy. Her father died when she was fifteen. She wished to become a nun but was advised to marry by her confessor. She married Antony Le Gras, who was in service to the queen and had the potential for a great future. They had a son, but her husband fell ill after twelve years and died. Louise had vowed not to marry again and to devote her life to God. She had met St. Vincent de Paul before her husband died. He agreed to become her confessor. While he felt that other helpful wealthy women were unfit to face the ugliness and suffering that true devotion would require, he found Louise to be made of sterner stuff. In 1629 he sent her to make a visitation of the "Charity" of Montmirail he had founded. Despite uneven health, Louise made many more such missions. Louise had rented a poor dwelling on the Rue des Fossé-Saint-Victor, and St. Vincent chose her to train women to care for the sick poor. In this home she lodged the first four candidates for noviceship, and they became the nucleus of the Sisters of Charity of St. Vincent de Paul. St. Vincent himself preferred the name "Daughters of Charity." Louise desired to draw up a rule of life, but St. Vincent waited for a sign from God. Finally assured of the dedication of Louise, in 1634, he permitted her to draft a rule, and it is, in essence, the rule that is followed to this day. Vows are taken for a year only, then are renewed each year. St. Vincent opened a foundling home, and the sisters undertook to teach the children. Louise oversaw all this activity, always showing great endurance despite her fragile health. She traveled all over France, establishing her sisters in hospitals, orphanages, and other facilities. At her death, more than forty houses had been founded. She died six months before St. Vincent. She is the patron of social workers. She is portrayed in art in the habit of the order—a gray wool tunic with a large headdress or cornette of white linen, the usual dress of Breton peasant women around the seventeenth century.

LUCY OF SYRACUSE. Martyr, virgin. d. 304. December 13. Her *acta* are unreliable. According to them, she was born in Syracuse, the daughter of noble and wealthy parents, and was brought up a Christian. Her father died while she was a child. She made a secret vow of virginity, but her mother pressed her to marry a pagan man. Her mother suffered from a hemorrhage, and Lucy convinced her to pray at the tomb of St. Agatha. Her mother was cured, and Lucy told her of her desire to give her fortune to the poor and devote her life to God. The man she was to have married became angry, and he reported her as a Christian to the governor. This was during the time of the persecutions of Diocletian. Lucy remained loyal to her faith, and the judge ordered that she be made a prostitute in a brothel. Miraculously, however, the guards found themselves physically incapable of carrying her there. An attempt to burn her was tried and failed. She was killed with a sword thrust into her throat. Other legends hold that she tore out her own eyes to discourage a suitor who admired them, or that they were gouged out by the judge; her eyes were then miraculously restored to her, even more beautiful than before. She was one of the most illustrious virgin martyrs honored in Rome during the sixth century. In Sweden, her feast falls on the shortest day of the year and has become a festival of light. On this day the youngest daughter in celebrating households, dressed in white, wakes the rest of the family with coffee, rolls, and a special song. Her relics are preserved in Venice, and a partially incorrupt body is alleged to be hers. She is the patron saint of sufferers from eye diseases, of glaziers, of sufferers from hemorrhages and throat infections, and of cutlers. She is depicted in art as a girl carrying her eyes on a platter, book, or shell; or with a gash in her neck; or a sword embedded in it; or carrying a sword and a palm.

LUKE. Evangelist. First century. October 18. According to St. Paul, Luke was a Gentile, a physician—who probably attended St. Paul—and a fellow worker. Eusebius said that Luke's home was at Antioch and that he was probably a Greek. It is likely that he was with St. Paul during his second imprisonment in Rome. Luke traveled with Paul and was an acute observer, as is shown by his accounts in the

Acts of the Apostles. Luke remained with St. Paul through his last days, as is revealed by St. Paul's letter to Timothy, which reads, "Only Luke is with me." Luke's life after the death of St. Paul is uncertain. According to tradition, he wrote his Gospel in Greece and died in Boeotia. His Gospel is believed to be the accurate account of the life of Christ. Translations of his relics were claimed by Constantinople and Padua. He is the patron saint of the medical profession, doctors, artists, painters, sculptors, lacemakers, notaries (because of his account of Christ's life), and butchers (because his emblem is the ox). In art he appears as a bishop or a physician, often accompanied by a winged ox (perhaps an allusion to the sacrifice in the Temple at the beginning of his Gospel); or as an evangelist, writing.

MALACHY O'MORE. Bishop. 1094–1148. November 3. He was born Mael Maedoc Ua Morgair (Malachy O'More is the anglicized version) and was brought up at Armagh, Ireland, where his father was a schoolmaster. A religious boy, he put himself under the care of a hermit, Eimar, after his parents died. At twenty-five, he was compelled and commissioned by St. Celsus, the archbishop of Armagh, to be ordained and to be a preacher. Before fulfilling this mission, he was instructed by St. Malchus, the bishop of Lismore, and Malachy acted as a minister in his church at the same time. In 1123, his uncle, a lay-abbot of the Abbey of Bangor in the county of Down, resigned the abbey to Malachy in the hopes that he might return it to regular observance. Malachy, however, in a spirit of humility that caused great objection, turned its lands and most of its revenues over to someone else. With ten members of Eimar's community, he rebuilt the house and ruled it for a year, during which time miracles were attributed to him. At thirty, he was made bishop of Connor and set about bringing the see's nominal Christians to a genuine devotion, searching them out in their homes and fields to bring them to church, and his method restored observance to a great degree. In 1127, the area around Bangor, where Malachy lived, was invaded by Norsemen, and Malachy and his monks moved first to Lismore and then to Iveragh in Kerry. In 1129 St. Celsus died. His see had become hereditary over the years, and to break this tradition, he left it to Malachy. His relatives, however, installed St. Celsus's cousin, Murtagh. Malachy refused to make efforts to occupy the see. His refusal was overruled by St. Malchus and Gilbert of Limerick, the papal legate, and he went to Armagh. He declared that he would stay only long enough to restore order, and he refused to enter the city or the cathedral, ruling from outside, because he did not wish to incite trouble by his presence. In 1134, Murtagh died, naming Niall, St. Celsus's brother, as successor. Both sides were supported by troops. Twelve of Niall's supporters were killed by lightning when they tried to surprise their adversaries during a thunderstorm. Malachy took possession of the see, but Niall had carried off two relics—a book (perhaps the *Book of Armagh*) and a crosier—and many people believed that these talismans made him the rightful bishop. One of the malcontents invited Malachy to a conference, intending to assassinate him. Malachy attended, despite his friends' opposition, thinking that to martyr himself would bring peace. His adversaries were impressed with his courage, however, and came to terms. A bodyguard accompanied him until he recovered the crosier and book and could be acknowledged the true bishop by all. Having accomplished the restoration of peace, he resigned the see. In 1137, he returned to his original see of Connor. He divided the diocese, consecrating another bishop for Connor, and ruled Down himself. He established the community Ibracense, a congregation of Augustinian canons, with whom he lived. This community acted to spread the custom of following a regular way of life. He traveled to Rome in 1139 to procure the *pallium* for the archbishops at Armagh and Cashel. In

York he met St. Waltheof of Kirkham, who gave him a horse, and he then traveled to Clairvaux. St. Bernard became his friend and admirer and would write his biography. Impressed with the spirit he found at Clairvaux, Malachy decided to join them, but Pope Innocent II would not permit this. He made Malachy his legate in Ireland and promised the *pallia* if they were applied for with all formality. At Ivrea in Piedmont, Malachy cured his host's child. On his way home, he visited Clairvaux again and left four of his companions, who returned to Ireland as Cistercians and founded the Abbey of Millifont. He traveled through Scotland and was asked by King David to cure his dangerously ill son, Henry. Malachy told the prince, "Be of good courage; you will not die this time," and sprinkled him with holy water. The following day, the boy was well. At a synod of bishops in 1148, it was resolved to make formal application for *pallia* for the two metropolitans, and Malachy set off to see Pope Eugenius III, who was in France. Slowed by the political strategies of King Stephen in England, by the time he reached France, the pope had returned to Rome. He took the opportunity to visit Clairvaux again. There he was felled by a fever, and though the monks nursed him faithfully, he told them that their pains were in vain because he would not recover. He demanded that he be taken downstairs to the church so that he might receive the last sacraments. He died in St. Bernard's arms and was buried at Clairvaux. Malachy is reputed to have made prophecies about the popes, consisting of personal characteristics and circumstances of their reigns, from Celestine II until the end of the world under "Peter the Roman," in the form of symbolical titles or mottoes, but this belief is held to be without grounds. He succeeded in replacing the Celtic liturgy with the Roman and is famous as a pioneer of Gregorian reform. His was the first papal canonization of an Irish saint. He is portrayed in art presenting an apple to a king, thus restoring his sight; or instructing a king in a cell.

MARGARET, OR MARINA. Martyr, virgin. Date unknown. July 20. Her *cultus* began in the East and spread to France, England, and Germany, making her one of the most popular virgin-martyr saints of the Middle Ages. Promises she had supposedly made about her powers of intercession contributed to her popularity. Her *acta* are completely unreliable, although it is likely that she was a maiden martyred under Diocletian. According to her *acta*, she was the daughter of a pagan priest of Antioch in Pisidia and was nursed by a Christian woman. She became a Christian and was consequently driven from home by her father. She lived with her nurse and became a shepherdess. She was admired by the prefect Olybrius, who wanted her either as a wife or a mistress, but she resisted him. He vindictively called her before his tribunal and accused her of being a Christian. She was tortured and thrown into prison. There the devil appeared to her in the form of a dragon and swallowed her, but she held a cross, which irritated his stomach, causing it to burst, and thus was freed. She confronted another demon and overcame it. The next day attempts were made to kill her by fire and water, but they failed. Thousands of spectators were converted during these attempts, and they in turn, were executed. She was finally killed by beheading. Her executioner fell dead at her feet after killing her, a reward for not wishing to carry out his task, for in this way he could join her in heaven. Her body was taken by Theotimus and buried by a noble widow. She is one of the Fourteen Holy Helpers and was one of the "voices" heard by Joan of Arc. Her alleged relics were stolen from Antioch in 980, brought to San Pietro della Valle, and were translated to Montefiascone in 1145. Some of her relics were translated to Venice in 1213, and many others are claimed throughout Europe. She is the patron saint of pregnant women and childbirth (probably because she emerged safely from the dragon's stomach and she is reputed to have promised that women who invoked her during childbirth would have safe deliveries), and of death (she is reputed to have promised that whoever invoked her as they were dying would escape the devil). She is depicted in art trampling or standing on a dragon; or emerging from its mouth; or piercing it with a cross-tipped spear.

MARGARET CLITHEROW. Martyr. c. 1556–1586. March 25. She was the daughter of a prosperous candle maker, Thomas Middleton, and was born in the city of York. He died when she was about nine, and her mother remarried. Margaret married John Clitherow, a grazier and butcher, in 1571. Her husband was well off and held civic offices. Margaret was a well liked, attractive, and witty woman. She had been brought up a Protestant, but three years after her marriage she became a Catholic. She was religiously vocal and active and was imprisoned for two years for not attending the parish church. While in prison she learned to read; after she was released, she organized in her house a small school for her children and her neighbors' children. In a specially built room she hid priests who sought refuge from penal laws, and her home became one of the most important hiding places of the time. Masses were given by the guests, and Margaret would station herself behind the others, nearest the door, possibly to give the alarm in case of discovery. She made barefoot pilgrimages to the execution places of martyred priests, doing so at night to evade spies. Her husband remained silent about these activities, but he was summoned before the court in 1586 to give an account of why his son, who was attending a Catholic college, was abroad. While he was thus occupied, his house was raided, but no trace of priests could be found. His children were interrogated and gave nothing away, but a Flemish student broke down under threats and revealed the secret room. Vessels and books were discovered, and Margaret was taken to prison. She was joined two days later by her friend, Mrs. Ann Tesh, whom the boy had also betrayed. She and her friend joked to keep up their spirits. When called before the judge, Margaret said, "I know of no offense whereof I should confess myself guilty. Having made no offense, I need no trial." She was urged to choose a trial by jury, but she resisted because she did not want her children, servants, and friends to have to testify, and thus have to perjure themselves or testify against her—and know that they had caused her death, which she knew was inevitable. One Puritan who had argued with her in prison courageously declared in court that to condemn someone on the charge of a child was contrary to the law of God and man. The judge wished to save her but was overruled by the council, and so he sentenced her to be pressed to death, the penalty for refusing to plead. She was not allowed to see her children, and she was still visited by people who tried to change her mind, including her stepfather. She saw her husband once. She went to her death smiling, and she prayed for the Catholic clergy, and for Queen Elizabeth, that God would change her faith and save her soul. She refused to pray with Protestants in attendance. She was made to strip and lie flat on the ground, with a sharp stone under her back, and her hands were bound to posts. A door was laid over her and weights totaling seven or eight hundred pounds were placed upon it. It took about fifteen minutes for her to die, and her last words were "Jesu, Jesu, Jesu, have mercy upon me!" She had sent her hat to her husband "in sign of her loving duty to him as to her head," and her shoes and stockings to her twelve-year-old daughter Agnes, that she should follow in her steps. The child became a nun at Louvain, and two of her sons became priests. Her biography was written by her confessor, Father John Mush. She is one of the Forty Martyrs of England and Wales. One of Margaret's hands is preserved in a reliquary at the Bar Convent, in York. She is depicted in art as an Elizabethan housewife, kneeling; or standing on a heavy wooden door.

MARGARET OF CORTONA. Tertiary. 1247–1297. February 22. She was born to a small farmer of Laviano in Tuscany, and her mother died when she was seven. Her father remarried when she was nine, and her unsympathetic stepmother treated the spirited child harshly. Margaret eloped with a young nobleman from Montepulciano and lived with him in his castle as his mistress for nine years. She did so flamboyantly, periodically riding into the town well dressed, mounted on a fine horse. She had a son and regularly begged his father to marry her. One day her lover did not return from an errand; his dog led her to his body. He had been murdered, thrown into a pit, and covered with leaves. She saw this as a judgment upon her from God. She sold what little she had, giving the money to the poor, and showed up at her father's house in a poor robe, with her son, begging forgiveness. At the instigation of her stepmother, her father rejected her. Initially in despair, she eventually thought to go to Cortona to the Friars Minor, whom she had heard were compassionate to sinners. Once there, unsure where to go, she was stopped by two ladies, Marinana and Raneria, who heard her story and took her home with them. They introduced her to the Franciscans, who became her spiritual directors, and she was guided especially by John da Castiglione and Giunta Bevegnati, who acted as her confessor and would write her biography. Her first three years were ones of difficulty and temptation, for she found it hard to put aside her old life. She earned her living by nursing ladies, but she eventually gave this up to increase her devotions and attend to the sick and poor. She moved to a small cottage and lived upon alms. When food was given to her she gave the best of it to the poor, keeping the scraps for herself. After becoming assured of her dedication, the friars gave her the habit of a tertiary, and she sent her son to school at Arezzo, where he remained until he joined the Franciscans. She began to receive what were said to be direct communications from Jesus in the form of ecstasies and visions. One directed her to warn Bishop William of Arezzo to change his life-style and to stop quarreling with those in his diocese, particularly the people of Cortona. She made efforts to avert war when in 1289 the bishop was in dispute with the Guelfs. She went to see the bishop in person, but he would not listen. He was killed in battle ten days later. Around this time, unflattering rumors circulated about her relationship with the friars, and Father Giunta was transferred. The accusations were later proved to be false. Before he died, the bishop had granted a charter that enabled her to nurse the sick poor on a permanent basis. She was joined in her work by several women, one of whom gave her a house, which Margaret put to use for nursing. She engaged the help of the city council to help her start a hospital, which was called the Spedale di Santa Maria della Misericordia. The nursing sisters were Franciscan tertiaries, and she formed them into a congregation called the Poverelle. She also founded the Confraternity of Our Lady of Mercy, which pledged to support the hospital and help the poor. As Margaret grew older, her mortifications grew more extreme. She slept little, praying much, and when she did sleep, it was on the bare ground. She ate sparingly of bread and raw vegetables, wore a rough hair cloth, and performed acts of bizarre self-mutilation. She apparently treated her son with great severity, and the friars frequently asked her to moderate the rigorousness of her austerities. She was reputed to have performed miraculous cures and was sought out by people from all over Italy. She was given the last rites by Giunta and was publicly acclaimed a saint on the day of her death, although she was not canonized until 1728. Cortona began building a church in her honor the year of her death. The present building contains only a window from the original church, but her body is buried under the high altar. There is a statue of her and her dog by John Pisano. She came to be called "The Magdalen of the Seraphic Order." She is shown in art in an ecstasy, with angels supporting her; or as a Franciscan nun, with a small dog at her feet; or contemplating a corpse; or with a skull at her feet and a dog plucking at her skirt.

MARGARET OF SCOTLAND. Queen. c. 1045–1093. November 16. She was the daughter of Edward d'Outremer and the sister of Edgar the Atheling, who took refuge from William the Conqueror at the court of King Malcolm Canmore in Scotland. Margaret accompanied him and was married to King Malcolm in 1070. Her influence on her husband helped to make him an admired ruler. She addressed herself to promoting the arts, education, and religion in the kingdom. She supplied priests and teachers through the realm, helped her husband to found churches, and organized an embroidery guild of ladies of the court to make vestments and church decorations. She revived the Abbey of Iona, and, with her husband, built the Church of Dunfermline—the Scottish equivalent of Westminster Abbey as a burial place for the royal family. She fought simony and usury, and she regulated the Lenten Fast and Easter Communion. She liberated Anglo-Saxon captives. She had six sons and two daughters, and she raised them religiously. Her daughter Matilda married Henry I of England and came to be called "Good Queen Maud," and her son David became a saint. Her husband loved her greatly; though he himself could not read, he had her books covered with gold and silver bindings. She lived austerely, sleeping little in order to pray. In 1093 the Alnwick castle was attacked by King William Rufus; Malcolm and her son Edward were killed. Margaret was dying at the time and died four days after her husband. Her biography was written by Turgot, the prior of Durham and bishop of St. Andrews. She was buried in the church of the Abbey of Dunfermline. During the Reformation, the bodies of Margaret and Malcolm were translated to a specially built chapel in the Escorial, Madrid. The Jesuits at Douai obtained her head. She is patron saint of Scotland. She is portrayed in art as a queen with gifts for the poor; or holding a cross; or praying her husband out of purgatory.

MARGARET-MARY ALACOQUE. Virgin. 1647–1690. October 16. She was the daughter of Claude and Philiberte

Lamyn and was born in L'Hautecour, Burgundy. Her father was a respected notary, who died when she was around eight. She was sent to school with the Poor Clares at Charolles. She fell ill with a painful rheumatic condition at the age of twelve and was bedridden until she was fifteen. The family home had been taken over by her sister, and her mother and she were treated almost like servants. At twenty, she was pressed to marry but refused. She was confirmed at twenty-two and took the name Mary. Her brother furnished her dowry and she joined the Visitation convent at Paray-le-Monial. She worked in the infirmary, and the slow-moving, awkward Margaret-Mary suffered much under the active and efficient infirmarian, Sister Catherine Marest. In 1673, as she knelt before the Blessed Sacrament, she experienced a vision in which the Lord told her that she would act as his instrument. She was visited by more visions, and in the final revelation, the Lord asked that a feast of reparation be instituted for the Friday after the octave of Corpus Christi. She told her superior, Mother de Saumaise, about the visions, was treated contemptuously and was forbidden to carry out any of the religious devotions that had been requested of her in her visions. She became ill from the strain, and the superior, searching for a divine sign of what to do, vowed to believe the visions if Margaret-Mary was cured. Margaret-Mary prayed and recovered, and her superior kept her promise. A group within the convent remained skeptical of her experiences, however, and the superior ordered Margaret-Mary to present her experiences to theologians. They were judged to be delusions, and it was recommended that Margaret-Mary eat more. Bl. Claud La Colombière arrived as confessor to the nuns, and in him Margaret recognized the understanding guide that had been promised to her in the visions. He became convinced that her experiences were genuine and adopted the teaching of the Sacred Heart the visions had communicated to her. He departed not long after for England. During the next years Margaret-Mary experienced periods of both despair and vanity, and she was ill a great deal. In 1681 Claud returned;

in 1682 he died. In 1684, Mother Melin became superior and elected Margaret-Mary her assistant, silencing any further opposition. Her revelations were made known to the community when they were read aloud in the refectory in the course of a book written by Bl. Claud La Colombière. Margaret-Mary became novice mistress and was very successful. Her revelations now in the open, she encouraged devotion to the Sacred Heart, especially among her novices, who observed the feast in 1685. The family of an expelled novice accused her of being unorthodox, and bad feelings were revived, but this passed, and the entire house celebrated the feast that year. A chapel was built at Paray in honor of the Sacred Heart, and devotion began to spread to the other convents of the Visitidines, as well as throughout France. Margaret-Mary became ill while serving a second term as assistant to the superior and died during the fourth anointing step of the last rites. She, St. John Eudes and Bl. Claud are called "saints of the Sacred Heart." She is portrayed clad in the habit of the order, holding a flaming heart; or kneeling before Jesus, who exposes his heart to her.

MARIA GORETTI. Martyr, virgin. 1890–1902. July 6. She was born at Corinaldo, a village about thirty miles from Ancona. She was the daughter of a farm laborer, Luigi Goretti, and his wife, Assunta Carlini. There were five other children. The family moved in 1896 to Ferriere di Conca, near Nettuno in the Roman Campagna. Soon after, Luigi died of malaria. His wife struggled to support the family, receiving much help and encouragement from Maria. In 1902, as Maria sat on the front step mending a shirt, an eighteen-year-old neighbor, Alexander, the son of her father's partner, beckoned Maria into a bedroom, but she refused to·go. He grabbed her and pulled her in. She struggled and tried to scream, but he choked her. She cried that she would rather be killed than submit. Alexander began to pull her clothes off and struck at her with a dagger. She cried out that she was being killed, and he repeatedly stabbed her in the back and ran away. She was taken to the hospital, but it was clear she would not live. In her last hours she forgave her murderer, whom it was revealed she had feared for a long time but did not want to cause trouble by naming. She died within a day of the attack. Alexander was sentenced to thirty years of penal servitude and for a long time was unrepentant. One night he had a dream in which Maria gathered flowers and offered them to him, and he experienced a change of heart. He served twenty-seven years, and his first act as a free man was to beg forgiveness from Maria's mother. In 1947 Maria was declared blessed by Pope Pius XII, who appeared on the balcony of St. Peter's with Maria's mother and three of her sisters and brothers. In 1950 she was canonized in front of the largest crowd ever gathered for a canonization. Alexander was still alive. She is the patron saint of teenagers, particularly girls, and of the Children of Mary.

MARIE BERNADETTE SOUBIROUS. Virgin. 1844–1879. April 16. She was the oldest of six children born to Francis Soubirous and Louise Casterot, and although she was baptized Marie Bernarde, she was called Bernadette. Her father was a miller, and the family was constantly on the edge of poverty. The family lived in the basement of a damp building in the rue des Petits Fossés. Bernadette was not strong, suffering asthma among other ailments, and she had become ill during the cholera epidemic of 1854. She was considered to be a slow student—even stupid—but was a kind, helpful, and obedient child. In six months, starting on February 11, 1858, when she was collecting firewood on the banks of the river, Bernadette had eighteen visions of the Virgin Mary at the grotto of Massabielle, Lourdes, by the River Gave. The Lady of the visions told Bernadette to have a chapel built on the spot so that pilgrims could come to wash and drink from the spring that had begun to flow from the spot where Bernadette was directed to dig. Miracles were soon reported at the spring. By March 4, 200,000 people were accompanying her to the site. In one vision, the Lady said, using the local dialect, "I am the Immaculate Conception." The last vision occurred on July 16, the Feast of Our Lady of Mount Carmel. Bernadette's simplicity and integrity were never questioned. Although the publicity that accompanied her visions helped her father to find work, Bernadette gained little more than the spiritual consolation of a few months, for people constantly questioned the girl, embarrassing her and leaving her little privacy. She resided with the nuns at the hospice for five years in order to escape the publicity, but people sought her out even there. She joined the sisters of Notre-Dame de Nevers in 1866; she had wished for entrance two years earlier but had been prevented by bad health. She was happy with the nuns. Her health remained fragile, and she was given the last sacraments within four months of her arrival; she was allowed to take her first vows through a special dispensation. She recovered, however, and worked first as infirmarian and later as sacristan. She died at the age of thirty-five. The spring at Lourdes became the greatest pilgrimage site in modern Europe. She is the patron saint of shepherds.

MARK. Evangelist. d. c. 75. April 25. It is generally believed that his mother was the Mary whose house in Jerusalem served as a rendezvous for the apostles. He was related to St. Barnabas, a Levite, and so was likely a Levite himself. Commentators tend to believe that Mark was the young man who followed Jesus after his arrest, was caught, and slipped out of his cloak, fleeing naked. St. Paul and St. Barnabas took Mark with them on their mission to Salamis in Cyprus, but Mark returned to Jerusalem while they continued to Perga. As a result of this, St. Paul refused to include Mark when St. Barnabas and St. Paul planned missions to Cilicia and the rest of Asia Minor. This caused a rift between St. Barnabas and St. Paul, and Barnabas separated from Paul and went with Mark to Cyprus. When St. Paul was imprisoned for the first time in Rome, Mark was with him. Mark appears to have been intimately associated with St. Peter, as well, and it is likely that the Gospel of Mark was written in Italy, perhaps in Rome. Tradition holds that he lived for several years in Alexandria and became bishop. It is likely that he was martyred in that city. Venice claims to have the body of Mark, which was reputedly brought there from Alexandria in the ninth century, although this claim has been questioned. He is the patron saint of Venice, secretaries, Spanish cattle breeders (for which there is no obvious explanation), Egypt, and notaries (tradition has it that the Gospel of Mark was an accurate record of St. Peter's memories of Christ). His symbol in art is the winged lion, and he is often depicted writing or holding his Gospel. He may have a halter around his neck.

MARTHA. Virgin. d. c. 80. July 29. Martha was the sister of Mary (usually identified in the West as Magdalene) and Lazarus. She lived with them at Bethany, a small town near Jerusalem. Jesus preached in Judea and visited their house often. Martha may have been the oldest, for she directed the household, and took special pains to make Jesus comfortable. Active in her ministrations, she asked Jesus to ask her sister, the more contemplative Mary, to help her serve him, and he replied, "Martha, Martha, thou art careful and troubled about many things; but one thing is necessary. Mary hath chosen the best part. Eternal salvation is our only concern." This is seen as a reminder that active works can distract one from God, while contemplation brings one closer. It was Martha who went out to meet Jesus after the death of Lazarus. She is the patron saint of housewives and servants, Italian hoteliers, waiters, waitresses, and cooks. She is shown in art dressed as a housewife, often bearing a distaff or any symbol of housework, such as a bunch of keys.

MARTIN I. Martyr, pope. d. 655. April 13. He was born at Todi, in Umbria, and became a deacon in Rome. He displayed a great intellect and charitableness, was sent as a nuncio to Constantinople, and was elected pope in 649. He held the council at the Lateran that condemned Monothelitism (the denial that Christ had a human will) and the *Typos*—the edicts of the reigning emperor Constans II, which favored it. Although he was supported by the bishops of Africa, England, and Spain, he was arrested by Constans and taken to Constantinople. He had taken refuge in the Lateran, but the officers broke in in order to capture him. His own letters give an account of how his health broke down under the long voyage, and that in prison he was given poor food and was prevented even from washing. He was tried for treason, although he was clearly being incarcerated for not accepting the *Typos*. He was condemned without being able to speak in his own defense. He was insulted publicly, flogged, and imprisoned. The intercession of the patriarch of Constantinople saved his life, but he was exiled to Chersonesus in the Crimea. From exile he wrote of the bad treatment he received and berated the Romans for forgetting him while he had prayed steadily for their faith to remain intact. It is likely that he died of starvation. He was the last pope to die a martyr. He is portrayed in art vested as a pope, holding money (alms); or with geese around him (possibly a confusion with St. Martin of Tours); or seen through prison bars.

MARTIN DE PORRES. Confessor. 1569–1639. November 3. He was born in Lima, Peru, the illegitimate child of John de Porres, a Spanish knight, and Anna Velasquez, a Panamanian free woman of color. Martin inherited the features and dark skin of his mother, which upset his father, but John acknowledged Martin and his sister as his children. He was left to the care of his mother, and at twelve he was apprenticed to a barber-surgeon. Three years later he received the habit of the Third Order of St. Dominic, was admitted to the Rosary convént of the Friars Preachers at Lima, and in time became a professed lay brother. He spent his nights in prayer and penance, and he experienced visions and ecstasies. He is reputed to have experienced bilocation and levitation. He nursed the sick of the city, including plague victims, regardless of race, and helped to found an orphanage and foundling hospital. He distributed the convent's alms of food to the poor and is said to have miraculously increased the supplies on occasion. He cared for the slaves that had been brought from Africa. He showed a great control of and care for animals—a care that apparently was inexplicable to the Spaniards—extending his love even to rats and mice, whose scavenging he excused on the grounds that they were hungry. He kept cats and dogs at his sister's house. His protégé, Juan Vasquez Parra, reveals him to have been a practical and capable man, attending to details ranging from raising his sister's dowry in three days, to teaching Juan how to sow chamomile in the manured hoofprints of cattle. Martin's close friends included St. Rose of Lima and Bl. John Massias. He was called the "father of charity" by the community, although he referred to himself as a "mulatto dog." He died of quatrain fever. The Spanish viceroy, the count of Chinchon, came to kneel at his deathbed and ask his blessing. Cures were claimed at his tomb. He is the patron saint of race relations, social justice, public education and TV in Peru, Spanish trade unionists (due to injustices workers suffered), Peru's public health service, people of mixed race, and Italian barbers and hairdressers.

MARTIN OF TOURS. Bishop. c. 316–397. November 11. He was born in Sabaria, a town in Pannonia, of pagan parents. The family moved to Pavia, Italy, when his father, an officer, was promoted in the army. At fifteen, because he was the son of a veteran, he was compelled to join the army against his will. Although he had not formally become a

Christian, he lived more the life of a monk than a soldier for several years. While stationed in Amiens, he met at the city gates on a terrible winter day a poor beggar, who was thinly clad and shaking with cold. Martin cut his cloak into two pieces and gave one half to the beggar. That night in a dream he saw Jesus wrapped in the half of the cloak that he had given away. When he was about twenty, barbarians invaded Gaul. When he was presented with his companions before Julian Caesar to receive a war bounty, Martin refused to accept it. Irritated by this stance, Julian accused him of being a coward. Martin replied that he was willing to go into battle unarmed and to advance against the enemy in the name of Christ. He was thrown into prison, but an armistice brought his discharge. He went to Poitiers, and Bishop St. Hilary took him as a disciple. Martin had a dream that called him home, and he returned, converting his mother and others during the visit. He opposed the Arians in Illyricum so vocally that he was publicly scourged and exiled. In Italy, he was driven away by Auxentius, the Arian bishop. He retreated with a priest to the island of Gallinaria in the gulf of Genoa and remained there until 360, when the banished St. Hilary was allowed to return to Poitiers. As he wished to live as a solitary, St. Hilary gave him some land, now called Ligugé, where he was joined by other hermits—and thus the first monastic community in Gaul was founded. It was a famous monastery until 1607, and was revived in 1852. He lived there for ten years, preaching and reputedly performing miracles in the area. Around 371, Tours chose him as bishop. He was unwilling to take the office; the people tricked him into visiting a sick person in the city and then took him to the church. His poor appearance did not impress the bishops who had come to assist at the election, but the people overruled their objections. He lived in a cell by the church but soon retreated from the city and its distractions to a place that would become an abbey at Marmoutier. It was a desert, with a steep cliff on one side and a river on the other. Before long, eighty monks had joined him. Every year he visited each of his parishes in rural regions, traveling by foot, by donkey, or by boat. He was an innovator in that he worked to convert rural regions, to which he introduced a crude parochial system. Previously, Christians had been confined primarily to urban areas. His biographer reported that he extended his apostolate from Touraine to Chartres, Paris, Autun, Sens, and Vienne. Although he is said to have ruthlessly destroyed pagan temples, his reputed miracles did much to aid his progress: he is said to have cured St. Paulinus of Nola of an eye disease, healed lepers, and raised a dead man to life. He was one of the greatest pioneers of Western monasticism before Benedict—who had a particular veneration for him. During this time, Priscillian, the leader of a Gnostic-Manichean sect, was attacked by Ithacius, the bishop of Ossanova, who accused him of sorcery and urged the emperor to put him to death. Martin did not support Ithacius because Ithacius wished to execute heretics and was invoking the emperor to deal with an ecclesiastical matter. Martin pleaded with Maximus not to execute the heretics but to simply allow them to be excommunicated. Ithacius then accused Martin of heresy. Maximus told Martin that he would execute no one, but after Martin left him, he was prevailed upon to commit the case of the sect to the prefect. The sect was found guilty and the members were beheaded, marking this as the first judicial death sentence for heresy. Martin returned to Trier to arbitrate for the Spanish Priscillianists—in danger of persecution—and for two followers of the late emperor Gratian. His delicate position led him to maintain an alliance with Ithacius, which troubled him greatly afterward. He became ill in a rural district of his diocese and died. He is buried at Tours. His successor, St. Britius, built a chapel over his grave, and it was later replaced with a basilica. He was one of the most popular saints of the Middle Ages, and his shrine was a great site of pilgrimage. In England, St. Martin's Summer is a spell of fine weather that sometimes occurs around the time of his feast. He is the patron saint of beggars, France, soldiers, infantrymen and cavalry, horses, horse riders, geese, and wine growers (his feast falls just after the vendange). He is portrayed in art as a soldier, dividing his cloak to clothe a beggar; or in armor, with episcopal symbols. His emblems are a globe of fire over his head as he says mass, or a goose, whose migration often coincides with his feast.

MARY MAGDALENE. First century. July 22. She was probably named for Magdala, a place on the western shore of the sea of Galilee. She is accepted as having been the sister of Martha and Lazarus. Jesus met her on his Galilean mission. St. Luke records that she was a notorious sinner—though nothing is said of her being a harlot—and that she came into a house where Jesus was eating and fell weeping before him, then wiped his feet with her hair and anointed them with ointment from an alabaster box. When the host remarked that it was unbecoming of Jesus to be so acquiescent to so great a sinner, Jesus said, "Many sins are forgiven her because she hath loved much." He then told her that her sins were forgiven. St. Luke says that she accompanied and cared for Jesus and his apostles on their ministry in Galilee, and she then went to live with her brother and sister in Bethany. On another occasion when she anointed Jesus' head and feet, she was disapproved of by Judas Iscariot and the others. Again Jesus chastised the accusers, saying, "She hath wrought a good work upon me. . . . She hath done what she could." She watched Jesus on the cross and saw the great stone rolled before the door of the tomb where his body was placed. She was the first to be greeted by the risen Christ when she came with spices to the sepulcher in the morning. According to some accounts, after the Pentecost she accompanied the Virgin Mary and St. John to Ephesus, where she eventually died and was buried. Other accounts say that she, Martha, Lazarus, and others evangelized Provence. These sources hold that she spent the last thirty years of her life in a cavern of La Sainte Baume in the Maritime Alps, and was miraculously transported just before her death to the Chapel of St. Maximin, from whom she received the last sacraments; and by whom she was buried. One of the tales of the Middle Ages was that she was engaged to St. John the Evangelist when Jesus called him, and that in anger "gave herself to all delight." Jesus, not wishing to damn her when the cause of her behavior was his calling of St. John, converted her to penance. Relics of hers have been claimed in various places at various times, but none of the stories can be authenticated. She is the patron saint of penitents. She is depicted in art with long, unbound hair and a pot of ointment; or in Gospel scenes of the Passion and Resurrection.

MARY MAGDALENE DEI PAZZI. Virgin. 1566–1607. May 25. She was born in Florence to a distinguished family and was baptized Catherine. She was educated at the St. John Convent in Florence. She was pressed to marry but refused, and at sixteen she joined the Discalced Carmelites at St. Mary of the Angels Convent in Florence in 1582. When she was professed, she took the name Mary Magdalene. She held various offices in the convent and was extremely capable, eventually becoming superioress. While seriously ill, she experienced many ecstasies. After recovering, she practiced extreme mortifications and then fell into a five-year depression. When she emerged from this period, she experienced ecstasies from then on; sisters copied down what she said while in ecstasies, and these accounts were later published. She believed that suffering brought one to a profound spiritual plane and helped to save one's soul. She was reputed to have the gift of prophecy and to be able to read minds and perform great cures. She was an invalid for the last three years of her life and died at the convent. Her body is at the Church of St. Maria degli Angeli in Florence and is claimed to be incorrupt. She is depicted in art receiving the Blessed Sacrament from Jesus; or receiving a white veil from the Virgin Mary; or being presented to or receiving a ring from Jesus; or crowned with thorns and embracing a cross, with rays falling on her from a monstrance; or with flames issuing from her breast.

MATTHEW. Apostle. First century. September 21. It is possible that his original name was Levi and that he took that of Matthew—"the gift of Yahveh"—when he became a disciple. He was apparently a Galilean, and, although he was a Jew himself, was a tax collector for the Romans, a profession that was abhorred by the Jews. In his own Gospel he recounts his conversion. Jesus had just cured a man who was sick of the palsy and, passing by, saw Matthew in his customs house. He said to him, "Follow me." Matthew did, abandoning all his interests and relationships in the process. This occurred in the second year of the public ministry of Jesus. Matthew is the author of the first Gospel. It is said that having made many conversions in Judea, he went on missions to the East, but this is uncertain. His alleged relics were translated to Salerno by Robert Guiscard from Brittany, to which they were reputed to have come from Ethiopia. He is honored as a martyr, but none of the details of his martyrdom are known. He is the patron saint of accountants, tax collectors, bankers, customs officers, and security guards. He is portrayed in art at a desk, with an angel, who may hold a pen or inkwell or be guiding his hand. He may be shown holding money, a bag of coins, money box, or a sword (a symbol of martyrdom). In the Middle Ages, he was shown with spectacles, presumably to help him read his account books.

MATTHIAS. Apostle. First century. May 14. After the Ascension, he was chosen by lot to take the place of the traitor Judas Iscariot among the apostles. The choice was between himself and Joseph Barsabas. Traditions of his life are inconsistent. Some accounts say he preached in Judea, Cappadocia, and on the coast of the Caspian Sea. He is believed to have suffered many persecutions and been martyred at Colchis or Jerusalem. His alleged relics were removed by Empress St. Helena and are now venerated at St. Matthias's Abbey, in Trier. He is depicted in art as an elderly man, holding or being pierced by a halberd or sword.

MAXIMILIAN MARY KOLBE. Martyr. 1894–1941. August 14. He was born at Zdunska-Wola, near Lodz, Poland, and was baptized Raymond. His parents were cottage weavers. The family was eventually driven to poverty under the Russian government, and his parents became Franciscan tertiaries. In 1907, he joined the junior seminary at Lwów, and in 1910, joined the Conventual Franciscans, taking the name Maximilian. His father joined Palsudski's patriots and was hanged for treason in 1914 at the age of forty-three. Maximilian studied at Rome and founded the Militia of Mary Immaculate in 1917 to further devotion to Mary. He was ordained in Rome in 1918, and after being diagnosed with tuberculosis in 1919, he returned to Poland. There he taught Christian history in a seminary. After recovering from a nearly fatal attack of illness, he founded a monthly bulletin, *Militia of the Immaculate Mary*, a magazine for Christian readers. Circulation reached 45,000, and the presses were worked by priests and lay brothers. After another episode of illness, he reestablished the presses at Niepokalanów ("cities of the Immaculate Conception") near Warsaw, and there he founded a community of Franciscans in 1927. Daily and weekly newspapers were now being published. He founded another similar community in Nagasaki, Japan. He returned to Niepokalanów in 1936 to become superior; the foundation grew to house about 770 friars. He harbored over 1,500 Jews and 3,000 Polish refugees during the German occupation. He had sent most of the friars home for their safety. He continued publishing his paper, which criticized the Third Reich, and he was arrested by the Gestapo in 1941. The officers who inspected the monastery were amazed at how little food the brothers subsisted upon. Maximilian was imprisoned at Auschwitz, and one of his duties was to move the bodies of the tortured. He took confessions whenever possible and smuggled in bread and wine for the Eucharist. He took the place of a family man who was one of the ten men randomly selected by the commandant to be executed in retaliation for the escape of a prisoner from their bunker. The men were to be starved to death. Two weeks later, the only one still conscious, he was injected with carbolic acid. When he was canonized, the man whose life he had saved was present.

MAXIMINUS OF TRIER. Bishop. d. c. 349. May 29. He was the brother of St. Maxentius of Poitiers and may have been a native of that city. He traveled to Trier as a young man, perhaps drawn there by the reputation of its bishop, St. Agritius. He completed his education, and he succeeded St. Agritius as bishop in 333. St. Athanasius went to Trier in exile in 336, was welcomed by Maximinus, and stayed for two years, writing during that time of Maximinus's courage, vigilance, and nobility. St. Paul, bishop of Constantinople, also sought refuge in Trier. Maximinus was reputed to have performed miracles. He convened the synod of Cologne, condemning Euphratas as a heretic and deposing him from his see. He cautioned the Emperor Constans, whose favorite home was at Trier, against the Arians. Since he was such a vocal opponent of Arianism, he was named with St. Athanasius in an excommunication the Arians declared. Although he was apparently a prolific writer, nothing of his work survives. St. Jerome describes him as "one of the most courageous bishops of his time." He is portrayed in art receiving St. Athanasius at Triers; or with a bear at his side; or commanding a bear to carry his baggage.

MAXIMUS THE CONFESSOR. Abbot. 580–662. August 13. As a young man he was placed at the imperial court in Constantinople and became the principal secretary of Emperor Heraclius. He resigned his post to become a monk at Chrysopolis (Scutari). He eventually became abbot, and there he wrote some of his mystical treatises. When St. Sophronius, patriarch of Jerusalem and Maximus's mentor, died in 638, Maximus took his place as an advocate of orthodoxy against Monothelitism. In doing this, he defied the views of Heraclius and his successor, Constans II. In 648, the Emperor Constans II issued a decree, the *Typos*, in favor of Monothelitism. Maximus was present at the synod summoned by Pope St. Martin I, at which the *Typos* was condemned. In 653, the pope was arrested and exiled, and later he died of mistreatment. Maximus stayed in Rome, and after arguing against the *Typos* in front of an imperial legate, he, too, was arrested and taken to Constantinople. He was tried and banished to Bizya, in Thrace. There harsh weather, neglect, and hunger caused Maximus, a man in his seventies, great suffering. Theodosius, the bishop of Caesarea in Bithynia, was sent to interview him, and Maximus articulated his beliefs so well that Theodosius was convinced. He gave him money and clothes, and he was moved to a monastery at Rhegium. Another deputation visited him there, promising him honors from the emperor if he would accept the *Typos*. He held fast, and for this he was insulted and his few possessions confiscated. He was taken to Perberis, where Anastasius the Abbot and Anastasius the Apocrisiarius were imprisoned as well. They remained incarcerated under terrible conditions for six years and then were returned to Constantinople to face a tribunal. They were condemned and sentenced to be scourged, to have their tongues and right hands cut off, to be pilloried in each of the twelve quarters of the city, and then be imprisoned for life. After a hard journey to Skhemaris, near Batum on the Black Sea, he died. He was a prolific theological and ascetic writer. He was a prominent exponent of Byzantine mysticism, and his work, *Mystagogia*, is a treatise on liturgical symbolism. His work also included *Quaestiones ad Thalassium*, sixty-five questions and answers on difficult passages of Scripture. He was a great upholder of the teaching authority of the Holy See.

MÉDARD. Bishop. c. 470–558. June 8. He was born in Salency in Picardy, to a Frankish nobleman and a Gallo-Roman mother. He was educated at Saint-Quentin. He was a layman for some years but was ordained at thirty-three. He became so recognized for his success as a missionary and preacher that he was chosen to succeed Bishop Alomer; he may have been consecrated by St. Remigius of Rheims. According to unreliable tradition, he moved his see from Saint-Quentin to Noyon after a raid by Huns, then united it with the diocese of Tournai. Allegedly Noyon and Tournai remained under one bishop for 500 years. He is known to have given the veil to Queen St. Radegund. He is credited with the institution of the old local observance of the Rosière. Each year where his feast is celebrated, the young girl who has been judged the most exemplary in the district is escorted by twelve boys and twelve girls to the church, where she is crowned with roses and given a gift of money. He is the patron saint of the corn harvest and vintage. He is depicted in art with a spread eagle over his head, an allusion to the legend that as a child, an eagle once spread its wings over his head to shelter him from rain. This belief may explain the origins of a peasant prediction that if it rains on his feast the next forty days will be wet, but if it is a good day, the next forty days will be fine as well. He is also depicted kneeling, with a dove over his head; or leaving footmarks on a stone; or with a colt or horses or a beggar near him. For unknown reasons, he was portrayed in the Middle Ages laughing with his mouth wide open (*"le ris de St. Médard"*), and he was invoked to cure toothache.

MEDERICUS, MERRY. Abbot. d. c. 700. August 29. He was born in Autun, and at thirteen entered a local monastery, perhaps St. Martin's, where the life-style of the monks was very regular. He was made abbot against his wishes, but he lived his life as a model to his brethren. He resigned his office after a time because he was afraid of becoming vain and because the office provided too many distractions. He retreated into a forest a few miles away and sustained himself by his own labor. His whereabouts were discovered, however, and after becoming ill, he returned to the monastery. He left the monastery again when he was quite elderly to make a pilgrimage to the shrine of St. Germanus of Paris—a fellow native of Autun. In the northern section of Paris he lived with St. Frou in a small cell adjoining a chapel dedicated to St. Peter. He remained there almost three years, patiently enduring a lingering illness, before dying. The Church of Saint-Merry stands on the location of his cell. He is portrayed in art teaching his monks; or holding chains with caltrops.

MICHAEL THE ARCHANGEL. September 29. Michael (''Who is like unto God'') is the chief of the archangels, the seven angels who stand before the throne of God. In the Book of Daniel, he is accounted ''one of the chief princes'' of the heavenly host and the special guardian of Israel. In the *Book of Revelation*, he appears as the principal soldier in the heavenly battle against the devil (or the dragon), ''who was cast unto the earth and his angels . . . thrown down with him.'' In the *Book of Henoch*, the most prominent of the Old Testament apocrypha, Michael is ''the great captain'' who is ''set over the best part of mankind,'' the chosen who are inheritors of the promises. It is he who is to explain the meaning behind God's judgments. In the *Testaments of the Twelve Patriarchs*, he is said to be merciful, and in the *Ascension of Isaias*, he is presented both as ''always interceding for the human race'' and as the scribe who records the deeds of men in the heavenly books. Michael is said to have had a direct confrontation with the devil over the dead body of Moses. When Moses died, Satan claimed the body on the grounds that since Moses had killed the Egyptian, he was a murderer. Michael replied, "The Lord rebuke thee, thou slanderer." The Christian *Shepherd of Hermas* portrays Michael as a majestic angel who presides over the awards when the willow twigs, some of which grow and others wither away, are brought for inspection and judgment. In the *Testament of Abraham* Michael appears as a character whose intercession is so powerful that souls can be rescued even from Hell. It is he who is said to conduct souls to God. The formal cult of Michael appears to have begun in the East; he was invoked for the sick, and Constantine built a church in his honor for this purpose at Sosthenion, near Constantinople. His alleged apparition on Monte Gargano in southeast Italy in the late fifth century, during which he pointed out a spot where a shrine in his honor was to be built, had a great deal to do with the spreading of his cult to the West. He was often made a patron of cemeteries. He is the patron saint of battle, security forces and paratroops, of Brussels, of banking, of radiologists and radiotherapists (the procedures are dangerous to the doctors themselves, so the intercession of the angel is invoked), of death, of England, Germany, Papua, New Guinea, and the Solomon Islands, of the sick, and of those possessed by the devil. He is depicted in art as an archangel in full armor, with a sword and pair of scales (to weigh souls); and standing over or fighting a dragon or devil with his lance.

MILDRED OF THANET. Abbess. d. c. 700. July 13. She was the daughter of Merewald, an Anglian ruler, and St. Ermenburga, a Kentish princess, and the granddaughter of Penda, the king of Mercia. Her sisters, Milburga and Mildgytha, and a brother were also saints. Egbert, king of Kent, arranged for the murder of her two brothers, his nephews. Afterward he repented and sent for Ermenburga to pay her the *wergild*, which the law demanded should be paid to the relatives of the victim. He gave her land in the Isle of Thanet, and Mildred founded the monastery Minster upon it. The monastery was to continually offer prayers for her brothers' souls. Mildred showed a vocation for the Church and was sent to the convent of Chelles, France, to be educated. A suitor aggressively pressed her to marry him, but she resisted him and returned to England. St. Theodore, the archbishop of Canterbury, gave her the Benedictine habit. Mildred appears to have been the first abbess of Minster. Her convent would become one of the oldest continuously occupied buildings in England. She fasted often and was very modest, and she did much to comfort and aid the poor and troubled. She died of a lingering illness. During the reign of Canute, her relics were stolen and taken to St. Augustine's abbey at Canterbury. Some of her relics were taken to Deventer in Holland; some were returned to Minster. She was one of the most popular saints in medieval England. The rock that St. Augustine was to have first walked upon was long known, not as his, but as St. Mildred's rock. There is an annual pilgrimage to Minster. She is portrayed in art habited as a Benedictine, accompanied by a white hart or holding a lamp.

MONICA. Widow. 332–387. August 27. She was probably born at Tagaste, in North Africa, to Christian parents. She was reared by a family retainer, who led her charges a strict life. One of the rules the servant made was that the children never drink between meals. She explained herself, saying, "It is water you want now, but when you become mistresses of the cellar you will want wine—not water—and the habit will remain with you." When Monica was given the duty of drawing wine for the family, she ignored this maxim and became secretly bibulous. One day she was seen drinking by a slave, who accused her of being a tippler. Monica was horrified and stopped drinking. She was married to a wealthy citizen, Patricius, who was short-tempered and dissipated. She bore his life-style with patience, however, and although he felt some contempt for her devoutness and generosity to the poor, he respected her. He never physically abused her, despite his explosive temper, and when other women showed her bruises from their husbands she told them that their tongues brought the treatment upon them. Her good example brought about the conversion of her husband and her difficult mother-in-law, who had previously meddled in the household. The marriage produced three living children, and Monica was widowed at forty. The oldest son, Augustine, who was extremely intelligent, had been marked by his parents for a fine future, but he pursued a self-indulgent life. When Monica heard that he was living dissolutely and had become a Manichean while a student at Carthage, she refused to allow him to live in her house. Then she had a vision, in which she seemed to be standing on a wooden beam, despairing of his fall, when a shining being asked her the reason for her lamentation. She answered, and he told her to stop crying. Looking toward the spot he indicated, she saw Augustine standing on the beam next to her. She told the dream to her son, and he replied playfully that they might easily be together if Monica would give up her faith. For nine years she prayed for his conversion, fasted, and pleaded with clergy to try to change his mind. A bishop told her that her son was young and stubborn, but that God's time would come. At twenty-nine, Augustine decided to go to Rome to teach rhetoric. Monica determined to accompany him, but Augustine tricked her and sailed alone. When she reached Rome, he had gone on to Milan. There Augustine came under the influence of St. Ambrose and was converted. In thankfulnes to St. Ambrose, she turned to him as her spiritual guide. She deferred to him in all religious quandaries, including questions of practice. In response to one of her questions about fasting, he gave the famous response, "When I am here, I do not fast on Saturday, but I fast when I am in

Rome; do the same, and always follow the custom and discipline of the Church as it is observed in the particular locality in which you find yourself." St. Ambrose had great respect for her, and she became one of the most devout women in Milan. Monica had tried to arrange a marriage for St. Augustine, but he declared after his complete acceptance of the Catholic faith that he would live a celibate life. He moved with his mother and some friends to a villa belonging to one of them, and there they lived a religious life in an environment of religious and philosophical discussion. Monica, who was well versed in the Scriptures, was an active participant. After Augustine was baptized in 387, the company departed for Africa. At Ostia, before boarding a ship, Monica died. Her relics are preserved at St. Augustine's Church in Rome near the Piazza Navona; other relics are at Arrouaise. She became a model to Christian mothers due to her care and anxiety for her son. She is the patron saint of married women and mothers. She is portrayed in art standing behind a kneeling St. Augustine, with a girdle, scarf, handkerchief, or book in her hand; or receiving a monstrance from an angel.

NICHOLAS. Bishop. d. c. 350. December 6. He is accounted to have been born at Patara in Lycia, a province of Asia Minor. He was chosen bishop of the then rundown diocese of the capital of Myra, which he ruled with great care and faith. Greek histories hold that he suffered imprisonment and made a famous confession during the persecution of Diocletian. He was present at the Council of Nicaea, where he condemned Arianism—one story holds that he actually slapped the heretic Arius. He died at Myra. By the time of Justinian, there was a basilica built in his honor at Constantinople. He was one of the most popular saints of all times, and he became the subject of many legends. These hold that he was a wealthy young man who decided to devote his money to charitable activities. A citizen of Patara had lost his fortune, and because he could not raise dowries for his three daughters, he was going to give them over to prostitution. After hearing this, Nicholas took a bag of gold and threw it through the window of the man's house at night. The eldest girl was married with it as her dowry. He performed the same action for each of the other girls. The three purses, portrayed in art with the saint, were mistakenly thought to be the heads of children, and thus originated the story that three children, murdered by an innkeeper and pickled in a tub of brine, were resuscitated by Nicholas. The three purses are also thought to be the origin of the pawnbrokers' symbol of three gold balls. Another legend holds that he appeared to sailors caught in storms off the coast of Lycia and led them safely into port. Churches built under his dedication are often placed so that they can be seen off the coast as landmarks. Yet another legend has it that he appeared to Constantine in a dream and thereby caused him to save three unjustly condemned men from death. When Myra fell into the hands of the Saracens, Italian cities seized the chance to acquire the relics of Nicholas. The relics were stolen by Italian merchants and came to Bari in 1087. A new church was built to shelter them, and Pope Urban II was present at their enshrining. The shrine became one of the great pilgrimage centers of medieval Europe. Many miracles were reputed to have been worked through his intercession. The popular cultural representation of "St. Nick" is based on a combination of a Low Countries custom of giving children presents on his feast day as their patron, and the Dutch Protestants of New Amsterdam linking this to Nordic folklore of a magician who punished naughty children and rewarded exemplary ones with presents. He is the patron saint of children, of brides and unmarried women, of pawnbrokers, of perfumers (from his shrine at Bari there was said to originate a fragrant "myrrh"), of travelers, pilgrims and safe journeys (because he reputedly traveled to the Holy Land and Egypt), of sailors and maritime pilots, Russia, Greece, Sicily, Lorraine, and Apulia. He is de-robed as a bishop, with three children in a tub at his feet; or with three gold balls on a book; or with three purses; or shown with a ship or an anchor; or calming a storm.

NICHOLAS OF TOLENTINO. Confessor. 1245–1305. September 10. He was born in Sant' Angelo, a town in the March of Ancona, supposedly the product of his middle-aged childless parents' prayers and their pilgrimage to the shrine of St. Nicholas at Bari. He was baptized with the name of his patron. He received minor orders as a boy and was given a canonry in the Collegiate Church of St. Saviour in his native town. Although his superiors wished him to aim for higher offices within the secular clergy, he wished for a life of contemplation. He overheard a sermon in an Augustinian church and this led him to join the order of Augustinian friars at Sant' Angelo. He was professed before he turned eighteen. He then went to San Ginesio to study theology. His overgenerous almsgiving at the monastery earned a complaint to the prior from the procurator. He was ordained in 1270 and made a resolution to preach every day. He became well known among the people, particularly in light of miracles he is reputed to have performed—in one case, curing a blind woman. He became novice master at Sant' Elpidio for a time. He was invited to stay for a while at a monastery near Fermo, but while praying at its church he seemed to hear a voice saying, "To Tolentino, to Tolentino. Persevere there." He was sent there soon afterward and remained the rest of his life. Tolentino had fallen into civil and moral disorder, and a street ministry was undertaken to regulate observance and to eradicate both extreme religious practices and dissolution. Nicholas's preaching produced results from the start. He worked selflessly in the slums, caring for the sick, settling fights, guarding children, and confronting notorious sinners. The individual nature of his ministry is illustrated by one woman's giving testimony in the cause of his canonization to the effect that he had reformed her husband who had abused her for years. He lived in the town for thirty years, and his final illness lasted a year. He rose once from his bed in the final months to absolve a penitent who he knew would confess to no one else. Fragments of his body were alleged to bleed just before great calamities, such as the fall of Constantinople in 1452. His relics, rediscovered in 1926, are in Tolentino. He is portrayed in art with a basket of rolls (called "St. Nicholas's bread," distributed to the sick or women in labor, to be soaked in water and swallowed); or as a hermit; or with stars or the sun on his breast or around his head.

NICHOLAS VON FLÜE. Hermit. 1417–1487. March 22. He was born near Sachseln in Unterwalden to a family of small farmers, who owned the Kluster Alp and the estate of Flüeli on the Sachsterberg, from which their surname was derived. His father held a civil post; his mother was very devout and brought up her sons to belong to the brotherhood of the Friends of God (*Gottesfreunde*). The society sought to live a strict life, to meditate on the passion of the Lord, and to seek a close relationship with God. They lived with their families in small communities or as hermits. Thus, Nicholas was pious from childhood. At twenty-two, he fought as a soldier in the war with Zürich, and he fought again fourteen years later when Thurgau was invaded. As the captain of a company, he prevented the destruction of a nunnery. He was appointed magistrate and judge and was sent as a deputy for Obwalden to councils. He was offered the office of governor many times but always refused. He married and continued the devout practices of his childhood, often praying all night. He is said to have experienced visions and revelations. At the age of fifty he decided to resign his offices and become a hermit. His wife, religious also, did not oppose him. He left barefoot and bareheaded, wearing a drab habit and carrying a rosary and a staff. He appears to have been headed for Strasbourg, where the headquarters of the *Gottesfreunde* lay. On his way, however, he was put up by a peasant who was a Friend of God, and the man told him that the Swiss were unpopular in Alsace and that he might not find there the life that he sought. That night during a thunderstorm, Nicholas looked at a little town beyond the frontier and saw that lightning made it appear to be in flames. He took this as a divine confirmation of the peasant's advice and turned back. One night he was felled by terrible stomach spasms (likely an ulcer) and from then on he lost all interest in and the ability to eat normal food and drink. Hunters brought news to his family that they had seen him living on his pastureland in a shelter of boughs. Family members went to beg him not to stay there and fall prey to exposure, and so he moved to Ranft, where the people of Obwalden built him a cell and a small chapel. He spent nineteen years in this lonely place, above a narrow gorge. He prayed much of the time and advised those who sought counsel from "Bruder Klaus" on spiritual and worldly matters. In response to questions about his eating nothing (with the exception of Holy Communion), Nicholas would reply, "God knows." Cantonal magistrates had his cell watched for a month to assure themselves of the fact that no one brought him food. The Emperor Frederick III himself came to know of him and respect him. Nicholas founded a chantry for a priest with donations and thus was enabled to assist at mass daily. At this time, the Swiss Confederation had gained its independence, and the rulers of Europe sought its alliance. Internal disputes threatened its solidarity, but an agreement was reached and put forth in the Edict of Stans. Still unresolved, however, was the issue of the inclusion of Fribourg and Soleure, and it caused such controversy that in 1481 civil war was feared. A parish priest of Stans recommended seeking a final opinion from Nicholas. This was agreed to, and he went to Nicholas. His counsel had been asked at various stages of the drafting of the edict, and it has even been said that it was drawn up in his cell. After the priest's return to Stans, the council arrived at a unanimous decision within an hour. Despite his lack of education and experience with the world, his mediation led to permanent national unity. He could not even write; he used a special seal as a signature. Letters of thanks to him from Berne and Soleure still survive. Six years later, he became ill for the last time. He suffered greatly for eight days, then died peacefully in his cell. He was buried at Sachseln. He is the patron saint of Switzerland.

NINO. Virgin. d. c. 320. December 15. She was perhaps a native of Colastri in Cappadocia. Tradition holds that as a young girl she was captured and carried off to the country, where she gained respect from the people through her strict life-style and devotion to prayer. One day a mother brought her sick child to Nino to ask her how it should be treated. Nino replied that Christ could heal the most desperate cases. She wrapped the baby in her cloak, prayed, and returned the baby to its mother in perfect health. News of this healing traveled to the sick queen of Iberia, and she sent for Nino. Nino refused to come, but the queen had her brought by force, and the queen was healed also. When the king got lost while hunting, he vowed that if Christ was God and would reveal his way home, he would believe in him. The mist cleared, and the king was converted. After being instructed by Nino, the royal couple announced to their people a change in religion, began to build a church, and permitted Nino to preach and instruct others. In the process of the building, a huge pillar, which men and oxen had been unable to move, turned itself onto its base, and after remaining suspended in the air, traveled to its place while a crowd watched. It is noteworthy that the Cathedral of Mtzkheta had always been known as the Church of the Living Pillar. The king told the Emperor Constantine what had happened and asked that bishops and priests be sent to the area. After overseeing the conversion of the area, Nino is said to have moved to a cell on a mountain at Bodbe in Kakheti. She was buried there and her tomb still remains in the cathedral of the episcopal see that was later established. She is honored as the apostle of Georgia.

NORBERT. Bishop, founder. c. 1080–1134. June 6. He was born in Xanten, in the duchy of Cleves. He was the youngest son of Heribert, count of Gennep, and Hedwig of Guise. As a young man he wished to live a comfortable and worldly life. He received minor orders and was presented the canonry in the Church of St. Victor in his native city, among other benefices. These appointments were probably received in the hopes of worldly advancement. He was appointed almoner by Emperor Henry V and took part in all the enjoyments of court life. While in a thunderstorm one day, he was thrown by his horse and lay unconscious for almost an hour. A voice supposedly told him to reform his life. He went to Xanten, where he contemplated his past life and prayed and fasted, then made a retreat at the Abbey of Siegburg. He was ordained a priest in 1115. Following another forty days' retreat he returned to Xanten where he aspired to live an evangelical and apostolic life. His behavior was somewhat extreme, however, and he made enemies; he was denounced as a hypocrite and innovator at the Council of Fritzlar in 1118 and was accused of preaching without a commission. He sold all his estates and gave the money to the poor, reserving only forty silver marks, a mule—which died soon afterward—and some ecclesiastical materials. Accompanied by two followers, he traveled barefoot to Saint-Gilles, where Pope Gelasius II was residing in exile. He confessed his misdeeds and offered to do any penance the pope demanded. The pope gave him permission to preach wherever he chose. Norbert set out barefoot in the snow. His followers fell ill and died at Valenciennes. There he was visited by Burchard, the archbishop of Cambrai, and Bl. Hugh of Fossés. Burchard was astonished at the change he saw in a man who had been a pleasure-loving courtier; and Bl. Hugh decided to become his follower and grew to be a trusted friend, who would succeed him as head of his order. Norbert went to Rheims to see Pope Callistus II, who had succeeded Gelasius II, in order to renew his sanction to preach. While there, Bartholomew, bishop of Laon, commissioned Norbert to help reform the Canons Regular of St.

Martin's at Laon. For this reason, his order gained a reputation more as a reforming order than as a new order. His actions caused a great deal of hostility, and there were two or three attempts on his life. After these, Norbert decided to leave the city for a time, but the people, censured by the Church and afraid of the emperor's anger, begged him to return. He succeeded in carrying out the majority of his reforms. At some point, as a result of his diplomacy in avoiding new disputes over investiture, the pope extended his metropolitan jurisdiction to all of Poland. He also continued to direct his Premonstratensian houses though Bl. Hugh. After Pope Honorarius II died, one group of cardinals elected Cardinal Gregory Papareschi pope (Innocent II) and another group elected Cardinal Pierleone (Anacletus II), causing a schism. Anacletus was favored by Rome, and Innocent fled to France. There, greatly due to the efforts of St. Bernard and St. Hugh of Grenoble, he was accepted as the legal pontiff. Norbert supported him, rallied favor for him in Germany, and convinced the emperor to endorse Innocent. Lothair was persuaded to raise an army to accompany Innocent into Italy, and in 1133, the emperor and the pope entered Rome, accompanied by Norbert and St. Bernard. Norbert was invested with the *pallium* and the emperor made him his chancellor. By this time, however, his health was suffering, and he died the following year. His relics were translated in 1627 by the Emperor Ferdinand II to the Premonstratensian Abbey of Strahov in Bohemia. He is depicted in art holding up a chalice with the Host in his right hand; or holding up a monstrance with St. Thomas Aquinas; or with an assassin making an attempt on his life with a dagger in a confessional.

OLYMPIAS. Widow. d. 408. December 17. She was born to a wealthy family in Constantinople. When she became orphaned, her uncle, the prefect Procopius, became her guardian and put her in the care of Theodosia, the sister of

St. Amphilochius. Procopius married her to Nebridius, prefect of Constantinople. St. Gregory Nazianzen wrote apologizing that he could not attend the wedding and enclosed a poem of good advice for Olympias. Nebridius died soon afterward, however, and Olympias was pursued again by many suitors. Emperor Theodosius urged her to marry a relative of his, but she told him that the early death of her husband was a sign from God that she should remain single. She resisted his entreaties and, angered, he ordered her fortune to be put in trust until she was thirty years old. She was prevented from seeing the bishop and attending mass. She wrote to the emperor, facetiously thanking him for easing for her the burden of managing and disposing of her money, and said that the favor would be complete if he had it divided between the Church and the poor. He restored her power over her estate in 391. Olympias then moved into a house with other maidens who wished to devote themselves to God, and she was consecrated a deaconess. She lived simply, was active in charity, and prayed a great deal. St. John Chrysostom warned her to moderate her almsgiving and to take care that she gave to those most deserving. After St. John became bishop of Constantinople in 398, he took Olympias and her followers under his protection. Under his direction she expanded abroad, and an orphanage and hospital were attached to the house. When banished monks from Nitria came to appeal against Theophilus of Alexandria, Olympias paid to lodge them. Her friends included St. Epiphanius, St. Peter of Sebaste, and St. Gregory of Nyssa. Her greatest friend, however, was St. John of Chrysostom, and when he was exiled in 404, she had to be forcibly dragged from his feet. She fell under persecution herself and was brought before Optatus, the prefect of the city, and charged with having set fire to the cathedral. The real object was to convince her to hold communion with Arsacius, the usurper of the see. She came safely through the interview and was released. She became ill, and was exiled, and moved about a great deal. In 405 she was brought back to Constantinople and sentenced to pay a heavy fine. Her community was dispersed. St. John comforted her in his letters, and she carried out certain commissions for him. She died in exile, in Nicomedia, the year after the death of St. John. Her body was taken to Constantinople. She is depicted in art kneeling, with a skull, crucifix, book, and rosary at her feet.

ONESIMUS. Martyr. d. c. 90. February 16. He was a slave of Philemon, a respected citizen of Colossae in Phrygia, who had been converted by St. Paul. Onesimus robbed his master and fled. He met St. Paul, imprisoned in Rome, who converted and baptized him. St. Paul gave him a canonical letter of recommendation to deliver to Philemon. In his letter, St. Paul asked Philemon to receive Onesimus as a brother. Perhaps making a play on Onesimus's name, which means "profitable," he told Philemon to acknowledge him as one who "was to thee unprofitable, but now profitable." Onesimus was pardoned, then was sent back to St. Paul, whom he served faithfully. St. Paul made him a bearer of his Epistle to the Colossians, later made him a preacher, and then a bishop. He is sometimes confused with St. Onesimus, the bishop of Ephesus, who showed charity to St. Ignatius on his journey to Rome in 107. The "Apostolic Constitutions" account Onesimus as bishop of Beroea in Macedonia, and his former master Philemon, bishop of Colossae. He is said to have been martyred. He is portrayed in art being stoned to death.

OSWALD. King, martyr. 604–642. August 9. He was the nephew of King St. Edwin. He was baptized at Iona during a period of exile in Scotland, after his father, Aethelfrith, had been killed by Raedwald and Edwin had seized the throne. After Edwin's death in 633 in the wars against Penda and Cadwallon, Oswald mustered a small number of troops and marched against Cadwallon, who had killed Oswald's brothers. The night before the battle, he erected a huge wooden crucifix into the ground and had his troops—among whom only a few were Christians—kneel down and pray that God would defend them. That night he had a vision in which St. Columba of Iona stretched his cloak over the sleeping troops and promised them victory. Although Cadwallon's troops were much greater in number, Oswald and his men won the battle. Oswald then began to work to spread Christianity and restore his kingdom to order. At his request, St. Aidan was sent to evangelize the country. Oswald gave him the isle of Lindisfarne for his episcopal see, and he himself acted as interpreter during St. Aidan's sermons until Aidan learned the language. His kingdom reached as far as the Firth of Forth and St. Adamnan called him the "Emperor of all Britain." He married Cyneburga, the daughter of Cynegils, the first Christian king of Wessex, to whom Oswald stood godfather at his baptism. After a few years, the pagan Penda of Mercia instigated battles again, and Oswald was killed on the field at Maserfield. As he saw his retreat cut off, he said a prayer for his soldiers, and for his bodyguard, who died with him. Oswald was mutilated and his head, arms, and hands hung upon stakes. For this reason, there have been many claims made of his relics. His head is in St. Cuthbert's coffin at Durham, where it was placed in 875. He is portrayed in art with a raven with a ring in its beak; or holding a bowl and trampling on his murderers; or blowing a horn; or carrying his own head on a sword; or as a king preaching from a pulpit; or with a dove over his head.

PACHOMIUS. Abbot. c. 290–346. May 9. He was born to pagan parents in the Upper Thebaîd, Egypt. At twenty, he was drafted into the emperor's army. The soldiers were treated with great kindness by the Christians of Latopolis while they were being shipped down the Nile under terrible conditions, and Pachomius was greatly struck by this. When the army disbanded, he returned to Khenoboskion and enrolled himself as a catechumen at a Christian church. After being baptized, he sought out an elderly desert hermit called Palaemon and asked to be his follower. They lived very austerely, doing manual labor, and often praying all night. One day while walking in the Tabennisi Desert on the banks of the Nile, Pachomius is said to have heard a voice that told him to begin a monastery there. He also experienced a vision in which an angel set out directions for the religious life. The two hermits constructed a cell there together, and Palaemon lived with him for a while before returning to solitude. Pachomius's first follower was his own brother, John, and within a short time, there were one hundred monks. He wrote the first communal rule for monks, an innovation on the common type of eremitical monachism. The life-style was severe but less rigorous than that of typical hermits. His rule influenced SS. Basil and Benedict; thirty-two passages of Benedict's rule are based on Pachomius's guidelines. He opened six other monasteries in the Thebaîd, and from 336 on lived primarily at Pabau, near Thebes, which outgrew the Tabennisi community in fame. He was an excellent administrator, and he acted as superior general. The communities were broken down into houses according to the crafts the inhabitants practiced, such as tailoring, baking, and agriculture. Goods made in the monastery were sold in Alexandria. All those in authority met each year at Easter and in August to go over annual accounts. He built a church for poor shepherds and acted as its lector, but he refused to seek ordination for the priesthood or to present any of his monks for ordination. He was an opponent of Arianism and was visited by St. Athanasius in 333. He built a nunnery for his sister on the other side of the Nile but would never see her. By his death, there were 3,000 monks in nine monasteries. He died in an epidemic. He is one of the most well-known figures in the history of monachism. He is shown in art with an angel appearing to him; or with an angel bringing the monastic rule; or walking among serpents.

PACIFICO, PACIFICUS OF SAN SEVERINO. Confessor. 1653–1721. September 24. He was born at San Severino in the March of Ancona to Antony Divini and Mary Bruni. He was baptized Charles Antony. He was orphaned at five and was taken into the household of his uncle, who treated him badly. At seventeen, he joined the Friars Minor of the Observance at Forano, and in 1670 he received the habit and took the name Pacifico. He studied and was ordained at twenty-five. He taught philosophy to the junior friars for two years. He believed that his true vocation was preaching, however, and he was sent out on missions in the area. His preaching was well received, and his reputation was enhanced by his ability to remind penitents of sins they had forgotten to confess. At thirty-five, he became deaf and blind, and he suffered ulcers in his legs that practically crippled him. He lived at Forano for a time and then moved to the friary of San Severino, where he acted as vicar and superior. He was known to make prophecies; on one occasion he predicted the victory of Prince Eugene of Savoy over the Turks at Belgrade. Despite his physical frailty, he practiced mortifications, including wearing a hair shirt and fasting so rigorously that his superiors had to restrain him. He often experienced ecstasies during mass. In 1721, as the bishop of San Severino was leaving after a visit, he cried out, "My lord—Heaven, Heaven! And I shall soon follow you." Fifteen days later the bishop died, and two months later, so did Pacifico. Miracles were reported at his tomb.

PASCHAL BAYLON. Confessor. 1540–1592. May 17. He was born at Torre Hermosa, on the borders of Castile and Aragon, to Martin Baylon and Elizabeth Jubera. He was born on a Whitsunday, and so was named "Paschal." He worked as a shepherd for his father and others until the age of twenty-four. At eighteen, after a vision, he had applied to join the Friars Minor at Loreto, 200 miles away, but the monks turned him down, knowing nothing of him personally. He applied again, a few years later, and was accepted, and he lived a strict life according to the recently initiated reforms of St. Peter of Alacantara. He worked mostly as a doorkeeper in various friaries in Spain. He spent long hours kneeling before the tabernacle, with his clasped hands outstretched. He was sent to France with a message to Father Christopher de Cheffontaines, the minister general of the Observants, and traveled wearing his habit during a dangerous time of religious wars. He was accosted several times and once narrowly escaped with his life, after he defended the doctrine of the Real Presence of the Holy Eucharist to a Calvinist preacher and a crowd. He was stoned by a party of Huguenots and suffered from the injury for the rest of his life. He was reputed to perform miracles. He died on a Whitsunday, in the friary at Villareal, just as the bell was tolling to announce the consecration at the high mass. He is the patron saint of shepherds, the Eucharist and Eucharistic guilds, societies and congresses, and of Italian women (there seems no obvious explanation for this except that his name—"Baylonna," in Italian—rhymes with "donna"). He is portrayed in art in the act of adoration before the host; or watching sheep.

PATERNUS. Hermit. d. 1058. April 10. He was probably born in Ireland, but he traveled to Westphalia, and became one of the first monks at the monastery of Abdinghof founded by St. Meinwerk. Wishing for solitude, he moved to a cell adjoining the abbey. He predicted that the city would be razed by fire within thirty days if the inhabitants didn't turn from their sins, but he was mocked as a visionary. On the Friday before Palm Sunday in 1058, fires broke out simultaneously in seven parts of the city. The city and the monastery were destroyed. The monks escaped, with the exception of Paternus, who, refusing to break the vows of enclosure, remained in his cell and was killed. His death made a great impression upon his contemporaries, St. Peter Damian and Bl. Marianus Scotus, who visited the ruins two weeks after his death, and prayed on the mat where he had died.

PATRICK. Bishop. c. 390–c. 461. March 17. It is unclear exactly where he was born—somewhere in the West between the mouth of the Severn and the Clyde—but this most popular Irish saint was born in Scotland, of British origin. His father, Calpurnius, was a deacon and a civil official, and his grandfather was a priest. At sixteen, Patrick was captured by pirates and became a slave in Ireland. He worked as a shepherd. After six years, he was told in a dream that he should be ready for a courageous effort that would take him back to his homeland. He ran away from his owner and traveled 200 miles to the coast. His initial request for free passage on a ship was turned down, but he prayed, and the sailors called him back. After a long journey, Patrick, then twenty-two or twenty-three, returned to his family. He received some kind of training for the priesthood, including study of the Latin Bible, but his learning was not of a high standard, and he was to regret this always. It is said that in visions he heard voices in the wood of Focult. There is no reliable account of his work in Ireland, where he had been a captive. Legends include the stories that he drove snakes from Ireland, and that he described the Trinity by referring to the shamrock, and that he singlehandedly—an impossible task—converted Ireland. He gathered many followers, including Benignus, who would become his successor, and he worked to evangelize the country, preaching, teaching, opening schools and monasteries, building churches, and converting chiefs and bards. He is alleged to have performed miracles, which helped in his conversions. There was some contact with the pope, and Patrick succeeded Palladius, the first Irish bishop. As the first real organizer of the Irish Church, Patrick is called the "Apostle of Ireland." According to the Annals of Ulster, the Cathedral Church of Armagh was founded in 444, and the see became a center of education and administration. Patrick organized the Church into territorial sees, raised the standard of scholarship (encouraging the teaching of Latin), and worked to bring Ireland into a closer relationship with the Western Church. His writings, including his *Confessio* (his autobiography, perhaps written in response to criticism he received), the *Lorica* (or "Breastplate"), and the "Letter to Coroticus," protesting British slave trading, are the first surely identified literature of the British Church. He may have died at Saul on Strangford Lough, where he had built his first church. Glastonbury claims his alleged relics. He is the patron saint of Ireland and of Nigeria (which was evangelized primarily by Irish clergy). He is depicted in art vested as a bishop, driving snakes before him or trampling upon them; or with a fire before him; or with a devil holding him in a fire.

PAUL. Apostle, martyr. c. 3–66. June 29. He was born in Tarsus in Cilicia, a Jew, and was given the name Saul. He received instruction in Jerusalem from Gamaliel, the famous Jewish rabbi. He was probably the best educated of the apostles and the New Testament writers. He worked as a tent maker. He became a persecutor of Christians and was present at the stoning and murder of St. Stephen, standing as a guard over the clothes of the murderers. He applied to the high priest for a commission to arrest all Jews at Damascus who confessed to Jesus Christ. On his way to Damascus, he and his band were surrounded by a great light, and he heard the words, "Saul, Saul, why dost thou persecute me?" He responded, "Who art thou, Lord?" and was answered, "Jesus of Nazareth, whom thou persecutest. It is hard for thee to kick against the goad." He was told to go on to Damascus where he would learn what was expected of him, and he was temporarily blinded. In Damascus, he was approached by Ananias, who said "Brother Saul, the Lord Jesus, who appeared to thee on thy journey, hath sent me that thou mayest receive thy sight, and be filled with the Holy Ghost." He recovered his sight as something like scales fell from his eyes. He was baptized and began to preach in synagogues that Jesus was the Son of God, amazing those who knew of his previous antipathy for Christianity. He spent three years as a solitary in "Arabia," and then returned to Damascus, where he preached zealously. He incurred so much hostility that he had to flee the city and was let down the city wall in a basket. He went to Jerusalem but returned to Tarsus when the opposition from the Jews became too great. He was sought out by St. Barnabas and accompanied him to Antioch in Syria on a mission. The community of believers gathered there became known, for the first time, as "Christians." In 44, Saul returned to Jerusalem with donations for the brethren who were suffering in a famine. He and St. Barnabas were ordained and set out on missions to Cyprus and Asia Minor. At this time, he took the name Paul. In Lystra, after healing a cripple, the two men were initially thought to be gods—Barnabas was believed to be Jupiter and Paul, Mercury, because he was "the chief speaker." The crowd's mood changed, however, and they were stoned, and Paul was left for dead; they escaped. In 49, Paul returned to Jerusalem and attended a meeting at which the attitude of the Christian Church toward Gentile converts was decided. From 49 to 52 he traveled on missions with Silas, gathering Timothy in Lystra. A vision summoned him to Macedonia, and he was joined by St. Luke. In Philippi Paul exorcised a girl, for which Paul and Silas were beaten and imprisoned but later released. At Athens Paul gave an address on the Areopagus, in which he made a reference to their altar dedicated "to the unknown god." He settled in Corinth for a year and a half. He returned to Jerusalem for a short time in 52, and set out on his third missionary journey. He traveled to Galatia, Mace-

303

donia, Achaia, and then returned to Jerusalem. During a winter at Ephesus his preaching interfered with the city's silversmithing trade, which made and sold images of Diana. He was arrested in Jerusalem and was sent into captivity in Caesarea for two years. Paul appealed, as a Roman citizen, for a hearing by the emperor. He was sent on a ship to Crete, but the ship was wrecked on Malta. He was transferred to another ship and brought to Rome. It appears that he was tried and acquitted in Rome after a long imprisonment. By some accounts, he traveled to Spain, but it is probable that he spent the winter of 65 in Nicopolis. Upon his return to Rome, he was again imprisoned. Tradition holds that he was beheaded on the Ostian Way, at Aquae Salviae (now Tre Fontane). His fourteen Letters, addressed mostly to churches he founded, belong to the deposit of divine revelation. His burial place is honored in the Basilica of St. Paul-Outside-the-Walls. He is the patron saint of the lay apostolate, the "Cursillo" movement and Catholic Action, and of Malta and Greece. In art he is shown as a thin-faced, elderly man with a high forehead, receding hair, and a long pointed beard, although the apocryphal *Acts of Paul and Thecla* say he was short, bald and bandy-legged. He usually holds a sword and a book; or has three springs of water near him.

PAUL OF THE CROSS. Founder. 1694–1775. October 19. He was born in Ovada, Italy, the oldest son of noble but impoverished parents. At fifteen, he began an extreme penitential regime at his home in Castellazzo, Lombardy. At some point, he turned down a chance for an inheritance. He joined the Venetian army and fought against the Turks in 1714. A year later he was discharged, and he returned to his life of devotion. He refused to marry and spent several years in retreat at Castellazzo. In 1720, he experienced a vision of the Virgin Mary in a black habit with the name "Jesus" and a cross in white on her chest. She told him to found an order devoted to preaching the Passion of Christ. He received permission to do so from the bishop of Alessandria, and during a retreat, Paul drew up the rule. With his brother, also his closest confidant, he went to Rome to seek papal approval. They were turned down, but they returned in 1725 and Paul was given permission to accept novices by Pope Benedict XIII, who ordained the brothers in 1727. They took a house on Monte Argentaro, but the severity of the rule cost them many of their first novices. They opened their first monastery in 1737 and received approval of a modified rule in 1741. The Barefooted Clerks of the Holy Cross and Passion—the Passionists—began to spread throughout Italy. Two main objectives were the ministry of the sick and dying, and the reconciling of sinners. Soon their preachers were much in demand. Paul was made the first superior general, against his will, at the first general chapter, and filled the office until his death. He preached to huge crowds throughout the papal states, scourging himself in front of them. He was one of the most famous preachers of his time, and he is said to have had the gift of prophecy and healing, and to have appeared to people in visions. Crowds fought to touch him and get a scrap of his clothing. The Passionists received final approval from Pope Clement XIV in 1769, and two years later, Paul opened a convent for nuns at Corneto. He lived mainly in Rome by the Basilica of SS. John and Paul, which Clement gave to the order. He was ill for three years before he died and is buried at the Basilica of SS. John and Paul.

PAUL MICKI. Martyr. 1562–1597. February 6. He was born in Tounucumada, Japan, the son of a Japanese military chief. He attended the Jesuit college of Anziquiama. He joined the Jesuits in 1580 and became known as an eloquent preacher. He was crucified with twenty-five others during the persecution of Christians under the *taikō*, Toyotomi Hideyoshi, ruler of Japan in the name of the emperor. Crucified at the same time was Francis, a carpenter who was arrested while watching the executions, and Gabriel, the nineteen-year-old son of the Franciscans' porter.

PAULA. Widow. 347–404. January 26. She was a wealthy descendant of the Scipios and the Gracchi, and she lived in Rome. She was married to Toxotius and had five children, including St. Eustochium, but her husband died when she was thirty-two. She grieved terribly until her friend, St. Marcella, suggested that she devote herself to God. She began to live very simply, giving up social activities, sleeping on the floor, and giving much to the poor. She acted as hostess to St. Epiphanius of Salamis and to Paulinus of Antioch when they visited Rome, and it was through them that she met St. Jerome. After her daughter, St. Blesilla, died suddenly, Paula fell into grief again, until St. Jerome wrote to her from Bethlehem to comfort her and to warn her against giving in to her mourning. At this time she decided that she wished to live as a hermit and devote herself fully to God. With St. Eustochium, she left her home and family for Africa in 385. She visited St. Epiphanius in Cyprus and met St. Jerome in Antioch. They pilgrimaged through Palestine and on to Egypt to visit the monks and hermits there. In 386 they came to Bethlehem. The women built a hospice, a monastery for men, and a convent for women. The sisters worked hard and lived austerely. Men were not allowed entrance. Paula built other buildings and churches, showing herself so generous in funding them that it caused her financial difficulty later in life. She attended St. Jerome, becoming his assistant as well as his confidante, for her knowledge of Greek and Hebrew proved a help to him in his writing. She convinced St. Jerome to take an interest in the dispute over Origenism. Her granddaughter Paula was put into her care and would one day succeed her as director of the convent. St. Jerome wrote her biography. She was buried under the Church of the Nativity, in Bethlehem. She is the patron saint of widows. She is portrayed in art as a pilgrim leading her daughter; or with a book and a black veil fringed with gold; or with a sponge in her hand; or prostrate before the cave of Bethlehem.

PAULINUS OF NOLA. Bishop. c. 354–431. June 22. He was born at or near Bordeaux. His father was prefect of Gaul and had lands in Italy, Aquitaine, and Spain. Paulinus was taught poetry and rhetoric by the poet Ausonius. He made a reputation for himself at a young age at the bar, and, according to St. Jerome, he was admired for his diction, imagination, and sentiments. He held several public offices and traveled extensively. He married a Spaniard, Therasia, and retired to a comfortable life on his estate in Aquitaine. There he met St. Delphinus, the bishop of Bordeaux, and Paulinus was converted by his wife and the saint and was baptized. The couple traveled to Spain to live on the wife's estate in 390. She bore a son, but the baby died a week later. The couple decided to live a more devout and charitable life, and they sold much of her property and gave the money to the needy. In 393, in keeping with the wish of the people, Paulinus was ordained a priest, although he had not even been ordained a deacon. He sold much of his property in Aquitaine and, despite the opposition of friends, again gave the money to the needy. They traveled to Italy, where he was well received by St. Ambrose, and he also became friends with St. Martin of Tours. In Rome, Paulinus met disapproval for the unorthodox method of his ordination, so they went on to Nola, where Paulinus had decided to settle. They moved into a large building near the tomb of St. Felix. He built a church for Fondi, an aquaduct and basilica in Nola, and supported many needy people, some of whom were lodged in the house. He and some followers lived a monastic life in the upper part of the building. Each year Paulinus wrote a birthday poem in St. Felix's honor. He succeeded as bishop of Nola in 409 and ruled until his death. He kept up a correspondence with the leading clergy of the day, among them St. Jerome and St. Augustine; Augustine wrote *On the Care of the Dead* in response to a question posed by Paulinus. He was buried in the church he built in honor of St. Felix. His relics were translated to Rome, then were returned to Nola by St. Pius X in 1909. He was considered to be the best Christian poet of his time after Prudentius. Thirty-two poems and fifty-one letters survive. He is portrayed in art preaching to the poor; or giving alms with a spade at his side; or holding a church.

PELAGIA. Martyr, virgin. d. c. 311. June 9. She was a disciple of St. Lucian at Antioch. During a persecution, probably under Diocletian, soldiers were sent to arrest her. She leaped from the top of her house into the sea to save her virginity. St. John Chrysostom wrote about her, praising her courage, and suggested that her suicide was divinely inspired. Various romances and legends have grown from this story. The most well known holds that Pelagia was a beautiful and flamboyant actress of Antioch, who was converted by the understanding St. Nonnus, and became a hermit in a cave on the Mount of Olives. She is portrayed in art falling from a roof or a window.

PETER. Apostle. d. c. 64. June 29. He was a Galilean, and his original home was at Bethsaida. He was the brother of St. Andrew. He was married and worked as a fisherman; he may have been the leader of a "cooperative" that included the sons of Zebedee. His name was Simon, but Jesus told him that his name would be Peter—"the rock." It is he who, speaking for the other apostles, said, "Thou art the Christ, the Son of the living God." To this, Christ responded, "You are Peter and upon this rock I will build my church . . . and I will give you keys to the kingdom of heaven." Peter made his boat always available to Jesus. He was present at the raising from the dead of Jairus's daughter, and the Transfiguration and Agony in the Garden. Together with St. John he was entrusted with the preparations for the Last Supper. The importance of Peter's position among the apostles is indicated by the great detail in which his three times denying Christ in the courtyard of Pontius Pilate's palace is related by all four evangelists. Christ appeared to Peter after the resurrection and told him of his mission to feed the flock and predicted his martyrdom. After the Ascension, Peter continued to take a leading part in all activities of the Church. All the details that are known of Peter come from the Acts of the Apostles and allusions in his and St. Paul's Epistles. He was the first apostle to preach to the Gentiles. He was also the first to perform a miracle, and he became the most celebrated miracle worker; his shadow was said to heal the sick. He was imprisoned by Herod Agrippa around 43, but he is said to have escaped, guided by an angel. The passion of St. Peter occurred in Nero's Rome, but there is no written account. Tradition has it that he was imprisoned in the Mamertine prison, and Tertullian says that he was crucified. Eusebius recounts that, according to his own wishes, he was hung head downward. The place of his crucifixion is believed to have been in the gardens of Nero, where many executions occurred. Tradition makes him Rome's first bishop, but the belief that his papacy lasted twenty-five years is unreliable. He is called the "Prince of the Apostles." His relics are beneath the high altar of St. Peter's in Rome. He is the patron saint of fishermen and popes. He is depicted in art as an elderly man of sturdy build, holding a key or keys, a ship, or a fish, and a book; or being crucified head downward; or robed as a pope with keys and a double-barred cross; or with a cock (a symbol of betrayal).

PETER CANISIUS. Confessor, doctor of the Church. 1521–1597. December 21. He was born in Nijimegen in Holland, the oldest son of Jacob Kanis, who was made a noble after tutoring the sons of the duke of Lorraine. After Peter's mother died, his father remarried, and his stepmother raised him religiously. He took his master of arts at Cologne at the age of nineteen. In keeping with his father's wish, he studied canon law in Louvain. He broke off his studies to realize his vocation, however, and he took a vow of celibacy and returned to Cologne to study theology. During a retreat held by Bl. Peter Faber, he vowed to join the Order of the Society of Jesus. He gave his inheritance to the poor, became a novice, and lived a community life in Cologne, visiting the sick and giving religious instruction. He began to write, his first publications being editions of the works of St. Cyril of Alexandria and St. Leo the Great. After being ordained, he earned a reputation as a preacher and attended two sessions of the Council of Trent as a delegate. He was summoned to Rome by St. Ignatius and worked with him for five months. He then went to Messina to teach in the first Jesuit school, but he returned shortly afterward to Rome. He was chosen to go to Germany in answer to a request from Duke William IV of Bavaria for Catholic professors to counteract heresy in the schools. Peter reformed the university and was made rector and then vice chancellor. He achieved a spiritual revival among the people through his preaching, catechizing, and his movement against the sale of immoral and heretical books. In 1552 he was called to Vienna on a similar mission by King Ferdinand. The churches were poorly attended when he arrived, but he earned the trust and following of the people by his efforts to relieve the sick and dying during an outbreak of the plague. He was appointed bishop to Vienna; he agreed to hold the office only for one year, without episcopal orders, title, or benefits. The parishes were virtually without clergy, the monasteries were deserted, and there had been no ordinations for twenty years. During this period he began work on his Summary of Christan Doctrine, and his *Catechism*, which became very popular. The *Catechism* passed through 200 editions before he died and was translated into fifteen European languages. He went to Prague to found a college and was made provincial, against his will, of a new province made up of South Germany, Austria, and Bohemia. The college gained such a fine reputation that Protestants sent their children to it, and in two years, Peter brought most of the city back to the faith. He moved to Augsburg in 1559 at the request of King Ferdinand, and he induced there a similar revival of the faith. He also influenced the Reichstag to restore public schools. Throughout his life he insisted upon the importance of schools and writing for publication; he is credited as one of the founders of the Catholic press. He wrote much during this period, composing a "Manual for Catholics," a martyrology, a revision of the Augsburg Breviary, and the General Prayer, which is still recited in Germany. At the end of his term as provincial, he moved to Dillingen in Bavaria, where he directed the university. He taught, acted as a confessor, and composed the first of a series of books he was commissioned to write as a reply against Protestantism. He acted as court chaplain for several years at Innsbruck and helped to resolve a rift between the emperor and Pope Pius IV. In 1577, he was relieved of the task of writing the book series as a result of ill health, although he continued to preach, make visitations as vice provincial, and give missions. In 1580, he was asked to go to Fribourg in Switzerland to build a college, which he did, raising funds and overcoming other problems in the process. The college became the University of Fribourg. For more than eight years he preached regularly, and he is credited with holding Fribourg to the faith during an uneasy time in history. His health broke down further, however, and in 1591 he suffered a paralytic seizure. He recovered enough to write, with the help of a secretary, and died six years later. He is considered to have been the leader of the Catholic Counter-Reformation in German lands, and he is called the "Second Apostle of Germany"—St. Boniface having been the first.

PETER MARY CHANEL. Martyr. 1803–1840. April 28. He was born in the diocese of Belley. At seven he became a shepherd to his father's sheep. The Abbé Trompier of the parish of Cras, having recognized his intelligence and devoutness, obtained permission to have Peter enter a small school he had started. Peter performed well and went on to the seminary. After his ordination, he was given the parish of Crozet, which had earned a bad reputation. Over three years, his attendance to the sick gained the parishioners' confidence, and he brought about a spiritual revival. In 1831, wishing to become a missionary, he joined the Marists, but he worked another five years in the seminary of Belley. In 1836, the Marists received papal approval, and Peter was sent with a small band of missionaries to the Pacific. With a companion, he went to the Islands of Futuna, under French sovereignty near Fiji, where cannibalism had previously flourished. They gained the confidence of the people by attending the sick, learned the language, and began to teach. The chieftain became jealous of their influence, however, and was further angered when his own son said he wished to be baptized. Peter was attacked by a band of warriors who killed him with a club and cut up his body with their hatchets. His martyrdom served his cause, however, for within a few months the island was Christianized. He is the patron saint of Oceania.

PETER CHRYSOLOGUS. Bishop, doctor of the Church. c. 406–c. 450. July 30. He was born in Imola, a town in eastern Emilia. He was ordained a deacon by Bishop Cornelius, and eventually he succeeded Archbishop John of Ravenna. His first sermon so impressed Empress Galla that from then on she generously endowed his building projects. Her son, the Emperor Valentinian III, and St. Leo the Great respected and supported him as well. He built a baptistery and a church dedicated to St. Andrew in Classis, the port of Ravenna. Although his discourses were all quite brief—he did not wish to strain the attention span of his hearers—on the basis of them he was declared a doctor of the Church by Pope Benedict XIII in 1729. He was called "Chrysologus" as an allusion to his "golden speech." Sometimes he would become so caught up in the excitement of his preaching that he would become momentarily speechless. He received St. Germanus of Auxerre in Ravenna in 448, and when Germanus died there, he officiated at his funeral. He was forewarned of his own death soon afterward and returned to Imola for his final days. He is shown in art being presented to Pope Sixtus III by SS. Peter and Apollinaris; or with a dish in his hand.

PETER CLAVER. Confessor. 1581–1654. September 9. He was born the son of a farmer in Verdu, in Catalonia. He attended the University of Barcelona, where he graduated with distinction. He received minor orders and joined the Society of Jesus at Tarragona. He then attended the college of Montesione in Palma, in Majorca, where he met St. Alphonsus Rodriguez. St. Alphonsus foretold Peter's work, and Peter approached his superior, asking to be sent to the West Indies. He was put off for the time and traveled to Barcelona to study theology. Two years later, he became the representative of the Aragon province on the mission of Spanish Jesuits to New Granada. They landed at Cartagena. He finished his studies at the house of Santa Fé, working there as a sacristan, porter, infirmarian, and cook. He was sent to the new house of the Society at Tunja for his tertianship. He returned to Cartagena in 1615 and was ordained. The port of Cartagena was one of the main centers of the slave trade, and the leader of work was Father Alfonso de Sandoval. He attended the incoming slaves with medicine and food, and tended to the ill among them. He ministered compassionately, despite the fact he couldn't communicate with them verbally. He had a company of seven interpreters and with them he taught the slaves and prepared them for baptism. He sought to make them feel that despite their rank as slaves, as Christians they retained dignity and worth. He is said to have baptized over 300,000 slaves in his forty years of ministry; in one year, he heard more than 5,000 confessions. He is said to have had the gift of reading hearts and prophesying. He himself performed severe personal penances. Each year he made a tour of the plantations to check on his charges, lodging in the slave quarters to see that the few laws for their protection were being enforced, and his presence was often unwelcome by the owners. But Peter continued his rounds, despite their, and some of his superiors', complaints. He visited the two main hospitals in Cartagena every week and was said to perform miracle cures. He also evangelized Protestant traders and sailors and converted an Anglican official whom he met while visiting prisoners of war on a ship. In 1650, he went to preach the jubilee among the Negroes along the coast, but illness forced his return to Cartagena. An epidemic had attacked the city, however, and he fell prey to it. After receiving the last sacraments he recovered, but for the rest of his life he suffered weakness and shaking. He was forced to retire, but he continued to hear confessions. He was largely forgotten in the monastery and was neglected by those looking after him, but he was faithfully visited by his good friend Doña Isabella de Urbina and her sister.

PETER DAMIAN. Bishop, cardinal, doctor of the Church. 1007–1072. February 21. He was born in Ravenna, was orphaned young, and grew up in the house of his brother, who treated him like a slave. He was made to tend swine as soon as he was capable. Another brother, the archpriest of Ravenna, felt sorry for him and had him educated. Peter appears to have taken his surname, Damian, after this kind brother. He went to school at Faenza and then Parma and performed very well. He began a regime of fasting and prayer, and he wore a hair shirt to remind himself to withstand temptations. He was generous to the poor and served them at his own table. He decided to seek out the life of a solitary. Two followers of St. Benedict from the Fonte Avellana of the reform of St. Romuald called upon him, and he decided to join their house. The hermits dwelt in pairs in cells, lived a very strict life, and devoted themselves mostly to prayer and reading. He became learned in the Scriptures and was induced to succeed the superior. He founded five other hermitages. He was always compassionate in his personal dealings, but he was uncompromising in his writing; he reprimanded bishops for playing chess and wealthy monks for wandering. He believed that communal life was less admirable than eremitic life. He preached against simony, clerical marriage, and laxity in the monasteries. For many years he carried out various commissions for the popes, and in 1057, Stephen IX made him cardinal-bishop of Ostia. Peter continually asked leave to resign the post, but it was not until Alexander II became pope that he was allowed to return to his solitary life, and then only with the understanding that the pope could employ him upon occasion. He became a simple monk, refusing to direct the communities. He made wooden spoons and other items when he was not praying or engaged in other work, not wishing to be unoccupied for a moment. In 1069, he persuaded the emperor Henry IV of Germany not to divorce his wife, Bertha. He was sent by the pope to Ravenna to calm the disorder after the excommunication of Henry, the archbishop. The archbishop died just before he arrived, but Peter made his accomplices recognize their guilt and gave them penance. On his trip home, he fell ill of a fever in a monastery outside Faenza and died. He was one of the forerunners of the Hildebrandine reform. He wrote prolifically and articulately; his poetry is among the best of the Middle Ages. He is depicted in art with a cardinal's hat by his side; or praying before a cross, with a miter and cardinal's hat on the ground.

PETER FOURIER. Founder. 1565–1640. December 9. He was born at Mirecourt, in Lorraine. At fifteen his father sent him to the university directed by the Jesuits at Pont-à-Mousson; Bl. William Lacey was a fellow student. After completing a course of studies, he opened a school in his home. At twenty, he joined the Canons Regular of St. Augustine at Chaumousey. He was ordained in 1589. He pursued further theological studies—exhibiting a remarkable memory—and obtained his doctorate. He was made procurator of his monastery and vicar of the parish, but his efforts to reform the observance of the abbey were badly received. In 1597 he chose to minister to the parish of Mattaincourt, having been told it was in deplorable shape. He lived very austerely, building a fire only when he had visitors. It was during this period that he came to see the importance of free education for children. His first efforts on behalf of boys were unsuccessful. He decided to concentrate on girls and had four women trained in the house of canonesses of Poussey in 1598. They opened a free school at Mattaincourt, where he instigated certain requirements for the girls' study. He urged that all poor children should be educated free in order to help them to live with dignity. The new congregation of nuns received papal approval in 1616 and were called the Canonesses Regular of St. Augustine of the Congregation of Our Lady. In 1628 Pope Urban VIII approved a fourth vow that bound the nuns to the free education of children. In 1622, Peter was appointed visitor to the canons regular by the Holy See. Mgr. John de

Porcelets de Maillane, the bishop of Toul, asked him to reform the houses of his order and unite them into one reformed congregation. His efforts were not welcomed, but by 1629 he had accomplished his mission. The Canons Regular of Lorraine merged into the Congregation of Our Savior, and Peter was unwillingly made superior general in 1632. The reformed canons, in keeping with his wishes, were willing to take up the work of teaching boys, but when this proposal was brought up in Rome in 1627, it was denied. The canons did direct several colleges, however, and in the eighteenth century, the Jesuits surrendered their colleges to the canons regular. In 1636 Peter was asked to make an oath of allegiance to King Louis XIII. As a supporter of the house of Lorraine and Duke Charles IV, he refused, and exiled himself to Gray in Franche-Comté. He became chaplain of a convent and taught in a free school he opened there. He died four years later.

PHILIP. Apostle. d. c. 80. May 3. Philip was a native of Bethsaida in Galilee and was a follower of St. John the Baptist. There is little mention of him in the synoptic Gospels except in the lists of apostles. St. John's Gospel relates that Philip was called by Christ the same day as St. Peter and St. Andrew. In the accounts of him, he emerges as a careful and rational man. When Bathanael asks, "Can anything good come from Nazareth?" Philip responds equably, "Come and see." When Jesus asks him where they can get bread to feed the 5,000, he responds, "Two hundred pennyworth of bread is not sufficient for them that every one may take a little." The evening before Christ's Passion, Philip asks him, "Lord, show us the Father, and it is enough for us." He is one of the apostles who spent ten days in the upper room waiting for the coming of the Holy Ghost. Nothing more of him is known for sure. After the Ascension, he is thought to have preached in Asia Minor and to have been martyred at Hierapolis in Phrygia under Emperor

Domitian. His alleged relics were translated to Rome and placed in the Basilica of the Twelve Apostles. He is the patron saint of Uruguay. He is depicted in art as an elderly, bearded man, holding a basket of loaves and a cross (upon which he is supposed to have been martyred upside down). The cross also may be an allusion to the weapon with which *The Golden Legend* says he drove away a dragon of the Temple of Mars.

PHILIP NERI. Founder. 1515–1595. May 26. He was born in Florence, the son of a notary, Francis Neri. His mother died when he was young, but his father remarried and the stepmother was good to the children. Philip was educated by the Dominicans at San Marco. At eighteen, he was sent to San Germano, to a relative who it was hoped would pass on his prosperous business to Philip. Soon after his arrival, however, he had a mystical experience that caused his conversion, and from then on he was indifferent to material things. He went to Rome, departing without money. He sought shelter there with Galeotto Caccia, a customs official, whose sons he tutored. He lived like a monk in the attic room for two years, praying for whole days and nights. He then began taking philosophy and theology at the Sapienza and at Sant' Agostino, and he studied for three years. He then abruptly abandoned his studies, sold most of his books, and began to preach. He spent his nights praying, primarily at the catacomb of St. Sebastian on the Appian Way. He preached from street corners, engaging in conversations with all ranks of people, and he influenced many to work with the sick in hospitals and to visit the Seven Churches. In 1544, he experienced a vision in which a globe of fire entered his mouth and dilated his heart; permanent physical effects of this experience were said to be found after his death. With his confessor, Father Persiano Rossa, he founded in 1548 a confraternity of poor laymen who met for spiritual exercises in the Church of San

Salvatore in Campo. The group popularized the devotion of the Forty Hours in Rome and looked after needy pilgrims. This work eventually evolved into the hospital of Santa Trinità dei Pellegrini, which in the jubilee year of 1575 cared for 145,000 pilgrims. He was ordained in 1551 and lived with Father Rossa at San Girolamo della Carità, where he worked primarily as a confessor. He was a witty and shrewd man, and aided by a gift for reading consciences, he converted many. He apparently delighted in practical jokes but was always very gentle. He considered going on foreign missions, but a Benedictine of St. Paul's convinced him that his apostolate was in Rome. He is said to have experienced ecstasies so often while saying mass that his servers sometimes left the church for a couple of hours and returned to continue serving after he had recovered. A room was built over the nave of San Girolamo for the people who attended his informal spiritual conferences. He and his priest followers grew to be called Oratorians, because they rang a little bell to summon attendees to the gatherings. The music called "Oratorio" was named for the Oratorians, because they used music in their services. During Philip's lifetime, he and his Oratory became a center of religious life in the city, and he became the most popular figure in Rome. He would later be called "the Second Apostle of Rome." A few years later, Philip sent five of his ordained disciples to the church of San Giovanni, the direction of which had been given to him by his fellow Florentines in Rome. Cesare Baronius, the historian, was among them. Philip drew up a simple rule of life, but he forbade them to bind themselves by vows or to give up their property. The congregation grew and in 1575 received approval from Pope Gregory XIII. The pope gave them the church of Santa Maria in Vallicella. Philip wished to rebuild the ancient church. Contributions flowed in for this work—including donations from Charles Borromeo and the pope. In 1577, the Congregation of the Oratory was transferred to the new church, the Chiesa Nuova. Philip remained in San Girolamo, having grown attached to his rooms, and did not move to the new location until 1584, when he did so according to the wish of the pope. Although he made himself available to his followers, he continued to live and eat alone. In 1593, he averted a conflict between France and the Holy See by influencing the decision to absolve the former Protestant Henry IV of Navarre. He died after a hemorrhage, his last act being to raise his hand to bless his followers. He was buried in the Chiesa Nuova. In art he is shown as a priest, usually in red, carrying a lily or with lilies around him.

PIUS V. Pope. 1504–1572. April 30. He was born Michael Ghislieri in Bosco, in the diocese of Tortona. He took the Dominican habit at the priory of Voghera at the age of fourteen. After being ordained, he acted as a lector in theology and philosophy for sixteen years, and for a time he was novice master and an administrator of the order. He was chosen bishop of Nepi and Sutri in 1556. In 1557 he was made inquisitor general against the Protestants in Italy and Spain. He was appointed cardinal the same year, in order, as he said, that irons should be riveted to his feet to prevent him from creeping back into the peace of the cloister. He was made bishop by Pope Pius IV of the war-depleted see of Mondovi, to which he soon brought order. In 1565, he succeeded Pius IV as pope, taking the name Pius V. Charles Borromeo had given Michael a great deal of support in the election, trusting that he would act as a much-needed reformer. His judgment proved true: on Pius's coronation, the money usually distributed to the crowds was given to the hospitals and the poor, and money for a banquet for the cardinals and other dignitaries was given to poor convents. One of Pius's first actions was to demand that bishops should live in their dioceses and parish priests in their parishes. His efforts at regulating his see embraced issues ranging from the abolition of bullfighting and prostitution, to cleaning out the Roman *curia* and eliminating nepotism, to cutting down the activities of bandits. He brought in shipments of corn during a famine at his own expense. He was, however, severely criticized for his harshness to heretics. The catechism ordered by the Council of Trent was completed during his rule, and he ordered translations made. He also commissioned the best edition to date of the writings of St. Thomas Aquinas; it was he who made Thomas a doctor of the Church. He had hoped to convert Queen Elizabeth of England, but in 1570 he felt compelled to excommunicate her, absolving her subjects of their allegiance to her as queen. This served only to endanger the Catholics in her realm, however, and many were accused of treason and martyred. Pius fell victim to a painful illness, which would kill him within the year. He is enshrined at Santa Maria Maggiore in Rome. He was one of the most important popes of the Counter-Reformation. He is shown in art reciting a rosary; or with a fleet in the distance; or with the feet of a crucifix withdrawn as he tries to kiss them.

PIUS X. Pope. 1835–1914. August 21. He was born in Riese in Venetia to a poor family and named Giuseppe Sarto. His father was the municipal messenger and postman. He attended the local school, went on to the school at Castelfranco, and then won a scholarship to the seminary at Padua. In his school days he would walk four miles barefoot to save his shoes. At twenty-three he was ordained, and engaged in a pastoral ministry for seventeen years. He became a canon of Treviso, and in 1884, the bishop of Mantua. In 1892 he was made a cardinal priest by Pope Leo XIII and was given the metropolitan see of Venice. In 1903 he was elected pope, after the favored candidate, Cardinal Puzyna of Cracow, withdrew his candidacy—the Emperor Franz Joseph of Austria having vetoed it. Pius's first action was to end the right of the civil power to interfere in a papal election. When the French government decreed the separation of church and state and proposed a method of dealing with ecclesiastical property, Pius broke off diplomatic relations with France, condemned the law of separation, and forbade the proposed method of property management. He encouraged Italian Catholics to become more active in politics. Pius made efforts to purge the Church of modernism, decreeing in 1907 that certain writers and propositions be condemned. Dangerous tendencies set out in the encyclical letter *Pascendi* were disciplined. He recommended daily communion when possible and directed that children receive communion at the age of seven, "the age of reason," and that communion be made available to the sick. He enacted instructions to restore the use of congregational singing of the Roman plainchant. He fostered the codification of canon law and reorganized the administration of the Holy See. He also commissioned the revision and correction of the Vulgate text of the Bible, and he founded the Biblical Institute for scriptural studies, which was placed under the direction of the Jesuits. He was greatly criticized, his uncompromising tactics raising much opposition in the Church itself. The outbreak of war in 1914 is said to have killed him. His will read, "I was born poor; I lived poor; I wish to die poor." Miracles have been attributed to his intercession. He is the patron saint of sick pilgrims, due to his establishment of the Unio Nationalis Italicae Traiciendis Aegrotis Lapurdum et ad Santuaria Internationalia, a society dedicated to taking sick people to the Italian shrine of Lapurdo.

POLYCARP OF SMYRNA. Confessor, martyr. c. 69–c. 155. February 23. He was a disciple of St. John the Evangelist and trained many other followers, including St. Irenaeus and Papias. He kissed the chains of St. Ignatius of Antioch on his way to martyrdom in Rome, and Ignatius asked him to watch over his church at Antioch and to write in his name to the churches of Asia that he could not attend himself. Polycarp sent a letter to the Philippians—which survives—soon after. Polycarp went to Rome to discuss with Pope St. Anicetus the timetable of keeping of Easter and other matters; they disagreed, but agreed to pursue their own customs. During the persecution in Asia in the reign of Marcus Aurelius, Polycarp hid, but he was betrayed by a slave who had been threatened with torture. He was arrested during a pagan festival. Realizing he was discovered, Polycarp refused to flee, saying "God's will be done." He met his pursuers at the door, ordered them dinner, and asked for some time to pray. He was taken before the tribunal of the proconsul but refused to speak against his faith. The people asked that he be thrown to lions, but the time of games was over. They then asked that he be burned alive. They tied his hands behind his back. It was said that there was a smell of incense as he burned, and he was then pierced with a sword, and a dove was said to come forth as well as enough blood to quench the fire. His body was burned to ashes to prevent the Christians from taking it. His martyrdom was written of by an eyewitness. The *Martyrium Polycarpi* is the oldest authentic example of the *acta* of a martyr. He is depicted in art trampling on a pagan; or with a funeral pyre near him; or stabbed and burned to death; or being burned in various ways.

PONTIAN. Martyr, pope. d. c. 235. August 13. He was a Roman and the son of Calpurnius. He succeeded Pope St. Urban I in 230. He convened a synod in Rome in 232 at which the condemnation of Origenism at Alexandria was confirmed. He was exiled to Sardinia during the persecution under Emperor Maximinus. He may have been sent to the mines. In Sardinia he met the exiled St. Hippolytus and brought him to a reconciliation with the Church. He resigned his office in 235 to allow the election of a nephew. It is most likely that he died of bad treatment, although a tradition holds that he was beaten to death.

PORPHYRY OF GAZA. Bishop. 353–420. February 26. He was born in Thessalonica, Macedonia. At twenty-five, he became a monk in the desert of Skete and spent five years living in a monastery. He lived for five years as a hermit in the Jordan Valley in Palestine, then moved to Jerusalem. He arranged for his friend and follower, Mark, to sell his inheritance, giving the money to the poor. He worked as a shoemaker, living very austerely, and at forty was ordained. He became bishop of Gaza in 396, but was much harassed by the pagans in his see. His position was aided by the Emperor Arcadius's order that a temple to Marnas, which had been a cause of great trouble to the Christians in Gaza, be destroyed. Other pagan temples and idols were destroyed as well. Riots resulted, and his life was threatened. He built a great church on the site of the razed temple to Marnas, and it was consecrated in 408. By the time he died, his see was free of paganism. His friend, Mark, who had become his deacon, wrote his biography.

PROSPER OF REGGIO. Bishop. d. c. 466. June 25. There is little known of him for certain; he appears to have been recognized chiefly for his charity. Tradition holds that he distributed his goods to the poor and died after ruling as bishop of Reggio in the province of Emilia for twenty-two years. He was buried in a church he had built in honor of St. Apollinaris outside Reggio. His relics were translated in 703 to a new church built in his honor by Thomas, the bishop of Reggio. He is the patron saint of Reggio.

RAPHAEL THE ARCHANGEL. September 29. He is one of the three archangels mentioned by name in the Bible. According to the history of Tobias, Raphael was sent by God to minister to the old Tobias, who was blind and ill, and to Sara, daughter of Raguel, whose seven bridegrooms had each died on the night of their wedding. When the young Tobias traveled into Media to collect money owed to his father, Raphael, in the form of a man named Azarius, accompanied him, helping him in his difficulties. From Sara, "he chased the evil spirit," and Tobias married her safely. The fact that he effected cures on his journey and that his name means "God has healed" had brought Raphael to be identified with the angel who moved the waters of the healing sheep pool (John v: 1–4). He is identified as an angel who "healed" the earth when it was tainted by the sins of the fallen angels in the apocryphal Enoch (10:7). He is the patron saint of travelers and safe journeys, of young people leaving home, of pharmacists, of blind people and against eye diseases (he gave young Tobias ointment to cure his father), and of health inspectors (he looked out for the bodily welfare of Tobias). In art he is shown as an archangel; or as a young man carrying a staff or a fish; or walking with Tobias; or holding a bottle or flask.

RAYMUND OF PEÑAFORT. Confessor. c. 1180–1275. January 7. He was born in Peñafort, Catalonia, into a family descended from the counts of Barcelona and allied to the kings of Aragon. By the age of twenty, he was teaching philosophy in Barcelona. He did this without pay and was greatly respected. At thirty, he went to Bologna to pursue studies in civil and canon law, took a doctorate, and again taught without pay. In 1219, he was made archdeacon by Berengarius, the bishop of Barcelona. In 1222 he took the Dominican habit. In response to his request for a penance to atone for the self-satisfaction with which he said he had taught, his superiors asked him to write a collection of cases of conscience for the use of confessors and moralists. The result was the *Summa*, the first work of its kind and one that exercised a great influence on the penitential system. He became famous for his preaching, traveling all over Spain to speak to Moors and Christians, who were returned from Moorish slavery. He was called to Rome in 1230 by Pope Gregory IX and was made his confessor. Raymund asked the pope for a penance to speed through all petitions made by the poor. Raymund was asked to assemble all the decrees of popes and councils since the collection made by Gratian in 1150, and in three years he compiled the five books of the "Decretals," which would remain the most authoritative codification of ecclesiastical legislation until 1917. He returned to Barcelona for his health and picked up his work as confessor and preacher. He filled various commissions at the request of the king and the pope. In 1235, he was chosen archbishop of Tarragona, but he refused the charge. In 1238, he was chosen master general of the order. He was very vocal about his unwillingness, but he obeyed. He made a visitation of his order on foot. He revised the Dominican constitution, adding commentaries on confusing passages. The code was approved in three general chapters. In 1240 he resigned his office with the excuse that, at sixty-five, he was too old. He set himself to oppose heresy and to work toward the conversion of the Moors in Spain. He asked St. Thomas Aquinas to write his work *Summa contra Gentiles,* worked to have Arabic and Hebrew taught in Dominican convents, and established monasteries in Tunis and Murcia. He wrote to the general of the order in 1256 that 10,000 Saracens had been converted. He helped to establish the Inquisition in Catalonia; he was accused, perhaps justifiably, of compromising a Jewish rabbi by deceit. He was visited by Alphonsus, the king of Castile, and James I of Aragon, one of his penitents, on his deathbed. He is the patron saint of lawyers, including canon lawyers (a result of his composing the *Summa de casibus poenitentialibus* and the "Decretals") and schools and faculties of law. He is shown in art in a boat, with a cloak for a sail; or with a key in his hand; or with the Virgin Mary and Infant appearing to him.

REGINA. Martyr, virgin. d. c. 286. September 7. Nothing is known of her for certain. Legends hold that she was the daughter of Clement, a pagan of Alise, in Burgundy. Her mother died in childbirth, and Regina was raised by a woman who brought her up to be a Christian. When her father discovered this, he refused to allow her to live with him, and she returned to her nurse and became a shepherdess. The prefect Olybrius presented himself as a suitor, but she refused him. Her father was willing to accept her as his daughter now that she had a distinguished suitor, but she refused his entreaties as well. Olybrius had her imprisoned, but when she remained firm, he vindictively had her tortured. That night in prison she had a vision of the cross, and a voice told her that her release would be soon. The next day she was ordered to be tortured again, then beheaded. Many onlookers were converted by the appearance of a dove hovering above her. She is portrayed in art in a boiling cauldron, with torches applied to her; or chained to a cross, with torches applied to her; or with lambs or sheep around her; or with doves.

RICHARD "THE KING." Confessor. d. 720. February 7. He was born in Wessex, England, and was the father of SS. Willibald, Winnebald, and Walburga. On a pilgrimage to Rome from Wessex with his two sons, he fell ill and died in Lucca, Italy. Miracles were reported at his tomb, and he became greatly venerated by the citizens of Lucca. The natives of the town amplified accounts of his life by calling him "King of the English." Even his real name is not known—"Richard" dates from the eleventh century.

RITA OF CASCIA. Widow. 1381–1457. May 22. She was born to elderly parents in Roccaporena in the central Apennines, and she showed great devotion from early childhood. She wished to enter an Augustinian convent, but she gave in to her parents' wishes and was married at the age of twelve. Her husband was a cruel and brutal man, well known in the neighborhood for his violent temper. For eighteen years she lived patiently with her contemptuous and philandering husband, forced to watch her sons becoming tainted by his influence. There came a point where he repented, however, and begged her to forgive him for his ill treatment; he was murdered shortly afterward in a vendetta. When her sons vowed to avenge their father's death, Rita prayed that they might die rather than commit murder. Both fell ill, and she nursed them and brought to them a spirit of forgiveness before they died. She applied three times to the Augustine convent at Cascia but was turned away because she was not a virgin. But in 1413, as a result of her persistence and strong faith, an exception was made, and she took the habit. She enforced hard austerities upon herself. She cared for the other nuns when they were ill and worked to return Christians who had neglected the faith back to observance. In 1441 she heard a sermon by St. James della Marc on the Crown of Thorns. Soon afterward, as she prayed, she became conscious of pain, as if a thorn had become embedded in her forehead. The location developed into an open wound, and it became so unattractive that she was separated from her sisters. The wound healed enough for her attend a pilgrimage to Rome in 1450, but it reappeared after her return and remained with her until her death, necessitating that she live in seclusion. She died of tuberculosis. Her body is said to have remained incorrupt until recent times. She is the patron saint of those in desperate situations (perhaps an allusion to her own life), of parenthood, and against infertility. In Spain she is the patron saint of desperate cases, particularly matrimonial difficulties. An Italian poll showed that her popularity is greater than that of the Madonna. Her symbol in art is roses, which are blessed on her feast day.

ROBERT BELLARMINE. Bishop, cardinal, doctor of the Church. 1542–1621. September 17. He was born in Montepulciano in Tuscany. His parents, Vincent Bellarmino and Cynthia Cervini, half sister to Pope Marcellus II, were of a noble but impoverished family. He was very intelligent, and as a boy displayed his ability in playing the violin and performing well in public disputations. He attended the Jesuit college at Montepulciano and was deemed by the rector to be very devout. He joined the Society of Jesus, with the support of his mother, for his father was initially against it. He went to Rome in 1560, and the father general of the order shortened his novitiate in order to allow him to attend the Roman College. Always fragile, after three years of study he was sent to Florence to recuperate. He taught boys and lectured on rhetoric and the Latin poets. A year later, he went to Mondovi in Piedmont to teach. He studied one day ahead of his students in Greek because he had not been taught the language himself. He preached well-attended sermons, and after overhearing one, his provincial superior had him transferred to Padua so he could attend the university to prepare for ordination. Before he finished his studies, he was asked to go to Louvain in Belgium to complete them there, in order that he might also preach to the undergraduates who were being exposed to dangerous doctrines by the chancellor, among others. Despite the fact that his sermons were in Latin, they were incredibly popular. Robert was so diminutive that he had to stand on a stool in the pulpit. He was ordained in Ghent in 1570 and became the first Jesuit to hold a professorship in the University of Louvain. He began a series of lectures on St. Thomas Aquinas's *Summa*. In a departure from the rhetorical conventions of the time, he never mentioned his opponents by name or attacked them personally in his teaching. He taught himself Hebrew and wrote a Hebrew grammar. He returned to Italy when his health became problematic, and there he was appointed to the chair of controversial theology at the Roman College. Robert held the chair for eleven years, in the process composing the four volumes of his *Disputations on the Controversies*. It displayed such a penetrating familiarity with the Bible that many of his opponents questioned whether he could have written it alone—proposing that his name was really an anagram for several Jesuits. The work became amazingly popular; in England, where the work was prohibited, a London bookseller said, ''I have made more money out of this Jesuit than out of all the other divines put together.'' In 1589 he was sent on a diplomatic embassy to France, then in a war between Henry of Navarre and the league. He was recalled to Rome by the death of Pope Sixtus V. Robert became the leader of a papal commission under Pope Clement VIII to edit and publish the new revision of the Vulgate Bible. He lived at the Roman College and became attached to St. Aloysius Gonzaga. He was with him at his deathbed, and he asked in his will that he be buried at Aloysius's feet. In 1592 he was made rector of the Roman College, and in 1594, provincial of Naples. In 1597 he came to Rome to act as theologian to Clement VIII, and he wrote two catechisms, one of which is still used in Italy. The catechisms are said to have been translated more often than any other literary work except the Bible and the *Imitation of Christ*. He was nominated a cardinal by Clement VIII in 1598. He was unwilling; although he had to occupy designated apartments, he continued to live with great austerity, living on bread and garlic and never lighting a fire. He used the wall hangings to make clothes for the poor. He was appointed archbishop of Capua in 1602. Although he had no pastoral experience, he set about preaching, and he initiated reforms decreed by the Council of Trent. He made visitations, catechized children, guided the clergy, and sought out those in need. When Paul V became pope in 1605, he recalled Robert and made him head of the Vatican Library, in addition to allowing him a part in the affairs of the Holy See. James I of England required an oath of the clergy denying the pope all jurisdiction over temporals, and Robert wrote responses to the two books James presented in defense of the oath. In his first response, Robert allowed himself some levity—making an allusion at one point to James's poor Latin—but his second response was a strong and uncompromising defense of papal supremacy. Robert did, however, hold moderate views on temporal supremacy, which dissatisfied radicals of both parties. He held that the pope's jurisdiction over foreign rulers was indirect. For this position he alienated Sixtus V, and because he denied the divine right of kings, his book *De potestate papae* was burned by the *parlement* of Paris. He was a friend of Galileo, and when he was asked to admonish the astronomer in 1616, he said only that he should present theories not yet proven as hypotheses. Galileo dedicated one of his books to him. In his later years he continued to write prolifically, completing a commentary on the Psalms and writing five spiritual books. He retired to the Jesuit novitiate of St. Andrew as he grew weaker and died there. He was notable as an ecclesiastical writer because he made rational arguments, rather than relying upon rhetoric and dogmatic claims. He is the patron saint of catechists and catechumens.

ROBERT OF NEWMINSTER. Abbot. 1100–1159. June 7. He was born in the Craven district of Yorkshire. He studied in Paris and wrote a commentary—since lost—on the Psalms. After being ordained, he became the rector of Gargrave. He then became a Benedictine at Whitby and joined a band of monks from St. Mary's Abbey, York, to establish a monastery in which the strict rule would be revived. They settled, in the middle of winter, in the valley of Skeldale on land given to them by Archbishop Thurston. The monastery became known as Fountains Abbey due to the presence of springs within its borders. The group became affiliated with the Cistercian reform, and the house became a model of its way of life. Robert was one of its most devout monks. The abbey became one of the centers of the White Monks in north England. Impressed by the establishment, Ralph de Merly, lord of Morpeth, built a Cistercian monastery on his own land, the Abbey of Newminster. He brought twelve monks from Fountains Abbey and appointed Robert abbot. The monastery flourished under Robert's rule, and he established a house at Pipewell in Northamptonshire in 1143, one at Sawley, and one at Roche. He is said to have had supernatural gifts, and visions and encounters with demons have been attributed to him. He fasted so rigorously during Lent that a brother asked him in concern why he would not eat. He responded that he might eat some buttered oatcake, but once it was placed before him, fearing gluttony, he asked that it be given to the poor. A beautiful stranger at the gate took it—and the dish. While a brother was explaining the loss, the dish suddenly appeared on the table before the abbot. It was thought that the stranger was an angel. He traveled again to France to see St. Bernard, after he was slandered by some monks about his relations with a pious woman. St. Bernard appears to have decided that the accusations were false. As a symbol of his belief in Robert's innocence, he gave him a girdle, which was kept at Newminster for performing cures. Before he returned home, Robert had an interview with Pope Eugenius III, who asked the bishop of Durham to give Robert some land at Wolsingham. Robert frequently visited St. Godric, and the night Robert died, Godric is said to have seen his soul ascending to Heaven like a ball of fire. His relics were translated to the church at Newminster. Miracles were reported at his tomb, including one in which a monk is said to have fallen unhurt from a ladder while whitewashing the dormitory. His tomb became a center of pilgrimage. He is depicted in art holding a church.

ROCH, ROCCO, ROQUE. Confessor. 1350–1390. August 17. There is no reliable history of his life. He appears to have been born in Montpellier. Legend has it that he was the son of the governor of Montpellier, a rich merchant. At the age of twenty he went on a pilgrimage to Rome. Italy was laid low by the plague, and he nursed the sick and is said to have effected miracle cures by making the sign of the cross over the diseased. He attended people in Acquapendente, Cesena, Rome, Rimini, and Novara. He fell victim to the disease himself and went out into the woods to die so as not to take up a hospital bed. He was said to have been fed by a dog, and when the dog's master discovered him, he cared for him. He recovered and returned to Piacenza, where he cured more people and cured their cattle as well. He eventually made his way back to Montpellier, where he was imprisoned as an imposter because his uncle did not recognize him. He died in prison five years later. When his body was examined, his true identity was revealed by a cross-shaped birthmark on his chest. Another more reliable account holds that he was arrested as a spy and died in prison in Angera in Lombardy. Miracles were reported at his tomb. His relics are claimed by Arles and Venice, where Tintoretto decorated his church with a series of paintings. He is the patron saint of infectious diseases, of physicians and surgeons, of cattle, of prisoners, and of Istanbul. He is depicted in art as a pilgrim with a staff, often with a plague spot on his thigh; or with a dog that is licking the spot or carrying a loaf of bread in his mouth.

RODERIC, RUDERICUS. Martyr. d. 857. March 13. He was a priest of Cabra. One of his brothers had become a Mohammedan; the other was a lapsed Christian. One night his brothers got into a fight, and Roderic tried to separate them. They turned on him and beat him unconscious. The Mohammedan had him placed on a litter and carried through the streets, while announcing that Roderic had apostatized and wished to be recognized as a Mohammedan before he died. Roderic heard all this in anguish but was too injured to speak. He escaped as soon as he was able. He ran into his Mohammedan brother on the streets later, and the brother accused him to the kadi of having reverted to Christianity after having declared himself a Mohammedan. Roderic denied ever having embraced Mohammedanism, but the kadi did not believe him and had him imprisoned in the most notorious prison in the city. There Roderic met another prisoner, Solomon, who had been incarcerated for the same reason. They comforted each other, while the kadi left them in prison for a long time, hoping to break them down. They were separated after it was ascertained that they would hold firm. Even alone, however, they remained stoic; they were condemned and beheaded. St. Eulogius witnessed the guards throw the bloodied pebbles into a stream so that the Christians could not collect them as relics.

ROMARIC, ROMARICUS. Abbot. d. 653. December 8. Romaric was a wealthy Merovingian nobleman who held a place of distinction at the court of Clotaire II. According to St. Amatus of Remiremont, it was he who brought about the conversion of Romaric, who consequently became a monk at Luxeuil. Romaric freed his serfs, and some of them became monks at Luxeuil, as well. In 620 Romaric and St. Amatus went to Romaric's estate at Habendum in the Vosges in 620 to found a monastery, which came to be known as Remiremont (*Romarici Mons*). St. Amatus became the first abbot, but he was succeeded by Romaric. Shortly before Romaric died, he heard that Grimoald, the son of his old friend, Bl. Pepin of Landen, was conspiring to keep Prince Dagobert from ascending the Austrasian throne. Romaric went to Metz, where he chastised Grimoald and the nobles who supported him. Afterward he returned to his monastery, where he died three days later, having ruled the abbey for thirty years. At Remiremont the *laus perennis* was performed by relays of seven choirs.

ROSALIA. Virgin. d. c. 1160. September 4. According to tradition, she left her home at a young age to live as a solitary in a cave on Mount Coschina, near Bivona in Sicily. Later she moved to a stalagmite grotto on Monte Pellegrino, near Palermo. There she is said to have died, and a stalagmite deposit eventually covered her body. An inscription attributed to her was found in the cave that read, *"Ego Rosalia Sinibaldi Ouisquine et Rosarum domini filia amore Domini mei Iesu Christi in hoc antro habitare decrevi"* — ("I, Rosalia, daughter of Sinibald, lord of Quisquina and Rosae, decided to live in this cave for the love of my Lord Jesus Christ"). Both the Benedictines and the Greek religious—more likely—have claimed her as a nun. In the Byzantine Archabbey of St. Savior at Messina there was a wooden crucifix inscribed "I, Sister Rosalia Sinibaldi, place this wood of my Lord, which I have ever followed, in this monastery." It now lies at Palermo. In 1624 the plague attacked Palermo. A victim had a vision of Rosalia and as a result, the cave was sought out and her bones were found. With them were found a terra-cotta crucifix, a silver Greek cross, and a crude rosary. Her remains were put into a reliquary and carried through the city; the plague epidemic ceased. In gratitude, the people built a church over her hermitage. She is the patron saint of Palermo. She is shown in art writing her name on the wall of a cave; or with or being presented with flowers; or holding a double Greek cross, distaff, book or palm.

ROSE OF LIMA. Virgin, tertiary. d. 1617. August 23. She was born in Lima, the daughter of Caspar de Flores and Maria del Oliva, people of the middle class. She was baptized Isabel but was called Rose and was confirmed with that name by St. Toribio, the archbishop of Lima. She appears to have used St. Catherine of Siena as her model of life, and she persisted in this despite the disapproval and mockery of her parents and acquaintances. She lived a strict life and practiced severe mortifications. She regularly rubbed her face with pepper to make it blotchy and thus deface her beauty. After someone complimented her on the loveliness of her hands, she rubbed them in lime; she was unable to dress herself for a month. Her parents lost a lot of money in an unsuccessful mining speculation, and Rose gardened and worked as a seamstress to earn money. She resisted their wishes that she marry, having taken a vow of virginity. She became a tertiary at the Third Order of St. Dominic and lived as a recluse in a hut in the garden. She wore on her head a circlet of silver, with sharp points facing inward. Her garden became the spiritual center of the city. When an earthquake struck, she was credited with saving Lima through her prayers. In addition to the persecution of friends, she suffered periods of depression and desolation. She was said to be gifted with supernatural powers and visions. She is said to have opened the first free clinic on the continent. She spent the last three years of her life with Don Gonzolo de Massa, a government official, and his wife, who was attached to her. She died in their home at the age of thirty-one. She became known as the ''Flower of Lima,'' a result of a poem written to celebrate her canon. She is the patron saint of Peru, Central and South America, the Philippines, India, the security forces and nurses of Peru, and florists and gardeners. She is shown in art as a nun of the Third Order of St. Dominic, with a garland of roses on her head; or with roses; or with roses and the Holy Infant.

ROSE-PHILIPPINE DUCHESNE. Blessed, virgin. 1769–1852. November 17. She was born in Grenoble, France, the daughter of a prosperous merchant. She was educated by the Visitation nuns of Sainte Marei d'en Haut, near Grenoble. At seventeen, against the opposition of her parents who wished to arrange a marriage for her, she joined the Visitation nuns. During the Reign of Terror in 1791, the nuns were repressed, and she returned home. There she nursed the sick, taught, and visited imprisoned priests. After the concordat of 1801, she attempted unsuccessfully to rebuild the convent where she'd been educated. In 1804, she convinced Mother Madeline Sophie Barat to accept it for her recently founded Society of the Sacred Heart. Rose became a postulant of the society and was professed the next year. Although she wished to be a missionary, she held administrative offices for fourteen years. In 1818, she was sent as superioress with four nuns to the United States, and she founded the first American Sacred Heart house at St. Charles, Missouri, in a log cabin. The company opened the first free school west of the Mississippi but moved to Florissant near St. Louis the next year. The community thrived after some initial difficulties, and by 1828, six houses had been established along the Mississippi River. She opened several schools in Missouri and Louisiana, insisting upon a high standard of education and compliance with French modes of behavior and discipline. She received some criticism for not learning English, but she was known to have an endearing personality. She resigned as head of the American branch in 1840 and began a school for the Pottowatomy Indians in Sugar Creek, Kansas. She did so at the request of the Jesuit Father De Smet. She was seventy-one at the time. The Indians called her the "Woman-Who-Prays-Always." After a year, her health forced her to leave the mission. She retired to St. Charles, where she died.

RUPERT OR HRODBERT OF SALZBURG. Bishop. d. c. 710. March 29. There have been varying opinions as to where Rupert was from. While a more reliable source makes him a Frank, another source makes him an Irishman. In any case, he was the bishop of Worms when he began his missionary work. He traveled to Regensburg with a small company around 697, perhaps with credentials from the French King Childebert III. They went to Duke Theodo, whose permission they needed to proceed. While Theodo was not a Christian, his sister is said to have been one. He agreed to listen to their preaching and was converted and baptized, along with many of his nobles. Pagan temples at Regensburg and Altötting were soon altered for Christian services. Other churches were built, and Regensburg became primarily Christian. The group continued down the Danube, converting many. Rupert made the old fallen-down town of Juvavum, given to him by the duke, his headquarters. The town was restored and he named it Salzburg. There Rupert founded a church and a monastery with a school. He made a trip home to gather more recruits. His sister, St. Erentrudis, entered a convent he founded at Nonnberg and became its first abbess. He did much to foster the operation of the salt mines. He is considered to be the apostle of Bavaria and Austria. His emblem is a barrel of salt. He may be shown holding a basket of eggs; or baptizing Duke Theodo.

SABAS. Abbot. 439–532. December 5. He was born at Mutalaska in Cappadocia, the son of an army officer. When his parents were posted in Alexandria he was left with his uncle, but his aunt treated him badly so he ran away to another uncle. Since he agreed to care for the child, the second uncle demanded to take over the administration of the family estate as well. The recriminations of the two uncles resulted in litigation, and Sabas fled to a monastery near Mutalaska. After ten years there, he went to Jerusalem to learn the way of life of the hermits. His uncles had wanted him to marry, but he resisted that. He stayed for a season in a monastery, but he wished for extreme solitude. St. Euthymius felt he was too young for such a life and suggested that he move to his monastery nearby, which was under the direction of St. Theoctistus. At the age of thirty, he was allowed to live five days a week alone in a desolate cave. He returned after the five days with fifty baskets he had made. After St. Euthymius died, he moved farther into the desert, where he lived for four years. He then moved to a cave in Cedron. In time, others came to join him. After initially resisting their request, he founded a laura, which came to be called Mar Saba ("Great Laura"), and his followers grew to 150. There was no priest in the laura because he felt it was unfitting for a hermit to pursue such a high calling. Some monks were discontented with this decision and appealed to the patriarch of Jerusalem. The patriarch did not disagree with Sabas, but he ordained Sabas in 491 in order to make peace. More followers were drawn to the laura, including Egyptians and Armenians, and special liturgies were introduced so they could worship in their own language. In time, the monastery would produce many saints, and it became one of the three or four oldest inhabited monasteries in the world. His mother joined him to live under his direction after his father died, and with the money she donated he built three hospitals and another monastery. In 493 he was made archimandrite over all the hermits of Palestine; St. Theodosius was made archimandrite of those who lived in communities. At the age of seventy, Sabas was sent by the patriarch Elias to help stop the persecution by Emperor Anastasius who was banishing orthodox bishops. He went to Constantinople and argued with the emperor. When Elias was deposed and replaced, Sabas and others went to Jerusalem and convinced the replacement not to renounce the Council of Chalcedon. Tradition has it that Sabas was with Elias when Elias died in exile, and he went on to preach in Caesarea, Scythopolis, and elsewhere. At the age of ninety-one, he was again asked to go to Constantinople, this time to negotiate a restoration of order after the Samaritan revolt. Justinian received him favorably and offered to endow his monasteries. Sabas politely declined this generosity but pleaded that the emperor stop taxing the people of Palestine, who were already burdened by losses from the revolt. Sabas said that he would build a hospital for pilgrims in Jerusalem and a fortress where hermits and monks could seek refuge from raiders, and that he would take action to put down the Samaritans. After he returned to his laura he became ill, and he was transported to a neighboring church where the patriarch himself cared for him. Before he died, Sabas asked to be returned to his laura, and there he appointed a successor. He died four days later, having asked to be left completely alone in order to contemplate. He is considered to be one of the founders of Eastern monachism. His reputedly incorrupt body was enshrined in Rome for centuries but was returned to Mar Saba after the Second Vatican Council. He is depicted in art with an apple in his hand; or living in a cave.

SALOME. Ninth century. June 29. In the middle of the ninth century, the abbot of the Ober Altaich monastery in Bavaria ordered a cell to be built onto the church with an opening into the choir. Here his relative, Salome, from England, came to live. Legend has it that she was an unmarried princess, niece to a king of England. On the way back from a pilgrimage to Jerusalem, she had lost her possessions, her attendants, and—for a time—her sight. She underwent many hardships, coming in time to Passau, where she remained for a short period, and then going on to Altaich. Later she was joined by a cousin or an aunt, Judith, who had been sent to find her by the king of England. Judith decided to remain at the monastery with Salome, and a second cell was attached to the first. Both lived there until their deaths, and they were buried next to each another. The only historical princess whose story seems to remotely resemble Salome's is Edburga, the beautiful, miscreant daughter of Offa of Mercia. She married Beorhtric, king of the West Saxons, and after murdering several of her husband's nobles, inadvertently poisoned him with a draught meant for someone else. She was expelled from England and sought harbor for a time in the court of Charlemagne. In order to restrain this woman, Charlemagne gave her a nunnery for women. Apparently she behaved badly there, too, however, and was driven out, and she wandered from city to city with a maid. She was said to have been seen begging in Patavium, which may have been a misspelling of Passau, thus placing her at Altaich. When the monastery of Altaich was razed by the Hungarians in 907, the relics of the two women were translated to Nieder Altaich.

SAVA. Bishop. 1174–1237. January 14. He was born Ratsko, the son of Stephen I, the founder of the dynasty of the Nemanydes of the Serbian state. He became a monk on the Greek peninsula of Mount Athos at seventeen and took the name Sava. He was later joined there by his father, who abdicated in 1196. They founded a monastery for Serbian monks, named Khilandari, which remains one of the seventeen ruling monasteries of the Holy Mountain. During the Middle Ages, it was the center of Serbian culture. Sava became abbot, and he was known for his gentleness and skill in training novices. He began to translate books into Serbian, and there is at Khilandari a psalter and ritual that are signed by the copier, "I, the unworthy, lazy monk Sava." In 1207 he returned home to find the country in a state of religious disorder. Clergy were scattered and mostly illiterate. Sava sent the monks who had accompanied him to do missionary and pastoral work. He settled at the monastery of Studenitsa and founded a number of smaller monasteries near the inhabited areas. He was sent by his brother, Stephen II, to Nicaea to see the Eastern emperor and patriarch, who had sought a harbor there from the Frankish invaders at Constantinople. Sava was designated the first metropolitan of the new hierarchy and was ordained bishop in 1219. He returned home, bringing books and more monks with him. He set about reforming and organizing the Church and in 1222, Sava crowned his brother archbishop; he is credited with giving the Serbians bishops of their own nationality. He also did much to further education in the country. He made two trips to Palestine and the Near East. On his way home from the second trip, he was taken ill and died at Tirnovo in Bulgaria. He is the patron saint of Serbia.

SCHOLASTICA. Virgin. c. 480–c. 543. February 10. She was the sister of St. Benedict and was said to be his twin. According to St. Gregory, she dedicated herself to God from an early age. Little is known of her life until after

St. Benedict moved to Monte Cassino. She moved to Plombariola and is said to have founded and become abbess of a convent about five miles from Monte Cassino. The convent is thought to have been under the direction of her brother; thus she is regarded as the first Benedictine nun. She visited her brother once a year, the two meeting in a nearby house because women were not allowed entrance to his monastery. According to St. Gregory, on their last visit, Scholastica asked her brother to stay until the next day, for she apparently had a presentiment that it would be the last time they would meet. St. Benedict resisted, because he did not wish to break his own rule by spending a night away from Monte Cassino. In response, she laid her head on the table and prayed that God would intercede for her. Just as she finished praying, a terrible storm began, which made travel impossible. St. Benedict remained the night, and they continued to talk. Scholastica died three days later, and her brother is said to have seen her soul rise to heaven in the shape of a dove. She is the patron saint of Benedictine nunneries and nuns, and she is invoked against storms. She is shown in art habited as a nun, with a crosier and crucifix; or with a dove flying from her mouth; or kneeling before St. Benedict's cell; or with a dove at her feet or bosom.

SEBASTIAN. Martyr. d. c. 288. January 20. There are no reliable accounts of his life. According to his *acta*, he was born at Narbonne in Gaul. He grew into a pious young man. He joined the army under Emperor Carinus around 283 in order to be able to assist the confessors and martyrs. Two martyrs, Marcus and Marcellian, were greatly bolstered in their faith by Sebastian while they were incarcerated. Sebastian also healed Zoë, the wife of Nicostratus, master of the rolls, of muteness. She, her husband, the parents of Marcus and Marcellian, the jailer, and sixteen other prisoners were converted. Chromatius, the governor of Rome, hearing that Sebastian had cured Marcus and Marcellian's father of the gout, sent for him, and was cured as well; he, too, was baptized, along with his son. He then discharged the prisoners, freed his slaves, and resigned his office. Emperor Diocletian, not realizing that Sebastian was a Christian, made him captain of a company of the pretorian guards. While Diocletian was away, his coruler Maximian extended to Sebastian the same patronage. As the persecutions grew worse, many of Sebastian's first group of converts were tortured and killed. Finally, Sebastian himself was arrested and Diocletian, angered by what he saw as betrayal, ordered that he be killed by archers. Sebastian was tied to a tree, shot with many arrows, and left for dead, but Irene, St. Castulus's widow, found that he was still alive and nursed him back to health. When he was well, instead of fleeing, Sebastian positioned himself on a staircase where he knew the emperor would pass. He then berated him for the persecution of the Christians. Taken aback for a moment at the sight of a man he thought was dead, Diocletian then ordered that he be beaten to death and his body thrown into the sewer. The order was carried out. After his death, Sebastian appeared to a woman named Lucina in a vision, and she buried him secretly in the *ad catacumbas*. In 367, Pope St. Damasus built the Basilica of St. Sebastian over the tomb; it is one of the seven principal churches of Rome. Sebastian is one of the Fourteen Holy Helpers. He is the patron saint of archers and soldiers, municipal police and neighborhood watch operations, contagious diseases (especially plague—he was reputedly successfully invoked against an outbreak of plague in Rome in 680), and physicians. He is portrayed in art as a naked youth tied to a tree, pierced with arrows.

SIDONIUS APOLLINARIS. Bishop. c. 423–480. August 21. He was born in Lyons, Gaul, to a noble family. He received a classical education at Arles and was taught by Claudianus Mamertus of Vienne. Around 450, he married

Papianilla, daughter of Avitus, the future emperor, and they had four children. They lived at the imperial court for several years, where he served under several emperors as a panegyrist. He left Rome for a period in 461 but returned and became prefect in 468. Later he retired to his estates at Auvergne, keeping up a large correspondence, which still survives and provides much insight into the times. In 469, he was named bishop of Arvernum (Clermont) against his will. He was probably still a layman at the time, and it appears that he was chosen mainly because it was thought he would be capable of maintaining Gallo-Roman power against the Visigoths. He gave up his luxurious life-style for an austere one, studied, and soon gained a reputation as an ecclesiastical authority. He was consulted often by other bishops. He endowed monasteries and charities and, in a terrible famine, fed thousands who had sought refuge from Burgundy; he then helped them to return to their homes. He led the people against King Euric of the Goths. When Clermont was defeated by the Goths in 474, Sidonius was exiled to a fortress near Carcassonne, where he remarked about two cranky women prisoners living down the hall. He returned in 476 and spent the rest of his life at Clermont, where he continued writing. He was a great orator and a celebrated poet; twenty-four of his poems survive. He is considered to be the last representative of the full classical culture before invasions altered the intellectual atmosphere of the West. He is portrayed in art appearing to a priest; or writing religious poems.

SILVERIUS. Martyr, pope. d. c. 537. June 20. He was the son of Pope St. Hormisdas born in Campania, Italy. When only a subdeacon he was made successor to Pope St. Agapitus I by Theoldehad, the king of Italy. The king made the appointment to circumvent a Byzantine candidate. He was eventually accepted by the Roman clergy, however, and when Empress Theodora asked him to recognize as patriarchs the monophysites Anthimus and Severus, he followed his conscience and refused. He is said to have commented at the time that he was signing his own death warrant. After the outskirts of Rome were plundered by the Ostrogoths, he and the senate, as the lesser of two evils, opened the gates to the Byzantine, Belisarius. The empress then sought her revenge. An attempt to trap him by a forged treasonous letter failed, so he was kidnapped and taken to Patara in Lycia in Asia Minor. The next day, Belisarius, spurred by his wife, named Theodora's choice for pope, the deacon Vigilius. When Emperor Justinian was informed of these actions, he ordered that Silverius be returned to Rome and an investigation opened. But Silverius was captured by the supporters of Vigilius when he landed, and he was taken to the island of Palmarola. Again, Belisarius had bent under pressure from his wife. It is presumed that Silverius died of starvation or murder. He was to some degree vindicated, because pope Vigilius ceased to support Theodora and held firm in the defense of orthodoxy. Silverius is depicted in art holding a church.

SIMON. Apostle. First century. October 28. Simon is surnamed "the Cananean" or "Zelotes" ("the Zealot") in the Holy Scriptures. The name was given in acknowledgment of the fervor with which he pursued Jewish law before his calling to Christianity. There is no mention of him in the Gospels except that he was one of the apostles. Tradition has it that after preaching in Egypt, he joined St. Jude, and they went on missions for some years in Persia, then suffered martyrdom. His emblems in art are a fish; a boat; an oar or a saw; or he is depicted being sawed in half (the tradition of the *Golden Legend* has it that he was killed in this way by pagan priests).

SIXTUS II. Martyr, pope. d. 258. August 7. It is possible that he was a Greek and a philosopher. He became pope in

257 and resumed the relations with St. Cyprian and the Churches of Africa and Asia Minor that had been ruptured by his predecessor, Pope St. Stephen I. The dispute over the validity of baptism by heretics was at its peak at this time; he supported the view that such baptisms were valid. According to St. Cyprian, Valerian sent an order to the senate calling for the death of bishops, priests, and deacons. While preaching in the catacombs of Praetexatalus during the celebration of the liturgy, Sixtus was seized with his deacons, Felicissimus and Agapitus and beheaded with a sword. He became one of the most greatly venerated of the early martyrs. He was buried in the catacombs of St. Callistus.

SOLANGIA. Martyr, virgin. d. 880. May 10. She was born at Villemont, near Bourges, to a family of poor vinedressers. At an early age, she vowed to serve God and remain a virgin. She worked as a shepherdess, watching her father's sheep. When her hour of prayer approached, she is said to have been attended by a guiding star that shone brightly over her head. She was said to have a great affinity for animals and to have the gift of healing. One of the sons of the count of Poitiers, hearing of her beauty, came to see her. When she resisted Bernard's advances, he pulled her up onto his horse by force. She extricated herself but was injured in the process, and he murdered her with his hunting knife. Legend had it that she then rose and carried her head in her hands to the Church of Saint-Martin-du-Cros. In its cemetery an altar was built in her honor in 1281. The field in which she liked to pray came to be called "Le Champ de Sainte Solange." She is sometimes called St. Genevieve of Berry. She is the patron saint of the province of Berry. She is portrayed in art stabbed or beheaded near a crucifix; or with her sheep and a distaff.

STANISLAUS. Bishop, martyr. 1030–1079. April 11. He was born at Szczepanow to noble parents who had been childless and had prayed for a child. They raised him religiously, encouraging him in his devotion to God. He was educated at Gnesen and was ordained a priest by Bishop Lampert Zula of Cracow. He was given a canonry in the cathedral and was later appointed preacher and archdeacon by the bishop. His expressive preaching and good example brought about a spiritual revival among his congregation, and he was sought out by clergy and laymen for his advice. He was generous to the poor and sought to bring about religious reforms. The bishop wished to resign his office to Stanislaus, but Stanislaus convinced him not to. When the bishop died, however, Stanislaus was chosen to succeed him; after Pope Alexander II endorsed the choice, he was consecrated in 1072. Stanislaus chastized Boleslaus II—"King Boleslaus the Cruel"—a sadistic and dissolute man, for his behavior, and the ruler was temporarily brought to repentance. But his good intentions did not last long, and he had the beautiful wife of one of his noblemen kidnapped and taken to his palace. Stanislaus was the only one of the clergy brave enough to confront Boleslaus, whom he reprimanded for his action. Finding this to be in vain, he excommunicated the king. When Boleslaus entered the cathedral of Cracow, Stanislaus halted the services. Enraged, Boleslaus followed him to the chapel of St. Michael outside the city and ordered his guards to kill him. The men returned and said that they could not kill him because he was surrounded by a divine light. The king himself entered the chapel and killed Stanislaus as he was celebrating mass. The guards cut the body up and scattered it to be eaten by wild animals. His remains were collected by cathedral canons and buried at the door of the chapel. It is probable that the murder was motivated by politics—some historians hold that Stanislaus was conspiring to dethrone Boleslaus—but this is unknown. Boleslaus's action, however, did speed his fall from power. Stanislaus is the patron saint of Poland and Cracow. He is depicted in art being hacked to pieces at the foot of an altar.

STEPHEN THE DEACON. First martyr. d. c. 35. December 26. He was a Jew and was likely a Hellenist of the Dispersion who spoke Greek. He was probably born abroad and later came to live in Jerusalem. He may have been educated in Alexandria. The circumstances of his conversion are unknown. The book of the Acts of the Apostles says that when there came to be many converts, the Hellenists complained against the Hebrews, claiming that their widows were being overlooked in the daily ministration. The apostles asked the faithful to choose seven men of good character who might superintend this business, for the apostles themselves had no time for it. Among the seven was Stephen, and the apostles ordained them the first deacons. Stephen was an effective speaker and was said to perform miracles. This provoked the hostility of the elders of some synagogues in Jerusalem, and they sought to undercut his power. They first disputed him, but he came out the superior. They then induced certain people to accuse him of blasphemy. Stephen was seized and taken to Sanhedrin. Although he was given no formal trial, he was allowed to speak, and he countered their accusations carefully and fully. He ended by saying, "Which of the prophets have not your fathers persecuted? And they have slain them who foretold of the coming of the Just One, of whom you have been now the betrayers and murderers. . . ." The audience was angered. Then he saw a vision, and said, "I see the heavens opened, and the Son of man standing on the right hand of God." The people took him outside the city and stoned him. The murderers laid their clothes on the ground to be guarded by Saul, who would become St. Paul. As Stephen died, he cried, "Lord, lay not this sin to their charge." His alleged relics, together with stones reputedly used at his martyrdom, were translated first to Constantinople and then to Rome. He is the patron saint of bricklayers (due to his death by stoning) and those in building trades, and deacons. He is invoked against headaches. He is portrayed in art vested as a deacon, holding a book or a palm; or carrying stones; or with stones resting on his book of the Gospels; or with stones gathered in the folds of his dalmatic.

STEPHEN HARDING. Abbot. d. 1134. April 17. He was born in southwest England. Nothing is known of his parentage. He was educated at the Abbey of Sherborne in Dorsetshire. He traveled to Scotland and then on to Paris, perhaps to study. On the way back from a trip to Rome, he and a friend came across a community of monks living a very austere and solitary life in a forest in Burgundy. Their rule of prayer and hard work attracted Stephen, and he joined them. Among the monks were St. Robert, the abbot, and St. Alberic. After some time, however, Stephen and some others felt that the original spirit of the community had lapsed. He accompanied St. Robert and St. Alberic to Lyons to ask the archbishop for permission to leave Molesmes. Permission was granted, and St. Robert and twenty others went to Cîteaux, a deserted area deep in a forest. Stephen built an austere monastery, which was opened in 1098. He became subprior. St. Robert returned to Molesmes soon after, and St. Alberic, who had replaced Robert as abbot, died in 1109. Stephen was elected abbot. He decreed that magnates could no longer hold their courts at Cîteaux, and thus cut off feudal sources of income, from which the abbey had derived most of its revenue. He also forbade the use of any expensive materials for the service of God. These changes put off visitors, which had been a source of new recruits. Combined with a disease that killed several monks, this caused the number of monks to dwindle significantly, and Stephen began to doubt his actions. One day, however, thirty men showed up and asked to become novices. They were noblemen, assembled and led by St. Bernard. From then on, the monastery thrived, and its reputation grew throughout France. Foundations were established at Pontigny, Morimond, and Clairvaux. Although St. Bernard was only twenty-four years old,

Stephen appointed him abbot of Clairvaux. Stephen ruled that the abbots of the monasteries must meet at Cîteaux each year, and that the abbot of the motherhouse must make a visitation of each abbey every year; these rules served to safeguard the original spirit and observance. In addition to being a biblical scholar, and perhaps an artist, Stephen was an excellent administrator. By 1119 there were ten monasteries, and Stephen drew up a constitution for the Cistercians—the Charter of Charity. His code would have a great influence on other orders. He also made emendations to the Vulgate Bible that were designed for the use of Cîteaux. He continued directing the monasteries until he was quite old and losing his sight, and he died at Cîteaux. He is shown in art with the Virgin Mary and the Infant appearing to him.

STEPHEN OF HUNGARY. King. c. 975–1038. August 16. He was born Vaik, the son of Geza, duke of the Magyars. His father had embraced Christianity mainly for political reasons. Vaik was baptized Stephen (Istvan) at the age of ten. At twenty, he married Gisela, the sister of St. Henry II of Bavaria. At twenty-two, he succeeded his father as ruler of the Magyars. After engaging in warfare to consolidate the country, he sent St. Astrik to Rome to get Pope Sylvester II's approval to organize an ecclesiastical hierarchy and to request that he confer upon him the title of king. Sylvester agreed and confirmed the religious establishments founded by Stephen as well as the election of bishops. Stephen became Hungary's first king in 1001; his crown was sent by the pope. He worked to establish sees, with Esztergom being designated the primary see. He built a church in Szekesfehervar where the kings of Hungary were afterward crowned and buried, and he completed the great monastery of Pannonhalma, which had been begun by his father. He prohibited pagan customs, punishing pagan-related superstitious practices severely;

and he punished blasphemy, murder, theft, adultery, and other crimes. He ordered that all persons marry except religious and churchmen, and he forbade the marriage of Christians to pagans. He eliminated tribal divisions, dividing the land into countries with a system of governors and magistrates, and thus solidified his people. Much of his governing groundwork lasted until recent times. He brought in many prominent foreign monks to help him, notably St. Gerard Sagredo, who tutored his son, Bl. Emeric. He made himself accessible to the people and was good to the poor, sometimes distributing alms in disguise—which proved to be a security risk on one occasion. He had intended to pass over much of his power to Bl. Emeric, but Emeric was killed in a hunting accident in 1031. Stephen spent the last years of his life in illness, while his family fought over the succession. He was buried beside Bl. Emeric at Szekesfehervar. Miracles were reported at his tomb. His crown was taken in World War II by the American army; it was returned in 1978. He is the patron saint of Hungary. He is depicted in art carrying a legate's cross; or with a church in his hand; or with a standard with the figure of the Virgin Mary upon it.

TARASIUS, THRASIUS. Bishop. d. 806. February 25. He was born of a noble family and was the uncle or great-uncle of Photius. A layman, he was secretary to the ten-year-old Constantine VI when he was named patriarch of Constantinople by the regent, Empress Irene. He was consecrated in 784, lived austerely, and became known for his acts of charity. In keeping with the resolutions of the General Council of Nicaea in 787, he restored statues and images to the churches and worked to eliminate simony. Constantine turned against him when Tarasius refused to sanction his divorce from Empress Mary, whom his mother had pressured him to marry. Constantine had even tried to coerce his support by deceit, but Tarasius remained firm. Constantine wished to marry Theodota, one of Mary's maids, and later did. Irene seized power and had Constantine imprisoned and blinded. After Nicephorus seized the throne five years later, Irene was exiled to Lesbos. Tarasius completed his twenty-one-year rule under Nicephorus. He worked to restore good relations between the Byzantine Church and the West. He is depicted in art with pictures of saints around him; or with the empress at his deathbed; or serving the poor at table.

TERESA OF AVILA. Doctor of the Church, virgin. 1515–1582. October 15. She was born at Avila in Castile to an aristocratic family. From childhood she was fascinated by the lives of the saints, once setting out with her brother for Moorish lands in the hopes of dying for the faith; they were met by an uncle at Adaja and returned to their parents. When she was fourteen, her mother died, and from then on she developed a great interest in romances and fashion, which worried her father. He sent her to the convent of Augustinian nuns in Avila. She became ill after a year and a half and returned home, but by this time she was reading St. Jerome's Letters and had decided to become a nun. Her father did not approve, and she believed she would have to await his death to carry out her wish. At age twenty, however, afraid that she might lapse in her devotion, she ran away to the Incarnation convent of Carmelite nuns outside Avila. Her father gave in, and she was professed a year later. She became ill, however, and her father removed her from the convent. Her friend, Sister Jane Suarez, accompanied her. Her illness, perhaps malaria, grew worse, but after three years, she recovered. Her convent, in keeping with the relaxed observance of the day, allowed visitors, and Teresa spent much of her time talking with visitors, to the point where she began to neglect prayer—she excused herself on the basis that she was not well. After her father died, his confessor brought her to recognize the danger of her lapse, and she returned to a regular practice of private prayer. During this period she read St. Augustine's *Confessions* and from then on her vocation was strong. She withdrew from her gregarious pursuits and began to experience visions, particularly one in which women warned her about being tricked by imagination and the devil. She told people about her visions, vowing them to secrecy, but word got out, making her an object of ridicule and persecution. She was introduced to a priest, who told her that she was being deluded by the devil—that divine visions were not granted to people who lived a life as flawed as hers. Alarmed, she was encouraged to consult a Jesuit. She did so, and the Jesuit assured her that her visions were divine, but that she must strengthen her mental life. He advised her to try to resist the visions, and she did so, but in vain. Another Jesuit, Father Balthasar Alvarez, recommended that she recite the *Veni Creator Spiritus* each day in the hopes of finding what God wished her to do. While doing so one day, she heard the words "I will not have you hold conversation with men, but with angels." She would frequently experience interior dialogues of great intensity, but under Father Alvarez she was persecuted. In 1557, she was visited by St. Peter of Alcantara, who told her that her visions were authentic but that she would never cease to suffer. She was said to levitate upon occasion. She experienced visions in which she was espoused to Christ in mystical marriages, and her heart was pierced. She made a vow that she would in everything do always that which seemed to be the most perfect and most pleasing to God. At this time, the Carmelites were very relaxed in their observance. They socialized with citizens and were free to come and go from the convent. When her niece began to talk of establishing a small community with a stricter life, Teresa took this to be a sign from God. She proposed to open such a house and was supported in her goal by her confessor St. Peter and others, but at the last minute, the prior provincial withdrew his permission due to opposition. She was secretly encouraged by a Dominican, however, and Teresa's married sister, Doña Juana de Ahumada, began to build a convent in 1561, pretending that it was to be a house for herself. Approval for the establishment finally came from Rome and the house of St. Joseph opened in 1562, with Teresa's niece among the thirteen nuns who joined. The townspeople were upset, suspicious of innovation, and apprehensive that the convent would be a financial burden. A Dominican persuaded them not to tear it down. Supporters sent a priest to speak for the monastery to the royal council, and eventually the opposition died down. The convent was strictly enclosed and followed a regime of austerity, including almost constant silence. The nuns wore coarse habits and sandals instead of shoes, and thus were called "Discalced" ("without shoes"). The prior general of the Carmelites, Father Rubeo, visited Teresa in 1567 and was so impressed with her that he gave her leave to found other convents. In addition, he gave her a license to found two houses of reformed friars— "Contemplative Carmelites." She lived at St. Joseph's for five years, then opened a second convent in Medina del Campo, and a third in the town of Malagon. She then traveled to Madrid. She founded convents at Valladolid and Toledo, and a monastery for men in the village of Duruelo in 1568, and another, and a nunnery, at Pastrana in 1569. She then passed over the responsibility for further houses for men to St. John-of-the-Cross. In 1570, she opened another foundation in Salamanca. In addition to being an able administrator, she was a very witty and kind woman. She thought it was of great importance to choose novices prudently. Intelligence was one of her top criteria. She always acted as a model to her nuns, doing household tasks along with the others, and never eating meat, and she wrote the *Way of Perfection* and the book of *Foundations* for their direction. Her mystic writing, the *Interior Castle,* was revolutionary, for it was the first work to point to the existence of states between prayer and contemplation. Teresa was asked to reform the convent of the Incarnation during the reformation movement of Pope St. Pius V. She was made prioress, and she found the nuns hostile to change, but she explained to them that she came to serve, not to coerce. Authorities who resisted her reforming efforts referred to her as "the roving nun." The prior general, who had supported Teresa, now turned against the reforms and held a general chapter to restrict it. St. John-of-the-Cross was imprisoned in a monastery, and Teresa was told to retire to one of her convents during the struggle. She appealed to contacts she had made in the world, and King Philip II came to her support. In 1580 an order from Rome exempted the Reformed from the jurisdiction of the Mitigated Carmelites; each division was to have its own provincial. By this time, Teresa's health had broken down. She opened her final house, her seventeenth, at Burgos, and wished to return to Avila, but was persuaded to visit Alba de Tormes at the request of the duchess. When she arrived, Teresa had to take to her bed. She died three days later. She was the first woman doctor of the Church. She is the patron saint of Spanish Catholic writers, the Spanish army and commissariat, and headache sufferers (perhaps due to her own chronic ill health). She is depicted in art wearing the habit of a Discalced Carmelite nun, her heart pierced by an arrow held by an angel; or holding a pierced heart, book, and crucifix. Her emblems are a fiery arrow and a dove above her head.

TERESA OF THE CHILD JESUS, OF LISIEUX. Virgin. 1873–1897. October 1. She was born in Alençon, the daughter of Louis Martin, a watchmaker, and Azélie-Marie Guérin, a maker of point d'Alençon lace. She was baptized Marie-Françoise-Thérèse. Her mother died in 1877, and the father moved the family to Lisieux, where the children could be overseen by their aunt. Her two older sisters became Carmelite nuns at Lisieux. When she was fifteen, Teresa wished to join the Carmelites, but she was refused on account of her age. A few months later in Rome during the jubilee of Pope

Leo XIII, as she knelt before the pope, she broke the rule of silence and asked him, "In honor of your jubilee, allow me to enter Carmel at fifteen." The pope was impressed by her fervor, but upheld the decision. At the end of the year, she entered. Her father suffered a nervous breakdown and was institutionalized for three years. Despite her fragile health, she lived the austere life faithfully and the autobiography she wrote at the request of her prioress, *L'Histoire d'une Âme* (The Story of a Soul), was revised and circulated to all the Carmelite houses. Her "little way" of searching for simplicity and perfection in all everyday tasks became a model for ordinary people. At twenty-two, she was appointed assistant novice mistress, although in actual fact she fulfilled the duties of novice mistress. After her father died in 1894, the fourth sister joined the convent. She contracted tuberculosis and hemorrhaged. She wished to join the Carmelites at Hanoi in Indochina at their invitation, but her illness became worse. She moved into the infirmary in 1897 and died at twenty-four. In contemplation of her death, she wrote, "I will let fall a shower of roses," meaning favors through her intercession; and she became known as "the Little Flower." Miracles were reported to have occurred through her intercession. She is the patron saint of foreign missions (due to her prayers for and correspondence with missions), all works for Russia, France, and florists and flower growers. She is portrayed in art as a Discalced Carmelite nun, holding a bouquet of roses or with roses at her feet.

TERESA OF JESUS JORNET E IBARS. Foundress, virgin. 1843–1897. August 26. She was born at Aytona (Lerida), Spain, the daughter of peasant farmers. She worked on the farm while qualifying to become a teacher. She joined the Poor Clares but was forced to leave due to fragile health. With Father Saturnino Lopez Novoa, she founded a congregation to care for the elderly at Barbastro—the Little Sisters of the Aged Poor—and became its superior general. She founded fifty-eight houses during her lifetime. The congregation received papal approval in 1887 and spread into other countries. She died in the motherhouse, which she had moved to Liria (Valencia). She is the patron saint of old people and old-age pensioners.

THEODORE AND THEOPHANES. Martyr and Bishop. c. 775–c. 841, c. 778–c. 845. December 27. They were brothers who were born in Kerak, across the Dead Sea, and grew up in Jerusalem. Both became monks in the monastery of St. Sabas and were admired for their intelligence and model behavior. The patriarch of Jerusalem urged Theodore to be ordained a priest, and when Emperor Leo the Armenian persecuted the worship of icons the patriarch sent Theodore to persuade the emperor not to interfere in ecclesiastical matters. Leo ordered that Theodore be scourged, and he exiled him with his brother to an island in the Black Sea where the two suffered the hardships of hunger and harsh weather. Not long afterward, however, Leo died, and the two were able to return to their monastery. But in 829, under the inconoclast, Emperor Theophilus, they were once again tortured and banished. In 831 they were recalled to Constantinople. After they refused discussions with the iconoclasts, Theophilus ordered that a twelve-line iambic verse be inscribed on their foreheads. The verse read, "These men have appeared at Jerusalem as vessels full of the iniquity of superstitious error, and were driven thence for their crimes. Having fled to Constantinople, they forsook not their impiety. Wherefore they have been banished from thence and thus stigmatized on their faces." The letters were cut into their foreheads, the operation taking two days. They were then banished to Apamea in Bithynia, where Theodore died. After Emperor Theophilus died, Theophanes was made bishop of Nicaea. The brothers came to be surnamed "Grapto" (the written-on). Theophanes wrote several hymns, one about his brother, and was called "the Poet" by the Greeks.

THEODORE OF CANTERBURY. Bishop. c. 602–690. September 19. He was born at Tarsus in Cilicia, a Greek. He was educated in Athens and became a monk. Oswy, king of Northumberland, and Egbert, king of Kent, sent a priest to Rome to be consecrated archbishop, but the priest died while still in the city. Pope St. Vitalian chose Adrian, an abbot, to replace him, but Adrian in turn suggested Theodore. Theodore agreed but requested that Adrian accompany him to Britain. Theodore was sixty-six at the time and had not been ordained. He was ordained subdeacon, then waited four months for his hair to grow, so that he might be tonsured in the Roman custom. He was then consecrated bishop. He and Adrian, accompanied by St. Benedict Biscop as their guide and interpreter, set out for Britain in 668. He wintered in Paris with St. Agilbert and began to learn English. He became ill, slowing the journey, but arrived in Canterbury in 669. With Adrian he made a visitation of all the churches in England. He confirmed the celebration of Easter, introduced the Roman chant in the Divine Offices, reformed and regulated observance, and ordained bishops where they were needed. In Northumbria he settled the dispute between St. Wilfrid and St. Chad as to who had the proper claim to the see of York. Theodore consecrated a church in honor of St. Peter at Lindisfarne, which had previously followed Celtic practices. He was the first metropolitan of England and the last metropolitan of foreign birth to occupy the metropolitan seat of Canterbury. Scholars were drawn to Theodore and Adrian, who knew both Latin and Greek—rare in Britain at that time. They arranged that the school at Canterbury teach sciences, including arithmetic (for calculating Easter) and astronomy, in addition to Scripture, the composition of Latin verse, Roman law, and music. Theodore held the first national council of the English Church at Hertford in 673. At this meeting he presented a book of canons, ten of which took special priority. They regulated the keeping of Easter, provided for the organization of the country into a diocesan system, and ordered an annual synod of bishops to meet at Clovesho. In 679 he acted as a peacemaker between King Egfrid and King Ethelred, successfully putting an end to their wars for some years. In 680 he held a provincial council to renounce monophysite error, and the council agreed to follow the five ecumenical councils. His greatest contribution was to create a missionary body and to consolidate into an ordered province of the Catholic Church the previously disorganized English Church. His arrangement of dioceses remains the foundation of the system used today. It is notable that when he began his work he was already an elderly man. He was buried in the Abbey of SS. Peter and Paul at Canterbury.

THOMAS. Apostle. First Century. July 3. He was probably born in Galilee to a humble family, but there is no indication that he was a fisherman. He was a Jew, but there is no account of how he became an apostle to Christ. His name is Syriac and means "the twin"; he was also called Didymus, which is the Greek equivalent. He is best known for his doubt that Christ had actually risen from the dead, and he said to the apostles, "Exept I shall see in His hands the print of the nails, and put my finger in the place of the nails, and put my hand into His side, I will not believe." Eight days later, Christ appeared to him and said, "Put in thy finger hither, and see my hands; and bring hither thy hand and put it into my side. And be not faithless, but believing." Thomas fell at his feet, saying, "My Lord and my God!" and Jesus replied, "Because thou hast seen me, Thomas, thou hast believed. Blessed are they that have not seen, and have believed." This incident gave rise to the expression "a doubting Thomas." Accounts of his missionary activities are unreliable, but the most widely accepted account holds that he preached in India. The *Acta Thomae* say that when the apostles divided up the world for their missionary labors, India fell to Thomas. He said he was not healthy enough and that a Hebrew could not teach Indians; even a vision of Christ could not change his mind. Christ then appeared to the merchant Abban and sold Thomas to him as a slave for his master, a king who ruled over part of India. When Thomas discovered this he said, "As thou wilt, Lord, so be it." At the court in India, Thomas, having admitted that he was a carpenter and builder, was ordered to build a palace. While the king was absent, however, Thomas did no building, and he used the twenty pieces of silver given to him by the King for charitable purposes. When the king returned, he imprisoned him, intending to flay him alive. At that point, the king's brother died, and when the brother was shown the place in heaven that Thomas's good works had prepared for the king, he was allowed to return to earth and offer to buy the spot from the king for himself. The king refused, released Thomas, and was converted by him. There exists a population of Christians along the Malabar Coast who were supposedly originally converted by Thomas, and their tradition holds that he built seven churches, was martyred by spearing on the "Big Hill" near Madras, and was buried in Mylapore. One account holds that he was killed for successfully persuading a woman, Mygdonia, to cease marriage relations with her husband, Charisius. In 1522 the Portuguese found the alleged tomb, and some relics now lie in the Cathedral of St. Thomas at Mylapore. The larger part of his relics appears to have been in Edessa in the fourth century, and the *Acta Thomae* say that they were taken from India to Mesopotamia. They were translated to several places and were finally taken to Ortona in the Abruzzi, where they are still honored. He is the patron saint of builders, building craftsmen and construction workers, architects and surveyors, blind people (due to his occasional spiritual blindness), India and Pakistan. He is portrayed in art as an elderly man, holding a lance or pierced by one; or kneeling before Jesus and placing his fingers in his side; or with a T-square.

THOMAS AQUINAS. Doctor of the Church. c. 1225–1274. January 28. He was born at the family castle of Roccasecca near Aquino. He was the son of Count Landulf of Aquino, a relative of the emperor and king of France, and Theodora. At the age of five, he was sent as an oblate to the Monte Cassino Monastery and was educated there until the age of thirteen. Around 1239, he attended the University of Naples, and he became a Dominican in 1244. His family was so upset by the fact that he had joined a mendicant order that they had him kidnapped by his brothers and returned to the castle, where they held him for two years in the hopes of changing his mind. He used the time to study religion, however, and he rejoined the Dominicans in 1245. He studied in Paris from 1245–1248 under St. Albert the Great. His nonparticipation at disputations and his large figure led him to be called "the dumb Sicilian ox." Thomas went with St. Albert to a new Dominican *studium generale* in Cologne in 1248 and was ordained. In 1252 he returned to Paris and lectured on the *Sentences* of Peter Lombard. He was master of theology in Paris in 1256. He then taught in Naples, Anagni, Ovieto, Rome, and Viterbo. During this period, from 1259–1268, he completed his *Summa contra Gentiles* and began his *Summa theologiae*, five volumes of his thoughts on all Christian mysteries. He experienced visions, ecstasies, and revelations. He was to break off writing the *Summa theologiae* because of a revelation he experienced while saying mass. He confronted the consternation of his bretheren by saying, "The end of my labors is come. All that I have written appears to be as so much straw after the things that have been revealed to me." Nevertheless, the work became the basis of modern Catholic theology. He was capable of intense concentration and was known to dictate to four secretaries at one time. He frequently used abbreviations in his writing because the friars did not have sufficient supplies of parchment. Always, he was a humble and prayerful man, and he was made a preacher general and was called upon to teach scholars attached to the papal court. In 1269, after returning to Paris, he became enmeshed in the dispute between the Order priests and seculars. During this time, St. Louis IX consulted him on matters of state. When a general strike took over the university, he was sent as regent to head a new Dominican school in Naples. He was appointed to attend the General Council of Lyons, but died on the way in the Cistercian Abbey of Fossa Nuova near Terracina, Italy. He is considered to have been the greatest Christian theologian and his work dominated Catholic teaching for hundreds of years. The amount of writing he accomplished is staggering. Among his works are *Quaestiones disputatae*, *Quaestiones quodlibetales*, *De unitate intellectus contra Averroistas*, and commentaries on the Lord's Prayer, the Apostles' Creed, and various parts of the Bible. He also wrote hymns, many of which are still used. He was called "the Angelic Doctor." His body lies in Toulouse, in the cathedral of Saint-Sernin. He is the patron saint of Roman Catholic schools, colleges, academies, and universities, scholars and students, apologists, philosophers, theologians, and booksellers (due to his patronage of education in general). He is depicted in art as a portly Dominican friar, carrying a book; or with a star of rays of light at his breast; or holding a monstrance with St. Norbert.

THOMAS BECKET. Bishop, martyr. 1118–1170. December 29. He was born in London, the son of Gilbert, the sheriff of London, and Matilda. He studied with the canons regular at Merton Priory in Surrey, then studied law in London. He continued his studies at the University of Paris. He joined the household of Archbishop Theobald of Canterbury and was sent by him on several missions to Rome.

He was sent to Bologna and Auxerre in 1144 to study cannon law and was ordained a deacon in 1154. He was nominated archdeacon of Canterbury by Archbishop Theobald. Henry of Anjou took a great liking to him after he convinced Pope Eugene III not to recognize the succession of King Stephen of Blois's son, thus endorsing Henry's right to the throne. The twenty-one-year-old King Henry II appointed him chancellor in 1155. They became great friends. Thomas was a cosmopolitan, active, and hot-tempered man, and he greatly enjoyed field sports; he became famed for his lavish life-style. When he joined Henry on a military expedition to Toulouse in 1159, it was at the head of his own troops. His judgments as chancellor were often at the expense of the Church. Henry nominated Thomas to succeed Archbishop Theobold, and he was elected in 1161 despite his strong distress. He resigned the office of chancellor and was ordained a priest the day before he was consecrated. He abandoned his luxurious life-style for a very austere regime, wearing a hair shirt under his cassock. Unfortunately for his friendship with Henry, he became more attentive to the state of Henry's soul. He was soon in disagreement with Henry over issues of Church and clerical rights. He refused to accept the Constitutions of Clarendon, which denied clerics the right to be tried in ecclesiastical courts and to appeal to Rome. This forced him to flee to France, where he appealed to Pope Alexander III. Thomas entered the Cistercian Abbey at Pontigny upon the pope's recommendation. When Henry threatened to eliminate all Cistercians from his realm if they continued to harbor Thomas, Thomas moved to St. Columba Abbey near Sens, which was under the protection of King Louis VII. Six years later, in 1170, with Louis as a mediator, Henry and Thomas came to terms, and Thomas returned to England. The king admitted the freedom of appeals to Rome, but the real power remained with him. They were soon embroiled in a new disagreement. Thomas refused to lift the excommunication of the archbishop of York and of those bishops who had taken part in the coronation of Henry's son—a violation of the rights of the archbishop of

Canterbury. He would do so only if the bishops swore obedience to the pope. Henry was enraged and is said to have questioned in consternation in the presence of his knights, how he could be rid of the troublesome priest. Four of his knights murdered Thomas in his cathedral, an act that horrified Europe. Thomas himself had opened the doors to the murderers although he knew he was in danger; when they ran in shouting, "Where is Thomas the traitor?" he responded, "Here I am, no traitor, but archbishop and priest of God." Henry performed a public penance. The shrine of St. Thomas became one of the most famous shrines in Christendom, and many miracles were reported there. Henry VIII would destroy the shrine, deface and forbid further images of Thomas, and order that his name be eliminated from liturgical books. Thomas is shown in art vested as an archbishop, with a wounded head; or holding an inverted sword; or kneeling before his murderers or before an altar.

THOMAS MORE. Martyr. 1478–1535. June 22. He was born in Cheapside, London, the son of a judge, John More, and Agnes. He attended St. Anthony's School in Threadneedle Street, and around the age of twelve he became a page in the household of Archbishop John Morton of Canterbury. Morton sent him to Oxford, where he studied at Canterbury College and later took a law degree at Lincoln's Inn. He was a superb student and became friends with Erasmus. He was admitted to the bar in 1501 and entered Parliament in 1504. He had considered becoming a Carthusian but decided against it, marrying Jane Holt in 1505. He wore a hair shirt, however, and engaged in regular devotions, and Erasmus said of him, "I never saw anyone so indifferent about food." He disallowed cards or dice in the house, invited poor people to eat with the family, and endowed a chapel in his parish church. The couple had four children. Their home soon became a salon of the intellectual figures of the day, including Linacre, Colet, Lilly, and Fisher.

More was very much in favor of the education of women; his own daughters were among the best-educated women in England—his favorite daughter, Margaret, being a particularly fine student. He was an outstanding scholar and became England's most prominent humanist. He wrote history, treatises, devotional books and prayers, poetry, and translated Latin. *Utopia*, his account of an imaginary society ruled by reason was most notable. He never espoused the punishment of heretics, however, saying he wished them not so much as "a fillip on the forehead." He held the office of undersheriff in London in 1519 and a year later, a month after his wife's death, he married a widow, Alice Middleton. She was a woman of great common sense; the only criticism he ever made of her was that she didn't get his jokes. Thomas was sent on several diplomatic missions by King Henry VIII and was appointed to the Royal Council in 1517. He was knighted in 1521, selected speaker of the House of Commons in 1523, and in 1529, he was made Lord Chancellor. He was somewhat wary of holding this office because he disapproved of Henry's defiance of the pope in his efforts to divorce Catherine of Aragon. He was clear-sighted about the loyalty he could expect from the capricious Henry, saying once, "If my head would win him a castle in France, it should not fail to go." His concern was shown to be warranted when he angered Henry by refusing to sign a petition to the pope requesting permission for Henry to divorce. He felt compelled to resign his office after tangling with Henry over measures being taken against the Church. He returned to his home in Chelsea in 1532, with little money, with the aim of living quietly and resuming his writing. He was arrested in 1534 after refusing to sign the oath in the Act of Succession that recognized the offspring of Henry's second wife, Anne Boleyn, as heir to the throne. He held fast to the opinion that Henry's first marriage was a true one. He was imprisoned in the Tower for fifteen months. While there, resisting the attempts of family and friends to make him concede, he wrote the *Dialogue of Comfort against Tribulation*. Much of his property was confiscated, and his wife had to sell her clothes to buy him necessities. When he was asked by Cromwell to comment on the Act of Supremacy, he did not reply, and so he was accused of treason. He was indicted and tried in Westminster Hall; he was so weak that he was allowed to sit during the proceedings. He was convicted and sentenced to be beheaded. Among his last words from the scaffold were, "I am the King's good servant but God's first." His head was exhibited on London Bridge; his daughter Margaret Roper pleaded for its return, and it was placed in the Roper vault in the Church of St. Dunstan. His body was buried in the Church of St. Peter ad Vincula in the Tower. He is the patron saint of lawyers. He is portrayed in art wearing Lord Chancellor's robes and the chain of office, and may carry a book or an ax.

THOMAS OF VILLANOVA. Bishop. 1488–1555. September 22. He was born at Fuentellana in Castile, the son of a miller. At sixteen he entered the University of Alcalá. After ten years, he was made a professor of philosophy. In 1516 he joined the Augustinian friars at Salamanca, where he taught moral theology at the university. In 1518 he was ordained a priest and preached and taught divinity in his convent. He served as prior of several houses and was named provincial of Andalusia and Castile in 1527, and again provincial of Castile in 1533. He acted as court chaplain to Charles V. It was he who sent the first Augustinian missionaries to Mexico. He was made archbishop of Valencia, despite his efforts to decline the office, and was consecrated in 1545. He preached throughout the diocese; his fine sermons would influence Spanish spiritual literature. He called the first provincial council in many years and worked to reform the clergy, whose abuses he had marked in his visitations. He came to be called "the Almsgiver" because of his generosity to the poor. Each day, several hundred poor were fed at his door. He took orphans under his special care and saw that destitute maidens were dowried and married. In 1550, pirates sacked a town in his diocese; he sent ducats to ransom the captives. He convinced the emperor to provide for the education of special priests to minister to the population of Moors who had been converted but had lapsed into apostasy, and he founded a college for the children of the newly converted, as well as a college for poor scholars. He wore a threadbare habit and prayed for hours at a time, sometimes experiencing ecstasies. He was said to have the power to heal and multiply food. He sent a representative to the Council of Trent and advised the bishops that working for a reformation in the Church should be as high a priority as acting against Lutheranism. Two of his suggestions were passed at the Council: one asked that benefices should be filled as much as possible by natives of the place, and that bishops should not be allowed to transfer from one see to another, believing as he did that a bishop should be wedded to his see as to a wife. In 1555 he was felled by heart trouble. He asked that his money be distributed among the poor and that all his goods be given to his college. He was buried in the church of the Austin Friars at Valencia. He is depicted in art as a bishop with a wallet in his hand, and beggars about him; or as a boy.

TIMOTHY. Bishop, martyr. d. 97. January 26. He was born in Lystra, Lycaenia, the son of a Greek father and a converted Jewish mother. When St. Paul preached at Lystra, Timothy replaced St. Barnabas. The two became close friends, and St. Paul would write of him affectionately as "the beloved son in faith." Since Timothy was the son of a Jewish woman, St. Paul permitted him to be circumcised to satisfy the Jews. He accompanied St. Paul on his second missionary trip. The opposition of the Jews compelled St. Paul to leave Berea, but Timothy remained behind. He was then sent to Thessalonica to investigate the status of the

Christians there and to shore up their faith in the face of persecution. His report was the basis of St. Paul's first letter to the Thessalonians. In 58, Timothy and Erastus went to Corinth to reinforce St. Paul's teachings. Then they accompanied St. Paul into Macedonia and Achaia. It is probable that Timothy was with St. Paul when he was imprisoned in Caesarea, and again in Rome, where he himself was imprisoned for a time. Tradition has it that he went to Ephesus, became its first bishop, and was there stoned and clubbed to death after denouncing the pagan festival of Katagogian, a celebration that honored Diana or Dionysus. St. Paul directed two letters to Timothy: one from Macedonia, and one while Paul was incarcerated in Rome, awaiting his own death. Timothy's relics were allegedly translated to Constantinople in 356; cures at the shrine are mentioned by St. Jerome and St. John Chrysostom. He is depicted in art with a club or stones; or being stoned to death.

TITUS. Bishop. First century. January 26. He was a Gentile probably born in Gortyna. He was converted by St. Paul and became one of Paul's favorite disciples. St. Paul refers to him as "my true child after a common faith." He acted as St. Paul's secretary and traveled with him to the Council of Jerusalem, where Paul refused to allow him to be circumcised. He was sent by St. Paul to Corinth to settle dissension, and again later to collect alms for the poor Christians of Jerusalem. St. Paul ordained him the first bishop of Crete. He met St. Paul in Epirus and later Paul sent a letter to him from Macedonia giving directions on spiritual matters and the proper performance of a good bishop. After traveling to Dalmatia he returned to Crete, where he probably died an old man. Some untrustworthy sources say he was a royal descendent born on Crete, and he went to Judea at the age of twenty after receiving a divine command; others say he was born at Iconium or Corinth. His head was brought to Venice after the invasion of the Saracens in 823, and it is venerated in St. Mark's. He is portrayed in art bareheaded, in a chasuble with a pastoral staff; or with a bright, smiling face.

TURIBIUS DE MOGROVEJO. Bishop. 1538–1606. March 23. He was born at Mayorga in Spain. Although he was devoted from a young age, he had no plans to become a priest. He studied law and was such an excellent student that he became a professor of law at the University of Salamanca. King Philip II made him chief judge of the ecclesiastical court of the Inquisition at Granada. When the authorities required an archbishop of strong character to work to convert the Peruvians in Lima, they selected him. He was horrified by this decision, and he presented the canons forbidding the promotion of laymen to Church offices to support his contention. He was overruled, however, was consecrated, and departed for Peru. He arrived in 1581 and confronted an enormous diocese—his first visitation took seven years—and one in which the Spanish were guilty of mistreatment of the native population. He fought injustice and vice, among the clergy as well as the laymen, championing the rights of the Indians, and succeeded in eliminating many of the worst abuses. At the same time, he helped Spaniards who were too proud to ask for help in such a way that they were not aware of his assistance. He founded many churches, religious houses, and hospitals; in 1591 he founded the first seminary in the New World. He continuously studied the various Indian dialects, and he succeeded in making many conversions. He is said to have confirmed St. Rose, St. Martin Porres, and St. John Massias. He was aided in his work by the Franciscan, St. Francis Solano. He fell ill at Pacasmayo but worked to the end, finally collapsing in Santa. He left his belongings to his servants and the rest of his property to the poor. He is the patron saint of bishops of Latin America.

ULRIC OF CLUNY, OR OF ZELL. Confessor. c. 1018–1093. July 14. He was born in Ratisbon and as a boy acted as a page to Empress Agnes. Wishing to pursue a religious life, he was received by his uncle Notker, the bishop of Freising. After being ordained to the diaconate, he was appointed archdeacon and provost of the cathedral. He regulated divine worship and the confessional. He was extremely generous, using his fortune to help those in distress. When he returned from a pilgrimage to Rome and Jerusalem, he found his offices had been filled by another. He decided to become a monk, and he went to Cluny, where in 1052 he received the habit from St. Hugh. He was ordained a priest, and after acting as confessor at Cluny for a time, he became chaplain to the nuns at Marcigny. The honor bestowed upon him by these offices caused jealousy among some of the brothers. He was also troubled by terrible headaches, and eventually he lost his sight in one eye. He returned to Cluny and was later sent to open a priory on the Rüggersberg. There he became involved in a dispute with the bishop of Lausanne, who was supporting the Emperor Henry IV against the Holy See. As a result, he was called back to Cluny and asked to establish a new monastery at Grüningen, near Breisach. Unhappy with the location, he instead founded the monastery in Zell, in the Black Forest. Backed by the bishop of Basle, he founded a convent of nuns as well, at Bollschweil. There he reputedly cured a girl of cancer. A great concern to him was that devotion be regulated among the monks. Found crying one day by one of his monks, he explained that he was weeping for the sins of his fellow monks. To remedy this, while acting as the novice master, he wrote the three books of the constitutions of the Abbey of Cluny—the Cluniac Customary, for the direction of the monastery. He was blind for the last two years of his life.

VALENTINE. d. c. 269. February 14. Little is known of him. He was a physician and priest in Rome, and he was beheaded under Claudius the Goth. On the day of his death another Valentine is celebrated in the Roman Martyrology: this Valentine was bishop of Interamna, sixty miles from Rome, and was scourged, imprisoned, and beheaded by order of the prefect Placidus. Many historians believe the two men to be the same. The custom of choosing a partner on Valentine's Day may have originated from the pagan Roman Lupercalia festival, which occurred in the middle of February, and during which partners chose each other by lot. There was also a medieval belief that birds pair on February 14. Valentine seems to have been buried on the Flaminian Way, and a basilica was erected to him. His relics were translated to the Church of St. Praxedes. He is the patron saint of lovers. He is portrayed in art as a priest bearing a sword; or holding a sun; or giving sight to a blind girl.

VERONICA. First century. July 12. In the Eastern Church she is identified with the woman who was healed by Christ of a hemorrhage condition that she'd suffered for twelve years. It is she who used her headcloth to wipe the face of Jesus when he fell beneath his cross on the road to Calvary, an incident that has been popularized in the traditional version of the Stations of the Cross. Legend has it that the imprint of his face was left on the cloth, and that Veronica came to Rome and cured the Emperor Tiberius with the relic. When she died, she left the cloth to Pope St. Clement. "Vera icon" ("true image") may have been transferred to her later in the form of a personal name—"Veronica." French legend holds that she was the wife of Zacchaeus, and after he became a hermit, she helped to evangelize southern France. Other accounts make her the same person as Martha, the sister of Lazarus, or a princess of Edessa, or the wife of an unknown Gallo-Roman officer. The alleged cloth of Veronica is in St. Peter's in Rome. She is depicted in art as a woman holding a cloth on which is imprinted the face of Jesus; or standing with a veil between SS. Peter and Paul.

VERONICA GIULIANA. Abbess, virgin. 1660–1727. July 9. She was born Ursula Giuliana at Mercatello in Urbino, the daughter of a family of breeding. She was devout from a very early age, beginning to give her food and clothing to the poor at six and pursuing a devotion to the Lord's Passion at eleven. Early on she was intolerant of those who were not as devoted as she, but this tendency was said to be tempered by a vision. She took great enjoyment in the increased station her father's promotion to a public office at Piacenza brought, and she reproached herself for it in later years. She decided to become a nun after experiencing a vision of the Virgin Mary, but her father opposed her plan. He insisted on introducing her to eligible suitors, which caused her to become ill from anxiety. Her father gave in, and she became a Capuchin nun in the convent of Città di Castello, in Umbria, taking the name Veronica. She became more intense in her devotion to the Passion of Christ and experienced a vision of Him bearing the cross. At this time, she began to experience a feeling of pain over her heart. In 1693, she experienced another vision in which the chalice of Christ's sufferings were offered to her. In 1694, the imprint of the Crown of Thorns appeared on her head, and in 1697, the *stigmata*. Medical treatment was given, but the wounds did not heal. Her wounds were examined by the bishop of Città di Castello and judged to be genuine. The wounds were bandaged, and the dressings fastened shut with the bishop's seal; she was separated from the other sisters, and she was watched carefully. The wounds remained. She acted as novice mistress for thirty-four years, forbidding the novices to read books of advanced mysticism, and she acted as abbess for the last eleven years of her life. She died of apoplexy. She had told her confessor that the instruments of the Lord's Passion were imprinted on her heart, and she drew their positioning for him more than once as she said they changed location over the years. A postmortem revealed the objects impressed in the area she had last indicated. An autobiographical account she had written was used in the process of her beatification. She is portrayed in art holding a heart marked with a cross.

VICTOR. Martyr. d. c. 290. July 21. What is known of him comes from legend. According to it, Victor was a Christian officer in the Roman army. When the Emperor Maximian entered Marseilles, Victor went at night from house to house, seeking to bring the frightened Christians to an acceptance of death, if God should will it. He was brought before the prefects and sent to Maximian. He held firm under the threats and anger of the emperor and was ordered to be bound and dragged through the streets. When he was returned, bruised and bloody, he continued to resist entreaties that he worship false gods. He was racked; while he was being tortured, Christ came to him in a vision. He was then thrown into a dungeon. At midnight, he was said to have been visited by angels, whose light filled the prison. Three frightened guards begged his pardon, and Victor called for priests and baptized them. The conversion enraged Maximian and he had all four brought to the marketplace. The three soldiers held fast to their faith and were beheaded. Victor was beaten and scourged and returned to prison. Three days later, he was brought again before Maximian and asked to burn incense at a statue of Jupiter. He kicked the statue over. The emperor ordered that his foot be cut off and that he be crushed to death under a miller's grindstone. When part of his body was crushed beneath the stone, the machine broke. Still alive, he was beheaded. The four bodies were thrown into the sea, but they were buried by Christians in a cave after they washed ashore. In the fourth century, St. John Cassian built a monastery over the site. Victor became one of the most celebrated martyrs of Gaul, and his shrine at Marseilles became one of its most popular pilgrimage sites. He is shown in art as a soldier, and he may stand near or hold a windmill.

VINCENT DE PAUL. Confessor, founder. 1581–1660. September 27. He was born in the village of Pouy, in Gascony, to farmers. He was placed in the care of the Cordeliers (Franciscan Recollects) at Dax. He attended the University of Toulouse and was ordained at the age of twenty. He became a chaplain to Queen Margaret of Valois, received the income of a small abbey, and at that time in his life wished for nothing more than a comfortable life-style. While he was visiting a friend, the friend was robbed; he accused Vincent. Vincent denied the theft, but he was the object of suspicion and rumor for six months until the real thief confessed. Legend has it that when he went to Marseilles to claim a legacy in 1605, he was captured by pirates, was taken to Tunis and sold as a slave, but escaped and returned to Paris. He became tutor to the children of Philip de Gondi and confessor to de Gondi's wife. After taking the confession of a dying peasant near the family's country seat at Folleville, Vincent discovered that the man had never been confessed in an orthodox fashion. Disturbed to think that the peasantry were being overlooked in this way, he was convinced to preach in the area and oversee the population's proper confession and penance. So many came to his confessional that he sent for the Jesuits of Amiens to assist him. He became pastor of Châtillon-les-Dombes and there converted many from lives of vice, including the count de Rougemont. He then went to Paris and ministered to the galley slaves in the Conciergerie and was eventually appointed chaplain to the galleys. He gave a mission in 1622 for the convicts at Bordeaux. Mme. de Gondi wished to found a company of missionaries to minister to the family's tenants, and her brother, the archbishop of Paris, gave the Collège des Bons Enfants for the new congregation. The members were to renounce ecclesiastical preferment and minister to small towns and villages. Vincent opened the house in 1625, attended the countess of Joigny until her death two months later, and then joined the new congregation. The priory of Saint-Lazare was given to the congregation and became its chief house in 1633. In this way the members came to be called Lazarists; later they assumed the name Vincentians, after their founder. St. Vincent founded twenty-five houses in his lifetime. He established confraternities to attend the sick in the parishes. With Louise de Marillac he originated the Institute of the Sisters of Charity, the first congregation of "unenclosed" women to devote themselves entirely to the poor and sick. He organized wealthy women to raise money for his works and founded several hospitals for the sick, foundlings, and the elderly. He raised money to relieve the victims in the wars in Lorraine. He sent missionaries to Poland, Ireland, Scotland, and the Hebrides; and he was responsible for ransoming over one thousand Christian slaves in North Africa. King Louis XIII sent for him on his deathbed, and the queen regent, Anne of Austria, consulted him on ecclesiastical affairs. During the Wars of the Fronde, he tried to convince her to give up her minister Mazarin. Anne appointed him a member of Louis XIV's Council of Conscience. He suffered ill health in his last years; he died while sitting upright in his chair. He is the patron saint of charities, Madagascar (where he sent missionaries), hospitals, and prisoners. He is portrayed in art garbed as a cleric of the sixteenth century, performing some act of mercy; or carrying infants in his arms; or surrounded by Sisters of Charity; or with ransomed slaves.

VINCENT FERRER. Confessor. c. 1350–1419. April 5. He was born of a noble family in Valencia and was raised religiously. He entered the Dominican priory of Valencia and received the habit in 1367. He was sent to Barcelona to study and was appointed reader in philosophy at Lerida before he was twenty-one. While there he published two treatises that were well received. He was sent to Barcelona to preach, despite the fact that he held only deacon's orders. The city, laid low by a famine, was desperately awaiting overdue ships of corn. Vincent foretold in a sermon that the

ships would come before night, and although he was rebuked by his superior for making such a prediction, the
ships arrived that day. He was transferred to Toulouse,
however, for a year, and continued his education. After
being called to his own country, he preached very successfully and became famed for his eloquence and effectiveness
at converting Jews—Rabbi Paul of Burgos, who became
bishop of Cartagena, being one—and reviving the faith of
those who had lapsed. He acted as confessor to Queen Yo-
landa of Aragon from 1391 to 1395. He was accused to the
Inquisition of heresy because he taught that Judas had performed penance, but the charge was dismissed by the antipope Benedict XIII, who made him his confessor. He was
also offered a bishopric, but he refused it. Distressed by the
great schism and by Benedict's unyielding position, he advised him to confer with his Roman rival. Benedict refused,
and the strain caused Vincent to become ill. During his
illness, he experienced a vision in which Christ and SS.
Dominic and Francis instructed him to preach penance. After recovering, he pleaded to be allowed to devote himself
to missionary work. He preached in Carpetras, Arles, Aix,
and Marseilles, with huge crowds in attendance. Miracles
were attributed to him; later, in the Netherlands, an hour
each day was scheduled for his cures. So effective a speaker
was he that, although he spoke only Spanish, he was thought
by many to be multilingual. His brother was the prior of
Grande Chartreuse, and as a result of Vincent's preaching,
several notable subjects entered the monastery. He returned
to Spain in 1407. Despite the fact that Granada was under
Moorish rule, he preached successfully, and thousands of
Jews and Moors were said to have been converted. His
sermons were often held outside because the churches were
inadequate to contain those who attended. He acted as a
judge to resolve the royal succession, and his influence
helped to elect Ferdinand king of Castile. Vincent went to
Perpignan to try to persuade Pope Benedict XIII to abdicate
during the schism, but he was unsuccessful. King Ferdinand, basing his actions on Vincent's opinion on the issue,

engineered the deposing of Benedict. He spent his last three years in France, and he died in Vannes after returning from a preaching trip to Nantes. He is portrayed in art as a Dominican holding an open book while preaching; or with a cardinal's hat or wings or a crucifix; or with Jewish and Saracen converts around him.

VINCENT PALLOTTI. Founder. c. 1798–1850. January 22. He was born in Rome, the son of a prosperous grocer. His schoolmaster said of him, "He's a little saint but a bit thick-headed." He grew more proficient at his studies as he grew older, however, and he was ordained at twenty-three. He took a doctorate in theology and became an assistant professor at the University of Rome. He was encouraged by his friendship with St. Caspar del Bufalo to resign his post and pursue pastoral work. He was popular as a confessor, and acted in this capacity at several Roman colleges. Unfortunately, he was disliked by the other clergy at the Neapolitan church to which he was appointed, and their malicious treatment of him inexplicably passed without comment from the authorities for ten years. Vincent gathered together a group of clergy and laymen to organize vocational schools. From this group would evolve the Society of Catholic Apostolate. The schools were intended to teach young people marketable skills such as shoemaking, tailoring, joining, and agriculture, and to instill in them a pride in their work. He worked from the premise that holiness is to be found not only in a religious life of prayer and silence, but also by filling any need in any part of life wherever one sees it. In 1837, during an epidemic of cholera, he cared for others despite the danger to himself. He went to great lengths to fulfill the spiritual needs of the people, once even impersonating an old woman in order to approach a bedridden man who had warned he would shoot any priest who came near him. He also performed exorcisms. His society contained only twelve members while he was alive, but it later spread worldwide. He is considered the forerunner of Catholic Action. It is interesting to note that when evidence was given during his beatification process, the vice rector of the Neapolitan church in Rome, who had been one of his severest persecutors, said that Pallotti was respectful and humble.

VINCENT OF SARAGOSSA. Martyr. d. 305. January 22. He was born in Huesca, Spain. He was educated by Bishop St. Valerius of Saragossa, and after he was ordained by him, he was commissioned to preach. During Maximian's persecutions, he and the bishop were arrested and imprisoned in Valencia. St. Valerius was exiled, but Vincent underwent terrible tortures; he had resisted turning over his church's sacred books and sacrificing to false gods. He converted his warden, and died of his injuries in prison. He was the protomartyr of Spain. His relics are claimed by Valencia, Saragossa, Lisbon, Paris, and Le Mans. He is depicted in art as a deacon holding a palm; or suffering on a gridiron; or being torn with hooks; or with a crow or raven or millstone.

VITUS. Martyr. d. c. 303. June 15. The identity of Vitus has become confused over time. There may have been two different Vituses: one in Lucania (southern Italy), and one in Sicily who was accompanied by companions. Legend has it that the Sicilian Vitus was the son of a senator. He became a Christian at the age of twelve. After gaining a reputation for conversions, Valerian, the administrator of Sicily, had him brought before him. His efforts to undermine his faith were unsuccessful, and Vitus, his tutor Modestus, and his nurse, Crescentia, fled to Rome. There Vitus exorcised Emperor Diocletian's son of a demon. When Vitus refused to sacrifice to pagan gods, he was accused of having cured the son by sorcery. He and his companions were tortured but remained unharmed. During a storm temples were razed, and an angel guided them back to Lucania, where they eventually died. Christians were martyred in Lucania, and the cult of the Lucanian Vitus is the oldest. An ancient church on the Esquiline at Rome was dedicated to him. He is one of the Fourteen Holy Helpers. His relics are claimed by Saint-Denis in Paris, and by Corvey, in Saxony, where a great following to him developed. He is the patron saint of epileptics, those suffering from St. Vitus' dance (named for him), dancers and actors (an offshoot of St. Vitus' "dance"), and he is invoked against storms.

WENCESLAUS OF BOHEMIA. Martyr. 907–929. September 28. He was born the son of Duke Ratislav of Bohemia and Drahomira. He was named Vaclav and was raised by his grandmother, St. Ludmila. She raised him religiously in a land that was still suspicious of Christianity. He was baptized by her chaplain, Paul, who had been a disciple of St. Methodias. After his father was killed in battle, Drahomira became regent, pursuing an anti-Christian policy. St. Ludmila, horrified to see the Christianizing efforts she and her husband had made being overthrown, urged Wenceslaus to seize power. She was murdered by nobles who wished to rob Wenceslaus of her support. Drahomira was driven from power by other circumtances, however, and Wenceslaus succeeded, immediately announcing that he would support the Church. His mother had been banished, but he recalled her to court. Wenceslaus sought to bring his people into closer contact with the West, and he pursued a friendly relationship with Germany, acknowledging King Henry I as his overlord. This move, together with the firm rein he kept on the abuses of the nobility, and his inclusion of clergy among his counselors, caused opposition. After he married and had a son, his resentful younger brother, Boleslaus, saw his chances of power slip further away. In 929 Boleslaus invited him to go to Stara to celebrate the feast of SS. Cosmas and Damian. On his way to mass at the Church of Alt Bunziau, Wenceslaus was attacked by Boleslaus. The brothers began to fight, and friends of Boleslaus killed Wenceslaus. Boleslaus had his relics translated to the Church of St. Vitus in Prague. The site became the center of his cult and a place of pilgrimage. From the year 1000 his picture was engraved on coins, and the crown of Wenceslaus came to be regarded as a symbol of Czech nationalism. The incidents described in the carol "Good King Wenceslaus Looked Out" are fabrications. Although he is the patron saint of brewers, wine is more directly associated with him; wine produced in his vineyards was used at mass. According to one legend, having a presentiment of his death, the night before he made a toast with wine to St. Michael the archangel, who guides souls to heaven. He is the patron saint of Bohemia, Czechoslovokia, Moravia, and of brewers (Czechs are famed for their beer, and thus their most famous saint became its patron). He is portrayed in art trampling on fire; or in a coffin carried by angels; or reaping corn for altar bread; or with Boleslaus asking his pardon.

WOLFGANG. Bishop. 924–994. October 31. He was born of a Swabian family. He was educated at the Reichenau Abbey, which was on an island in Lake Constance. There he met a nobleman, Henry, the brother of the bishop of Würzburg, and the two went on to the school at Würzburg that the bishop had opened. Wolfgang performed so well there that he sometimes provoked jealousy. He went on with Henry to become a teacher in the cathedral school of Trier after Henry was made archbishop in 956. There he met the reforming monk, Ramuold, and Wolfgang joined Henry in his efforts to strengthen the faith of the see. After Henry's death in 964, Wolfgang became a Benedictine at Einsiedeln. He was appointed director of the monastery school and was ordained by St. Ulric in 971. Under his direction, the school became one of the most flourishing institutions of its kind in the country. He traveled as a missionary to the Magyars in Pannonia, but he did not accomplish as much as he hoped. In 972 he was appointed bishop of Regensburg by Emperor Otto II. Although he resisted, wishing to return to his monastery, he was consecrated. He initiated a reform of the clergy and the monasteries in his diocese. He encouraged the canons to return to a regular life and made Ramuold abbot of St. Emmeram, an abbey that had been ill-managed by the bishops. He continued to preach and was known for his generosity to the poor; he was called the *"Eleemosynarius Major"* (the "Great Almoner"). He never abandoned his monastic habits. On one occasion he attempted to leave his see in order to seek a life as a hermit but was compelled to return. He accompanied the emperor on a trip to France. He ceded part of his see in Bohemia to set up a new diocese, that of Prague. He acted as tutor to Duke Henry of Bavaria's son, who later became emperor. He died at Puppingen, near Linz. In art he is depicted with a church in his hand; or holding a hatchet; or tormented by devils; or striking a fountain from the ground with his crosier.

WULFSTAN, WULSTAN, WOLSTAN. Bishop. 1008–1085. January 19. He was born in Long Itchington, in Warwickshire. He studied at the monastery of Evesham and later at Peterborough. Under the direction of Brihtheah, the bishop of Worcester, he was ordained a priest. He was offered a rich church but declined it, wishing to become a monk. He became a novice in the monastery of Worcester and was considered to live a model life. His attention at mass was once broken by the smell of roasting meat, and he vowed never to eat it again. He began as an instructor of children, and then he became precentor and later treasurer of the church. Against his will he was made prior of Worcester, and in 1062, bishop. He was the first English bishop to make a systematic visitation of his diocese. He promoted clerical celibacy, repressed the Bristol slave trade, and demanded the use of stone—not wooden—altars. His sermons were said to move people to tears. Under his hand, Worcester became one of the most prominent centers of Old English literature and culture. He gained the respect of King William the Conqueror, and he was the only English bishop—and one of the few authorities of any kind—who was allowed to retain his position after the Conquest. He helped William against the barons and later would support William II against the barons and the Welsh, providing for the defense of the castle of Worcester. He remained always humble, teaching others to be the same; he had the young novices personally serve the poor at table. He rebuilt the cathedral at Worcester, but his greatest concern was always that of saving souls. He died while washing the feet of twelve poor men, a rite he performed daily. Miracles were reported at his tomb, and William Rufus had it covered with gold and silver. King John asked to be buried near him. In 1216 the precious metals of his tomb were removed to pay a levy of 300 marks to Prince Louis of France. A translation was made to an even more magnificent shrine in 1218. At this time, the abbot of Albans removed one of the saint's ribs, took it back to his abbey, and built a shrine over it.

ZACHARY, ZACHARIAH. Prophet. First century. November 5. He was the father of St. John the Baptist and the husband of St. Elizabeth. He was a priest of the Old Covenant. The couple had reached middle age and were without children when one day in the Temple Zachary experienced a vision of an angel, who told him that in answer to the couple's prayers they would be granted a son "to whom thou shalt give the name John,'' who should be filled with the Holy Ghost even in his mother's womb, and who should bring back many of the sons of Israel to the Lord their God. Zachary doubted the truth of this and was struck temporarily dumb. His speech was restored after the birth of St. John. Tradition has it that Zachary was martyred, killed in the Temple "between the porch and the altar" by order of Herod because he refused to reveal the whereabouts of St. John. He is depicted in art holding a lighted taper.

ZITA. Virgin. 1218–1272. April 27. She was born in Monte Sagrati, near Lucca, to devout parents. Her sister became a Cistercian nun and her uncle Graziano was a hermit who was regarded by the local people as a saint. At twelve she became a servant in the town of Lucca in the house of Pagano di Fatinelli, a wool and silk merchant. She gave her food to the poor, frequently slept on the ground after giving her own bed to a beggar, and prayed much. She was eventually made housekeeper and took over the rearing of the children of the house. She became the confidante of the family and was the only person who could deal with her master's violent temper. She came to be so well regarded that she was discharged of many of her duties in order that she might visit the sick, the poor, and prisoners. She spent a great deal of time comforting and praying for prisoners awaiting execution. She died after serving the family for forty-eight years. She is the patron saint of housewives and servants. In England she was known as Sitha and invoked particularly when housewives and servants lost their keys or were in danger from rivers or crossing bridges. She is depicted in art in working clothes, with a bag and keys; or with loaves and a rosary.

Bibliography

Baring-Gould, Rev. S., THE LIVES OF THE SAINTS; Edinburgh: John Grant, 1914.

Benedictine Monks of St. August Abbey, Ramsgate, A DICTIONARY OF SERVANTS OF GOD, Wilton, CT: Morehouse Pub, 1989.

Cross, F. L., and E. A. Livingstone, eds., THE OXFORD DICTIONARY OF THE CHRISTIAN CHURCH, London: Oxford University Press, 1974.

Delaney, John J., DICTIONARY OF SAINTS, Garden City, NY: Doubleday & Co., Inc., 1980.

Drake, Maurice and Wilfred, SAINTS AND THEIR EMBLEMS, Burt Franklin, NY: Lenox Hill Pub. & Dist. Co., 1971.

Farmer, David Hugh, THE OXFORD DICTIONARY OF SAINTS. 2nd ed., London: Oxford University Press, 1987.

Reed, Daniel, Robert Linder, Bruce Shelley, Harry Stout, eds., DICTIONARY OF CHRISTIANITY IN AMERICA, Downers Grove, IL: Intervarsity Press, 1990.

Reed, Olwen, AN ILLUSTRATED HISTORY OF SAINTS AND SYMBOLS, Buckinghamshire, England: Spurbooks Ltd., 1978.

Tabor, Margaret E., THE SAINTS IN ART, Detroit: Gale Research Co., 1969.

Thurston, Herbert, and Donald Attwater, eds., BUTLER'S LIVES OF THE SAINTS, New York: P. J. Kenedy & Sons, 1956.

Walsh, Michael, ed., BUTLER'S LIVES OF THE PATRON SAINTS, Kent: Burns & Oates, 1987.

Feast Days of Saints

January 2 Basil the Great, Gregory Nazianzen
3 Genevieve
4 Elizabeth Bayley Seton
5 John Nepomucene Neumann
7 Raymund of Penafort
9 Adrian of Canterbury
12 Benedict of Biscop
13 Hilary of Poitiers
14 Sava
15 Ita
17 Antony the Abbot
19 Wulfstan
20 Fabian, Sebastian
21 Agnes
22 Vincent Pallotti, Vincent of Saragossa
24 Francis de Sales
26 Paula, Timothy, Titus
27 Angela Merici
28 Charlamagne, Thomas Aquinas
29 Gildas the Wise
30 Bathildas
February 1 Brigid
3 Ansgar, Blaise
5 Agatha
6 Paul Micki
7 Apollonia, Richard "the King"
8 Jerome Emiliani
10 Scholastica
14 Cyril and Methodius, Valentine
16 Gilbert of Sempringham, Onesimus
19 Conrad of Piacenza
21 Peter Damian
22 Margaret of Cortona
23 Polycarp of Smyrna
25 Tarasius
26 Porphyry of Gaza
27 Gabriel Possenti
March 3 Cunegund
4 Casimir of Poland
5 John Joseph of the Cross

6 Colette
7 Felicity
8 Apollonius, John of God
9 Dominic Savio, Frances of Rome
13 Roderic
15 Louise de Marillac
17 Joseph of Arimathea, Patrick
18 Cyril of Jerusalem
19 Joseph
20 Herbert
22 Nicholas von Flue
23 Turibius de Mongrovejo
24 Catherine of Sweden
25 Margaret Clitherow
29 Rupert of Salzburg
31 Benjamin
April 2 Francis of Paola
3 Irene
5 Vincent Ferrer
8 Julia Billiart
10 Fulbert, Paternus
11 Gemma Galgani, Stanislaus
13 Martin I
16 Benedict Joseph Labre, Marie Bernadette Soubirous
17 Kateri Tekakwitha, Stephen Harding
21 Anselm
23 George the Great
24 Fidelis of Sigmaringen
25 Mark
27 Zita
28 Peter Mary Chanel
29 Catherine of Siena, Joseph Cottolengo
30 Pius V
May 2 Athanasius
3 Philip, James the Less
4 Florian
8 Benedict II
9 Pachomius

386

10	Solangia
11	Francis di Girolama
13	Andrew Hubert Fournet
14	Matthias
15	Dympna, Isidore the Farmer
16	John Nepomucen
17	Paschal Baylon
19	Dunstan, Ivo of Kermartin
20	Bernardino of Siena
21	Godric
22	Rita of Cascia
23	John Baptist de Rossi
25	The Venerable Bede, Gregory VII, Mary Magdalene dei Pazzi
26	Philip Neri
27	Augustine of Canterbury
29	Maximinus of Trier
30	Ferdinand III, Joan of Arc
June 1	Justin Martyr
2	Elmo
3	Charles Lwanga, Kevin
4	Francis of Caracciolo
5	Boniface
6	Norbert
7	Robert of Newminster
8	Medard
9	Columba, Pelagia
11	Barnabus
13	Anthony of Padua
15	Germaine of Pibrac, Vitus
16	Guy, John Francis Regis
17	Herve
18	Gregory Barbarigo
20	Silverius
21	Aloysius Gonzaga
22	John Fisher, Paulinus of Nola, Thomas More
23	Etheldreda
24	John the Baptist
25	Gohard, Prosper of Reggio
26	Anthelm
27	Cyril of Alexandria
28	Irenaeus of Lyons
29	Paul, Peter, Salome

July 3	Bernardino Realino, Thomas
4	Elizabeth of Portugal
5	Antony Mary Zaccaria
6	Maria Goretti
9	Veronica Giuliani
11	Benedict
12	John Gualbert, Veronica
13	Henry the Emperor, Mildred of Thanet
14	Bonaventure, Camillus de Lellis, Ulric of Cluny
19	Arsenius the Great
20	Margaret
21	Laurence of Brindisi, Victor
22	Mary Magdalene
23	Apollinaris of Ravenna, Bridget of Sweden
24	Christina the Astonishing, Boris and Gleb
25	James the Greater
26	Anne, Joachim
29	Martha
30	Peter Chrysologus
31	Ignatius of Loyola, Justin de Jacobis
August 1	Alphonsus Mary Liguori
2	Eusebius of Vercelli
4	John Baptist Vianney
7	Cajetan, Sixtus II
8	Dominic
9	Oswald
10	Laurence of Rome
11	Clare of Assisi
13	Hippolytus, Maximus the Confessor, Pontian
14	Maxmilian Mary Kolbe
15	Hyacinth
16	Stephen of Hungary
17	Clare of Montefalco, Roch
18	Helena
19	John Eudes
20	Bernard of Clairvaux
21	Pius X, Sidonius Apollinaris
23	Rose of Lima

387

24	Bartholomew	18	Luke
25	Genesius the Comedian, Joseph Calasanz, Louis IX of France	19	Paul of the Cross
		24	Antony Mary Claret
		25	Gaudentius of Brescia
26	Teresa of Jesus Jornet E Ibars	28	Jude, Simon
		31	Wolfgang
27	Caesarius of Arles, Monica	November 3	Malachy O'More, Martin de Porres
28	Augustine of Hippo	4	Charles Borromeo
29	Medericus	5	Elizabeth, Zachary
31	Aidan of Lindisfarne	6	Leonard of Noblac
September 1	Fiacre, Giles	7	Engelbert
3	Gregory the Great	8	Godfrey
4	Ida of Herzfeld, Rosalia	10	Leo the Great
		11	Martin of Tours
7	Regina	12	Josaphat
8	Adrian of Nicomedia	13	Frances Xavier Cabrini
9	Isaac the Great, Peter Claver	15	Albert the Great
		16	Gertrude of Helfta, Margaret of Scotland
10	Nicholas of Tolentino		
16	Cornelius, Cyprian	17	Elizabeth of Hungary, Rose-Philippine Duchesne
17	Robert Bellarmine		
18	Joseph of Cupertino		
19	Januarius, Theodore of Canterbury	22	Cecilia
		23	Clement I
21	Andrew Kim Taegon, Matthew	25	Catherine of Alexandria
		26	Leonard Casanova of Port Maurice
22	Thomas of Villanova		
24	Pacifico	28	Catherine Laboure, James of the March
25	Finbar		
26	Cosmas and Damian	30	Andrew
27	Vincent de Paul	December 1	Edmund Campion, Eligius
28	Wenceslaus of Bohemia		
		2	Bibiana
29	Gabriel the Archangel, Michael the Archangel, Raphael the Archangel	3	Francis Xavier
		4	John Damascene
		5	Sabas
30	Jerome	6	Nicholas
October 1	Teresa of the Child Jesus of Lisieux	7	Ambrose
		8	Romaric
3	Gerard of Brogne	9	Peter Fourier
4	Francis of Assisi	11	Damasus I
5	Flora of Beaulieu	12	Jane Frances Fremiot de Chantal
6	Bruno		
9	Denis, John Leonardi	13	Lucy of Syracuse
13	Gerald of Aurillac	14	John of the Cross
14	Callistus	15	Nino
15	Teresa of Avila	16	Adelaide
16	Gerard Majella, Hedwig, Margaret-Mary Alacoque	17	Olympias
		21	Peter Canisius
		23	John of Kanti
17	Ignatius	24	Adela

Category of Saints

Adela   Widow
Adelaide   Widow
Adrian of Canterbury   Abbot
Adrian of Nicomedia   Martyr
Aidan of Lindisfarne   Bishop
Agatha   Martyr, Virgin
Agnes   Martyr, Virgin
Albert the Great   Bishop, Doctor of the Church
Aloysius Gonzaga
Alphonsus Mary Liguori   Bishop, Blessed, Doctor of the Church
Ambrose   Bishop, Doctor of the Church
Anastasia   Martyr
Andrew   Apostle, Martyr
Andrew Hubert Fournet   Confessor
Andrew Kim Taegon   Blessed, Martyr
Angela Merici   Virgin
Anne   Mother of Our Lady
Anselm   Bishop, Doctor of the Church
Ansgar   Bishop
Anthelm   Bishop
Anthony of Padua   Doctor of the Church
Antony Mary Claret   Bishop
Antony Mary Zaccaria
Antony the Abbot
Apollinaris of Ravenna   Bishop, Martyr
Apollonia   Martyr
Apollonius
Arsenius the Great
Athanasius   Bishop, Doctor of the Church
Augustine of Canterbury   Bishop
Augustine of Hippo   Bishop, Doctor of the Church
Barnabus   Apostle, Martyr
Bartholomew   Apostle, Martyr

Basil the Great   Doctor of the Church
Bathildis   Widow
Bede, the Venerable   Doctor of the Church
Benedict   Founder
Benedict II   Pope
Benedict Joseph Labre   Confessor
Benedict of Biscop   Abbot
Benjamin   Martyr
Bernard of Clairvaux   Abbot, Doctor of the Church
Bernardino of Siena   Confessor
Bernardino Realino
Bibiana   Martyr, Virgin
Blaise   Bishop, Martyr
Bonaventure   Cardinal-Bishop, Doctor of the Church
Boniface   Bishop, Martyr
Boris and Gleb   Martyrs
Bridget of Sweden   Foundress, Widow
Brigid   Abbess, Virgin
Bruno   Founder
Caesarius of Arles   Bishop
Cajetan   Founder
Callistus   Martyr, Pope
Camillus de Lellis   Founder
Casimir of Poland   Confessor
Catherine Laboure   Virgin
Catherine of Alexandria   Martyr, Virgin
Catherine of Siena   Doctor of the Church, Virgin
Catherine of Sweden
Cecilia   Martyr, Virgin
Charlemagne   Blessed
Charles Borromeo   Bishop, Cardinal
Charles Lwanga   Blessed, Martyr
Christina the Astonishing   Blessed, Virgin

389

Clare of Assisi Foundress, Virgin
Clare of Montefalco Virgin
Clement I Martyr, Pope
Colette Virgin
Columba Abbot
Conrad of Piacenza Confessor
Cornelius Martyr, Pope
Cosmas and Damian Martyrs
Cunegund Empress
Cyprian Bishop, Martyr
Cyril and Methodius Bishops
Cyril of Alexandria Bishop, Doctor
  of the Church
Cyril of Jerusalem Bishop, Doctor of
  the Church
Damasus I Pope
Denis Bishop, Martyr
Dominic Founder
Dominic Savio Confessor
Dunstan Bishop
Dympna Martyr, Virgin
Edmund Campion Blessed, Martyr
Eligius Bishop
Elizabeth
Elizabeth Bayley Seton Foundress,
  Widow
Elizabeth of Hungary Queen, Tertiary
Elizabeth of Portugal Queen,
  Tertiary, Widow
Elmo Bishop, Martyr
Engelbert Bishop, Martyr
Etheldreda Abbess, Queen
Eusebius of Vercelli Bishop
Fabian Martyr, Pope
Felicity Martyr
Ferdinand III King
Fiacre Abbot
Fidelis of Sigmaringen Martyr
Finbar Bishop
Flora of Beaulieu Blessed, Virgin
Florian Martyr
Frances of Rome Widow
Frances Xavier Cabrini Foundress,
  Virgin
Francis de Sales Bishop, Doctor of
  the Church
Francis di Girolama Confessor
Francis of Assisi Founder
Francis of Caracciolo Confessor,
  Founder
Francis of Paola Founder
Francis Xavier Confessor
Fulbert Bishop
Gabriel Possenti

Gabriel the Archangel
Gaudentius of Brescia Bishop
Gemma Galgani Virgin
Genesius the Comedian Martyr
Genevieve Virgin
George the Great Martyr
Gerald of Aurillac Confessor
Gerard Majella Confessor
Gerard of Brogne Abbot
Germaine of Pibrac Virgin
Gertrude of Helfta Virgin
Gilbert of Sempringham Confessor,
  Founder
Gildas the Wise Abbot
Giles Abbot
Godfrey Bishop
Godric Hermit
Gohard Bishop, Martyr
Gregory Barbarigo Bishop, Blessed,
  Cardinal
Gregory VII Pope
Gregory Nazianzen Bishop, Doctor
  of the Church
Gregory the Great Doctor of the
  Church, Pope
Guy Blessed, Tertiary
Hedwig Widow
Helena Empress, Widow
Henry the Emperor Emperor
Herbert Hermit
Herve Abbot
Hilary of Poitiers Bishop, Doctor of
  the Church
Hippolytus Martyr
Hyacinth Confessor
Ida of Herzfeld Widow
Ignatius Bishop, Martyr
Ignatius of Loyola Founder
Irenaeus of Lyons Bishop
Irene Martyr
Isaac the Great Bishop
Isidore the Farmer Confessor
Ita Virgin
Ivo of Kermartin Confessor
James of the March
James the Greater Apostle
James the Less Apostle
Jane Frances Fremiot de Chantal
  Co-foundress, Widow
Januarius Bishop, Martyr
Jerome Confessor, Doctor of the
  Church
Jerome Emiliani Confessor, Founder

Joachim   Patriarch
Joan of Arc   Virgin
John Baptist de Rossi   Confessor
John Baptist Vianney   Confessor
John Damascene   Confessor, Doctor of the Church
John Eudes   Founder
John Fisher   Bishop, Cardinal, Martyr
John Francis Regis
John Gualbert   Abbot
John Joseph of the Cross   Confessor
John Leonardi   Founder
John Nepomucen   Martyr
John Nepomucene Neumann   Bishop, Founder
John of the Cross   Doctor of the Church
John of God   Founder
John of Kanti   Confessor
John the Baptist   Martyr, Prophet
John the Evangelist   Apostle
Josaphat   Bishop, Martyr
Joseph   Patriarch
Joseph Calasanz   Founder
Joseph Cottolengo   Confessor, Founder
Joseph of Arimathea   Confessor
Joseph of Cupertino   Confessor
Jude   Apostle
Julia Billiart   Foundress, Virgin
Justin Martyr   Martyr
Justin de Jacobis   Bishop, Blessed, Confessor
Kateri Tekakwitha   Blessed, Virgin
Kevin   Abbot
Laurence of Brindisi   Confessor, Doctor of the Church
Laurence of Rome   Martyr
Laurence Ruiz   Martyr
Leo the Great   Doctor of the Church, Pope
Leonard Casanova of Port Maurice   Confessor
Leonard of Noblac   Abbot
Louis IX of France   King
Louise de Marillac   Co-foundress, Widow
Lucy of Syracuse   Martyr, Virgin
Malachy O'More   Bishop
Luke   Evangelist
Margaret   Martyr, Virgin
Margaret Clitherow   Martyr
Margaret-Mary Alacoque   Virgin

Margaret of Cortona   Tertiary
Margaret of Scotland   Queen
Maria Goretti   Martyr, Virgin
Marie Bernadette Soubirous   Virgin
Mark   Evangelist
Martha   Virgin
Martin I   Martyr, Pope
Martin de Porres   Confessor
Martin of Tours   Bishop
Mary Magdalene
Mary Magdalene dei Pazzi
Matthew Apostle
Matthias Apostle
Maximinus of Trier   Bishop
Maximinus the Confessor   Abbot
Maxmilian Mary Kolbe   Martyr
Medard   Bishop
Medericus   Abbot
Michael the Archangel
Mildred of Thanet   Abbess
Monica   Widow
Nicholas   Bishop
Nicholas of Tolentino   Confessor
Nicholas Von Flue   Hermit
Nino   Virgin
Norbert   Bishop, Founder
Olympias   Widow
Onesimus   Martyr
Oswald   King, Martyr
Pachomius   Abbot
Pacifico   Confessor
Paschal Baylon   Confessor
Paternus   Hermit
Patrick   Bishop
Paul   Apostle, Martyr
Paul Micki   Martyr
Paul of the Cross   Founder
Paula   Widow
Paulinus of Nola   Bishop
Pelagia   Martyr, Virgin
Peter   Apostle
Peter Canisius   Confessor, Doctor of the Church
Peter Chrysologus   Bishop, Doctor of the Church
Peter Claver   Confessor
Peter Damian   Bishop, Cardinal, Doctor of the Church
Peter Fourier   Founder
Peter Mary Chanel   Martyr
Philip   Apostle
Philip Neri   Founder
Pius V   Pope
Pius X   Pope

Polycarp of Smyrna   Confessor,
  Martyr
Pontian   Martyr, Pope
Porphyry of Gaza   Bishop
Prosper of Reggio   Bishop
Raphael the Archangel
Raymund of Penafort   Confessor
Regina   Martyr, Virgin
Richard "the King"   Confessor
Rita of Cascia   Widow
Robert Bellarmine   Bishop, Cardinal,
  Doctor of the Church
Robert of Newminster   Abbot
Roch   Confessor
Roderic   Martyr
Romaric   Abbot
Rosalia   Virgin
Rose of Lima   Tertiary, Virgin
Rose-Phillipine Duchesne   Blessed,
  Virgin
Rupert of Salzburg   Bishop
Salome
Sabas   Abbot
Sava   Bishop
Scholastica   Virgin
Sebastian   Martyr
Sidonius Apollinaris   Bishop
Silverius   Martyr, Pope
Simon   Apostle
Sixtus II   Martyr, Pope
Solangia   Martyr, Virgin
Stanislaus   Bishop, Martyr
Stephen Harding   Abbot
Stephen of Hungary   King
Stephen the Deacon   Protomartyr

Tarasius   Bishop
Teresa of Avila   Doctor of the
  Church, Virgin
Teresa of Jesus Jornet E Ibars
  Foundress, Virgin
Teresa of the Child Jesus of Lisieux
  Virgin
Theodore and Theophanes   Bishop,
  Martyr
Theodore of Canterbury   Bishop
Thomas   Apostle
Thomas Aquinas   Doctor of the
  Church
Thomas Becket   Bishop, Martyr
Thomas More   Martyr
Thomas of Villanova   Bishop
Timothy   Bishop, Martyr
Titus   Bishop
Turibius de Mongrovejo   Bishop
Ulric of Cluny   Confessor
Valentine
Veronica
Veronica Giuliani   Abbess, Virgin
Victor   Martyr
Vincent de Paul   Confessor, Founder
Vincent Ferrer   Confessor
Vincent of Saragossa   Martyr
Vincent Pallotti   Founder
Vitus   Martyr
Wenceslaus of Bohemia   Martyr
Wolfgang   Bishop
Wulfstan   Bishop
Zachary   Prophet
Zita   Virgin

Patron Saints

Abandoned children: Ivo of
  Kermartin, Jerome Emiliani
Abortion (protection against):
  Catherine of Sweden
Accountants: Matthew
Actors: Genesius the Comedian, Vitus
Advertisers and advertising:
  Bernardino of Siena

Advocates: Ivo of Kermartin
African Catholic Youth Action:
  Charles Lwanga
Algeria: Cyprian
Apologists: Catherine of Alexandria,
  Justin Martyr, Thomas Aquinas
Apulia: Nicholas
Aragon: George

Archeologists: Cyril of Jerusalem
Archers: Sebastian
Architects: Benedict, Thomas
Armourers: Dunstan
Arms dealers: Adrian of Nicomedia
Army and commissariat (Spanish):
Teresa of Avila
Artists: Luke
Asiatic Turkey: John the Evangelist
Astronauts: Joseph of Cupertino
Asylums: Dympna
Austria: Florian, Joseph
Aviators: Joseph of Cupertino
Bankers: Matthew
Banking: Michael the Archangel
Barbers: Cosmas and Damian
Barbers and hairdressers (Italian):
Martin de Porres
Barra (Outer Hebrides): Finbar
Basket makers: Antony the Abbot
Battle: Michael the Archangel
Beekeepers: Ambrose
Beggars: Martin of Tours
Belgium: Joseph
Bell-founders: Agatha
Benedictines (English): Benedict of
Biscop
Benedictine nunneries and nuns:
Scholastica
Benedictine Oblates: Henry the
Emperor
Berry (the province of): Solangia
Bishops: Ambrose
Bishops (Latin American): Turibius
de Mongrovejo
Blacksmiths: Brigid, Eligius
Blind: Cosmas and Damian, Raphael
the Archangel, Thomas
Bohemia: John Nepomucen, Joseph,
Wenceslaus of Bohemia
Booksellers: John of God, Thomas
Aquinas
Boys: Dominic of Savio
Brewers: Wenceslaus of Bohemia
Bricklayers: Stephen the Deacon
Brides: Nicholas
Bridges: John Nepomucen
Brittany: Anne, Ivo of Kermartin
Brussels: Michael the Archangel
Builders: Stephen the Deacon,
Thomas
Building craftsmen: Thomas

Butchers: Adrian of Nicomedia, Luke
Button makers: Louis IX of France
Cabinetmakers: Anne
Canada: Joseph
Canon lawyers: Raymund of
Penafort, Ivo of Kermartin
Carpenters: Joseph
Catechists and catechumens: Charles
Borromeo, Robert Bellarmine
Catholic Action: Paul
Catholic Action (African): Francis of
Assisi
Catholic Action (in Italy, young
people involved in): Gabriel
Possenti
Catholic press: Francis de Sales
Catholic writers (Spanish): Teresa of
Avila
Catholic youth: Aloysius Gonzaga
Cattle: Roch
Cattle (diseased): Blaise
Cattle breeders (Spanish): Mark
Cavalry: Martin of Tours
Cavalry (Italian): George
Cemeteries: Michael the Archangel
Central America: Rose of Lima
Charities (Catholic): Elizabeth of
Hungary, Vincent de Paul
Chemists: Cosmas and Damian
Childbirth: Gerard Majella, Leonard
of Noblac, Margaret
Childless women: Anne, Antony of
Padua
Children: Nicholas
Children of Mary: Maria Goretti
Choirboys: Dominic of Savio
Choirs: Dominic of Savio
Clergy: Gabriel Possenti
Clergy (parochial): John Baptist
Vianney
Coin collectors: Eligius
Confessors: Alphonus Mary Liguori,
John Nepomucen
Construction workers: Thomas
Cooks: Laurence of Rome, Martha
Cork: Finbar
Corn harvest: Medard
Cracow: Stanislaus
Craftsmen: Eligius
Cramp, colic (especially in children):
Elmo
Cursillo movement: Paul
Customs officers: Matthew

Cutlers: Lucy of Syracuse

Cyprus: Barnabus

Czechoslovakia: Cyril and Methodius, John Nepomucen, Wenceslaus of Bohemia

Dairymaids: Brigid

Dancers: Vitus

Deacons: Stephen the Deacon

Death: Margaret, Michael the Archangel

Death (happy): Joseph

Degree candidates: Joseph of Cupertino

Desperate situations: Jude, Rita of Cascia

Denmark: Ansgar

Dentists: Apollonia

Diplomatic services (of Spain and Argentina): Garbriel the Archangel

Disasters: Genevieve

Doctors and physicians: Cosmas and Damian, Luke, Roch, Sebastian

Domestic animals: Antony the Abbot

Doubters: Joseph

Drought: Genevieve

Drowning (those in danger of): Florian

Dublin: Kevin

Dying: James the Less

Dying (invoked against): Benedict

Ecologists and ecology: Francis of Assisi

Editors: Francis de Sales

Egypt: Mark

Elderly: Teresa of Jesus Jornet E Ibars

Embroiderers: Clare of Assisi

Emigrants: Frances Xavier Cabrini

Engineers: Benedict, Ferdinand III

England: George, Michael the Archangel

Epileptics: Dympna, Vitus

Equestrians: Martin of Tours

Eucharist and Eucharistic guilds, societies and congresses: Paschal Baylon

Europe: Benedict, Benedict II, Cyril and Methodius

Exegetes: Jerome

Eye trouble: Herve, Lucy, Raphael the Archangel

Farmers: George, Isidore the Farmer

Farmers (Italian): Benedict

Farm workers: Benedict, Isidore the Farmer

Fathers: Joseph

Fever: Genevieve

Finland: Henry the Emperor

Fire (invoked against): Agatha

Firefighters: Agatha

Fishermen: Andrew, Peter

Flemish men: Antony of Padua

Flood and water (those in danger from): Florian

Florists: Rose of Lima, Teresa of the Child Jesus of Lisieux

Flower growers: Teresa of the Child Jesus of Lisieux

Foresters: John Gualbert

France: Denis, Joan of Arc, Martin of Tours

France (works for): Teresa of the Child Jesus of Lisieux

Franciscan tertiaries: Louis IX of France

French Army Commissariat: Ambrose

Gaeta: Elmo

Gardeners: Fiacre, Rose of Lima

Gas station and garage workers: Eligius

Geese: Martin of Tours

Genoa: George

Germany: Ansgar, George, Michael the Archangel

Gibraltar: Bernard of Clairvaux

Glaziers: Lucy of Syracuse

Goldsmiths: Dunstan, Eligius

Greece: Andrew, Nicholas, Paul

Guatemala: James the Greater

Hairdressers: Cosmas and Damian

Harvests: Antony of Padua

Headaches: Denis, Stephen the Deacon, Teresa of Avila

Healers: Brigid

Health inspectors: Raphael the Archangel

Hemorrhage sufferers: Lucy of Syracuse

Hemorrhoid sufferers: Fiacre

Hoarseness: Bernardino of Siena

Homeless: Benedict Joseph Labre

Horses: Eligius, Hippolytus, Martin of Tours

394

Hospitals: John of God, Vincent de Paul
Hoteliers (Italian): Martha
Househunters: Joseph
Housewives: Anne, Martha, Zita
Hungary: Stephan of Hungary
Iceland: Ansgar
Illegitimate children: John Francis Regis
India: Francis Xavier, Rose of Lima, Thomas
Infantrymen: Martin of Tours
Infectious diseases: Roch, Sebastian
Influenza sufferers: Giles
Ireland: Brigid, Columba, Patrick
Istanbul: George, Roch
Italian knights of labour: Benedict
Italy: Catherine of Siena, Francis of Assisi
Jewelers: Dunstan, Eligius
Journalists: Francis de Sales
Journeys (safe): Nicholas, Raphael the Archangel
Judges: Ivo of Kermartin
Juvenile delinquents: Dominic of Savio
Kings: Henry the Emperor
Lacemakers: Luke
Law schools and faculties: Raymund of Penafort
Lawyers: Raymund of Penafort, Ivo of Kermartin, Thomas More
Lay apostolate: Paul
Learning: Catherine of Alexandria
Lepers: Giles
Leprosy: George
Librarians: Catherine of Alexandria, Jerome
Libraries: Catherine of Alexandria
Lithuania: Casimir, Cunegund, John of Kanti
Locksmiths: Dunstan
Lorraine: Nicholas
Lost articles: Antony of Padua
Lovers: Valentine
Luxembourg: Cunegund
Madagascar: Vincent de Paul
Madrid: Isidore the Farmer
Malta: Paul
Marble workers: Louis IX of France
Maritime pilots: Nicholas
Marriage: John Francis Regis

Married women: Monica
Masons: Louis IX of France
Matrimonial difficulties: Rita of Cascia
Medical profession: Luke
Mental illness: Dympna
Merchants (Italian): Francis of Assisi
Metalworkers: Eligius
Mexico: Joseph
Migrants: Frances Xavier Cabrini
Miners: Anne
Missions: Francis Xavier
Missions (Chinese): Joseph
Missions (foreign): Teresa of the Child Jesus of Lisieux
Missions (parish): Leonard Casonova of Port Maurice
Mixed race (those of): Martin de Porres
Mohammedans (invoked against): James the Greater
Monarchy (French): Louis IX of France
Mongolia (Outer): Francis Xavier
Monks: Benedict, John the Baptist
Moravia: Wenceslaus of Bohemia
Moscow: Boris
Mothers: Gerard Majella, Monica
Motorists: Frances of Rome
Mt. Aetna (invoked against eruption of): Agatha
Music: Cecilia, Gregory the Great
Musicians: Cecilia
Mystics: John of the Cross
Naples: Januarius
Naval officers: Francis of Paola
Navigators: Francis of Paola
Neighborhood watch operations: Sebastian
Nicaragua: James the Greater
Nigeria: Patrick
North Africa: Cyprian
Notaries: Ivo of Kermartin, Luke, Mark
Nurses: Agatha, Camillus de Lellis, Casimir, Catherine of Alexandria, John of God
Nurses (Italian): Catherine of Siena
Nurses (Peruvian): Rose of Lima
Nurses (psychiatric): Dympna
Nursing associations: Casimir
Oceania: Peter Mary Chanel

Opposition to atheistic communism: Joseph

Oppressed: Antony of Padua

Order of the Garter: George

Orphans: Ivo of Kermartin, Jerome Emiliani

Padua: Antony of Padua

Painters: Luke

Pakistan: Francis Xavier, Thomas

Palermo: Rosalia

Papua New Guinea: Michael the Archangel

Paratroops: Michael the Archangel

Paris: Denis, Genevieve

Park-keepers: John Gualbert

Pawnbrokers: Nicholas

Pelota players of Argentina: Francis Xavier

Penitents: Mary Magdalene

Pensioners: Teresa of Jesus Jornet E Ibars

Perfumiers: Nicholas

Peru: Joseph, Rose of Lima

Pets: Antony the Abbot

Pharmacists: Cosmas and Damian, Raphael the Archangel

Philippines: Rose of Lima

Philosophers and philosophy: Catherine of Alexandria, Justine Martyr, Thomas Aquinas

Physicians: Cosmas and Damian, Luke, Roch, Sebastian

Pilgrims: Nicholas, James the Greater

Plague: Adrian of Nicomedia, George, Gregory the Great, Sebastian

Plasterers: Bartholomew

Poets: Brigid

Poison (protection against): Benedict, John the Evangelist

Poland: Casimir, Florian, John of Kanti, Stanislaus

Police: Sebastian

Poor: Antony of Padua, Ferdinand III

Popes: Peter

Portugal: George

Possessed: Cympna, Michael the Archangel

Pregnant women: Margaret

Priests: John Baptist Vianney

Printers: John of God

Prisoners: Ferdinand III, Leonard of Noblac, Roch, Vincent de Paul

Prisoners of war: Leonard of Noblac

Prison guards: Adrian of Nicomedia

Public education and television (Peruvian): Martin de Porres

Public health service (Peruvian): Martin de Porres

Pueri Cantors: Dominic of Savio

Race relations: Martin de Porres

Radio: Gabriel the Archangel

Radiologists: Michael the Archangel

Rain (excessive): Genevieve

Reggio: Prosper

Retreats: Ignatius of Loyola

Robbers and brigands (those in danger from): Leonard of Noblac

Rulers and ruling authorities: Ferdinand III

Ruptures (particularly hernia): Conrad of Piacenza

Russia: Andrew, Basil the Great, Casimir, Joseph, Nicholas

Russia (works for): Teresa of the Child Jesus of Lisieux

Sailors: Elmo, Francis of Paola, Nicholas

St. Antony's Fire (sufferers of): Antony the Abbot

St. Vitus' Dance (sufferers of): Vitus

Savings and savings banks: Antony Mary Claret

Scientists: Albert the Great

Scholars: The Venerable Bede, Thomas Aquinas

Scholars (of scripture): Jerome

Schools (Christian): Joseph Calasanz

Schools and universities (Roman Catholic): Thomas Aquinas

Scotland: Andrew, Margaret of Scotland

Scruples (those troubled by): Ignatius of Loyola

Sculptors: Louis IX of France, Luke

Secretaries: Mark

Security forces: Michael the Archangel

Security forces (French): Genevieve

Security forces (Peruvian): Rose of Lima

Security guards: Matthew

Seminarians: Charles Borromeo, Gabriel Possenti

Serbia: Sava

Servants: Martha, Zita

Shepherds: Marie Bernadette Soubirous, Paschal Baylon

Sicily: Nicholas

Sick: Casimir, John of God, Michael the Archangel

Sick pilgrims: Pius X

Signals regiments (of Italy, France, and Columbia): Gabriel the Archangel

Silesia: Hedwig

Silversmiths: Eligius

Single women: Nicholas

Skin diseases: Antony the Abbot

Slander (invoked against): John Neposmucen

Sleepwalkers: Dympna

Smithies: Giles

Social justice: Martin de Porres

Social workers: John Francis Regis, Louise de Marillac

Soldiers: George, Martin of Tours, Sebastian

Soldiers (French): Joan of Arc, Louis IX of France

Solomon Islands: Michael the Archangel

South America: Rose of Lima

South Vietnam: Joseph

Spain: James the Greater

Speleologists (Italian): Benedict

Spiritual exercises: Ignatius of Loyola

Stonemasons: Louis IX of France

Storms (invoked against): Scholastica, Vitus

Students: Joseph of Cupertino

Students in Jesuit colleges: Aloysius Gonzaga

Students (particularly women students): Catherine of Alexandria

Students (particularly college): Gabriel Possenti

Surgeons: Cosmas and Damian, Roch

Surveyors: Thomas

Sweden: Bridget of Sweden

Switzerland: Nicholas Von Flue

Syphilis: George

Tanners: Bartholomew

Tax collectors: Matthew

Taxi drivers: Fiacre

Teenagers (particularly girls): Maria Goretti

Telecommunications: Gabriel the Archangel

Television: Clare of Assisi, Gabriel the Archangel

Theatrical profession: Genesius the Comedian

Theologians: Augustine of Hippo, Thomas Aquinas

Theologians (moral): Alphonsus Mary Liguori

Throat-complaint sufferers: Blaise

Throat trouble: Lucy of Syracuse

Toothache: Apollonia, Medard

Tourism (Spanish): Francis Xavier

Trade unionists (Spanish): Martin de Porres

Tramps: Benedict Joseph Labre

Travelers: Joseph, Nicholas, Raphael the Archangel

"Trinity House": Clement I

Undertakers: Joseph of Arimathea

United States National Catholic Rural Conference: Isidore the Farmer

Universal Church: Joseph

Upper Auvergne: Gerald of Aurillac

Uruguay: Philip

Venereal-disease sufferers: Fiacre

Venice: George, Mark

Veterinarians: Eligius

Vintage: Medard

Virginal innocence: Agnes

Waiters, waitresses: Martha

Weavers: Anastasia, Antony Mary Claret

West Indies: Gertrude of Helfta

Wet nurses: Agatha

Wheelwrights: Catherine of Alexandria

Widows: Frances of Rome, Paula

Wine growers: Martin of Tours

Women in labor: Elmo

Women (Italian): Paschal Baylon

Wool combers: Blaise

Workers: Joseph

Writers: Francis de Sales

Young women: Catherine of Alexandria

Young people (Lithuanian): Casimir

Young people leaving home: Raphael the Archangel

Yugoslavia: Cyril and Methodius

Symbols and Iconography of Saints

Adelaide: Escaping from prison in a boat; or holding a church in her hand.

Adrian of Nicomedia: With an anvil, sword, lion, or hammer; or being thrown off a cliff into the sea; or being brought to land by dolphins.

Aidan of Lindisfarne: Giving his horse to a beggar; or calming a storm and extinguishing a fire with prayer; or with a stag at his feet; or as a bishop holding a crosier, with his right hand upheld in benediction or holding a torch.

Agatha: Perhaps wearing a long veil, and holding a dish containing breasts; or with a knife or shears.

Agnes: With a lamb; or with a palm; or with a dove with a ring in its beak.

Albert the Great: Wearing a Dominican habit, often with St. Thomas Aquinas.

Aloyius Gonzaga: In a black habit, with a crucifix, lily, and discipline.

Alphonsus Mary Liguori: With rays shining upon his face from an image of the Virgin Mary; or reciting the rosary.

Ambrose: With a scourge; or with a beehive and bees.

Anastasia: Burning at a stake; or on a funeral pyre.

Andrew: With a saltire cross (St. Andrew's Cross) or the Latin cross; and/or with a fishing net.

Angela Merici: With an image of virgins ascending a ladder; or with St. Ursula and companions appearing to her.

Anne: Teaching her little daughter to read the Bible; or greeting St. Joachim at the Golden Gate.

Anselm: As an archbishop or Benedictine monk, admonishing an evildoer; or with Our Lady appearing to him; or with a ship; or exorcising a monk.

Ansgar: With converted Danes near him.

Anthelm: In a Carthusian habit, with a miter at his feet, and above his head a lamp with the Divine Hand pointing to or kindling the flame.

Anthony of Padua: Carrying the Infant Jesus on his arm; or holding a lily; or with a flame of fire in his hand or at his breast; or holding corn.

Antony the Abbot: As an old man with long white hair, scantily clad, with a T-shaped Egyptian cross; or with a raven; or with a torch; or with a pig.

Apollinaris of Ravenna: As a bishop, holding a sword or club, standing on hot coals; or being beaten by the devil.

Apollonia: Bearing a pair of pincers that hold a tooth; or with a gold tooth; or with a tooth suspended from a necklace.

Apollonius: On a funeral pyre; or drowning in the sea; or being crucified.

Arsenius the Great: Weaving baskets of palm leaves.

Athanasius: In a group of the Greek fathers, distinguished by name; or in a boat on the Nile; or with heretics under his feet.

Augustine of Canterbury: In the Augustinian habit, with a pen or book (one of his own works); or with a bishop's miter and crosier; or baptizing Ethelbert; or obtaining by prayer a fountain for baptizing.

Augustine of Hippo: Among the four Latin doctors, in episcopal vestments, with a pastoral staff; or with a burning heart.

Barnabus: Carrying the Gospel in his hand, with a pilgrim's staff and sometimes a stone; or being stoned; or being burnt to death; or in company with SS Paul or Mark, holding Mark's Gospel in his hand.

Bartholomew: With a butcher's flaying knife; or carrying on his arm the skin of a man with the face attached; or with the Gospel of St. Matthew.

Basil the Great: With a dove on his arm or hand, giving him a pen; or with the Church in his hand; or in company with the Greek Fathers, usually distinguished by name.

Bathildis: As a crowned nun; or with a ladder to heaven; or carrying a broom.

Bede, the Venerable: As an old monk, with a book or pen; or with a jug; or writing at a desk; or dying amidst his community.

Benedict: Holding a book, with a broken chalice or a sieve, and with an open copy of his own rule, open at the first word, *"Asculta"*; or with a raven with a bun in its beak.

Benedict Joseph Labre: As a beggar, sharing his alms with other poor.

Benedict of Biscop: In episcopal vestments, holding a crosier and an open book, and he may be standing by the River Tyne, with two monasteries in sight.

Bernardino of Siena: Holding up a sign bearing the legend "IHS," from which rays shine forth; or as a habited friar with three miters at his feet.

Blaise: With wool combs, or blessing wild beasts; or extracting an impediment from a child's throat; or in a cave with wild animals.

Bonaventure: With a cardinal's hat and a ciborium.

Boniface: With a book, pierced with a sword or ax; or felling an oak tree; or with a miter and staff.

Bridget of Sweden: Wearing the Bridgettine habit, bearing a pilgrim's staff, holding a heart marked with a cross, with the Saviour near her; or holding a chain, or a pilgrim's flask or wallet.

Brigid: With a cow lying at her feet; or holding a cross and casting out the devil.

Bruno: In a Carthusian habit, with a shaven head; or seated with a miter, crosier and olive branch, perhaps with a crucifix before him or a scroll with *"O bonitas"* issuing from his mouth.

Caesarius of Arles: With the image of angels extinguishing flames in a burning city.

Cajetan: With a lily in his hand; or with the Virgin Mary placing the Infant Jesus in his arms.

Callistus: Wearing a red robe with a tiara; or being thrown into a well with a millstone around his neck; or with a millstone around his neck.

Camillus de Lellis: Ministering to the sick.

Casimir of Poland: Crowned, holding a lily; or praying at a church door at night.

Catherine of Alexandria: With a spiked wheel, which may be broken; or as a young, beautiful woman, crowned, or with a palm, book or sword in her hand; or with Christ placing a ring on her finger.

Catherine of Siena: In a Dominican habit, holding a heart and a book, wearing a crown of thorns; or with a lily; or accepting a marriage ring from the Infant Jesus.

Catherine of Sweden: With a hind.

Cecilia: Sitting at an organ; or playing a harp; or holding a palm; or crowned with roses, with a roll of music.

Charles Borromeo: With an archbishop's crosier, generally barefoot, with a rope around his neck; or with a casket and crucifix near him; or communicating with plague patients.

Clare of Assissi: With a pyx or monstrance, and perhaps holding a cross or lily.

Clement I: With the emblem of an anchor, sometimes robed as a pope, with a tiara and a cross with three branches.

Colette: Holding a crucifix and a hook; or with SS Francis and Clare appearing to her.

Columba: With devils fleeing from him.

Conrad of Piacenza: With small birds fluttering about him; or with stags and other animals surrounding him.

Cornelius: Vested as a pope, holding a cow's horn or with a cow near him.

Cosmas and Damian: As doctors of medicine with robes and instruments contemporary with the depictions; or being martyred in various ways; or in various depictions of alleged incidents of their lives, such as the grafting of a white leg onto the body of a black man with cancer.

Cunegund: Walking over hot ploughshares or carrying one in her hand; or holding a lily with St. Henry; or holding a model of the church of St. Stephen.

Cyprian: As a bishop, holding a palm and a sword.

Cyril and Methodius: Cyril with Bulgarian converts around him; or Cyril in a long philosopher's coat; or both brothers holding a church.

Cyril of Alexandria: With the Greek Fathers, distinguished by name; or with the Virgin Mary appearing to him.

Cyril of Jerusalem: With a purse in his hand.

Damasus I: Holding a ring; or holding a screen with *"Gloria Patri"*, etc., upon it; or with a church door behind him.

Denis: As a headless bishop, carrying his own mitered head, with a palm, sword or book, and his vestments may be covered with fleur-des-lis.

Dominic: In the Dominican habit (a white tunic and scapular and a black cloak), holding a lily, often with a star shining above his head; or with a dog; or with a globe, with fire; or with a rosary; or holding a tall cross.

Dunstan: As a bishop holding the devil with a pair of pincers, often grasping him by the nose; or with a crucifix speaking to him.

Dympna: Being beheaded by a king; or praying in a cloud surrounded by a group of lunatics bound with golden chains.

Eligius: With metal-working images, such as a hammer and horseshoe or a shod horse's leg; or wearing armour, standing on an anvil; or dressed as a bishop, holding a metal-working or goldsmith's tool.

Elizabeth: Clad as an elderly lady, holding the infant St. John the Baptist; or pregnant, greeting the Virgin Mary.

Elizabeth of Hungary: Performing an act of charity; or wearing a double crown; or weaving a crown and holding two others; or with a cloak full of roses, perhaps carrying a basket of food.

Elizabeth of Portugal: Carrying roses in her lap in winter; or as a nun of the third order of St. Francis, sometimes with a beggar near her or with a rose or jug in her hand.

Elmo: With a large opening in his body through which his intestines have been wound, or are being wound, around a windlass; or vested as a bishop holding a winch or windlass.

Engelbert: In archiepiscopal vestments, a crosier in his hand, and an upraised sword piercing a crescent moon in his other hand.

Etheldreda: As an abbess, crowned, with a pastoral staff and two does.

Fabian: With a dove by his side; or with a tiara and a dove; or with a sword or club; or kneeling at a block.

Felicity: With a wild cow by her side, perhaps with St. Perpetua.

Ferdinand III: With the emblem of a greyhound; holding a sword or an orb; or as a king with a cross on his breast; or on horseback, with a Moorish prince kneeling to him.

Fiacre: Carrying a shovel; or digging in a garden; or with a spade and an open book, sometimes with a hind at his feet.

Fidelis of Sigmaringen: With a club set with spikes or a whirlbat.

Florian: His hand resting on a millstone; or being thrown into a river with a stone around his neck.

Frances of Rome: Habited in black with a white veil, accompanied by her guardian angel, often carrying a basket of food or a book of the Office of the Virgin.

Francis de Sales: A sacred heart crowned with thorns above him; or with a heart in his hand.

Francis of Assisi: In a Franciscan habit, usually with the stigmata and a winged crucifix before him; or preaching to the birds; or propping up a falling church; or kneeling before a crib.

Francis of Paola: With the word "Caritas" in a circle of rays, perhaps standing on his cloak in the sea.

Francis Xavier: With a pilgrim's staff and beads, sometimes holding a lily; or exclaiming "*Satis est Domine, satis est!*"; or dying on a mat in a shed; or with angels bearing to him a crown; or carrying an Indian on his shoulders.

Gabriel the Archangel: As a young archangel, vested with an alb and girdle, with a lily, kneeling and holding a scroll emblazoned with "*Ave Maria.*"

Genesius the Comedian: As a player being baptized on a stage, with angels around him; or as a player holding a violin or a sword; or with a clown's cap and bells.

Genevieve: As a shepherdess, usually holding a candle, which the devil is trying to extinguish; or with a coin suspended around her neck.

George the Great: As a youth in armour, often mounted, killing or having killed a dragon, with a shield and lance decorated with a red cross on a white ground.

Gerard of Brogne: With St. Peter consecrating his church; or with SS Peter or Eugenius appearing to him; or holding the Church in his hand.

Germaine of Pibrac: As a shepherdess, with flowers in her apron, planting her distaff to keep her sheep while she goes to Mass; or with a distaff and spindle, with sheep at her side.

Gertrude of Helfta: Clad as an abbess, holding a flaming heart, and perhaps accompanied by a mouse or mice.

Gildas the Wise: With a bell near him.

Giles: With the emblem of a hind, sometimes with an arrow piercing his breast or leg.

Godfrey: Serving the sick; or embracing a poor man.

Godric: Dressed in white, kneeling on grass and holding a rosary, while above him the Blessed Virgin and Jesus appear, teaching him her song.

Gohard: Being beheaded on an altar.

Gregory VII: With a dove upon his shoulder.

Gregory Nazianzen: With Reading, Wisdom and Chastity appearing before him.

Gregory the Great: Vested as a pope, carrying a double-barred cross, and a dove may sit on his shoulder or hover near his ear, dictating to him; or writing, reading, or kneeling before an altar, behind which the emblems of the Lord's Passion appear.

Hedwig: With the Church and a statue of the Virgin Mary in her hands; or washing the feet of the poor; or barefoot with her shoes in her hands; or in a religious habit with the robes and crown of a princess near her.

Helena: Dressed as an empress, holding or supporting a cross, with an open book.

Henry the Emperor: Holding a lily with St. Cunegund; or holding a globe with a dove on it; or holding a church and a palm, with devils in the air; or asleep, with St. Wolfgang appearing to him; or holding the cathedral of Bamberg and a sword.

Herve: As a blind man, with a wolf and Guiharan, his child guide, and perhaps with frogs appearing near him.

Hilary of Poitiers: Holding an open book of the Gospel; or as a bishop with three books; or with a child (sometimes in a cradle at his feet, raised to life by him); or with a pen or stick.

Hippolytus: Dressed in armour, holding a palm or bearing a lance; or dragged and torn by horses; or holding keys as a jailer; or burying the body of St. Laurence; or holding an instrument resembling a curry comb.

Hyacinth: Sailing on the sea on his cloak; or curing the bite of a scorpian; or restoring a drowned youth to life; or with the Virgin Mary, or she and the Infant Jesus, appearing to him.

Ida of Herzfeld: Filling a tomb with food for the poor; or with a dove over her head; or carrying a church.

Ignatius: Regarding a crucifix, with a lion at his side; or standing between two lions; or in chains; or holding a heart with "IHS" upon it; or with a heart with the "IHS" torn out by lions.

Ignatius of Loyola: With his hand on the book of his constitutions, with "IHS" above him in light; or with Christ appearing to him, bearing his cross.

Irenaeus of Lyons: With a book or casket, with a lighted torch in his hand.

Isidore the Farmer: Before a cross; or with an angel and white oxen near him; or holding a hoe or rake.

James of the March: With a cup and a serpent near it.

James the Greater: As an elderly, bearded man, with a hat with a scallop shell; or with a shell or shells around him; or as a pilgrim with a wallet and staff; or with or being beheaded by a sword.

James the Less: Being beaten with a fuller's club; or with a fuller's club; or with a book.

Jane Frances Fremiot de Chantal: Holding a heart inscribed with "IHS."

Januarius: Wearing episcopal robes, holding a palm, with Vesuvius behind him; or being thrown into a fiery furnace; or being tied to a tree, a heated oven beside him; or with vials of his blood upon the book of the Gospels; or praying in the midst of flames; or lighting a fire.

Jerome: Robed as a cardinal, with a lion in attendance; or stripped of robes, sometimes in a monastic cave, beating his breast; or as a scholar writing; or with a pen and inkwell.

Jerome Emiliani: Delivering a possessed child, with a chain in his hand; or with the Virgin Mary and Child appearing to him; or in a black habit, holding a key and a shackbolt.

Joachim: Meeting St. Anne at the Golden Gate of Jerusalem; or leading Mary as a child; or with an angel announcing the birth of Mary.

Joan of Arc: As a bareheaded girl in armour, with a sword, a lance, or a banner with the words *"Jesus, Marie"* upon it; or wearing an envisored helm.

John Fisher: Robed as a cardinal, with haggard ascetic features; or with an ax or his hat at his feet.

John Gualbert: Clothed as a Vallombrasan Benedictine; or with a crucifix bending toward him; or with a church or a picture of Jesus in his hand; or standing on the devil.

John Nepomucen: Standing on a bridge; or with a bridge and river near him; or with a padlock and a finger to his lips; or with the empress confessing to him, with stars around his head; or floating on a river under a bridge; or in prison, manacled, with angels; or in a doctor's four-horned biretta, with his finger to his lips and stars around his head.

John of the Cross: With a large cross on his shoulders; or as a Carmelite with a pen and manuscript, looking at a crucifix; or with Jesus appearing to him, bearing his cross.

John of God: Carrying a pomegranate with a cross at the top; or with an alms chest; or carrying sick persons; or as a pilgrim, washing Jesus' feet.

John of Kanti: Giving his garments to the poor.

John the Baptist: As a lean and ascetic man, with a rough robe or the skin of a camel, carrying a lamb or with a lamb nearby, and a tall staff often ending in a cross; or carrying his own head; or baptizing Jesus; or carrying a book or a dish with a lamb upon it; or with the wings of a messenger (in Greek art).

John the Evangelist: Holding a chalice from which a snake or dragon is emerging; or with an eagle; or in a cauldron of boiling oil.

Josaphat: With a chalice or crown; or as a winged deacon.

Joseph: As an old man carrying a lily or some instrument of carpentry, usually with Mary or Jesus.

Joseph Calasanz: Holding a lily and miter, with a cardinal's hat before him, perhaps with the Virgin Mary and Infant appearing to him.

Joseph of Arimathea: As a very old man, carrying a pot of ointment or a flowering staff or a pair of altar cruets.

Joseph of Cupertino: Raised above the ground before an image of the Virgin Mary.

Justin: With an ax or a sword.

Kevin: With a blackbird.

Laurence of Rome: With a gridiron; or with a purse; or carrying a long cross on his shoulder and a Gospel book in his hand.

Leo the Great: With SS Peter and Paul, confronting Attila; or on horseback, with Attila and his soldiers kneeling before him; or praying at the tomb of St. Peter.

Leonard of Noblac: Vested as an abbot, holding chains, fetters or locks, freeing prisoners.

Louis IX of France: Clad in royal robes, often decorated with fleur-des-lis, holding a cross, crown of thorns or other emblems of the Savior's Passion.

Louise de Marillac: In the habit of the Daughters of Charity (a grey wool tunic with a large headress or cornett of white linen).

Lucy of Syracuse: As a girl carrying her eyes on a platter, book or shell; or with a gash in her neck; or with a sword embedded in her neck; or carrying a sword and a palm.

Luke: As a bishop or a physician, often accompanied by a winged ox; or as an evangelist, writing.

Malachy O'More: Presenting an apple to a king; or instructing a king in a cell.

Margaret: Trampling or standing on a dragon; or emerging from a dragon's mouth; or piercing a dragon with a cross-tipped spear.

Margaret Clitherow: As an Elizabethan housewife, kneeling; or standing on a heavy wooden door.

Margaret-Mary Alacoque: Clad in the Visitation habit, holding a flaming heart; or kneeling before Jesus, who exposed his heart to her.

Margaret of Cortona: In an ecstasy, with angels supporting her; or as a Franciscan nun, with a small dog at her feet; or contemplating a corpse; or with a skull at her feet and a dog plucking at her skirt.

Margaret of Scotland: As a queen with gifts for the poor; or holding a cross; or praying her husband out of purgatory.

Mark: With a winged lion; or writing or holding his Gospel, perhaps with a halter around his neck.

Martha: Dressed as a housewife, often bearing a distaff or any symbol of housework, such as a bunch of keys.

Martin I: Vested as a pope, holding money; or with geese around him; or seen through prison bars.

Martin of Tours: As a soldier, dividing his cloak to clothe a beggar; or in armour, with episcopal symbols; or with a globe of fire over his head as he says Mass; or with a goose.

Mary Magdalene: With long, unbound hair and a pot of ointment; or in Gospel scenes of the Passion and Resurrection.

Mary Magdalene dei Pazzi: Receiving the Blessed Sacrament from Jesus; or receiving a white veil from the Virgin Mary; or being presented to or receiving a ring from Jesus; or crowned with thorns and embracing a cross, with rays falling on her from a monstrance; or with flames issuing from her breast.

Matthew: At a desk, with an angel, who may hold a pen or inkwell or be guiding his hand; or holding money, a bag of coins, a money box, or a sword.

Matthias: As an elderly man, holding or being pierced by a halberd or sword.

Maximinus of Trier: Receiving St. Athansius at Triers; or with a bear at his side; or commanding a bear to carry his baggage.

Medard: With a spread eagle over his head; or kneeling, with a dove over his head; or leaving footmarks on a stone; or with a colt or horses or a beggar near him; or laughing with his mouth opened wide.

Medericus: Teaching his monks; or holding chains with caltrops.

Michael the Archangel: As an archangel in full armour, with a sword and a pair of scales; or standing over or fighting a dragon or devil with his lance.

Mildred of Thanet: Habited as a Benedictine, accompanied by a white hart or holding a lamp.

Monica: Standing behind a kneeling St. Augustine, with a girdle, scarf, handkerchief or book in her hand; or receiving a monstrance from an angel.

Nicholas: Robed as a bishop, with three children in a tub at his feet; or with three gold balls on a book; or with three purses; or with a ship or an anchor; or calming a storm.

Nicholas of Tolentino: With a basket of rolls ("St. Nicholas' bread"); or as a hermit; or with stars or the sun on his breast or around his head.

Norbert: Holding up a chalice with the Host in his right hand; or holding up a monstrance with St. Thomas Aquinas; or with an assassin making an attempt on his life with a dagger in a confessional.

Olympias: Kneeling, with a skull, crucifix, book and rosary at her feet.

Onesimus: Being stoned to death.

Oswald: With a raven with a ring in its beak; or holding a bowl and trampling on his murderers; or blowing a horn; or carrying his own head or a sword; or as a king preaching from a pulpit; or with a dove over his head.

Pachomius: With an angel appearing to him; or with an angel bringing the monastic rule; or walking among serpents.

Paschal Baylon: In the act of adoration before the Host; or watching sheep.

Patrick: Vested as a bishop, driving snakes before him or trampling upon them; or with a fire before him; or with a devil holding him in a fire.

Paul: As a thin-faced, elderly man with a high forehead, receding hair and a long pointed beard, usually holding a sword and a book; or with three springs of water near him.

Paula: As a pilgrim leading her daughter; or with a book and a black veil fringed with gold; or with a sponge in her hand; or prostrate before the cave of Bethlehem.

Paulinus of Nola: Preaching to the poor; or giving alms with a spade at his side; or holding a church.

Pelagia: Falling from a roof or a window.

Peter: As an elderly man of sturdy build, holding a book and a key or keys, a ship, or a fish; or being crucified head downwards; or robed as a pope with keys and a double-barred cross; or with a cock.

Peter Chrysologus: Being presented to Pope Sixtus III by SS Peter and Apollinaris; or with a dish in his hand.

Peter Damian: With a cardinal's hat by his side; or praying before a cross, with a miter and cardinal's hat on the ground.

Philip: As an elderly bearded man, holding a basket of loaves and a cross.

Philip Neri: As a priest, usually in red, carrying a lily or with lilies around him.

Pius V: Reciting a rosary; or with a fleet in the distance; or with the feet of a crucifix withdrawn as he tries to kiss them.

Polycarp of Smyrna: Trampling on a pagan; or with a funeral pyre near him; or stabbed and burnt to death; or being burned in various ways.

Raphael the Archangel: As an archangel; or as a young man carrying a staff or a fish; or walking with Tobias; or holding a bottle or flask.

Raymund of Penafort: In a boat, with a cloak for a sail; or with a key in his hand; or with the Virgin Mary and Infant appearing to him.

Regina: In a boiling cauldron, with torches applied to her; or chained to a cross, with torches applied to her; or with lambs or sheep around her; or with doves.

Rita of Cascia: With roses.

Robert of Newminster: Holding a church.

Roch: As a pilgrim with a staff, often with a plague spot on his thigh; or with a dog that is licking the plague spot or carrying a loaf of bread in his mouth.

Rosalia: Writing her name on the wall of a cave; or with or being presented with flowers; or holding a double Greek cross, distaff, book or palm.

Rose of Lima: As a nun of the third order of St. Dominic, with a garland of roses on her head; or with roses; or with roses and the Holy Infant.

Rupert of Salzburg: With a barrel of salt, perhaps holding a basket of eggs or baptizing Duke Theodo.

Sabas: With an apple in his hand; or living in a cave.

Scholastica: Habited as a nun, with a crosier and crucifix; or with a dove flying from her mouth; or kneeling before St. Benedict's cell; or with a dove at her feet or bosom.

Sebastian: As a naked youth tied to a tree, pierced with arrows.

Sidonius Apollinaris: Appearing to a priest; or writing religious poems.

Silverius: Holding a church.

Simon: With a fish, a boat, an oar, or a saw; or being sawed in half.

Solangia: Stabbed or beheaded near a crucifix; or with sheep and a distaff.

Stanislaus: Being hacked to pieces at the foot of an altar.

Stephen Harding: With the Virgin Mary and the Infant appearing to him.

Stephen of Hungary: Carrying a legate's cross; or with a church in his hand; or with a standard with the figure of the Virgin Mary upon it.

Stephen the Deacon: Vested as a deacon, holding a book or a palm; or carrying stones; or with stones resting on his book of the Gospels; or with stones gathered in the folds of his dalmatic.

Tarasius: With pictures of saints around him; or with the empress attending his deathbed; or serving the poor at table.

Teresa of Avila: Wearing the habit of a Discalced Carmelite nun, her heart pierced by an arrow held by an angel; or holding a pierced heart, book and crucifix; or with a fiery arrow and a dove above her head.

Teresa of the Child Jesus of Lisieux: As a Discalced Carmelite nun, holding a bouquet of roses or with roses at her feet.

Thomas: As an elderly man, holding a lance or being pierced by one; or kneeling before Jesus and placing his fingers in his side; or with a T-square.

Thomas Aquinas: As a portly Dominican friar, carrying a book; or with a star

of rays of light at his breast; or holding a monstrance with St. Norbert.

Thomas Becket: Vested as an archbishop, with a wounded head; or holding an inverted sword; or kneeling before his murderers; or before an altar.

Thomas More: Wearing Lord Chancellor's robes and the chain of office, perhaps carrying a book or an ax.

Thomas of Villanova: As a bishop with a wallet in his hand and beggars around him; or as a boy.

Timothy: With a club or stones; or being stoned to death.

Titus: Bareheaded, in a chasuble with a pastoral staff; or with a bright, smiling face.

Valentine: As a priest bearing a sword; or holding a sun; or giving sight to a blind girl.

Veronica: Holding a cloth on which is imprinted the face of Jesus; or standing with a veil between SS Peter and Paul.

Veronica Giuliani: Holding a heart marked with a cross.

Victor: As a soldier, perhaps standing near or holding a windmill.

Vincent de Paul: Garbed as a cleric of the 16th century, performing some act of mercy; or carrying infants in his arms; or surrounded by Sisters of Charity; or with ransomed slaves.

Vincent Ferrer: As a Dominican holding an open book while preaching; or with a cardinal's hat, or wings, or a crucifix; or with Jewish and Saracen converts around him.

Vincent of Saragossa: As a deacon holding a palm; or suffering on a gridiron; or being torn with hooks; or with a crow or raven; or with a millstone.

Wenceslaus of Bohemia: Trampling on fire; or in a coffin carried by angels; or reaping corn for altar bread; or with Ratislav asking his pardon.

Wolfgang: With a church in his hand; or holding a hatchet; or tormented by devils; or striking a fountain from the ground with his crosier.

Zachary: Holding a lighted taper.

Zita: In working clothes, with a bag and keys; or with loaves and a rosary.

405